D0913902

One Show Interactive

Advertising's Best Interactive and New Media

Volume V

President	John Butler
Executive Director	Mary Warlick
Interactive Director	Kevin Swanepoel
Editor	Kevin Swanepoel
Contributing Editors	Steve Marchese
	Kyle McKenna
DVD Production	Scream DVD, Mark Ashkinos (Producer)
	Click 3X
Creative Director	Kevin Swanepoel
Design and Layout	Joy Robles
	Kyle McKenna
Cover / Divider Pages	
Executive Producers	Tetsuya Watanabe, Yuma Sakata,
	Taihei Yamanishi, Tomoko Inokuma (Dentsu Inc.)
Art Director and Designer	Takashi Okazaki
Planner and Producer	Saitoh (GONZO DIGIMATION)
Coordinator	Yoko Kawahara (GONZO DIGIMATION HOLDING K.K.)
Copyright © 2002	Takashi Okazaki
Publisher	One Club Publishing LLC
	21 East 26th Street
	New York, NY 10010
Telephone	+ 1 (212) 979 1900
Fax	+ 1 (212) 979 5006
E-Mail	publishing@oneclub.com
Web Site	www.oneclub.com
In Association With	The One Club for Art & Copy Inc.
Distributed in the USA by	Sterling Publishing Co., Inc.
	387 Park Avenue South
	New York, NY 10016-8810
Telephone	+ 1 (212) 532-7160
Fax	+ 1 (212) 213-2495
Web Site	www.sterlingpub.com
Distributed in Canada by	Sterling Publishing
	c/o Canadian Manda Group
	One Atlantic Avenue, Suite 105
	Toronto, Ontario M6K 3E7
Distributed Internationally	
Excluding North America by	AVA Distribution
Telephone	+41-78-600-5109
E-Mail	sales@avabooks.ch
Wedsite	www.avabooks.ch

Copyright © 2002	A collection by The One Club for Art & Copy Inc. All Rights Reserved. No part of this book or DVD may be reproduced in any way by any means whatsoever without express permission in writing from the owners.

First Printing	0-929837-19-3
Book Production	AVA Singapore Pte Ltd
E-Mail	production@avabooks.com.sg
Printed	Singapore

Contents

The One Club

Based in New York City, The One Club was founded in 1975 and is a non-profit organization dedicated to maintaining the highest standards of creativity in advertising. Its 1,000 members include many of advertising's most respected art directors and copywriters, as well as students of advertising.

Mission

As part of its mission to promote high standards of creative excellence, The One Club produces the advertising industry's most prestigious awards program, The One Show. Judged by a panel of the advertising industry's elite creative directors, this annual event acknowledges excellence in art direction, design, and copywriting in a variety of categories, including television, radio, newspapers, magazines, billboards and public service. The coveted One Show "Gold Pencils" are regarded as the zenith of achievement in the advertising world.

In 1998, The One Club launched One Show Interactive, the first awards show dedicated exclusively to advertising in new media. With the One Show Interactive awards,The One Club extended its mission of recognizing creative excellence to the new media field.

Now in its sixth year One Show Interactive is recognized as the most prestigious competition for advertising in new media.

Programs

The One Club regularly produces a variety of events and programs that encourage aspiring advertising professionals to hone their craft. These programs include:

- "Gold on Gold" lectures (award-winning industry professionals discuss the creative process)
- Portfolio Reviews
- The One Show College Competition
- Creative Workshops
- *one. a magazine* — a quarterly publication by and for advertising creatives
- One Club Gallery Exhibitions
- The One Show Annual, the indispensable hard cover reference showcasing the best advertising worldwide
- One Show Interactive Annual, the first book of its kind, highlighting the best new media advertising

Education

In 1995, The One Club established an education department, dedicated to fostering the creative talents of advertising students nationwide. The department sponsors educational programs and events, and administers scholarships to outstanding students in advertising programs at a select number of colleges and advertising schools throughout the country.

John Butler – President
The One Club

Welcome to One Show Interactive, Volume V.

One Show Interactive is proud to be the first show dedicated solely to creative excellence in new media. In many ways, those of you whose work appears in this book have tougher jobs than your offline advertising peers. The very nature of your canvas is much more experiential than print, TV, radio, or outdoor advertising. After all, the average consumer can't click on a print ad or a TV commercial, moving from mere information to the delivery of product. The best work in your space not only communicates a brand message, but every banner, Web site, or CD-ROM you create offers the possibility of being a transaction medium itself. I don't envy you. Simply put, you have a lot more to think about. Certainly there is a lot more for clients to demand and assume.

As the interactive industry matures, it seems the term, "new media," is fast becoming dated; these days it's pretty much expected that a client will have a presence on the Web. The expansion of internet advertising has been more rapid than any other traditional medium, and that goes for the level of creativity employed as well. Take a trip to the Museum of Broadcasting in New York and view some of the commercials from 1949 – when television was in its nascent stages – and you'll see what I mean. But the level of creativity in new media, since the first One Show Interactive in 1998, continues to impress me.

The work that appears in this annual shows a true commitment to The One Club's passion for breakthrough work. Thank you for meeting – and exceeding – the creative challenges of your medium. And now I invite you to enjoy these 200 pages and accompanying DVD, featuring the best new media of the year.

Kevin Swanepoel – Interactive Director
The One Club

This, the sixth year of One Show Interactive, will be remembered as ushering in an age of unparalleled integration. We have evolved dramatically from the beautiful yet static, advancing into a new stage of brand integration and increased user interactivity. It is expected, especially in this industry, that each year's work will take a massive technological leap forward — a result of improved software and more efficient hardware.

This year's work was not only technically and creatively dynamic, it was strikingly intelligent — capturing the spirit of the client's branding, motives and services unlike ever before. The work surfaced from a more focused, goal-oriented environment, where the purpose and utility of new media was finally realized after years of creative experimentation, economic booms, and confidence-shattering busts. Today, clients are smarter and savvier, and creatives have the years of experience to fully translate brand images online.

Not only does the work of the 2002 One Show Interactive annual look beautiful and function seamlessly, it also resonates with a meaning and understanding of the relationships that make good advertising work — between the client and the agency, the programmer and the designer, the brand and the medium.

Interactive Director – The One Club

Jan Leth – One Show Interactive Jury Chairman
Executive Creative Director
OgilvyInteractive, North America

It's been a pivotal year in the digital world. As the dust has settled from the dot-com bust – with the over hyping a thing of the past, and the glee of some in the non-digital world receding – we find that the internet continues to boom, with more and more people making it a genuinely mainstream medium. While the evolution of the medium continues there is a great degree of maturity showing. The work honored this year reflects that maturity in the original thinking, brilliant design, concept and execution on display here.

The fact that the internet has "arrived" was best demonstrated by the team at Fallon with their BMW Films work. No longer a support vehicle, the internet became their showcase for engaging consumers in the most novel way in memory. The fact that this campaign has created unbelievable angst in all other creative departments around the world speaks for itself.

Hewlett Packard's "Invent" campaign renews our faith in banners. Like fine Indian miniatures, these beautifully crafted works leverage the unique interactive capabilities of the Web to leave the user with a sense of wonder at the potential for invention, and the campaign's message firmly embedded in their brain.

While the internet began as a means for distributing in-depth information, sites like VW's Autoshow and Mid-Tokyo Maps not only expand the possibilities for exploration, but create harmonious, enlightening experiences involving users well beyond what they may have first sought out. The passion, inspiration and attention to detail given these sites is self evident.

My thanks to my fellow jurors for their many long hours spent evaluating the entries. I am sure they came away from the experience feeling just as inspired and rejuvenated as I did.

2002 One Show Interactive Judges

Erik Blair	Kevin°, New York
Tim Brunelle	Arnold Commmunications, Boston
Benjy Choo	Kinetic Interactive, Singapore
Hillman Curtis	hillmancurtis, New York
Toshiya Fukuda	Hakuhodo Inc., Hakuhodo i-studio Inc., Tokyo
Abby Greensfelder	Discovery.com, New York
Penny Hardy	Fuel North America, New York
Brad Johnson	Second Story, San Francisco
Jason Kuperman	TBWA\Chiat\Day, Los Angeles
Jason Lucas	TBWA\Chiat\Day, New York
Richard Mellor	Hyperinteractive, London
Matt Owens	One9ine, New York
Paulo Jorge Pereira	AgênciaClick, São Paulo
Thomas Romer	Chopping Block, New York
Anette Scholz	Scholz & Volkmer, Weisbaden
Aaron Sugarman	Freelance, New York
Oliver Viets	Elephant Seven GmbH, Hamburg
Chris Wiggins	Fallon Interactive, Minneapolis

Benjy Choo
Kinetic Interactive, Singapore
Judges' Choice – Allied Works Architecture
Client – Allied Works Architecture

What struck me most was the gridless navigation of the Allied Works Architecture Web site, one that's easy to adapt to. Much thought was put into how the layout and flow of each element came together on screen. You will never find a jarring blink as each item transits into the page in layers, drawing the eye and educating the mind.

The site also manages to achieve a balance between art and technology, judiciously using just the right amount of programming to get the idea across, leaving the simplicity of the layout to bring out the well-written copy. Even loading times and a careful selection of images show the attention to detail put into the design of this site.

All these add up to the overall experience, one that not only shows brilliant information design, but more importantly, restraint.

Tim Brunelle
Arnold Commmunications, Boston
Judges' Choice – HP "Invent" Banner Campaign
Client – Hewlett-Packard

(You mean aside from all the work we did for Volkswagen?)

Obviously Fallon's BMW Films idea was truly amazing. The site was easy to use. The downloadable application was smart. And then the DVD showed up in the mail. If only a few more clients saw the need to take such relevant, calculated risks. I thought the Ensenda site www.ensenda.com was well conceived and neatly designed as well. A definite high water mark for sites of any kind. And the HP "Invent" banner campaign stood well above the rest of the work in that category.

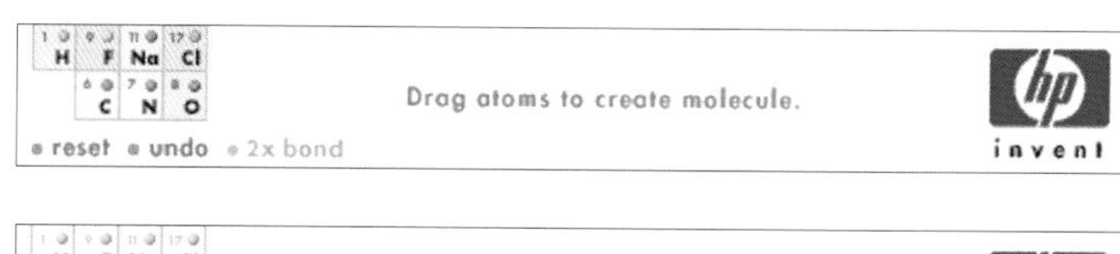

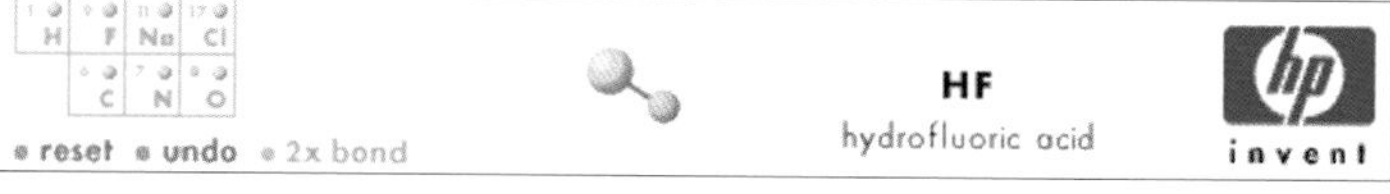

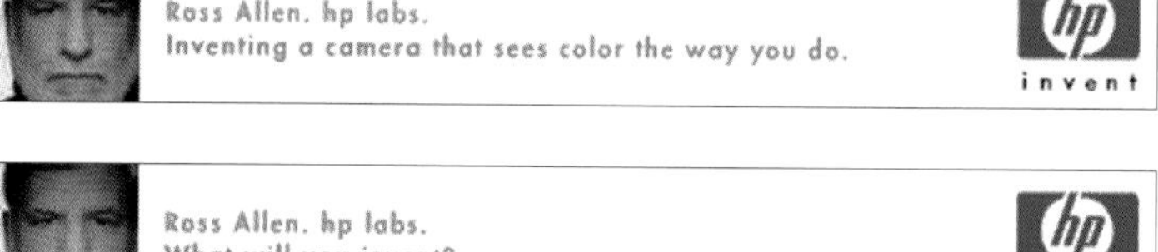

Brad Johnson
Second Story, San Francisco
Judges' Choice – Mid-Tokyo Maps
Client – Mori Building Co., Ltd.

The HP Invent ad campaign was the first time I ever wanted to see *more* ad banners. *Born Magazine* is a place I'll keep coming back to, and Allied Works Architecture is where I want to live. Wengenmayer's site is brilliantly simple, and Sandstrom's is simply brilliant. Picking one piece from so many good ones with completely different purposes was tough.

In the end, it was a piece that will for me inspire new ways of thinking about future projects — one that contributes to the ongoing evolution of our medium: Mid-Tokyo Maps. It is brilliant information design. I have seen great mapping resources online, but never such a thorough, comprehensive or exhaustive examination of a single subject. From one view of Tokyo, hundreds of gels, overlays, and data sets allow users to "filter" the city, studying it historically, architecturally, culturally, seismically, environmentally, or in terms of its population, transportation, density — it just doesn't stop! With a wealth of contextual panels, informative text and info graphics, the site is a great resource for broad audiences — from specialized city planners to a general visitor.

Toshiya Fukuda
Hakuhodo Inc., Tokyo
Judges' Choice – Breast Exam
Client – American Cancer Society

This banner ad for the American Cancer Society made me think deeply about the meaning of interactiveness.

Just wonderful.

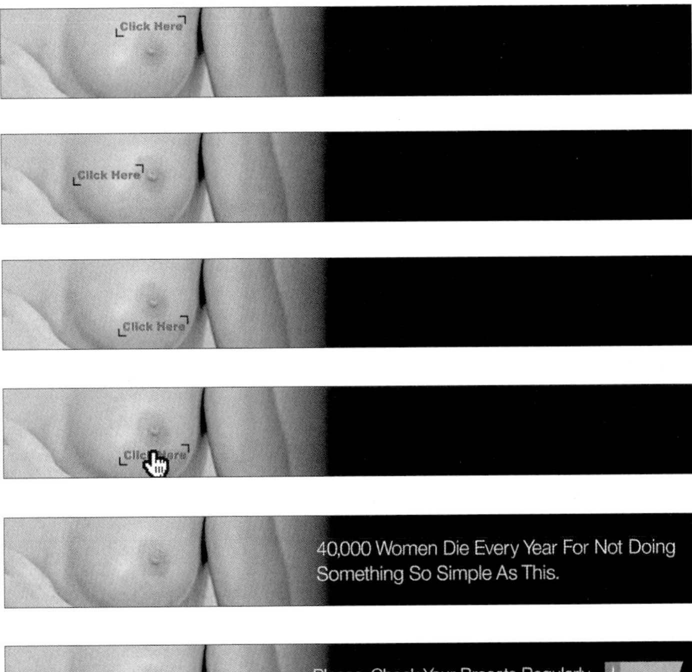

Jason Kuperman
TBWA\Chiat\Day, Los Angeles
Judges' Choice – Rain Forest
Client – O' Boticario

Okay, maybe the execution could have been art directed a little bit better, but the concept was exceptionally clever. I found the roar of the chainsaw and the opportunity to wield it pretty irresistible, so I would imagine that this piece did well in attracting initial interaction. Once I realized I was cutting down trees I started to do exactly what the banner was intended to make me do – think about deforestation. It is so simple, but it evoked an emotional reaction by allowing me to interact with it in a way that made a point. I can't say I have seen a lot of interactive work that does this, so just for that fact alone, I would consider it my choice for Best of Show.

Matt Owens
One9ine, New York
Judges' Choice – Detroit Auto Show
Client – Mercedes Benz

My favorite of the sites presented was the Mercedes Benz Web site for the Detroit Auto Show. It was one of the few sites I spent a long time with. The environmental nature of the site gave a real sense of space and time unfolding and I really enjoyed this dimension of the project. The site went above and beyond my expectations and presented more than just the information. The sensitivity to detail was great and overall, I stopped thinking about an online experience and just wanted to see more. I was unable to go to the auto show in Detroit, but the Mercedes site gave me a great impression of Mercedes Benz' contribution to the show.

Erik Blair
Kevin°, New York
Judges' Choice – The Hire: BMW Films
Client – BMW of North America

BMW Films is an exciting first in both project size and content for the Web. Never have such large media stars (Guy Ritchie, Madonna, David Fincher, Ang Lee...) all been attached to such a convincing and cohesive piece of branded content, Web-based or otherwise.

The campaign was a pointed branding success. Associating its products with some of the most respected names in film and music, BMW created a media spectacle which drew savvy (and demographically "correct") consumers...then kept them around with easy and fun links to information on their featured products.

Secondary games, mixers, screensavers and the like can detract from the coherence of any consumer Web site experience. By offering easily digestible, high-impact entertainment coupled with similarly "pop" product pages (and little else), BMW Films did more this year to promote the Web as an important branding media than any other advertising campaign.

Jason Lucas
TBWA\Chiat\Day, New York
Judges' Choice – The Hire: BMW Films
Client – BMW of North America

As a stand-alone piece of online communication, BMW Films is a compelling, entertaining experience. Having been exposed to the entire campaign, including print, television, online and outdoor, I have to say this was a bold stroke of integrated creative work. Rather than simply rehash the same executions for each medium, specific creative was developed for each, making a greater sum of all parts. Moving forward, it's up to all of us to learn from BMW Films, but the real challenge when making such rich consumer experiences will be to make them more inclusive and interactive rather than passive.

Penny Hardy
Fuel North America, New York
Judges' Choice – The Hire: BMW Films
Client – BMW of North America

Why?

BMW Films pushed what is expected as an integrated marketing campaign. It's not just about making the work offline and online match visually. It's about an idea of how to market this car to a different audience, an audience that embraces the internet.

Consumers have forced us to change our approach to advertising online. It's more complex than just pushing information at the user. We have to create experiences that they want and raise their hand asking for more. BMW Films has done this.

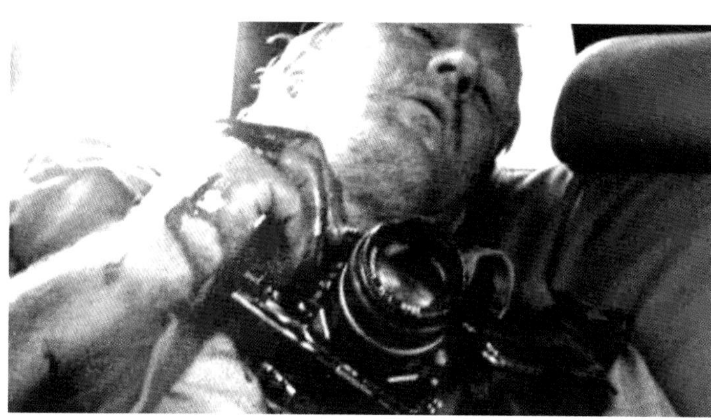

Hillman Curtis
hillmancurtis, New York
Judges' Choice – The Hire: BMW Films
Client – BMW of North America

My Best of Show is "The Hire" by BMW Films and Fallon Interactive. The player works great, the interface is very nice, though I could have done without the flash intro. The films themselves were for the most part disappointing, but I think this entry excited me because I am such a huge believer in presenting film and video narrative on the Web. All in all a wonderful concept presented with no shortage of creativity.

Paulo Jorge Pereira
AgênciaClick, São Paulo
Judges' Choice – The Hire: BMW Films
Client – BMW of North America

My personal Best of Show choice is the BMW Films.

The reason is probably the same as that which made it become the official Best of Show: when I saw it for the first time, a couple months before the judging sessions, my first thought was "I wish I had done this!" Not only because of the clever idea or the awesome execution, but also because of the courage they had to battle for such a project with the client. It's clearly an example for our industry.

Thomas Romer
Chopping Block, New York
Judges' Choice – http://www.lobo.cx
Client – Lobo Filmes

Simple but gorgeous interface, very easy to use and pleasing to view. I have a hard time separating the work in the portfolio from the reasons I like the site. It's all top notch work and really since it is mostly Spanish-based, mostly stuff I have never had the opportunity to be exposed to.

Aaron Sugarman
Freelance, New York
Judges' Choice – Nike Freestyle
Client – Nike

Unlike many Nike forays into interactive media, which are ambitious but somehow off the mark, the Freestyle Web site is a perfect swish for the swooshers. It builds from what is often a tenuous concept–that consumers could love an ad so much that they want to dive headlong into it. Nike's hypnotic Freestyle campaign is genius, the exception that proves the rule. The interactive extension takes flight with an interface that mercifully eschews the confusion-equals-art approach, delivering straightforward options and proper user feedback. While the type and images are nicely bold and graphic, it's the clever use of sound and motion that pack the real punch. Sometimes the hardest part is figuring what not to include, and Freestyle gets it just right here–all of the flava with none of the fat. The downloadable goodies are downright desirable, the info nuggets tasty and brand-enhancing. Nike Freestyle got game.

Oliver Viets
Elephant Seven GmbH, Hamburg
Judges' Choice – Iberia
Client – Iberia

When producing online campaigns that use the good old pop-up format, one should really always keep in mind that it is the user who gets screwed: we decide what to do with the user's time and money. Sometimes, I myself become victim of my own work. How absurd.

Yet it is exactly those moments that I wish that more brands and advertisers understood the importance of establishing a more subtle kind of online advertising. But to persuade our clients of the strength of the online medium as an advertising platform, one needs ideas that are as convincing in their charm and simplicity as the example for Iberia.

Chris Wiggins
Fallon Interactive, Minneapolis
Judges' Choice – thetruth.com
Client – American Legacy Foundation

There was a lot of good stuff this year, and making a personal choice for Best of Show isn't easy. I'll exempt myself from commenting on BMW Films since I worked on it, but of the others I'd have to say I really liked thetruth.com site. The art direction of the whole campaign is wonderful, and the online execution is slick and appropriate for the medium. Once you start to explore, you find that interacting with the site is almost as addictive as the product it's about. Because the TV spots are very aggressive and memorable, the site has a lot to live up to and I believe it holds up very well. And of course it's hard not to love the fact that they've been able to bring that much creativity to a not-for-profit cause and elevate it to such a high. Well done.

Now Iberia's Business Class offers you much more room between the seats.

Always thinking about you.

Best of Show

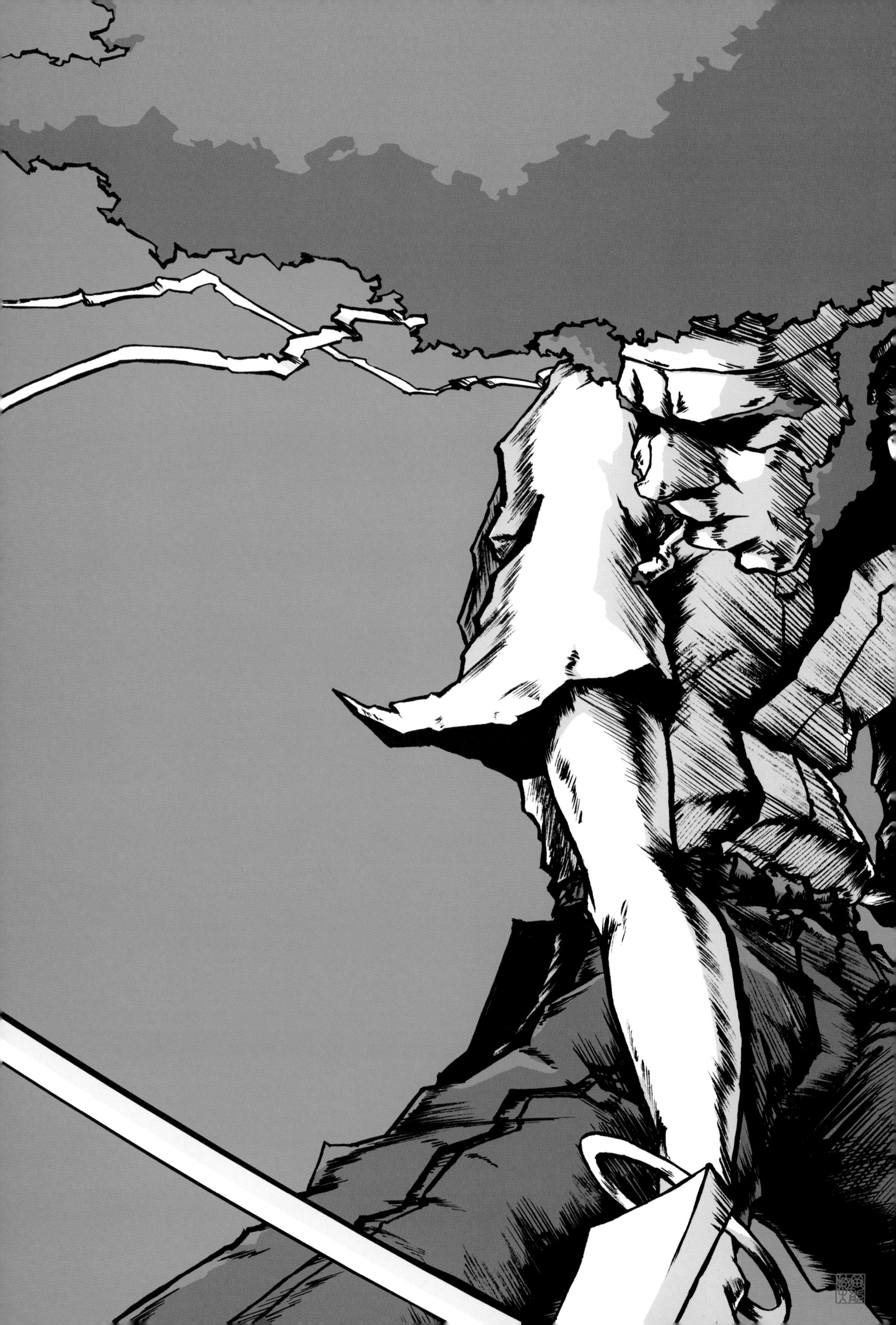

Agency	Fallon Minneapolis
Client	BMW of North America
Art Director	Kevin Flatt
Writers	Joe Sweet, Chuck Carlson
Creative Director	Kevin Flatt
Designer	Brooke Posard
Photographer	Mark LaFavor
Information Architect	Matt Heinrichs
Programmers	George Hilal, Marc Gowland, Josh Hagen Chris Wiggins
Producers	Jennifer Bremer, Cori Van Brunt Jane Petersen
Digital Artists/Multimedia	Christian Erickson, Chris Wiggins Chris Stocksmith, Laurie Brown
Music/Sound	Elements
ID	02040N
URL	www.bmwfilms.com

Best of Show

Page	xx

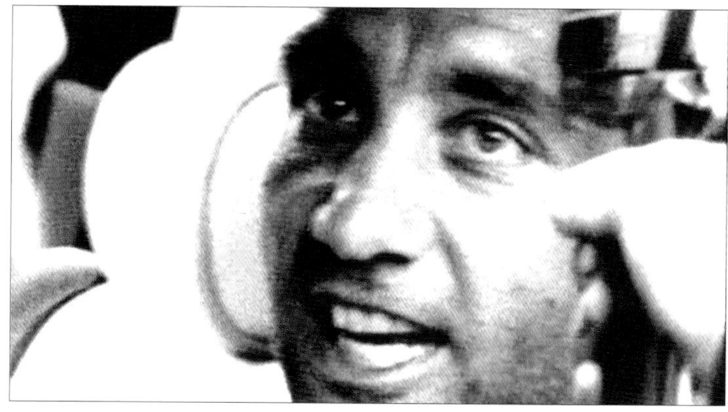

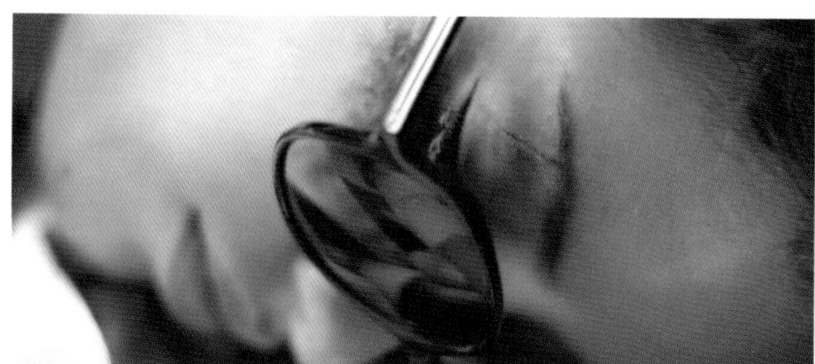

Driving into a New Advertising Future

It began as an advertising brief. But advertising wasn't the answer. We were frustrated that traditional commercials didn't let us show what BMWs could really do. BMW customers increasingly weren't watching television, yet they had embraced the Web in astounding numbers.

Then, our clients agreed to throw away the rule book.

Why not, instead, create something so entertaining, so rewarding, that people would actually seek it out? Why not take the money saved on media and put it on the screen? Why not create an interactive experience more akin to home theater?

What resulted was BMW Films: a series of short films directed by and starring A-list Hollywood talent. Each film revolved around a central character called The Driver, the world's best when it came to transporting people out of dangerous situations. The Driver's character traits — his youthfulness, integrity, passion, and willingness to take risks — reflected on both the brand and the audience. Each film featured The Driver using a BMW to complete his missions, showcasing BMW's true performance. The films were distributed at an entertainment-focused Web site, making them "found" treasures, yet they were still accessible to anyone at anytime.

In the end it took one brave client, more than a hundred people working in every discipline at Fallon, and the wisdom and commitment of our production partners at Anonymous to pull it off. And it worked in every possible way.

Perhaps it doesn't fit everyone's definition of advertising today. Hopefully, neither will the next thing Fallon does.

Pencil Winners

Agency | Goodby, Silverstein & Partners
San Francisco
Client | Hewlett-Packard
Art Director | Jeff Benjamin, Rick Casteel
Writer | John Matejczyk
Creative Director | Steve Simpson
Designer | Keith Anderson
Producer | Danaa Zellars
ID | 02001N
URL | www.goodbysilverstein.com/2002/invent.html

Award | Gold
Category | Banner – Single
Page | 2

Inventing, Composing, Enlightening

We both lie silently still
In the dead of the night
Although we both lie close together
We feel miles apart inside

Was it something I said or something I did
Did the words not come out right
Though I tried not to hurt you
Though I tried
But I guess that's why they say

Every rose has its thorn
Just like every night has its dawn
Just like every cowboy sings his sad, sad song
Every rose has its thorn

Yeah it does.

This rich-media banner was designed to bring the HP Invent campaign online. We took advantage of the medium and invited users to connect with the HP brand and their own inventive spirit.

Users can create any song imaginable just by dragging notes onto a music bar. Although, after hearing our art director compose, "Every Rose Has Its Thorn" we aren't sure if this is a good thing.

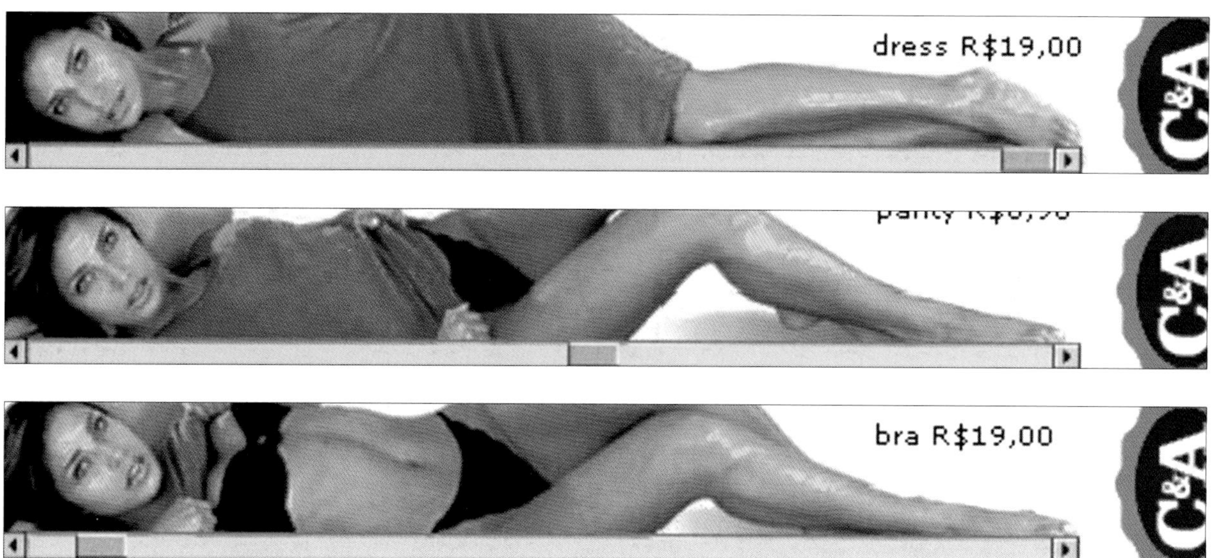

Agency | Agenciaclick - São Paulo
Client | C&A
Art Director | Rodrigo Buim
Writer | Suzana Apelbaum
Creative Director | PJ Pereira
Technical Director | Abel Reis
Photographer | Argos Estudio
Programmer | Jefferson Russo
Producers | Thais Lyro, Darcio Vilela
ID | 02002N

A True Revelation

This banner with scroll shows a beautiful and well-dressed woman. She takes off her clothes depending on the position of the scroll, and ends up in only lingerie with the scroll all the way to the right. This banner was created for the popular Brazilian store C&A, to advertise both the clothes and the lingerie.

Award | Gold
Category | **Banner – Single**

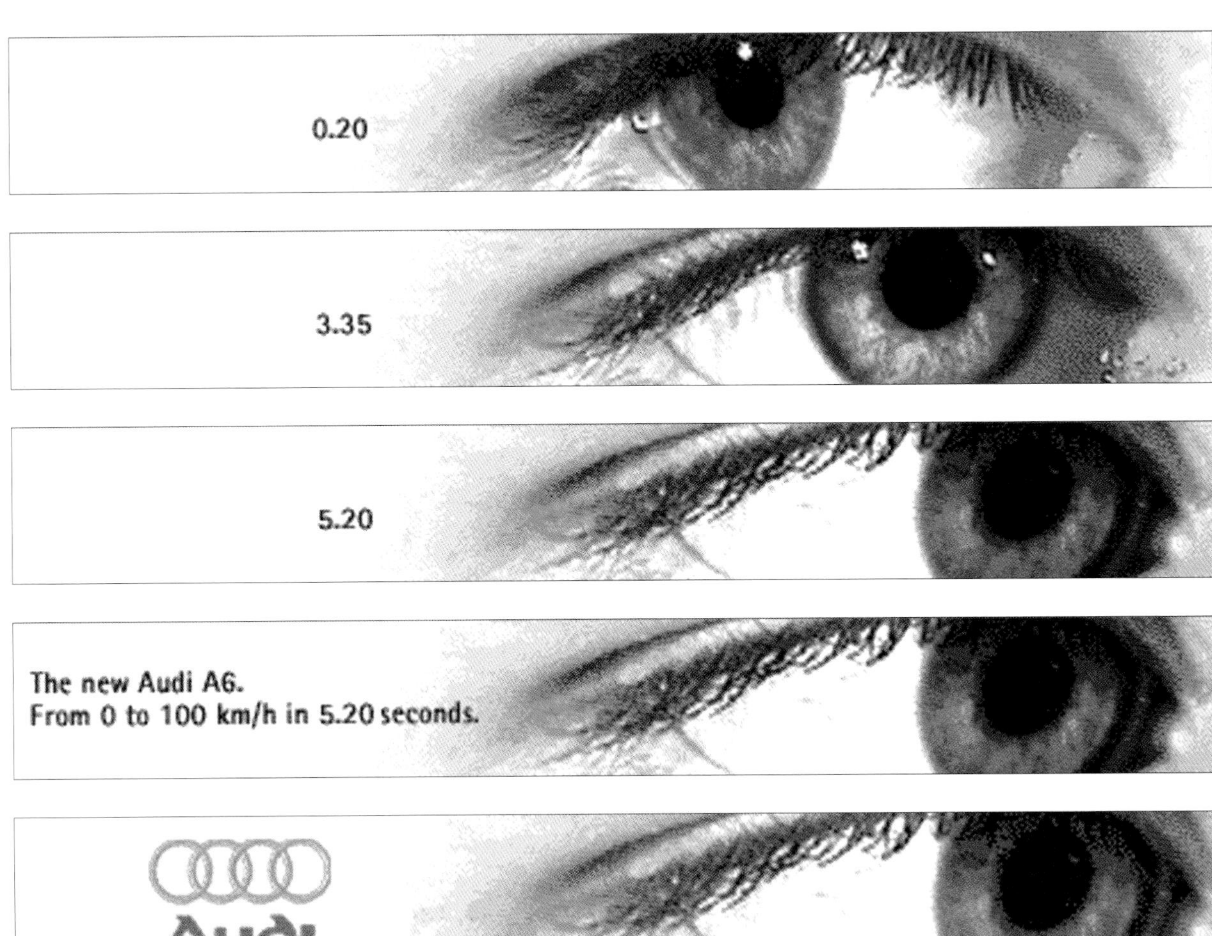

Agency	AlmapBBDO - São Paulo
Client	Audi
Art Director	Luiz Sanches
Writer	Roberto Pereira
Creative Directors	Marcello Serpa, Eugênio Mohallem
Technical Directors	Abel Reis, Régis Amaral
Designers	Fabio Costa, Eduardo Foresti Diego Martins
ID	02003N
URL	www.almapbbdo.com.br/oneshow/audi/eye

The Look of Genuine Speed

Designed to communicate the launch of the new Audi A6, the idea behind this banner is as simple as the category in which it is competing. This idea was adapted for the Internet from a print ad in such a way as to show the real movement and speed of the car in action.

Award	Silver
Category	Banner – Single
Page	4

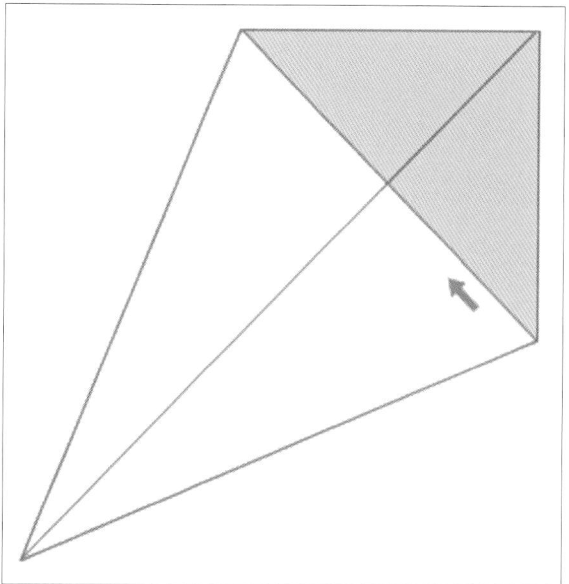

Agency	Agenciaclick - São Paulo
Client	WWF
Art Directors	Ricardo Landim, Raphael Vasconcellos
Writer	Daniel Cariello
Creative Directors	PJ Pereira, Raphael Vasconcellos Ricardo Figueira
Designers	Ricardo Landim, Raphael Vasconcellos Marcelo Eduardo
Producer	Ricardo Landim
ID	02004N

Origami

The Internet user follows the origami step-by-step without knowing that a golden-lion-tamari will appear. The user will only discover it after the final fold has been completed. The last frame of the banner includes the WWF logo and the message to "Save the golden-lion-tamari."

Award Silver

Category **Banner – Single**

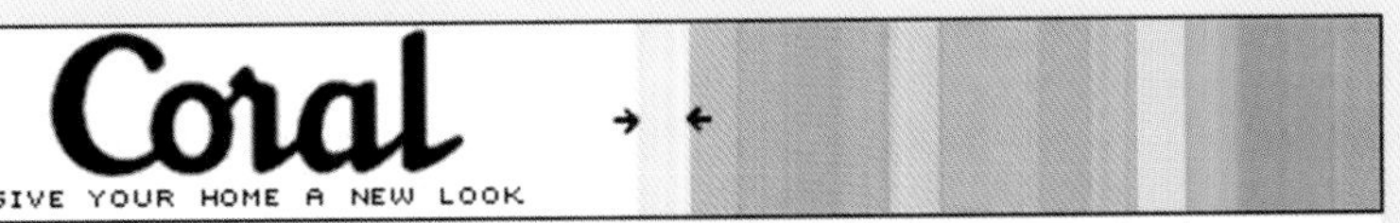

Agency	AlmapBBDO - São Paulo
Client	Intas Coral
Art Directors	Ricardo Abellan, Paulo Lemos
Writer	Caroline Freire
Creative Directors	Fabio Costa, Eduardo Foresti
Programmer	Paulo Lemos
ID	02005N
URL	www.almapbbdo.com.br/oneshow/coral/color

Creative Color Control

Our greatest challenge in creating this banner for Coral ICI Paints was to get users to interact with it so that we could show them the entire color range of a new line of paints being launched for home use. We used the background of the home page of the leading Brazilian portal (UOL) as if it were the wall of the visitor's home. When interacting with the banner, users color the background of the page — in other words, they test colors by "painting a wall in their home."

Award	Bronze
Category	**Banner – Single**
Page	6

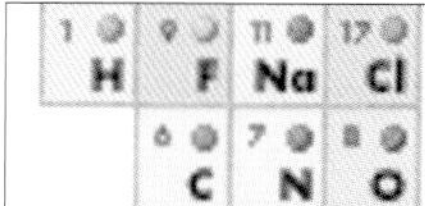

Drag atoms to create molecule.

reset undo 2x bond

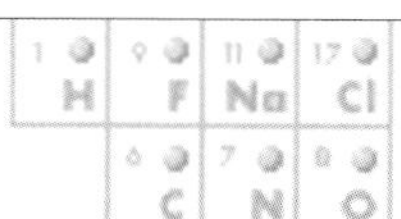

HF
hydrofluoric acid

reset undo 2x bond

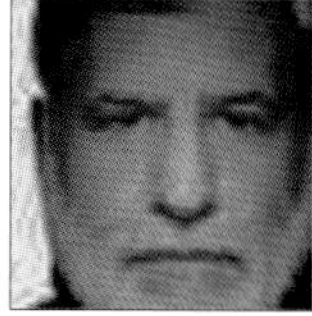

Ross Allen. hp labs.
Inventing a camera that sees color the way you do.

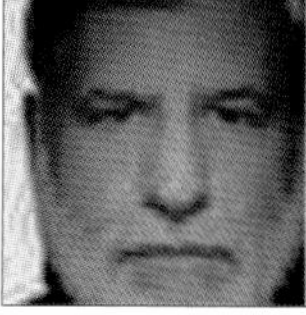

Ross Allen. hp labs.
What will you invent?

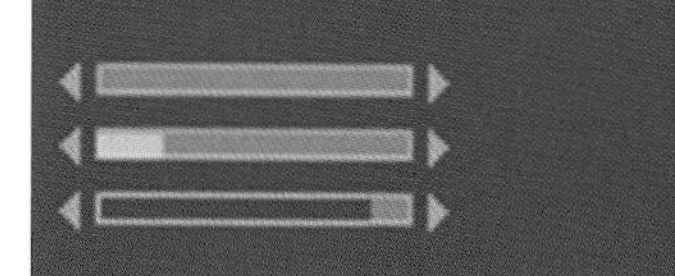

red=0% green=20% blue=86%

Agency	Goodby, Silverstein & Partners San Francisco
Client	Hewlett-Packard
Art Directors	Jeff Benjamin, Rick Casteel
Writers	Will Elliott, John Matejczyk
Creative Director	Steve Simpson
Designer	Keith Anderson
Producer	Danaa Zellers
Production Co.	Freestyle Interactive, Orange Design
ID	02006N
URL	www.goodbysilverstein.com/2002/invent.html

Entering the Labs of HP Inventors

Who knew being an inventor was this much fun.

These rich-media banners invite users into the labs of HP Inventors, allowing them to do their own inventing while interacting with the HP brand.

Molecular scientist Stan Williams invites users to create their own molecule. Users confront the challenges and yes, even the fun of chemistry. Valences, bonds and double bonds — a few of the things HP scientists confront as they work to invent the world's first molecular computer.

Color and imaging scientist Ross Allen invites users to interact with the elements of color, adjusting quantities of red, green, and blue to create their own color.

In Music Composer users can create any song imaginable just by dragging notes onto a music bar. Although, after hearing our art director compose "Every Rose Has Its Thorn" we aren't sure if this is a good thing.

Award	Gold
Category	Banner – Campaign

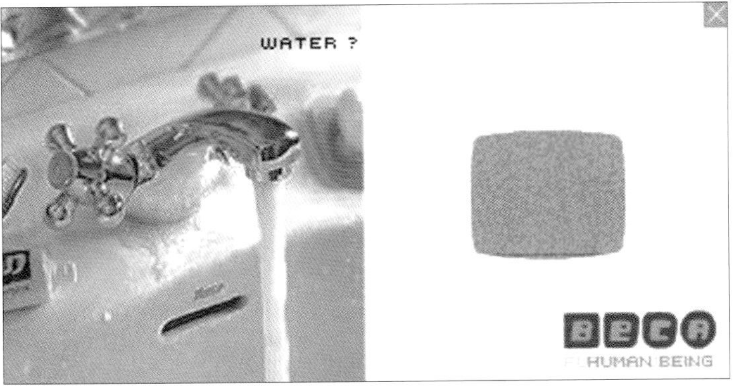

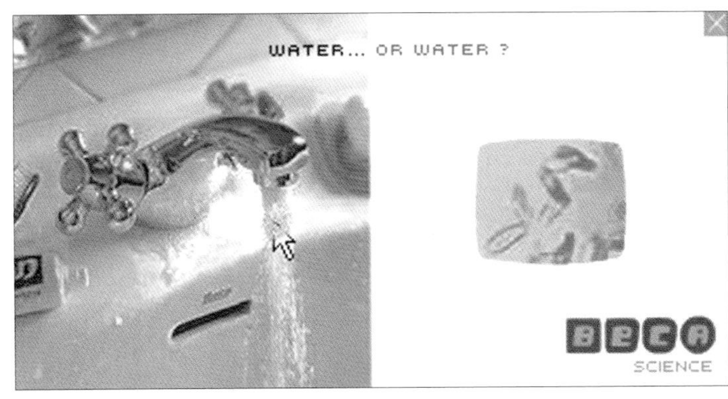

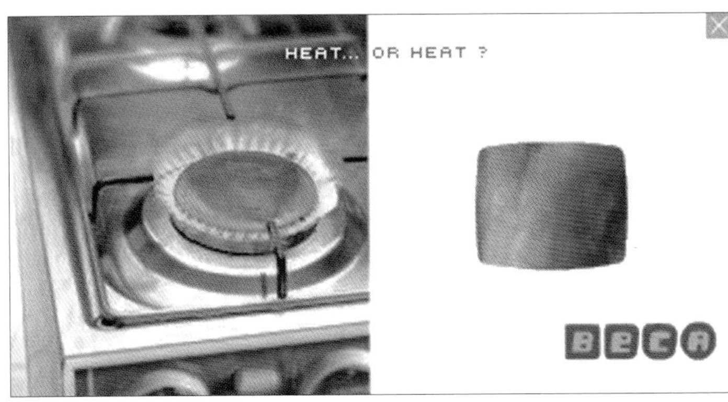

Agency	Herraiz Soto & Co. - Madrid
Client	Planeta 2010
Art Director	Sergi Mula
Writer	Rafael Soto
Creative Directors	Angel Herraiz, Rafael Soto
Illustrator	Siscu Soler
Programmer	Carles Sanz
Music/Sound	Sergi Mula
ID	02007N
URL	www.herraizsoto.com/festivales/beca_i
Award	Silver
Category	**Banner – Campaign**
Page	8

Stay Curious

We've been told so many times "Hey, kid! Don't touch that!" that now we're all totally repressed. I myself, for example, would love to touch a load of things that I daren't touch just to make sure I stay in line with social order. But, luckily, on the Internet there isn't any social order or authority watching over us. On the Internet we can touch anything we want. And that little pleasure we get out of experiencing new sensations is what we wanted to exploit with this piece. Put your finger in water and fire and see what happens.

Free of charge? Well, not so free. That's really all just part of a publicity idea.

Beca is a cultural channel in Spain (a kind of National Geographic). This channel really offers a profound knowledge of the things which surround us so that, in time, you end up seeing things from a wiser point of view.

So the water which comes out of the tap is no longer water. Not any more. Now it is an atomic formula with bacteria and minerals. The flame in the kitchen is no longer something trivial. Now it reminds you of a vibrating display of nature.

That's what knowledge is all about, you see things from a different point of view. And that is what the Internet has and luckily it can be touched.

THE SMALLEST WAY TO SHARE YOUR VISION

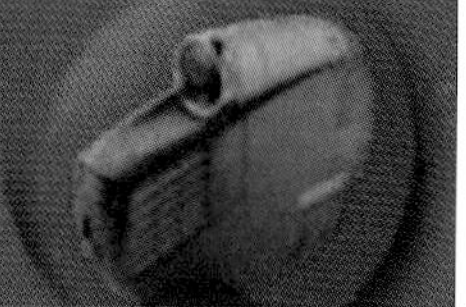

Inspiration Technology

click

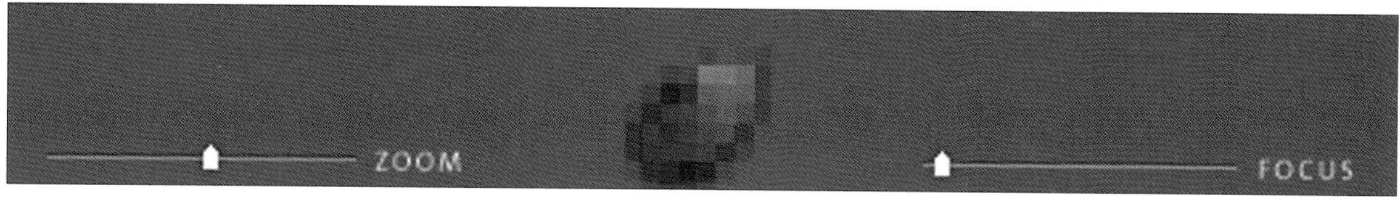

THE MP2800 MICROPORTABLE PROJECTOR

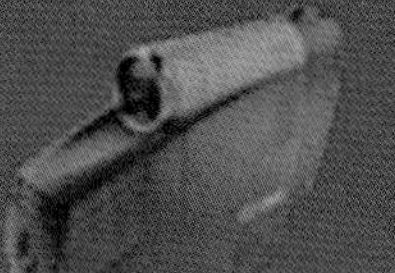

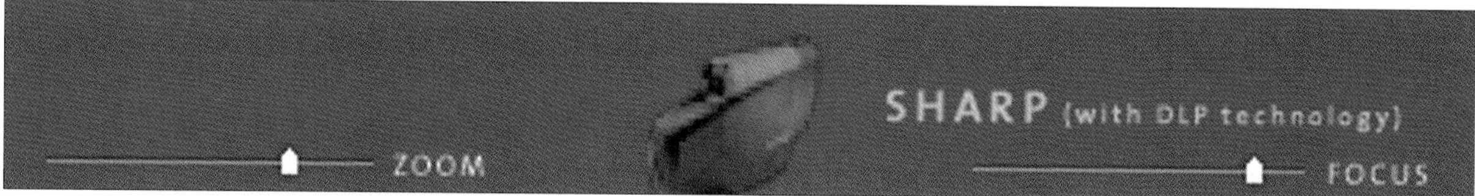

Agency	Foote Cone & Belding - San Francisco
Client	Compaq
Art Director	Steve Vranakis
Writer	Liz Campanile
Creative Director	Steve Vranakis
Designer	Edd Patton
Programmer	Freestyle Interactive
Producer	Brenda Jackson
ID	02008N
URL	clients.sf.fcb.com/Awards/one/

Portable Projecting Power

Our main objective in this campaign was to convey the size and precision of Compaq's revolutionary MP2800 Microprojector. And what better way to do so than by practicing what we preach in a 468 x 60 space? By enabling users to adjust both image size and clarity with controls right in the banner, we were able to provide an interactive sense of how small — but mighty — the Microprojector truly is.

Award	Bronze
Category	**Banner – Campaign**

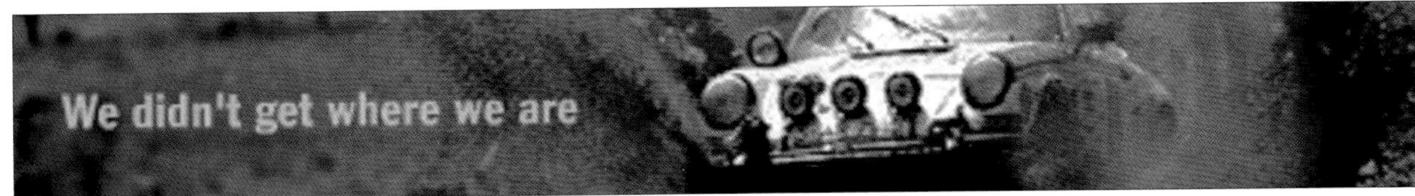

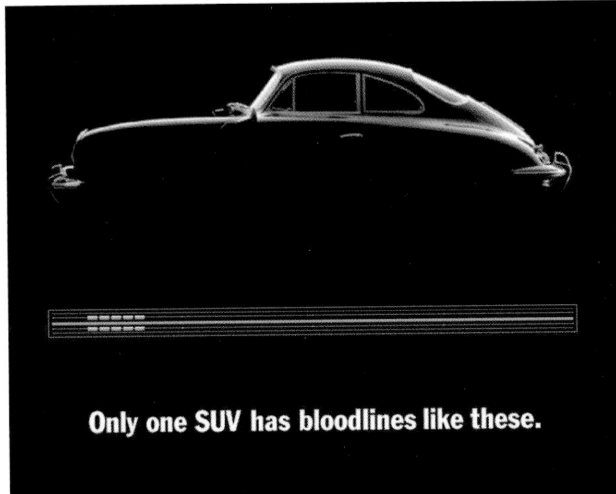

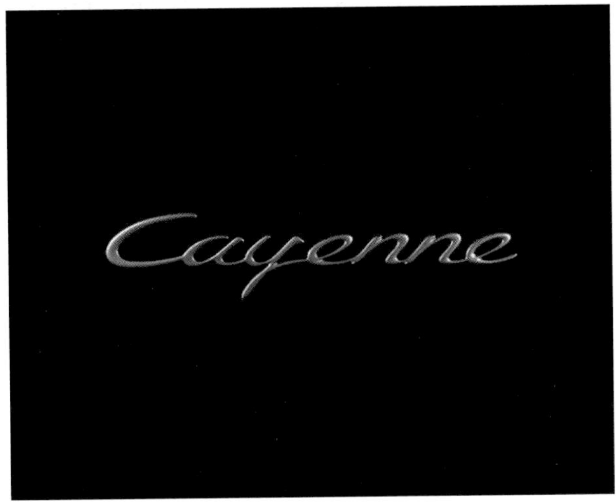

Agency	Carmichael Lynch - Minneapolis
Client	Porsche
Art Directors	Randy Hughes, T. Scott Major
Writer	Steve Casey
Creative Director	Jud Smith
Designer	T. Scott Major
Programmers	Donn Ha, T. Scott Major
Producer	Steve Diedrich
Digital Artists/Multimedia	T. Scott Major, Jesse Kaczmarek
ID	02009N
URL	http://carmichaellynch.com/portfolio/clients/oneshow/porsche-cayenne/

Award	Bronze
Category	Banner – Campaign
Page	10

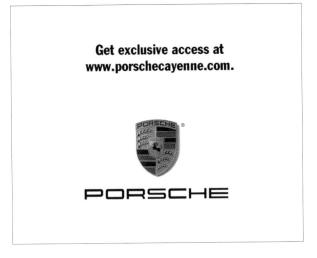

We didn't write the book on off-roading.

Just the racy chapters.

Cayenne

Get exclusive information
at porschecayenne.com.

Writing the Book on Off-Roading

Strategy & Rationale

To build anticipation and interest for Cayenne over the long timeframe leading up to the official launch of the vehicle in September 2002, it was decided to develop a three-phased campaign. The first phase, "Heritage," focused on Porsche's rich off-road and racing history in order to build credibility and highlight their expertise in this area, making Cayenne seem like a natural extension of their sports car line.

Reaching Top Prospects Online

The online advertising portion of the campaign supported these ideas along with direct mail, print advertising and Web. The Heritage campaign continued into 2002 and will be followed with the "Development" and "Launch" phases, which will gradually unveil more details of the vehicle.

Creative Execution Brings Porsche Heritage To Life

The creative reflects the Porsche heritage and off-road and racing experience. The visual aspects take advantage of the electronic medium by employing dynamic, animated movement, copy and image transitions and interactivity to catch the audience's eye. The call to action motivates the audience to go to the microsite created specifically for Cayenne, porschecayenne.com. At the site, prospects register to get access to the inside story, unveiled in "chapters" throughout the year, to learn more about Cayenne.

Agency	AlmapBBDO - São Paulo
Client	Iberia
Art Director	Victor Aragão
Writer	Caroline Freire
Creative Directors	Fabio Costa, Eduardo Foresti
Designer	Diego Martins
Programmers	Paulo Pacheco, Claudio Bellanga
ID	02010N
URL	www.almapbbdo.com.br/oneshow/iberia/business

Award	Gold
Category	**Beyond the Banner**
Page	12

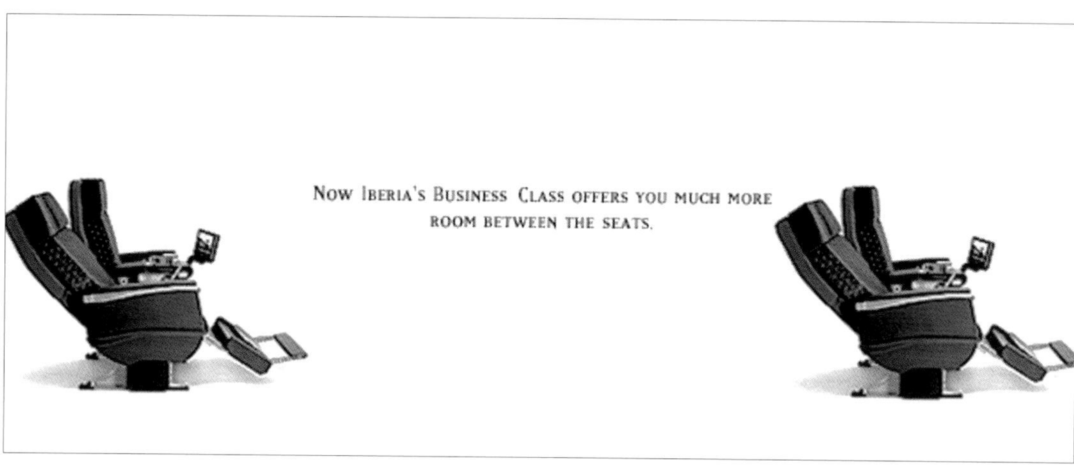

Now Iberia's Business Class offers you much more room between the seats.

Always thinking about you.

Reading Between the Lines

Iberia has only two classes of service on its flights. So our biggest challenge was to demonstrate the comfort, tranquility and quality of the Executive Class of service without resorting to the usual language employed by the other airlines. We chose this non-conventional format so that we could "play" with the title and the seats. Our intention was for the title to be readable only after the animation sequence.

03

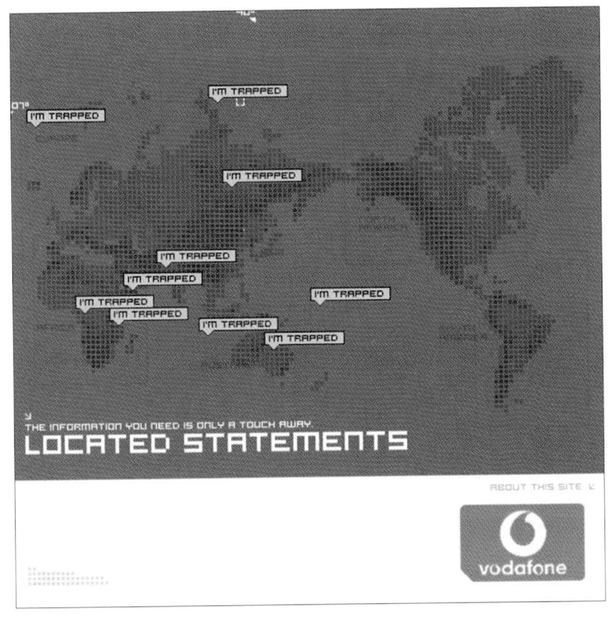

Agency	Wieden + Kennedy - Amsterdam
Client	Vodafone Ltd. UK
Art Directors	Marius Gronvold, Robert Lindström
Writers	Jenna Hall, Carlos Furnari
Creative Directors	Anita Lozinska, Ned McNeilege
Information Architects	Erik Loyer, David Eriksson
Programmers	Klaas Kroon, Joakim Lindkvist
Digital Artists/Multimedia	Marcus Ericsson, Mikael Forsgren Leong Kin Fei
Producers	Katie Raye, Marlene Eriksson Guido van den Meersche
Music/Sound	Dandy Warhols
ID	02011N
URL	http://howareyou.vodafone.com

Award	Gold
Category	**Beyond the Banner**
Page	14

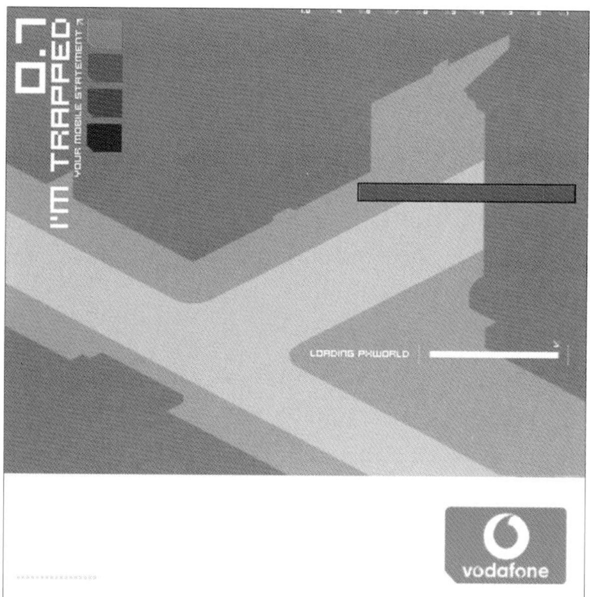

Understanding What Lies Behind a Connection

At the heart of the Vodafone brand is an understanding of the human need for communication. People want to connect with others and share how they're feeling whenever they need to, no matter where they are. The global launch of the Vodafone advertising campaign shared this idea with people by using the simple line, "How are you?"

An important element of the launch online was the perfect forum to ask "How are you?" and have people respond. From the Vodafone perspective, online communities aren't formed by geography or nationality, but instead around common interests and experiences. It's not about connecting with other German or Spanish people. It's about connecting with other people who feel gorgeous or free or lost. In this mood based experience, we want to give people immediate contact with the community that suits them, and let them explore that mood in an involving and unexpected way.

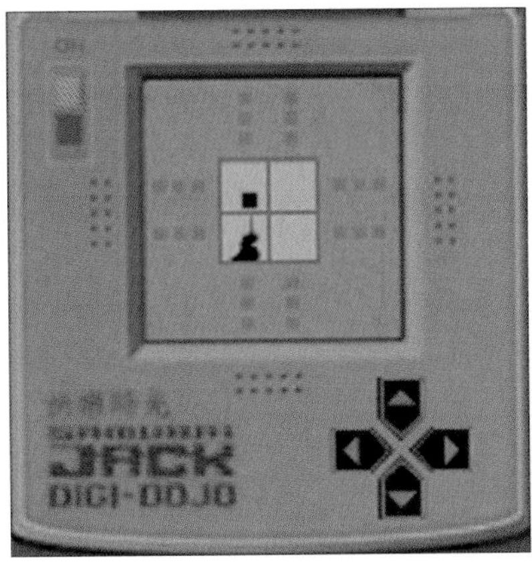

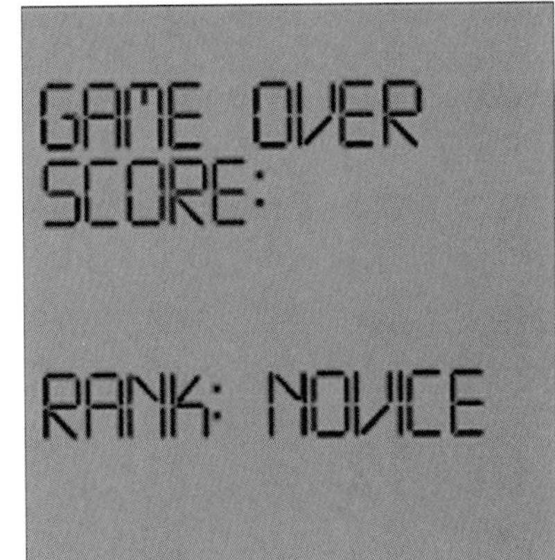

Agency | POP - New York
Client | Cartoon Network
Creative Director | Vincent Lacava
Designers | Geoffrey Fowler, Tristan Spence
Vander McClain
Game Designer | Frank Lantz
Programmer | Veronique Brossier
Producer | Maureen Reilly
Music/Sound | Mark Thompson
ID | 02012N
URL | www.popnyc.com/contest/orbit.html

03

Award | Silver
Category | **Beyond the Banner**
Page | 16

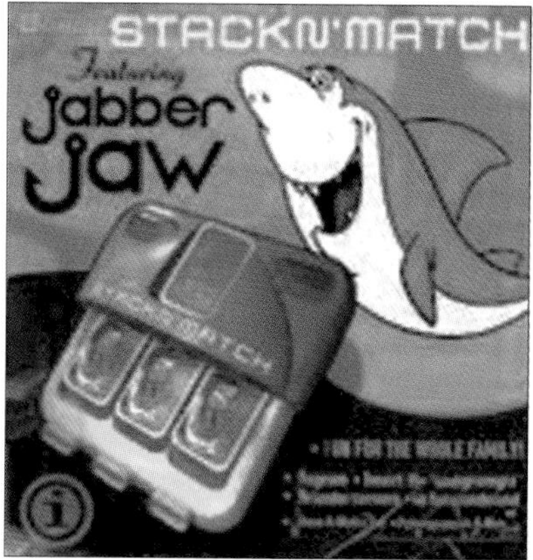

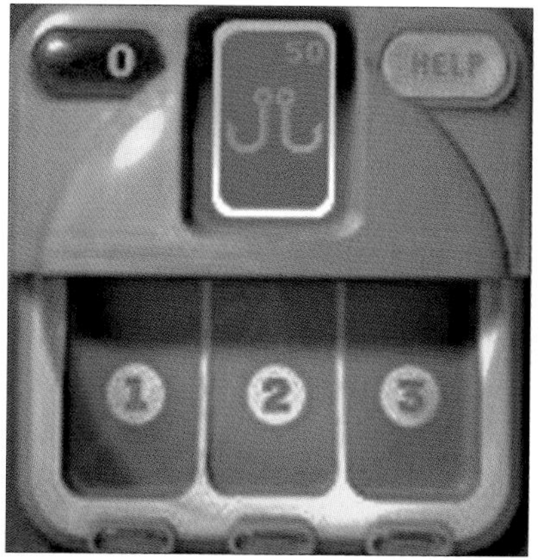

Mini Games, Mighty Gaming

They used to be made of plastic and come in cereal boxes or gumball machines. Often they broke or got lost. But they were great on long family car trips, after "I Spy with my Little Eye" got tedious. Usually they were stamped, "Made in Japan," at least before those words signified chic design and the priciest upper strata of luxury goods. Inspired by our love of classic hand-held games, each of the eight mini-games we devised for Cartoon Network are simple, but together they'll give kids a well-rounded workout of hand, eye and gaming skills. One features Samurai Jack, outnumbered by his foes, engaged in mortal combat. In another, kids get to exercise their fashion sense on an unsuspecting Snagglepuss. There are memory games, card games, and a somewhat surreal Bugs Bunny Chia head.

Agency	Herraiz Soto & Co. - Madrid
Client	Mahou Beer
Art Director	Andreu Colomer
Writer	Rafael Soto
Creative Directors	Angel Herraiz, Rafael Soto
Designer	Andreu Colomer
Illustrator	Siscu Soler
Programmer	Javier Álvarez
Music/Sound	Sergi Mula
ID	02013N
URL	www.herraizsoto.com/festivales/game_i

Award Bronze

Category **Beyond the Banner**

Page 18

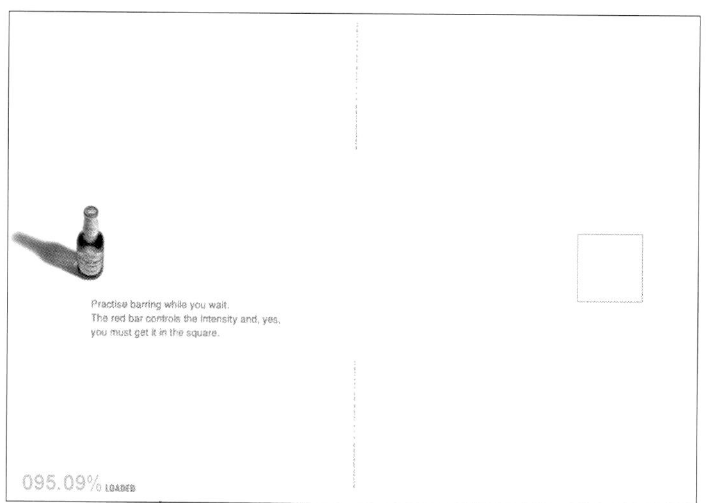

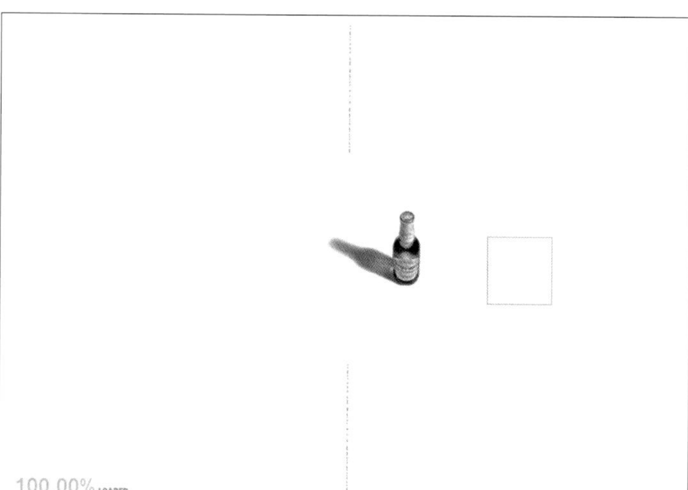

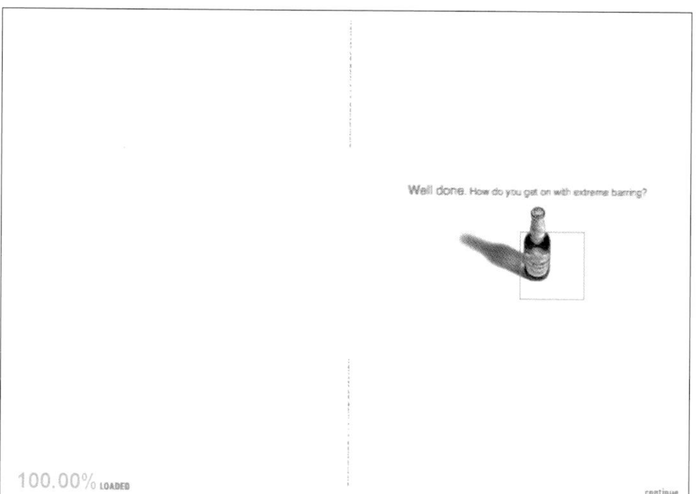

Football for the Fans

There's the football (soccer) of the stars. That of the newspaper headlines. That of the slow motions with drops of sweat and impossible manoeuvres. Prime time football. That of the gods.

But there is another football. One which is even better. That of the fan. The one who shouts in front of the telly. The one who is on his feet in the stadium. The one who crosses his fingers.

This piece wanted to hit the mark with those fans. With those who have football in their heads all the time.

Of course, they don't see peas, they see footballs. Okay, so let's play football.

And that's how the idea of making a game of football out of everyday objects came about. First things first – if you can play football with something, why eat it?

But without a challenge, football isn't football. So, to make things more difficult, we offered the possibility of setting up a goal using the glass and the tin, being able to make it as big or small as you want according to the points you want to score. The same with the salt and pepper which act as fullbacks and, the more you want them to bother you, the more points you score.

Ah, and of course, this is only the beginning. Coming soon, changes of stadium; a Chinese restaurant with sushi and an airplane with a food tray. Bon apétit.

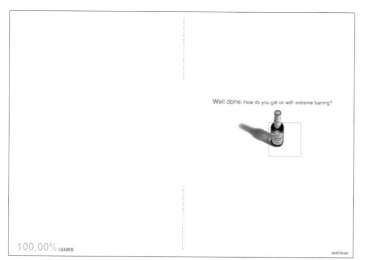

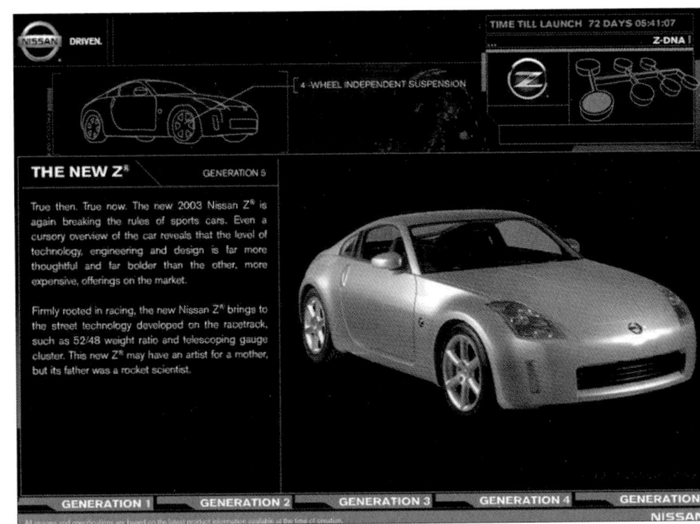

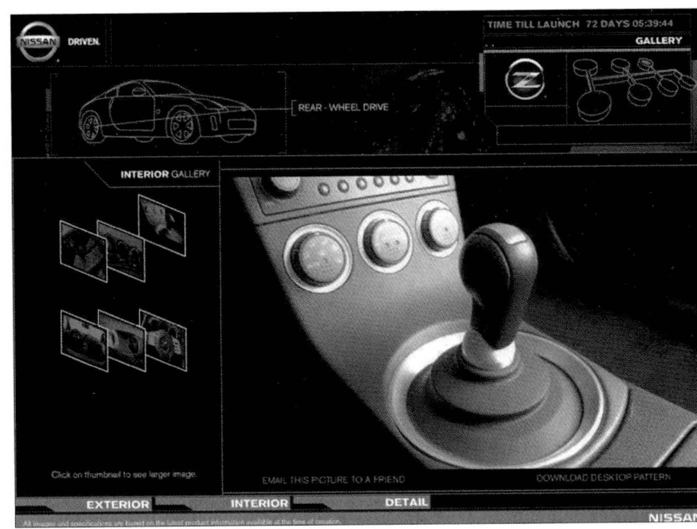

Agency	TBWA/Chiat/Day - Los Angeles
Client	Nissan North America
Art Director	Shervin Samari
Writer	Jason Rappaport
Creative Directors	Gary M. Smith, Rob Schwartz Chris Graves
Designers	Dan Lareau, Pat Cinco, Brian Kiel
Information Architect	Gary M. Smith
Programmers	Dan Lareau, Brian Kiel
Producer	Jill Savage
ID	02014N
URL	richter.tbwachiat.com/oneshow

Award	Gold
Category	**Beyond the Banner**
Page	20

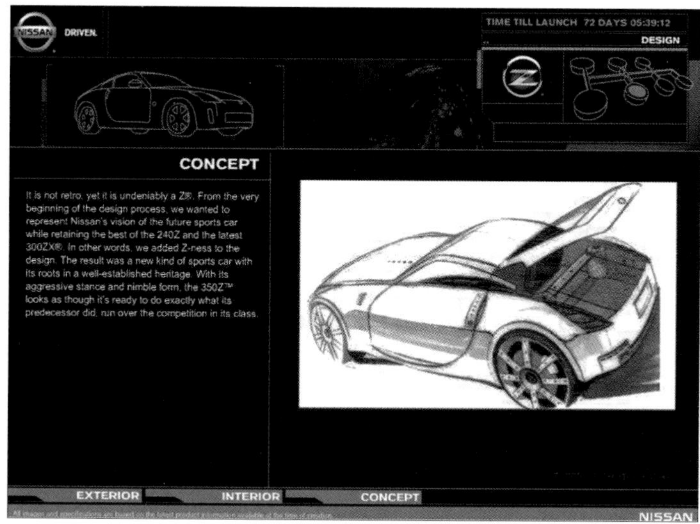

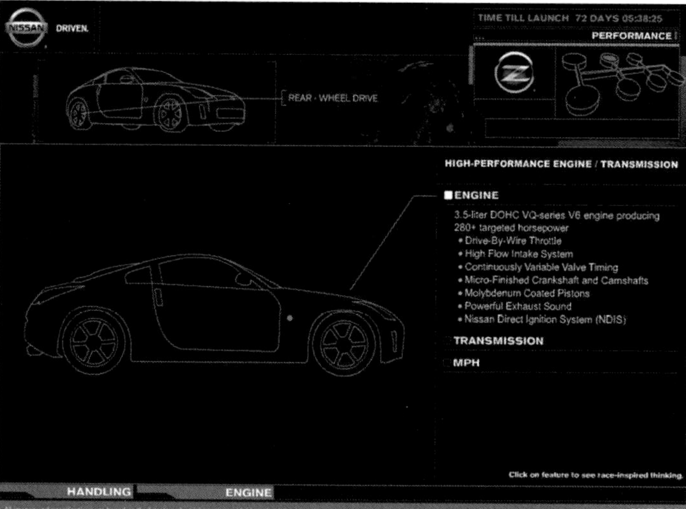

Exploring the FutureZ

The reason for FutureZ was to re-introduce the New Nissan Z to the public while re-enforcing the heritage of a tremendously popular sports car.

Technically, the site was designed in a full flash interface, which re-enforced the innovation that the Z car carries with it.

The site was meant to give an exploratory, yet very informative user experience without too many bells and whistles, while enticing previous (as well as first time Z enthusiasts) to acquire more information on the car and eventually pre-order one.

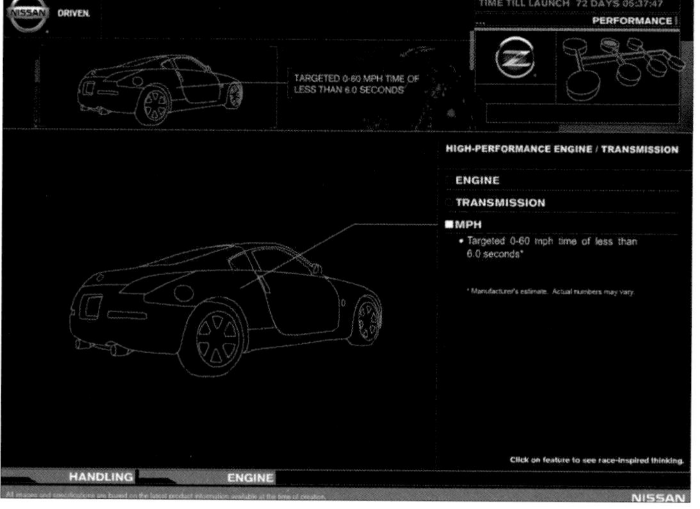

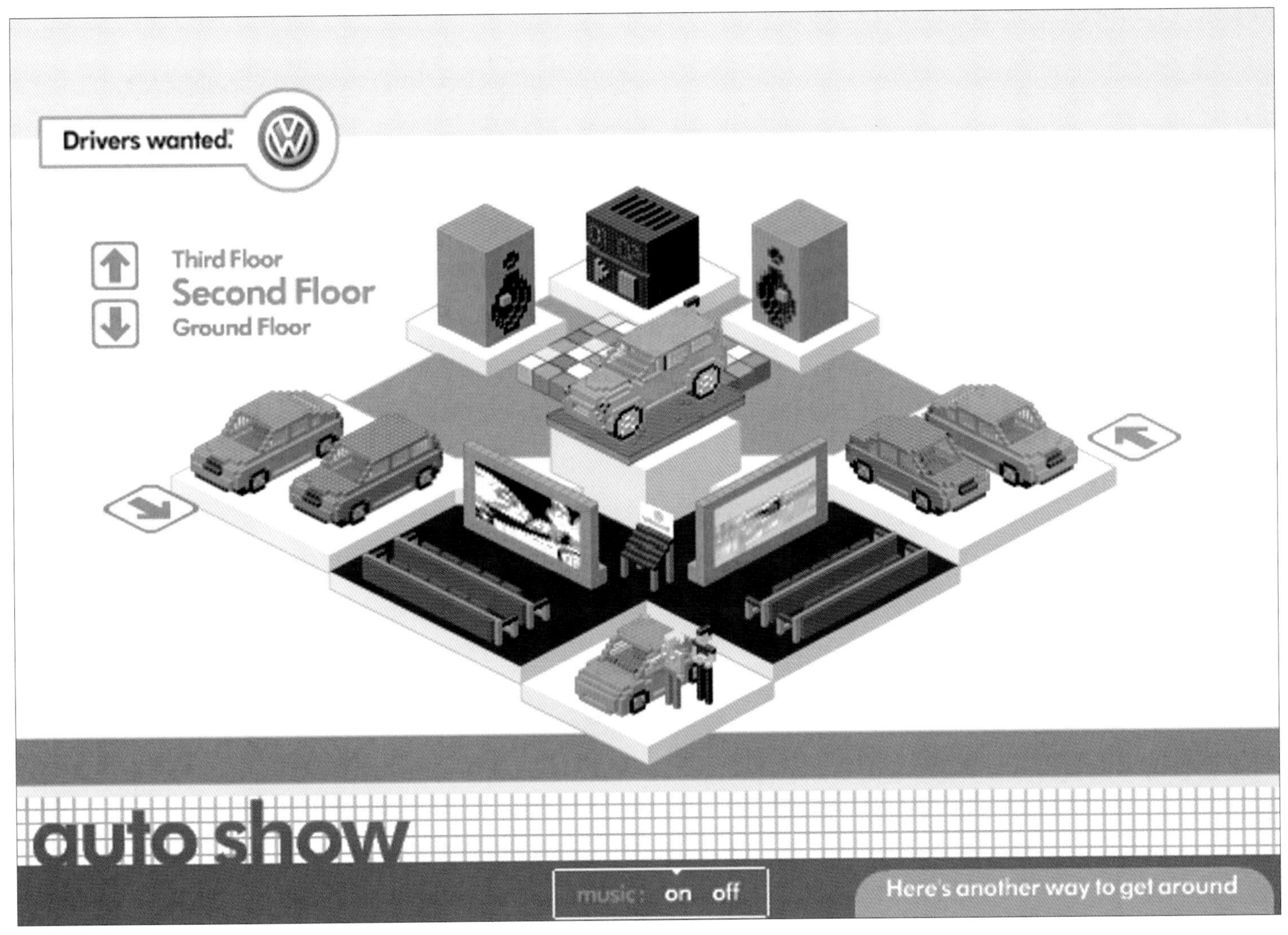

Agency	Arnold Worldwide - Boston
Client	Volkswagen of America
Art Director	Dmitri Cavandar
Writer	Kerry Lynch
Creative Directors	Ron Lawner, Alan Pafenbach, Tim Brunelle Chris Bradley
Mechanical Supervisor	Claudine Kaprielian
Technical Director	Jonathan Groves
Production Company	Heavy Productions
Designer	Samiah Abdul Basir
Flash Programmer	Joe Cartman
Programmer	Silverline Technologies
Producer	Jennifer Phillips-Bruns
ID	02015N
URL	vw.com/autoshow

Award	Gold
Category	**Promotional Advertising — Web Sites**
Page	22

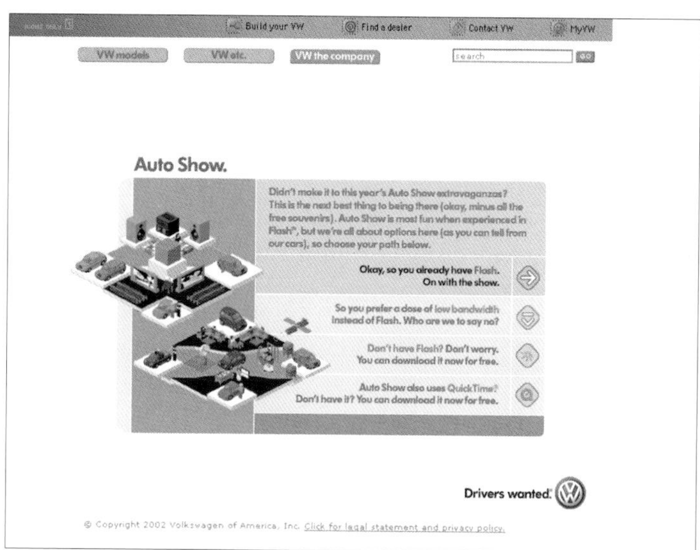

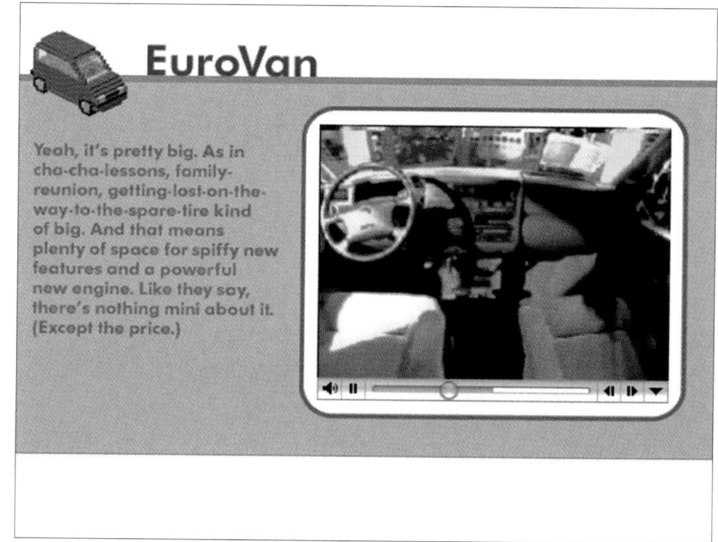

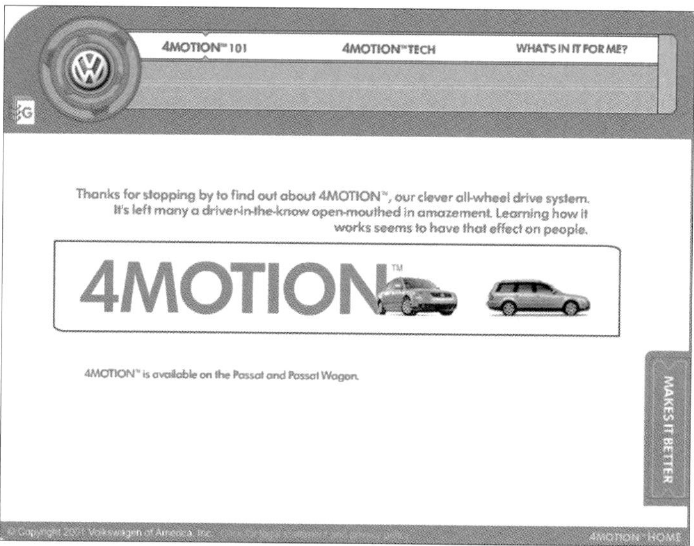

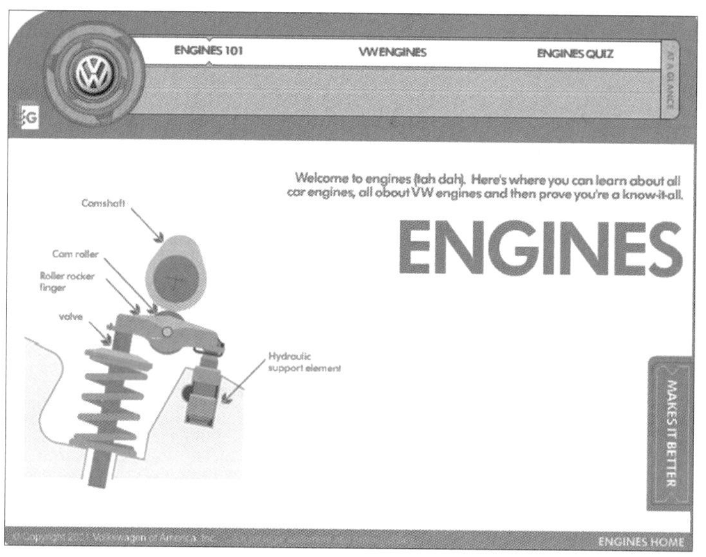

A Multi-Tiered Metaphor that Works

After Dmitri and Kerry picked up their Gold Pencils at the awards ceremony, they didn't seem very impressed with the achievement. So Pete Favat leaned over and said, "Hey, it took me ten years to even get into the book! Show some enthusiasm fer chrissakes!" So Dmitri politely raised his award and softly uttered "Woo hooo."

Kids today. They don't know how good they have it.

Chris Bradley
Tim Brunelle

The site is one of those Web metaphors that actually works: a virtual three-story auto show which gives users a taste of a real auto show. The navigation is dirt simple. We shot "live" videos of each car from Detroit and LA (thanks to Martin Albert, our DP). And the 3-D "lego" design keeps everything in perspective. Particularly saucy is the weirdly recognizable 3-D engine on the ground floor.

Dmitri Cavander
Kerry Lynch

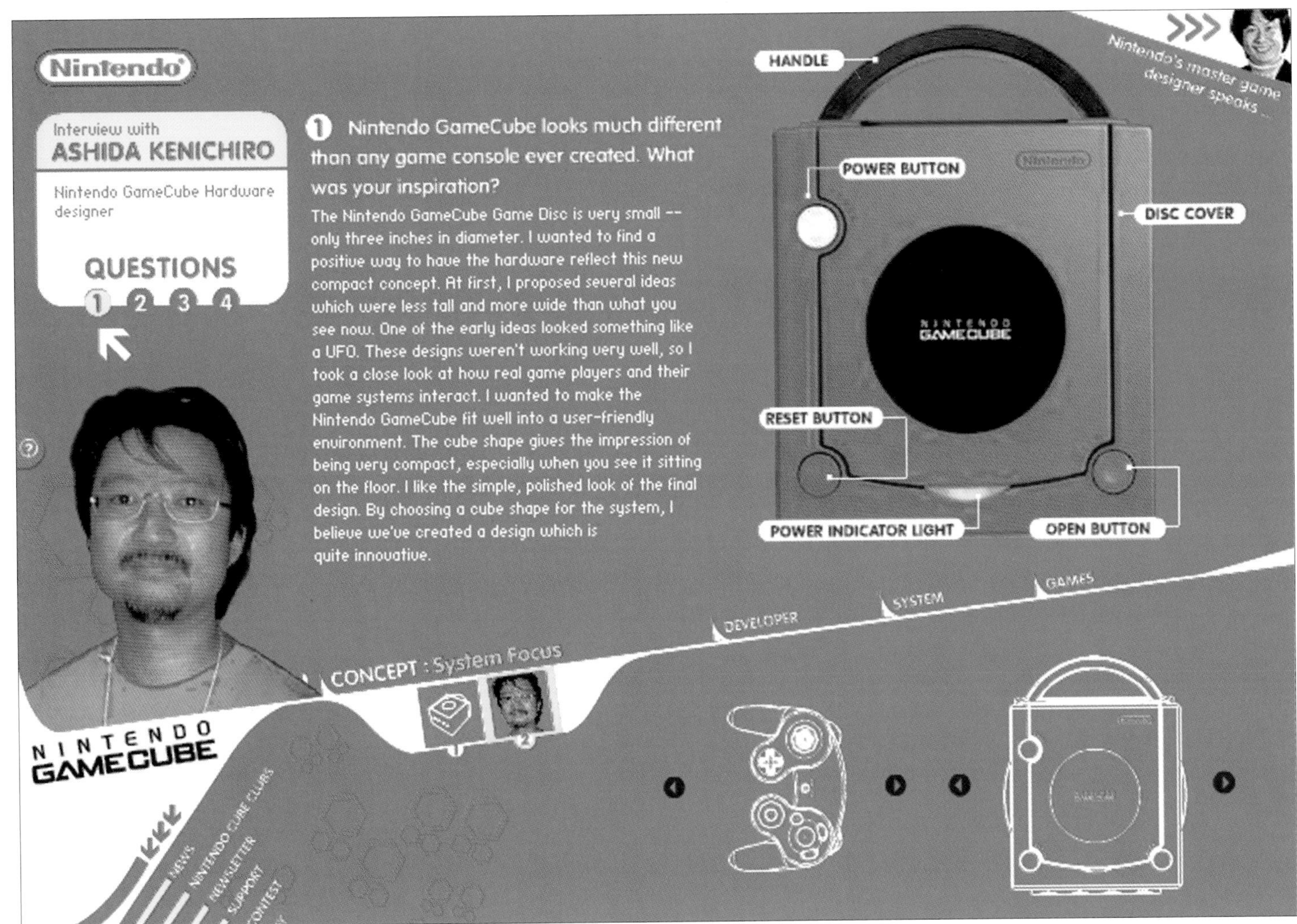

Agency	Blast Radius - Vancouver
Client	Nintendo of America
Art Director	David Wharton
Writers	Peter Alexander, Judy Renouf
Creative Director	Kaye Puhlmann
Designers	Andre Matarazzo, Aimee Croteau Brent Hopkin, Hyung Bin Im, Tyler Payne Lilli Wong
Programmers	Cory Christians, Diane Kim, Ryan Klak Jade McClure, Valerie McDonald, Bart Millar Graeme Dimmick, Ian Schumacher
Information Architects	Ali Grayeli, Julian Richards
Producer	Andy Hartpence
ID	02016N
URL	www.nintendogamecube.com

04

Award	Silver
Category	**Promotional Advertising — Web Sites**
Page	24

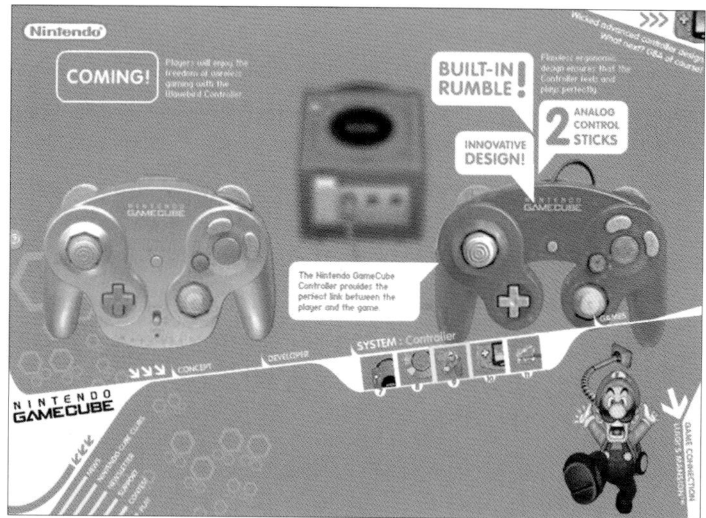

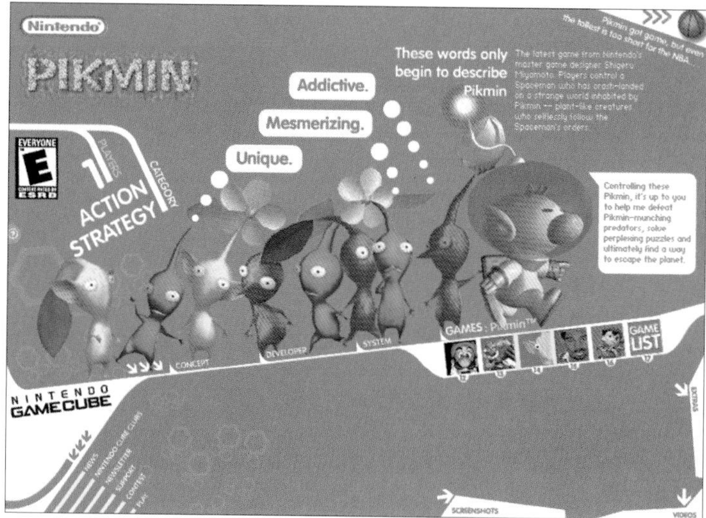

Innovation Cubed

As part of an integrated marketing campaign for the Fall 2001 launch of the new Nintendo GameCube console, Nintendo of America partnered with Blast Radius to develop the interactive components of the campaign, which included teaser Web sites, interstitials, superstitials, a CD-ROM and a full promotional Web site.

Blast Radius conveyed the Nintendo GameCube brand by creating online experiences that are user-friendly and playful, much like the console itself, and by appealing to a gamer's need for a wealth of game and system information.

Featuring sections on game Developers, the System and Games, the site provides video clips and images of games, a game list, a variety of angle shots of the console and controller, and system details.

For those who just want to play, there are five activities on the site that illustrate distinctive system features. When played successfully, the activities reward players with exclusive wallpaper downloads.

We needed to create a site that would appeal to all-ages, create a buzz with Nintendo advocates, capture the interest of the general gaming population and provide deeper information for those driven to the site by offline channels. We began with playful teasers to build hype around the site, establish a personality for Nintendo GameCube and communicate key features of the console such as the wireless controller.

To introduce the console to the market for the launch phase we wanted to communicate the incredible depth of Nintendo's games, the thought process that went into creating them and most importantly, how much fun the games are to play. This was accomplished by telling the story of Nintendo GameCube in a semi-linear format starting with the initial concept, moving on to the developers and the system, then culminating in the games themselves.

Ultimately, the best thing about the site is how the various disciplines on the team came together and worked with Nintendo to create an experience that captured the fun and excitement of playing the Nintendo GameCube.

Kaye Puhlmann
Creative Director

Agency	Scholz & Volkmer - Weisbaden
Client	Mercedes-Benz
Art Director	Christa Heinold
Writer	Chris Kohl
Creative Director	Anette Scholz
Designer	Christa Heinold
Digital Artists/Multimedia	Mario Dold, Michael Dralle Samuel Ruckstuhl
Programmer	Thorsten Kraus
ID	02017N
URL	www.mercedes-benz.com/detroit2002

04

Award	Bronze
Category	**Promotional Advertising — Web Sites**
Page	26

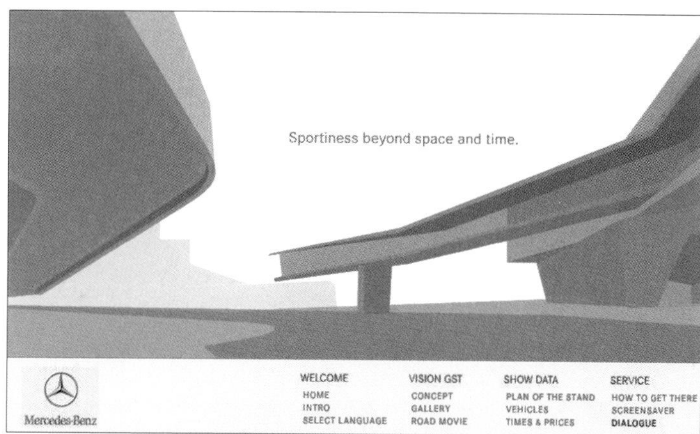

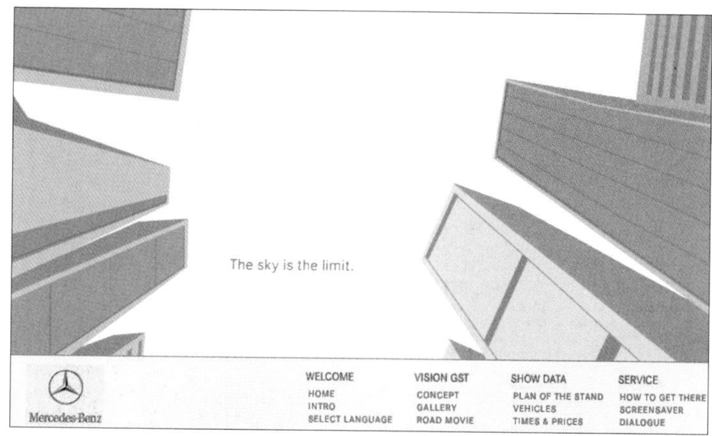

Show and Tell: The Vision GST

A show Web special for Mercedes-Benz was developed on the occasion of the "North American International Auto Show 2002" in Detroit.

In the focus of the show and thus also of the Internet appearance is the presentation of a new type of Mercedes-Benz vehicle, of the "Vision GST" (Grand Sport Tourer).

The site offers emotional as well as informative access. The new room concept of the "Vision GST" is in the center of the emotional presentation. The viewer is taken through animated landscapes into the new automobile's own world. Apart from that, information about every exhibited car of Mercedes-Benz, about the show stand, the opening hours, the show prices, and a route description can be quickly requested.

The Internet appearance addresses Mercedes-Benz customers and those interested in getting information about the Show and the activities of Mercedes-Benz.

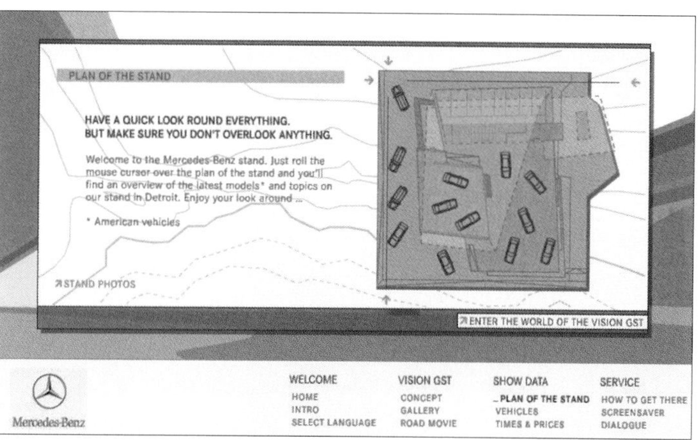

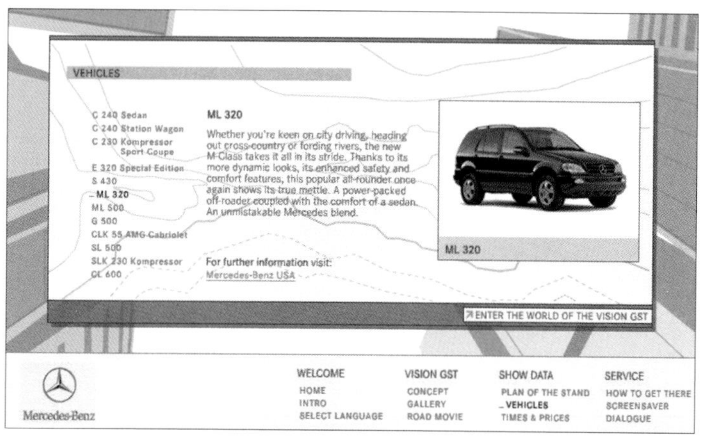

04

Agency	PeñaBrand/Butler Shine & Stern Sausalito
Client	Digitango
Art Director	Luis Peña
Designer	Luis Peña
Illustrator	Luis Peña
Programmer	Luis Peña
ID	02018N
URL	www.penabrand.com/digitango/ digitango.html

Award	Silver
Category	**Promotional Advertising — CD-ROMs**
Page	28

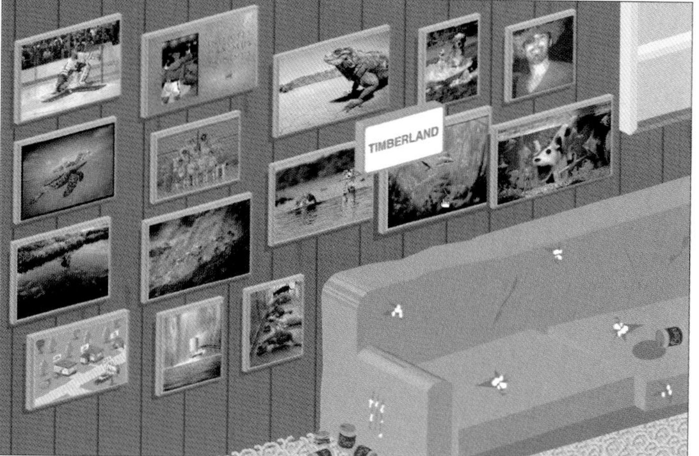

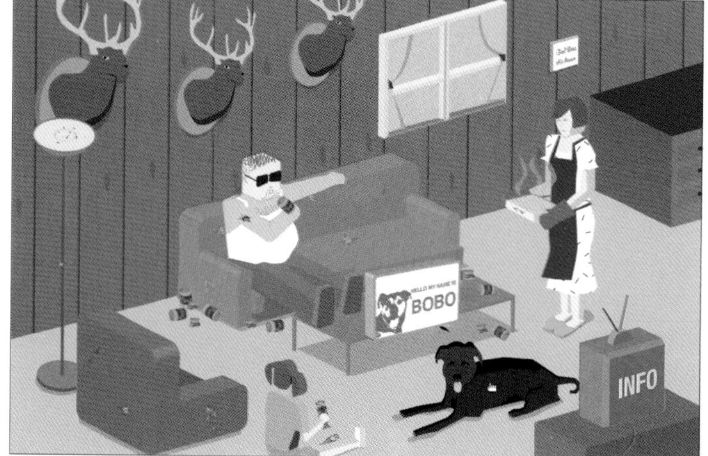

Square Dancing in Tango Town

Digitango is a high end image creation shop in San Francisco. Their clients include art directors and creative directors throughout the country. For their portfolio they wanted a CD-ROM that highlighted their work and told the story of how their work is created. They wanted the CD to communicate their sense of humor and 'cool' mood of their office space. I came up with a "trailer park" motif, which reflects the sensibility of their office space, and using 'comic based' illustrations I created a unique interface which implements an environment rather than the typical menu bar.

Agency | TBWA Hunt Lascaris - Johannesburg
Client | BMW
Art Directors | Paul Warner, Peter Khoury
Writer | Avital Pinchevsky
Creative Director | Tony Granger
Designer | Peter Khoury
Programmers | Preston Thomas, Olivier Schildt
ID | 02019N

Award | Gold
Category | **Promotional Advertising — Other Digital Advertising**
Page | 30

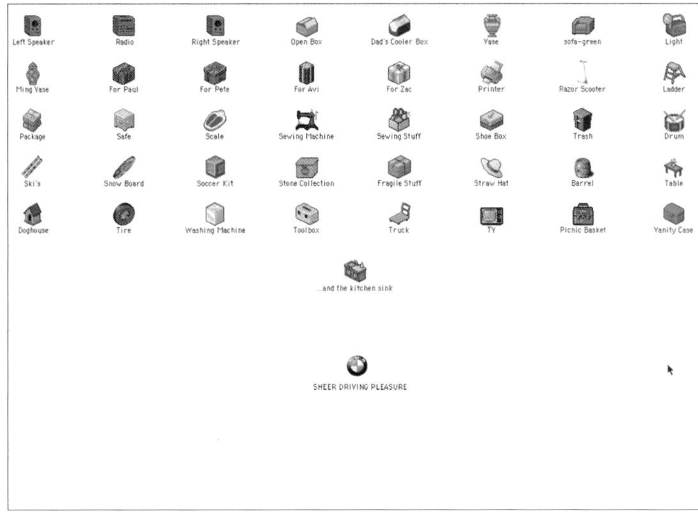

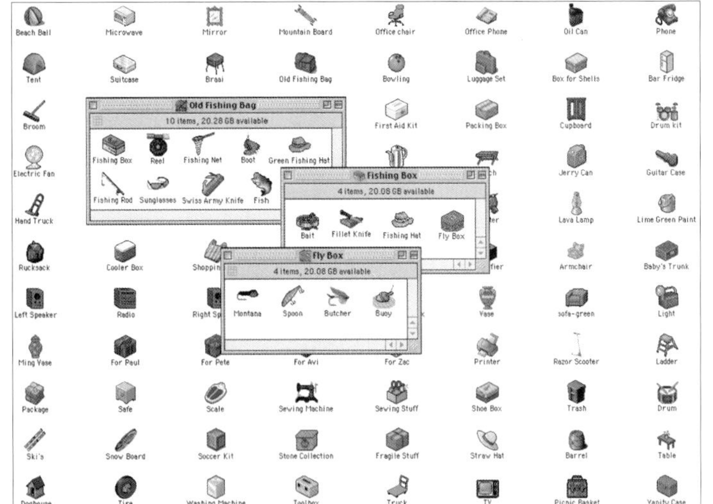

...and the Kitchen Sink

The New BMW Touring's USP is the fact that it has 200% more boot space. Our primary goal was to illustrate this massive boot space. The secondary was to bring potential buyers to the BMW Web site and expose them to this car. The mailer was sent to people on the BMW database. Upon opening the e-mail, an invisible folder would download onto the viewer's desktop. The viewer would then see a BMW Touring icon and click on it. Upon clicking, a folder would open and fill the screen with many icons representing the things you'd find in the boot.

The icons themselves were files too, some up to 3 layers deep. For example, An old fishing bag' could be opened to reveal 10 items that the fishing bag contained including things like a reel, a fishing net, a fishing box and more. The fishing box would then open to reveal 4 items including a flybox. The flybox would then open to reveal 4 fishing flies.

The viewer would scroll down and see the BMW logo, and wouldn't be able to get out of the folder until clicking on the logo. That, in turn would take the viewer directly to the BMW Web site.

MID-TOKYO MAPS

make it better

[素顔の東京]

TOKYO UNDRESSED → To the map

Mid-Tokyo Maps shows Tokyo in ways she has never been seen before.
We invite everyone to participate in thinking about where she should go from here.

TAMACHI HAMAMATSUCHO SHINBASHI YURAKUCHO TOKYO KANDA AKIHABARA OCHANOMIZU SUIDOBASHI IIDABASHI ICHIGAYA YOTSUYA SHINANOMACHI SENDAGAYA YOYOGI

Library

Return to latest issue

Top Page About "Mid-Tokyo Maps" Viewers' voices Inquiries

Copyright (c) 2001 Mori Building Co., Ltd.

Agency	Transform - Tokyo
Client	Mori Building Company
Art Director	MID-TOKYO MAPS Creative Team
Writer	Nanba Hitomi
Creative Directors	Hisayoshi Tohsaki Yoshiaki Nishimura Naoki Sato
Designers	Momoko Takaoka, Yusuke Shibata Rio Hashimoto, Jun Awano, Kazuo Soma Taku Enjoji , Yoko Washimine
Programmer	Jun Kuriyama
Producers	Masahiro Watahiki Hiroko Sakomura
ID	02020N
URL	http://www.mid-tokyo.com/
Award	Gold
Category	**Corporate Image B2C — Web Sites**
Page	32

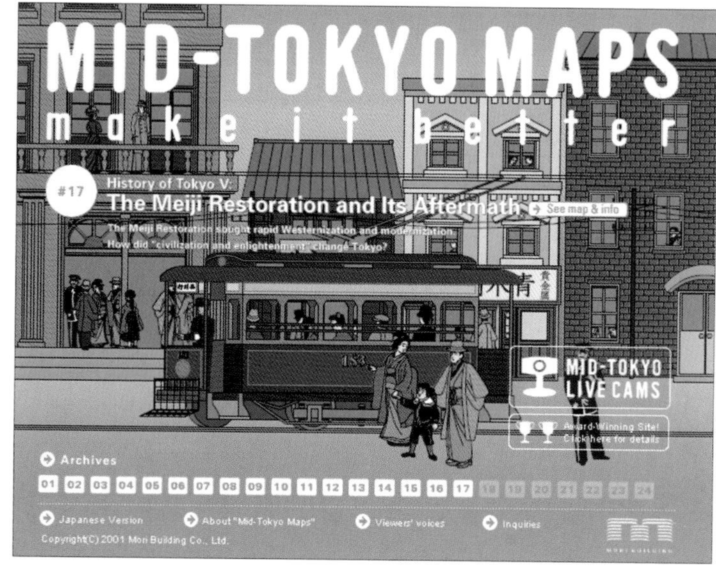

Mapping a Better Tomorrow

Mid-Tokyo Maps thinks about Tokyo as a world city — how we can re-make it into an attractive place to live, one that will hold its own in today's global competition.

"Make It Better." Based on this theme and centered on Mid-Tokyo, twenty-four maps in five series formed the basis for our discussions of: "Urban Parallels," which compared Tokyo with other major metropolises; "Urban Appeal," which looked at what a city needs to attract residents; the "History of Tokyo"; "Urban Lifestyles" and "Developing 21st Century Cities."

Interactive maps were used in order to make the tremendous amount of city planning information in each map easy to understand and fun for the casual viewer, as well as a resource for the specialist.

In Japan, the revitalization of our cities is now seen as a central pillar in revolutionizing our country and economy — but we hope that Mid-Tokyo Maps will contribute to a discussion about cities not only in Japan, but also around the world.

Agency	Framfab - Copenhagen
Client	Nike Europe
Art Director	Rasmus Frandsen
Writer	Jamie McPhee
Creative Director	Lars Bastholm
Designers	Tue Wesnæs, Rasmus Michelsen
Producer	Anne-Sofie Hahn-Pedersen
Information Architect	Jens Christiansen
Programmer	Thomas Weiss
ID	02021N
URL	http://freestyle.framfab.dk

Award	Gold
Category	**Corporate Image B2C — Web Sites**
Page	34

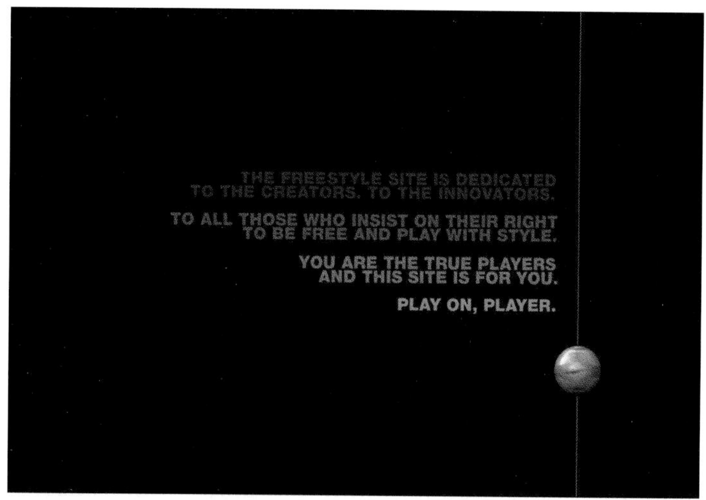

Kicking (and Dribbling) it Freestyle

The Concept

Giving respect to the true players, nike.com/freestyle celebrates the creativity and style that athletes bring to their own game. To bring it to life online, the site's aim is to give users the opportunity to create, personalize and participate. It's improvisational, innovative and totally original. In other words, freestyle.

The Tone

To merge street ballers, both football and basketball, with pro players, Freestyle is set in an undefined space where the players make it happen. The look is minimal and the voice is casual to emphasize the "just doing our thing" attitude.

The Site

The Crew: Features bios and behind-the-scenes clips from the Nike Freestyle shoots.
The Mixer: Allows users to create their own customized screensaver by mixing clips from the Freestyle commercials.
Show Off: Gives a heads up to what Freestyle events are happening and how to get the heads up when they're heading your way.
Nike iD: Lets users create their own shoes by choosing the color, texture and personalized tag.

Agency	Moonwalk Stockholm / St. Lukes Sweden - Stockholm
Client	Speedy Tomato
Art Directors	Johan Mogren, Jakob Westman, Ysabel Zu
Writers	Fredrik Lundgren, Nathan Cooper
Creative Directors	Calle Sjonell, Tim Hearn
Designer	Linus Niklasson
Programmers	Felix af Ekenstam, Didde Brockmann
Content Strategists	Robert Thorgren, Nicole van Rooij-Ekstr
Production Co.	Fido Film
ID	02022N
URL	http://www.moonwalk.se/eng/campaign/ monsterwithoutamouth/

Award	Silver
Category	**Corporate Image B2C — Web Sites**
Page	36

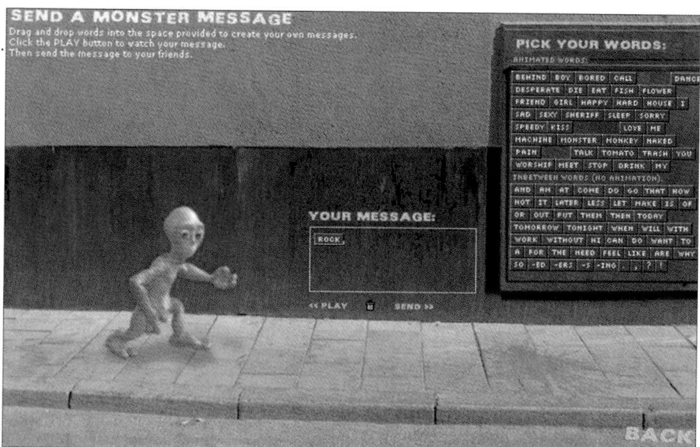

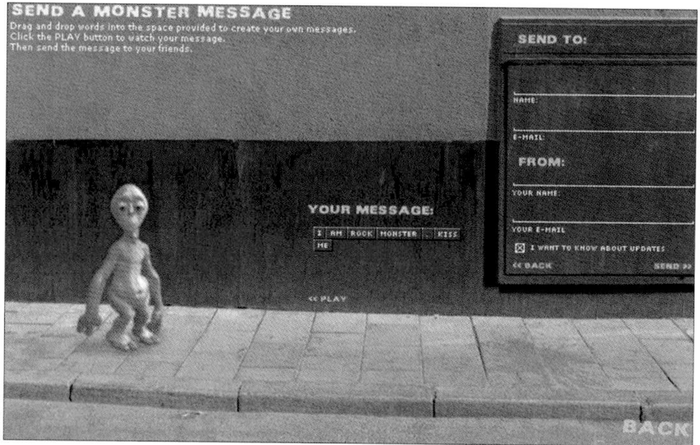

Communicating a Monster of a Message

Speedy Tomato wanted to reach trendsetters in Europe to sign up for their mobile community. They thought that if they could persuade the trendsetters, a lot of others would follow their footsteps. The concept was based on the creation of a personality that was the total opposite to Speedy Tomato – in other words someone who was really bad at communication. The answer was the Monster Without a Mouth. He has no mouth and no ears, which makes him really bad at making himself understood.

We wanted to get the visitors to interact with bad and confusing communication through the Monster to understand the importance of good communication – and sign up for Speedy Tomato's mobile community. To create curiosity and to get visitors to discover the Monster for themselves first, the site was released without any advertising for the first two months.

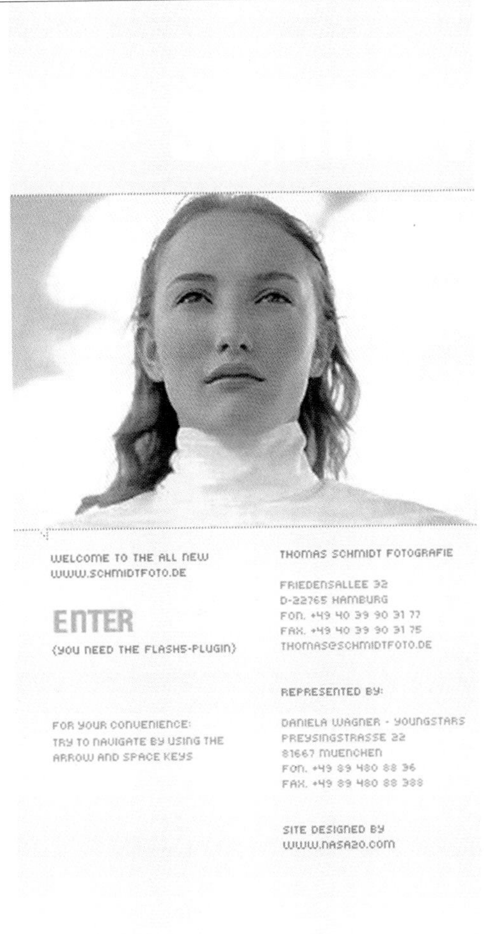

Agency | n.a.s.a.2.0 - Hamburg
Client | Thomas Schmidt
Art Director | Oliver Hinrichs
Creative Director | John Eberstein
Designer | Oliver Hinrichs
Content Strategist | John Eberstein
Photographer | Thomas Schmidt
Programmers | Ronald Böhling, Oliver Hinrichs
Malte Büchmann
Digital Artist/Multimedia | Oliver Hinrichs
ID | 02023N
URL | www.schmidtfoto.de

05

Award | Silver
Category | **Corporate Image B2C — Web Sites**
Page | 38

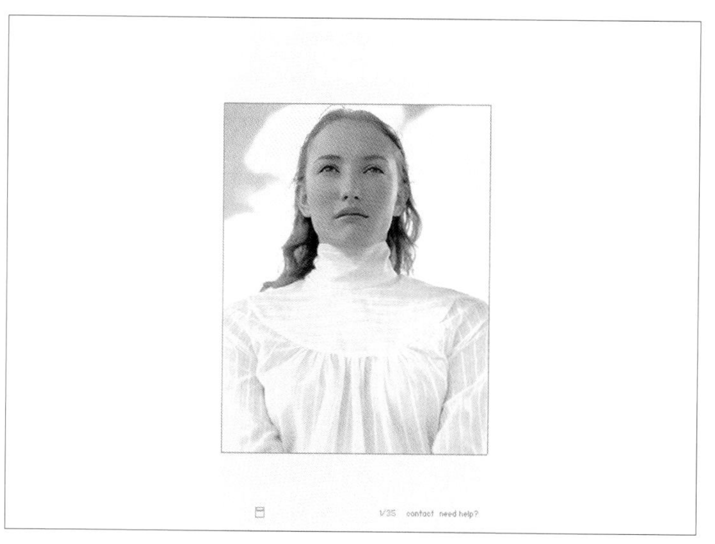

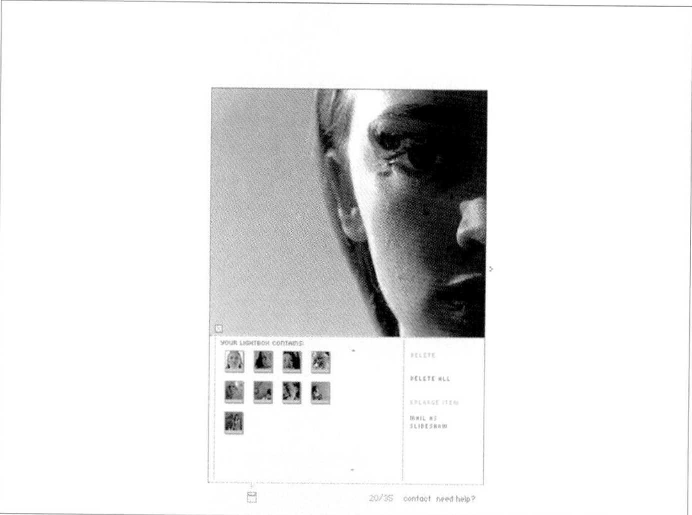

A Focus on Form and Functionality

Task

German artist and photographer Thomas Schmidt is always looking to reveal 'the third dimension beyond' his pictures. The look and feel of his work is very special indeed: His photos are pure, modern, almost spiritual. Keywords for his site as well. Thomas Schmidt asked for as little distraction from his pictures as possible, for less loading time, more focus on the pure work.

Realization

Sometimes a menu or even a mouseclick is one too many. Functionality is wanted and available, just when and where it is necessary. Pure keyboard controlling, if wanted, offers more ease of use and less visual distraction. A custom-built admininstration tool enables Thomas Schmidt to easily update photos himself – no flash knowledge necessary. The site itself takes full advantage of Flash 5 and a php4 backend is used to store all the user information in a database.

VOLVO
for life

LET THE JOURNEY BEGIN

voc©copyright 2001

Agency	Ogilvy Interactive - Singapore
Client	Volvo
Art Director	Dominic Goldman
Writers	Mak Kye Li, Tan Kim Lee, Graham Kelly
Creative Director	Graham Kelly
Photographer/Illustrator	Dominic Goldman
Designer	Dominic Goldman
Programmers	Chandra Barathi, Dominic Goldman
Producer	Yow Pin Fern
Digital Artist/Multimedia	Dominic Goldman
Music/Sound	Ben James Galvin
ID	02024N
URL	www.volvocarsasia.com/museum/home.html

05

Award	Bronze
Category	**Corporate Image B2C — Web Sites**
Page	40

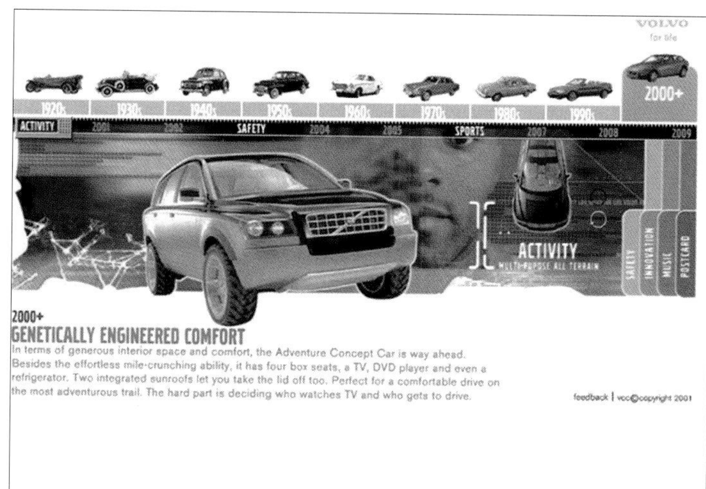

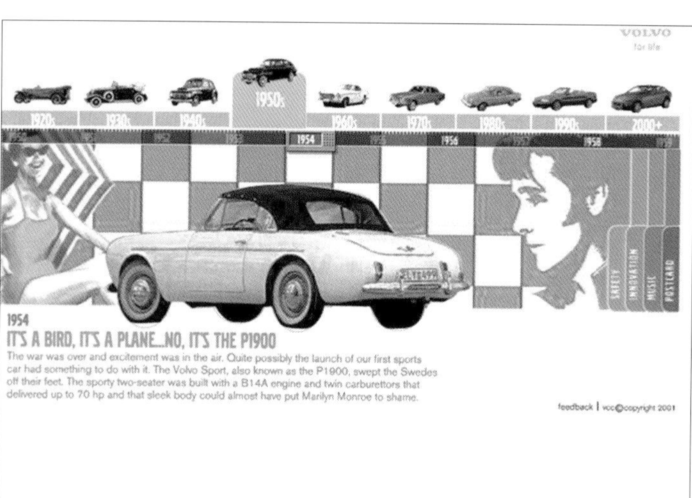

The Past, Present, and Future of Volvo

The objective was to deepen Volvo owners' relationship with the brand and attract potential buyers to the brand. We decided to do this by drawing on the heritage of Volvo. Specifically, by demonstrating how, throughout its history, Volvo has remained true to its key values of safety, innovation and environmental awareness.

These values are highlighted in each era. But rather than just listing them alongside shots of cars, we wanted to put the information in the context of its time. The solution was a simple-to-navigate site that immerses the visitor in the sights and sounds of each decade.

For example, in the section on the Sixties the cars are surrounded by visual cues from the decade, such as psychedelic patterns and lava lamps. Not to mention clips of a classic Volvos in action, which you view on a vintage TV. The strains of a Sitar playing in the background added to the groovy mood.

To spread the word about the site, there's a viral component. You can send friends e-postcards from your favorite era: past, present or future.

05

Agency	Scholz & Volkmer - Weisbaden
Client	Mercedes-Benz
Art Director	Heike Brockmann
Writer	Katharina Schlungs
Creative Director	Michael Volkmer
Designers	Michael Dralle, Dominik Lammer Philipp Bareiss, Elke Grober Kathrin Schüler, Anne Wichmann Jutta Ottmann
Programmer	Peter Wolfrum
Digital Artists/Multimedia	Tim Leydecker, Diane Preyer Das Werk (Frankfurt)
Music/Sound	J. Jochen Helfert, Mark A. Frank
ID	02025N

05

Award	Gold
Category	**Corporate Image B2C — CD-ROMs**
Page	42

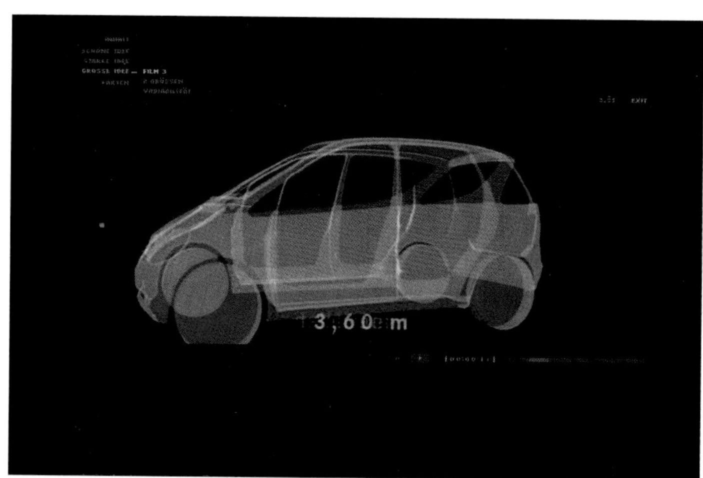

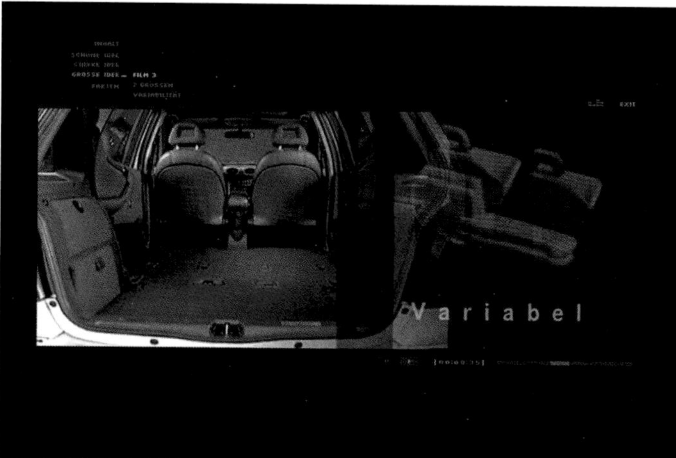

At the Head of the Class

Scholz & Volkmer produced the CD-ROM by order of Mercedes-Benz. The target was to communicate the measures of model maintenance of the A-Class, the safety concept and the introduction of a new long-wheelbase version. Apart from that, the CD-ROM should function as an emotional appetizer stimulating and strengthening the user's interest in the A-Class.

Finer, stronger, bigger

First, an introduction puts the user in the right mood for the topic and the basic idea of the CD-ROM. Afterwards, he/she gets to the homepage focusing on three highlights: the new styling of the exterior and the interior, the even better safety and the long-wheelbase version of the A-Class for those who need some more space.

Films rouse the interest in more

The interactive test-drive starts with three films, one for each chapter. The mixture of real takes and animations with music composed for this very special purpose provides the user with information in an emotional and entertaining way. This principle takes effect on the whole CD-ROM.

Get in, try out and leave

The CD-ROM continues in a playful and interactive manner. By Quicktime VR, the user gets an idea of the new interior and exterior design of the A-Class. Different crash-test videos and three-dimensional animations on the down-gliding motor illustrate the safety concept. In order to experience the variability of the A-Class and the new long-wheelbase version, the user can, for example, remove and shift the seats, and measure the A-Class completely.

Facts, facts, facts

The fourth topic complex is for those who want to know it in detail. Here are all the details on equipment, technical data, the three different lines, colors and gearing.

05

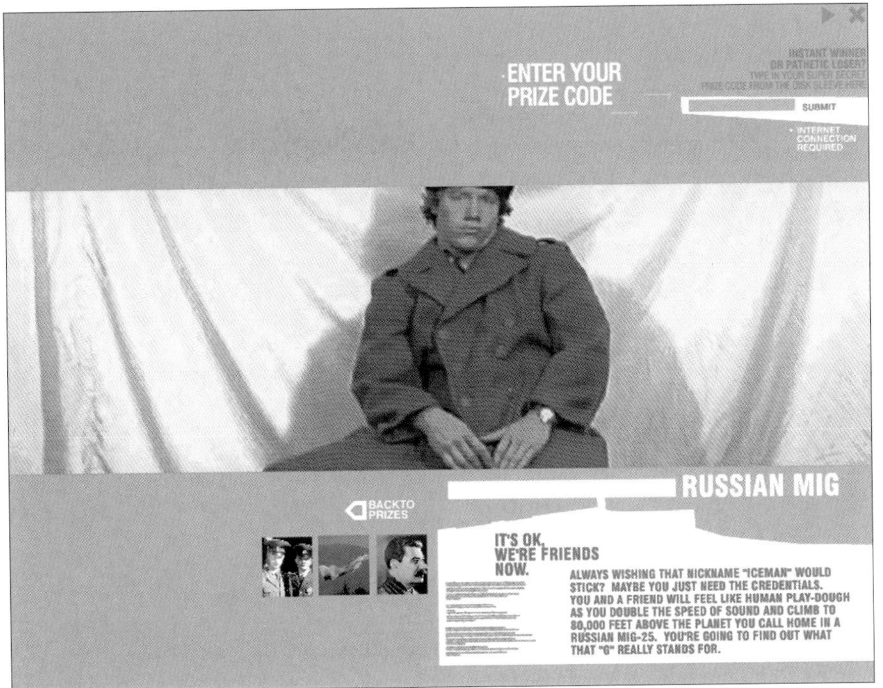

Agency	Archrival - Lincoln
Client	Nebraska Book Company
Art Director	Clint! Runge
Writers	Clint! Runge, Joe Goddard, Caleb Jensen Charles Hull
Creative Director	Clint! Runge
Designers	Clint! Runge, Bart Johnston
Photographers/Illustrators	Clint! Runge, Joe Goddard
Programmer	Bart Johnston
Digital Artists/Multimedia	Cass Kovanda, Bart Johnston
Producer	Joe Goddard
Music/Sound	Charles Hull
ID	02026N

Award	Gold
Category	**Corporate Image B2C — CD-ROMs**
Page	44

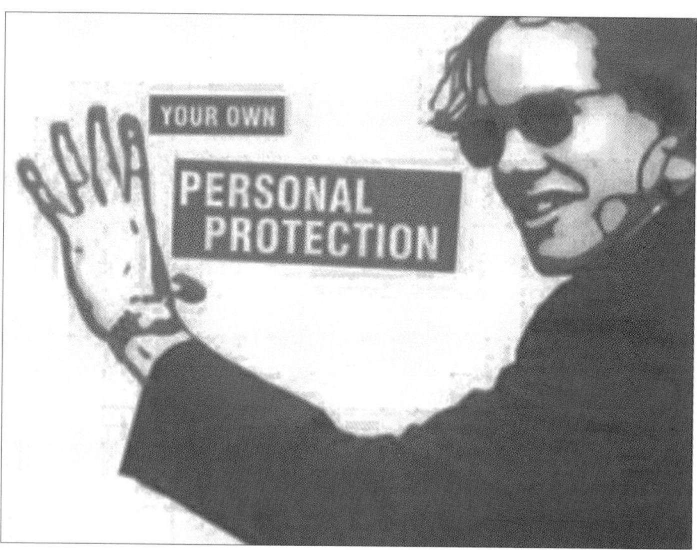

A Compelling Reason To Bring Back Your Books

Got Used was a campaign idea about giving college students a reason to bring back their books. Many bookstores give away prizes they think are "cool" like a home stereo system or a DVD player or something like that. Sure, those prizes are great and you would love to win one of them, but would you really go out of your way to register for it? I mean, who doesn't give something like that away. It's what we termed as "corporate cool." So instead, we needed to come up with a list of grand prizes that were unlike anything before.

To college students, what's cool are experiences and irreverent things that make your friends wonder why the heck you have one of those. So, here's a sample of the ten grand prizes — a NYC hotdog cart; a trip to hunt Bigfoot with wacky scientists in Canada; an opportunity to run with the bulls in Spain; a flight in a Russian Mig; personal protection from two professional bodyguards for one week; and much more.

All of the Got Used material featured two "real" college students who, in much to the form of a 70's detective show, searched for books to return to their bookstore. The I-card starts with a small movie of these two, along with featuring the ten grand prizes. You'll notice the two students go undercover for each prize.

The "home" design of the card features the two exchanging books (conceptually this is what bringing back your textbooks is like, from one student to the next, they all exchange). When the user rolls over to find out more info on the prizes, the students turn and kung-fu-face the prizes. At any point, the user can enter in a number (printed on the outside of the i-card) to find out if they've won.

This interactive piece was especially challenging because the design was almost entirely based on large, full-screen animations, making the presentation very RAM intensive. In its initial stages, the playback on older machines was almost unbearable. To avoid making major compromises to the design, Archrival designed the presentation to incrementally simplify the animations as needed, based on the user's system. The result is a presentation that performs well on multiple platforms and configurations, while still providing a rich and consistent user experience.

05

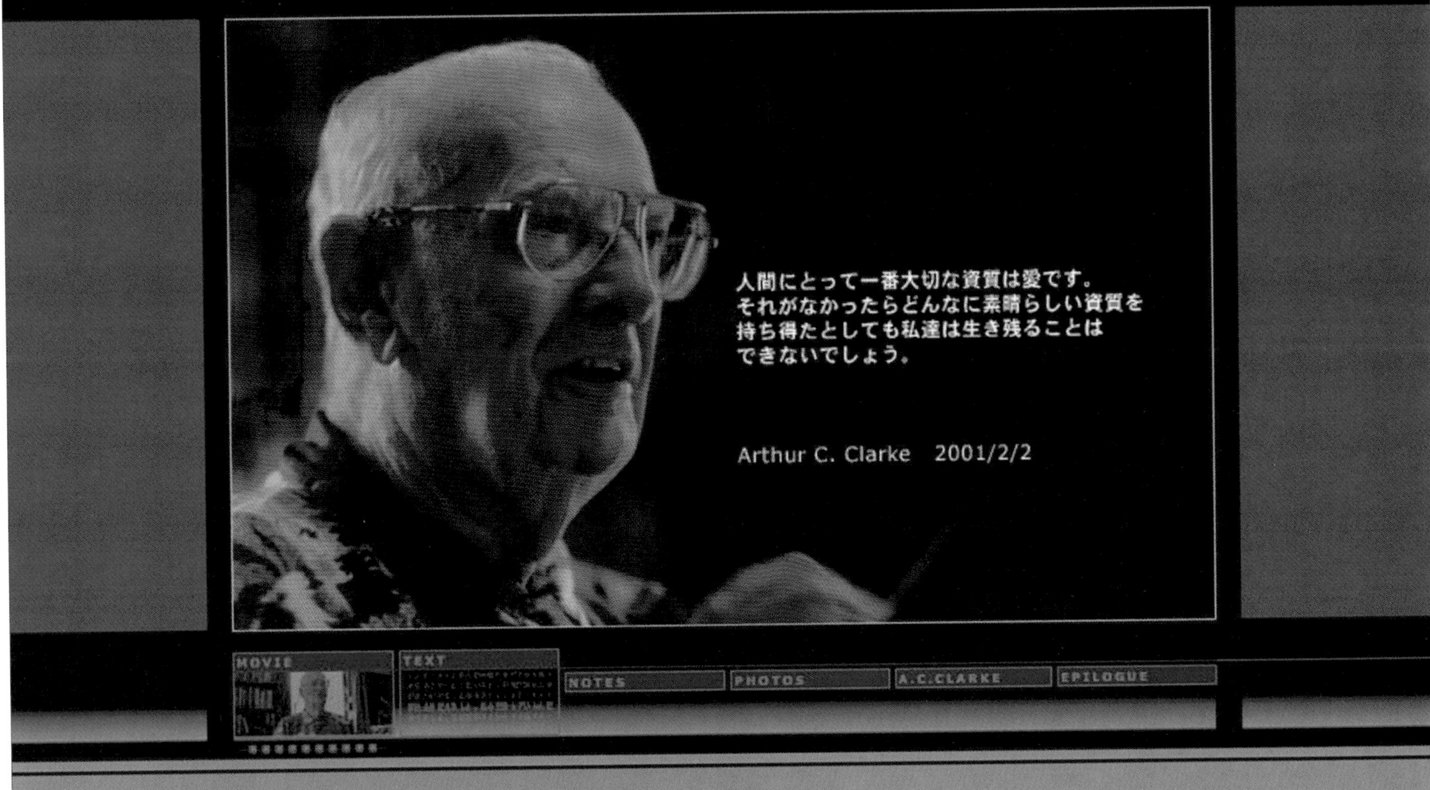

Agency	Hakuhodo - Tokyo
Client	Sony Marketing Japan
Art Director	Tom Vincent
Writer	Tomomi Maeda
Creative Directors	Toshiya Fukuda, Moses Koizumi
Designer	Tom Vincent
Producers	Chiaki Watanabe, Kuniyuki Marumo
	Takuya Kawai, Yukimasa Okada
Programmer	Perez Ito
Digital Artist/Multimedia	Koji Shibata
ID	02027N

Award	Bronze
Category	**Corporate Image B2C — CD-ROMs**
Page	46

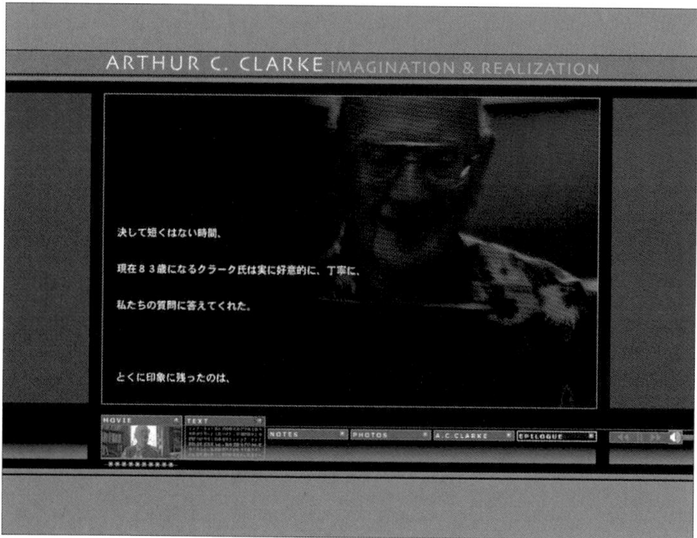

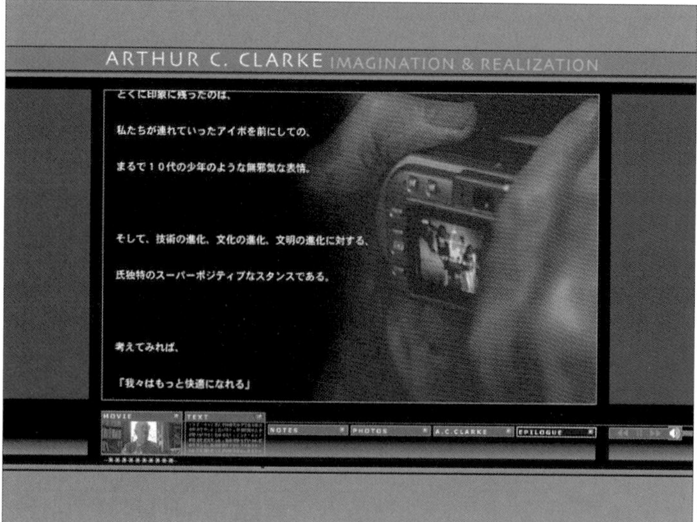

Imagination & Realization

In February, 2001, to coincide, of course, with the classic of all science fiction movies, "2001 - A Space Odyssey," Sony sent a small group of people to Colombo, Sri Lanka, to record a magazine interview with the grand master of science fiction, Arthur C. Clarke. Armed with a trunk-full of Sony's latest gadgets, they spent a couple of days talking with the octogenarian about his thoughts on the future of our planet, while his dogs played cautiously with Aibo in the background.

"Imagination & Realization" was built from the low-quality video taken as a back-up during the interview. The challenge was to build a broadband video Web site entirely in Flash, to allow the viewer to flick between the main video of Clarke on one hand and text and photographs on the other. A full transcript of his speech, a biography and list of works, notes to shed light on the multitude of scientific and historical references, and photographs of his home and workplace all help the viewer to get a little bit closer to the workings of one of the most inventive minds of the 20th century as he lays out his vision for the 21st century, and beyond.

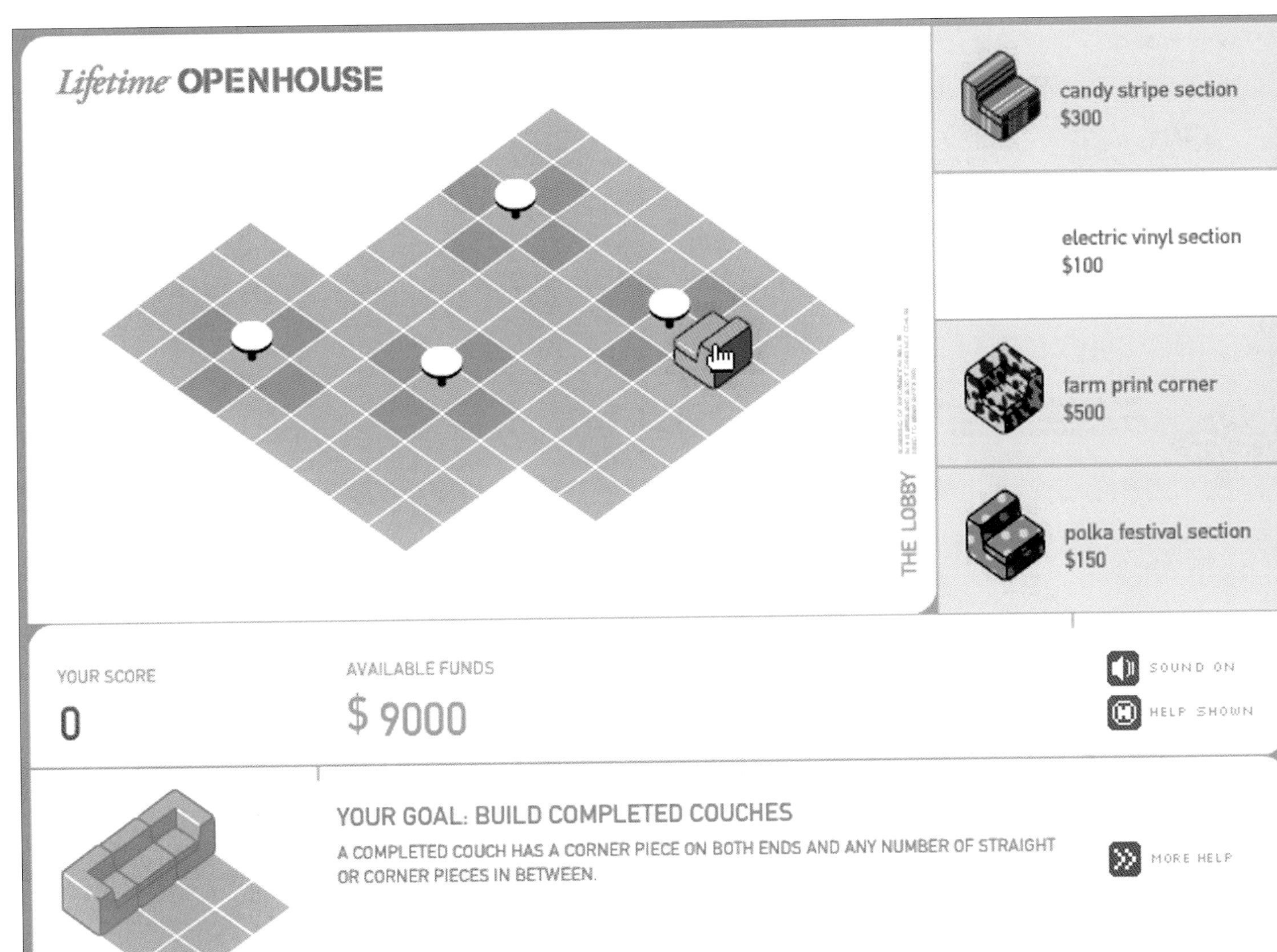

Agency	POP - New York
Client	Lifetime Television
Art Director	Lesli Karavil
Creative Director	Vincent Lacava
Designers	Geoffrey Fowler, Scott Gursky
Game Designer	Frank Lantz
Producer	Demetri Detsaridis
Programmer	Veronique Brossier
Digital Artist/Multimedia	Motomichi Nakamura
Music/Sound	Michael Sweet
ID	02028N
URL	www.popnyc.com/contest/openhouse.html

Award	Silver
Category	**Corporate Image B2C — Other Digital Advertising**
Page	48

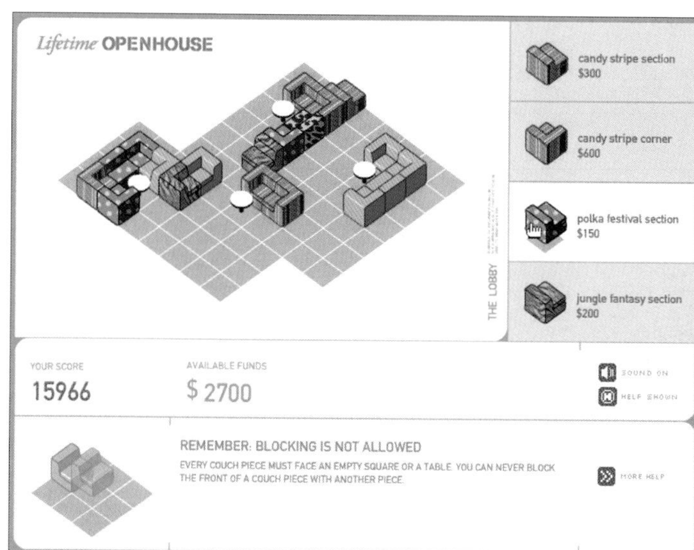

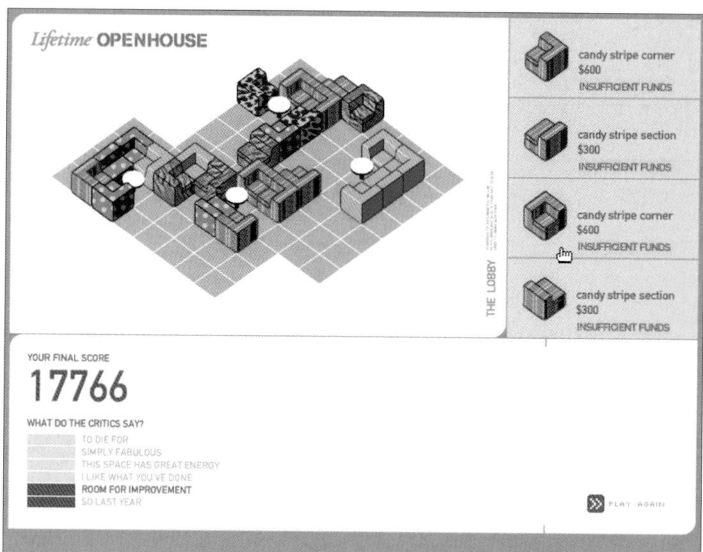

An Online Guide to Digital Feng Shui

If you're anything like us, you know it's not nearly enough for the true connoisseur of good design just to buy the right objects. They must be arranged just so. And with furniture, particularly at home, nothing is more essential. We have occasionally found ourselves lying awake in the middle of the night thinking, "You know, maybe if we moved the table and try the side chairs by the window, House & Garden would call."

Open House is our attempt to capture the compulsive urge of this will to decorative perfection. Naturally, there are useless nooks where nothing fits, bulky chairs, unwieldy sectional sofas that only seem to grow, and fabric patterns that clash with unexpected violence if juxtaposed injudiciously. The game is of course quite as addictive as the real thing. We're still trying to figure out where the armless circa 1960 blue vinyl desk chair really ought to go.

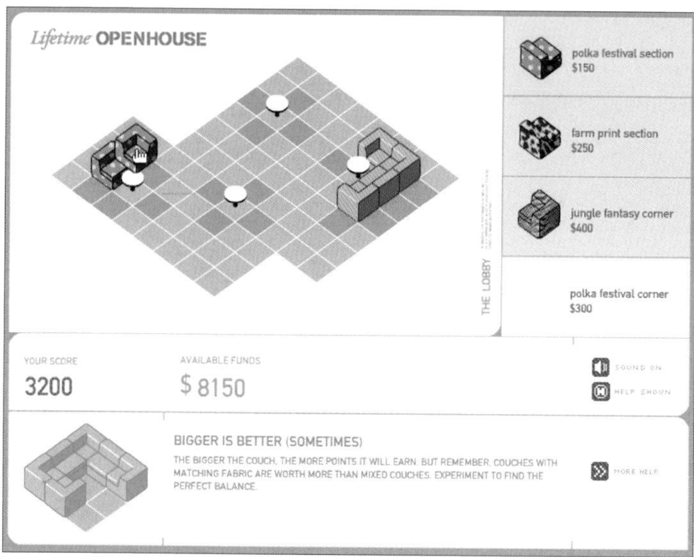

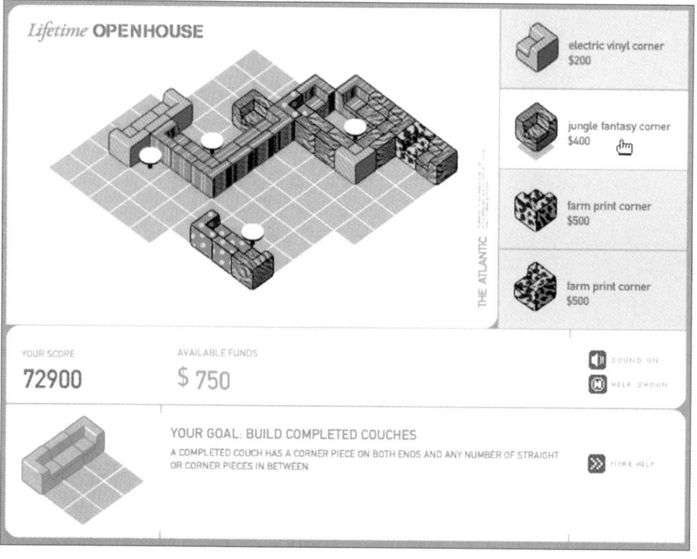

ERROR 404

The requested URL could not be found

You may have typed in the wrong address. Don't worry, we all make mistakes, especially when we're a bit tired. So click on the button below to see how Brand's Essence of Chicken gives you a physical and mental boost.

PACFusion.com Error Message: Generated Mon, 11 Sep 2000 09:54:24 GMT by palo2.pacific.net.sg (Squid/2.4.DEVEL2)

Agency	Ogilvy Interactive - Singapore
Client	Cerebos
Art Director	Gina Sim
Writer	Graham Kelly
Creative Director	Graham Kelly
Designer	Gina Sim
Producer	Ho Lian Shi
Programmer	Gina Sim
Digital Artist/Multimedia	OgilvyOne
ID	02029N
URL	http://www.our-work.com/brands/

05

Award	Bronze
Category	**Corporate Image B2C — Other Digital Advertising**
Page	50

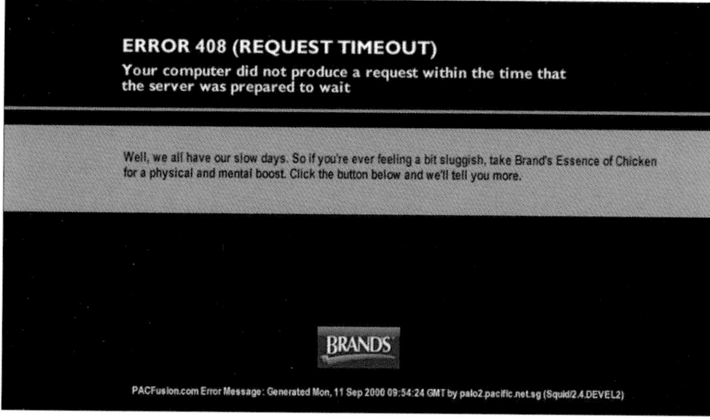

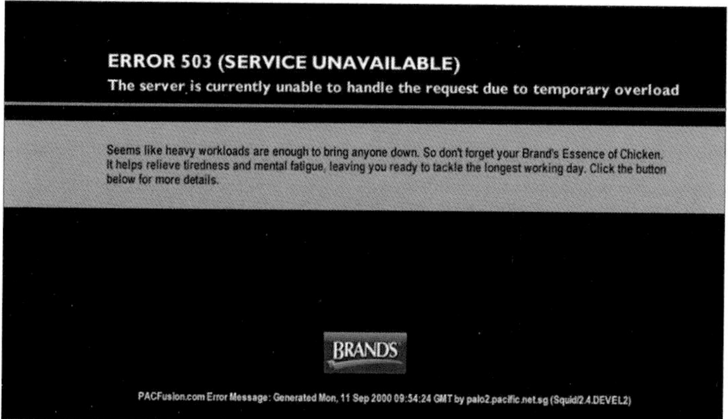

The Essence of an Idea

Brands Essence of Chicken has been going strong in Asia for 165 years. So its key benefits – that it gives you a physical and mental boost – are old news. Our brief was to communicate these benefits online. To give this a more thought-provoking twist we "hijacked" Internet error messages.

The first in the series involved tweaking the "404" error message, which is displayed whenever you type in a wrong Web address (URL). Working with Yahoo Singapore, the agency changed the portal's standard error messages so that in addition to the standard "Error 404. The requested URL could not be found" headline, was copy which stated "Don't worry we all make mistakes, especially when we're a bit tired."

Readers were then invited to click on a button at the foot of the page, which took them to the Brands Web site – specifically a section on how Brand's Essence of Chicken provides that much-needed mental and physical boost. In effect, it was "moment of truth" advertising: delivering product information when the consumer really needs it.

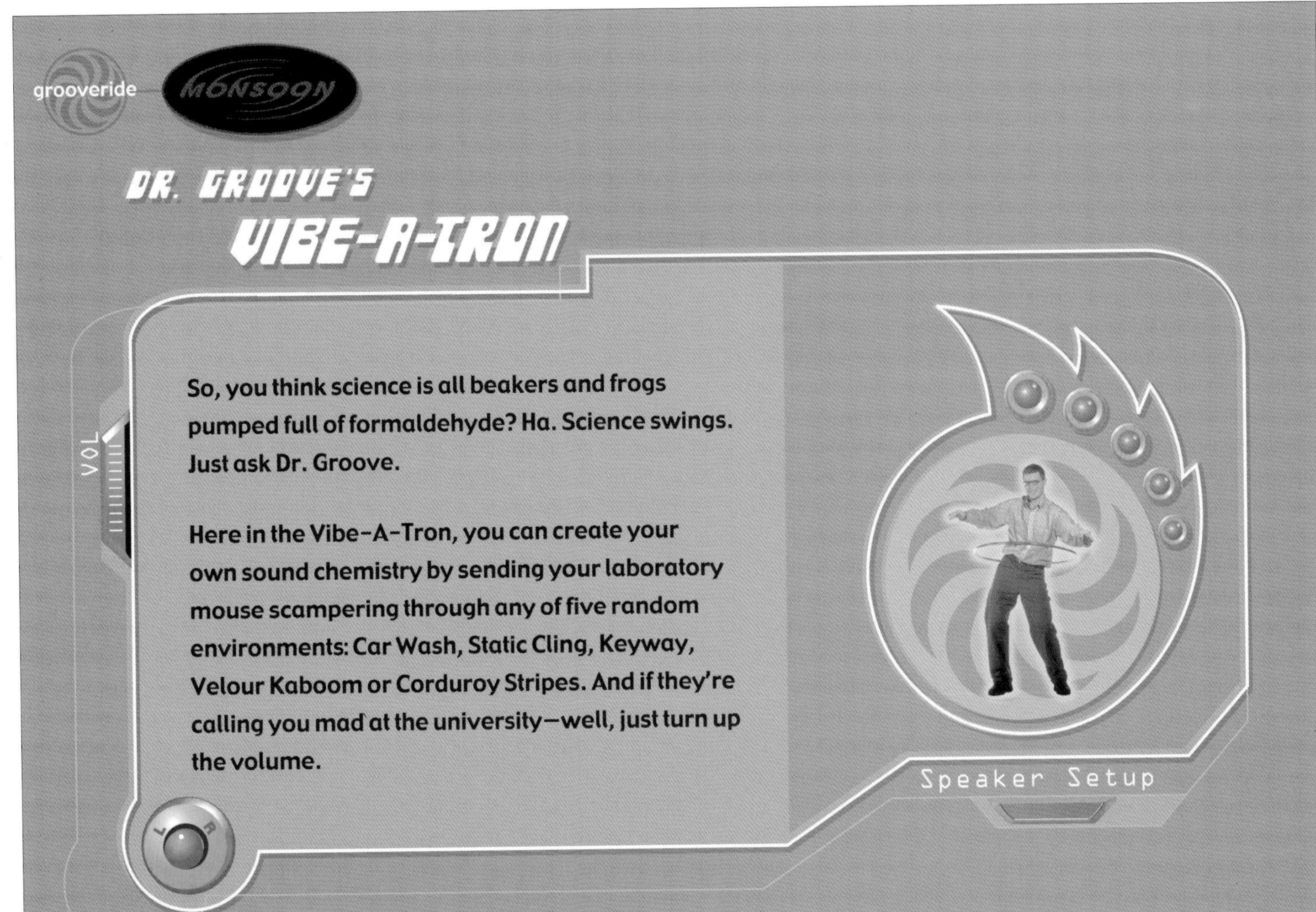

Agency	Young & Laramore - Indianapolis
Client	Monsoon Audio Systems
Art Director	Dana Root
Writers	Evan Finch, Colin Dullaghan
Creative Director	Carolyn Hadlock
Content Strategists	Dana Root, Carolyn Hadlock
Programmers	Gabriel Interactive, Perry Board
Music/Sound	Dana Root, Arnie Benton
	Aaron Kohn
ID	02030N

205

Award	Bronze
Category	Corporate Image B2C — Other Digital Advertising
Page	52

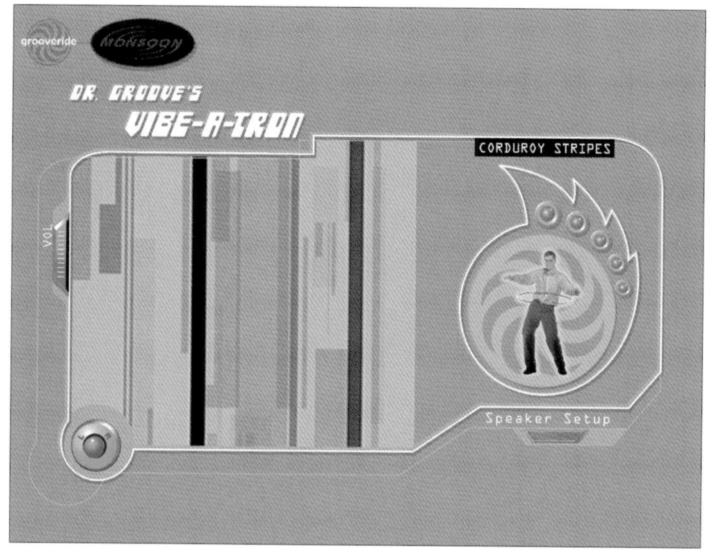

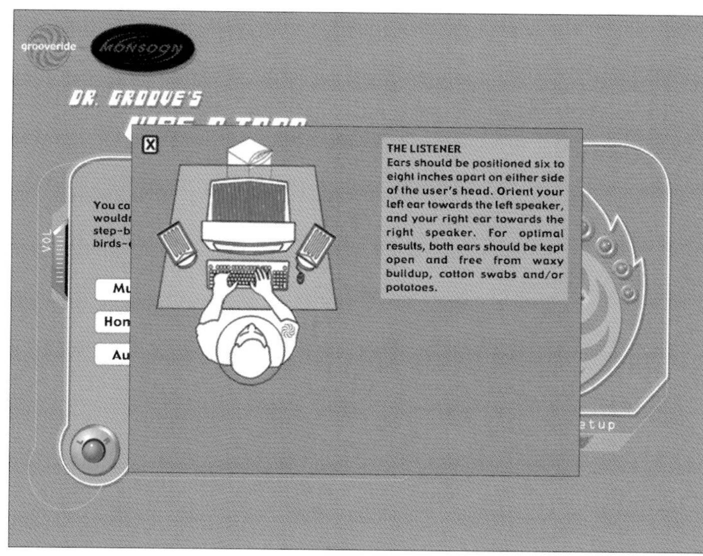

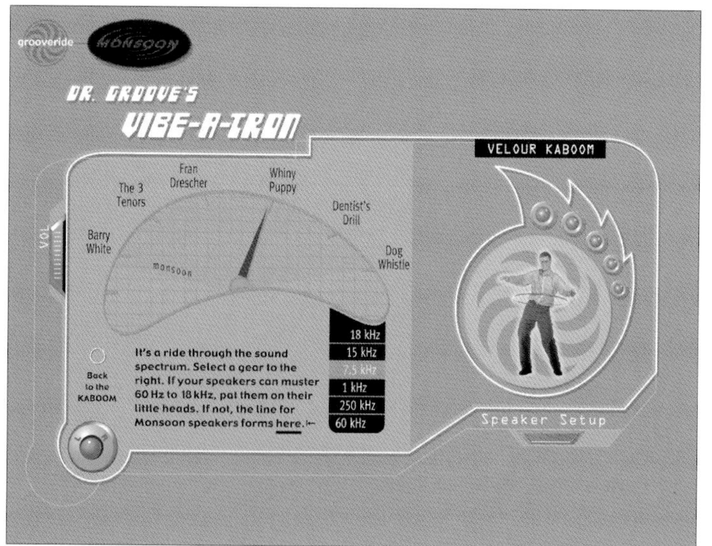

Feeling the Vibe

If all interactive projects could be like this, art directors and writers everywhere would be clamoring to work on them. Think about it– create a digital sound chemistry lab called Dr. Groove's Vibe-a-tron. Work with a client who sees the potential of such an idea. Do a music score that has train tracks, a didgeridoo, violins, and thunder. All in the name of product demonstration for an audio system called Monsoon.

Working on this was an amazing experience. It was Phase 2 of the very first interactive work that we did at the agency. Lines blurred. Egos faded. And the result was a wonderfully hi-tech, charming virtual lab that you could experiment with for hours. And people did. The technology was so fluid that the mouse virtually disappeared. Corduroy Stripes and Car Wash are some of our favorite compositions.

alliedworksarchitecture

At allied works we endeavor to create enduring and evocative architecture that fully engages the cultural forces of our time. We seek insight into every project, believing that significant work depends upon intense discovery. We find creative genesis through understanding existing phenomena, and we strive to discover what is inherent in a place or activity. This inquiry is driven by an aspiration, a question formed in collaboration with the client. We resist the temporality of novelty, and search for the archetypal in a new cultural and historical context.

Agency	Paris France - Portland
Client	Allied Works Architecture
Writer	Doug Lowell
Creative Directors	Jeff Faulkner, Doug Lowell
Designer	Jeff Faulkner
Producer	Jason Davis
Digital Artists /Multimedia	Erik Falat, Sophie Schmidt
ID	02031N
URL	www.alliedworks.com

Award	Gold
Category	**Corporate Image B2B — Web Sites**
Page	54

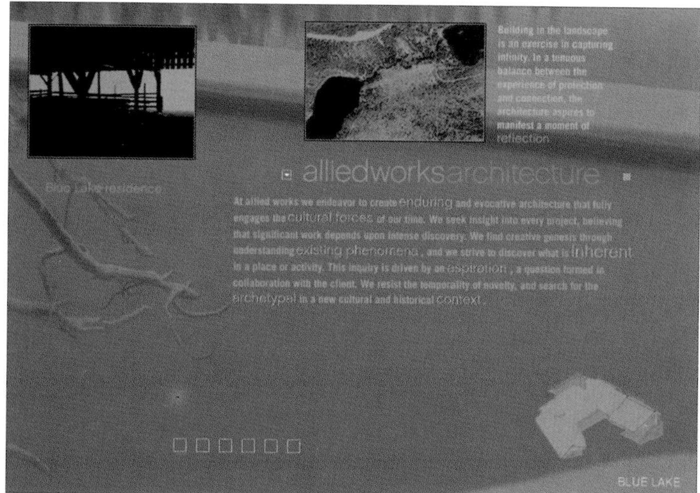

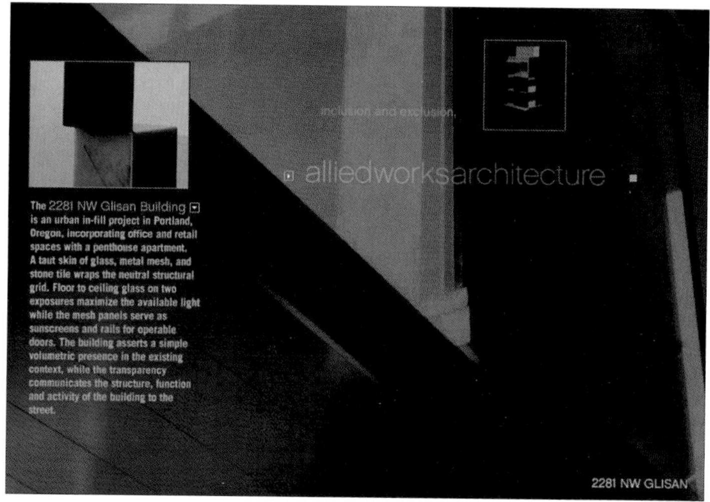

The Architecture of the Integrated Whole

This site is designed to be an unified experience that expresses the spirit of Allied Works Architecture. It speaks to architecturally-savvy prospective clients, the kind of people that might be on the board of directors of an important art museum or cultural institution. It also speaks to the architectural community, including critics, curators, theoreticians, and practitioners. Our client wanted more of an artistic statement than a marketing tool.

The inspiration for the Allied Works site came from working very closely with Brad Cloepfil, founder and chief architect of Allied Works. The site needed to be a statement of Brad's and Allied Works' vision of architecture at every level. It was an intensely collaborative process throughout.

The idea for the site came from reading through written material Brad had given us. We discovered a one-paragraph statement that was a densely and carefully constructed summary of everything Allied Works stood for. We decided that this paragraph should be the navigation, and that everything in the site should unfold from there.

The site actually utilizes one of the oldest innovations and conventions of interactivity — the hyperlink. But, whereas the hyperlink usually leads to a dead end, we wanted the hyperlink to open a door that led to another door, etc.

At the same time, Brad didn't want a separate portfolio section for the site. He wanted his philosophy and work to be contained within a whole, to be integrated, as they are in his everyday world. So the site was created as one integrated whole, versus a variety of sections with separated content.

Agency	Kinetic Interactive - Singapore
Client	Ad Planet
Art Director	Sean Lam
Writers	Alfred Teo, Catherine Phua
Content Strategists	James Chua, Sean Lam
Producer	James Chua
Designer	Sean Lam
Information Architects	James Chua, Sean Lam
Programmer	Sean Lam
Music/Sound	Victor Low
ID	02032N
URL	www.adplanet.com.sg

Award	Silver
Category	**Corporate Image B2B — Web Sites**
Page	56

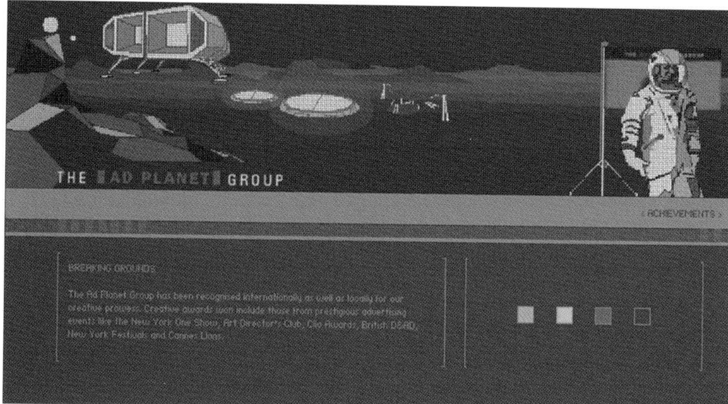

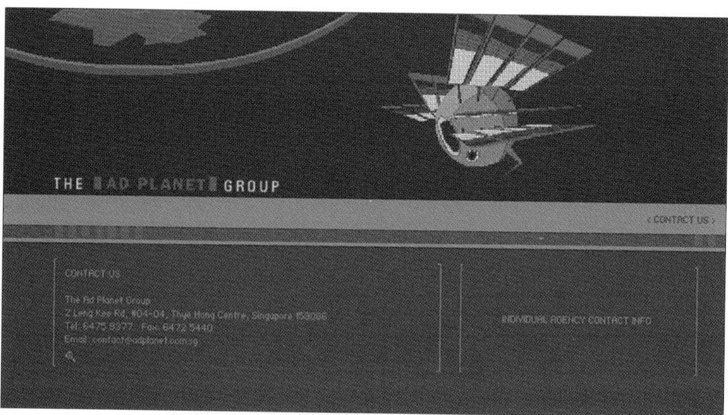

Belief Creates Possibilities

Playing up on the sci-fi theme that the client's name evokes, a Web site based on the concept of "galactic-space" was created. Literal as it may seem, the approach simply and objectively portrays the client's image and philosophy.

Being a group that consists of several agencies, the Web site is essentially a launch pad/transit area, hence the idea of a space-portal. As a local company that is fiercely proud of it's achievements, an inspiring and emotive mood was set with the help of the appropriate background soundtracks and a purposefully consistent use of red (the clients corporate color) throughout the entire site.

Finally, the infinitely undiscovered expanse that is the universe also echoes the client's motto whereby nothing is impossible.

06

Agency	a.k.a. Euro RSCG - San Francisco
Client	Ensenda
Art Directors	Andrew Lau, Larry Yannes
Writers	John Egan, John Mattingly
Creative Directors	Scott Ex Rodgers, Kevin McCarthy
Designers	Mark Arcenal, Nicholas Macias
Producer	Sila Soyer
Music/Sound	Jerome Wilson
ID	02033N
URL	www.ensenda.com

06

Award	Silver
Category	**Corporate Image B2B — Web Sites**
Page	58

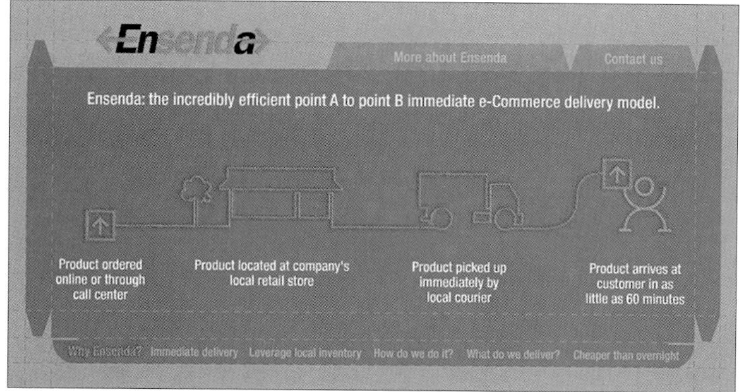

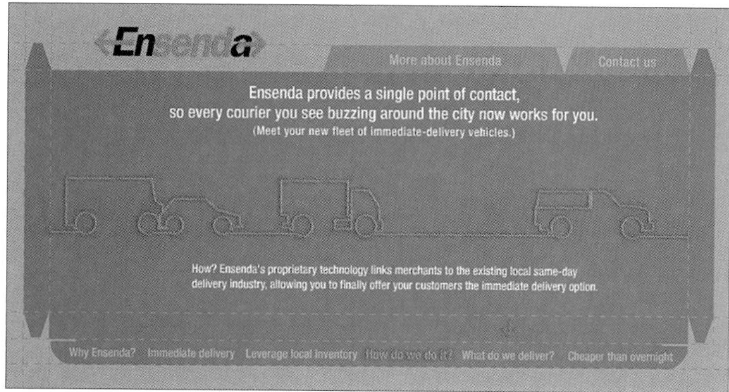

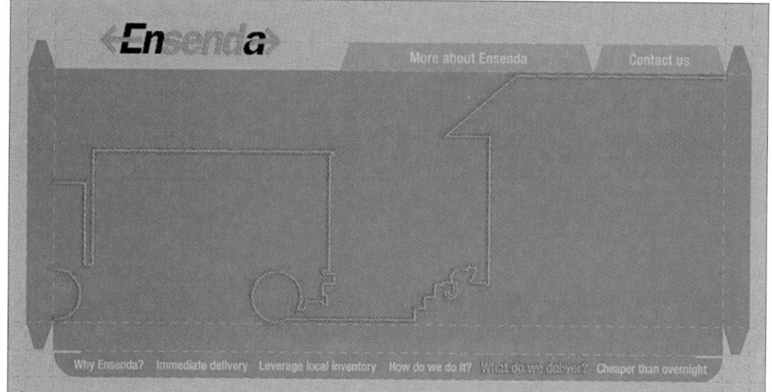

Delivering an Immediate Idea

Want that Palm Pilot you ordered online in your palm in an hour instead of three days and cheaper than overnight? Ensenda enables retailers to deliver online purchases in as little as 60 minutes. How? By eliminating all unnecessary steps between customer and their purchase.

The design vehicle to communicate this? A straight line. The challenge, and opportunity, was to make the whole site function using only this line. Here's an idea, we thought, that can truly take advantage of this medium we're all strangely obsessed with. We set our art directors loose. "Take this line and run with it."

Fast forward to two weeks later (what kind of deadline should we have expected from an immediate delivery client?), throw in some slightly mischievous sound effects and an Easter egg or three (press 'c' on the 'How Do We Do It' screen), and there it was. In the spirit of immediate delivery, even the site arrives quickly. Using flash, the entire thing weighs in at only 800k.

The end result is the product of true collaboration and something we're collectively quite proud of. In that spirit, this project was the ultimate realization of what a.k.a. was created to be about.

Agency	Kinetic Interactive - Singapore
Client	The Picturefarm
Art Director	Jason Chan
Writer	Alex Goh
Designer	Jason Chan
Information Architects	James Chua, Jason Chan
Producers	James Chua, Adeline Tan
Programmer	Benjy Choo
Digital Artist/Multimedia	Jason Chan
Music/Sound	Victor Low
ID	02034N
URL	www.picturefarm.com.sg
Award	Bronze
Category	Corporate Image B2B — Web Sites
Page	60

Welcome to the Farm

The Picturefarm is an award-winning film production company focused on establishing itself as an unconventional setup. The concept for the site came out of the intention to reflect this ideal, and from a literal interpretation of the company's namesake.

The whole farm backdrop provided us with a truckload of gags and puns to work with. The sections of the site are metaphorically represented by farm-related illustrated elements, and a suitably appropriate soundtrack was written to complement the concept. The finished product is indicative of a refreshing, forward-thinking, non-conservative approach to a film production company's Web site.

Note: No cows were harmed in the creative process.

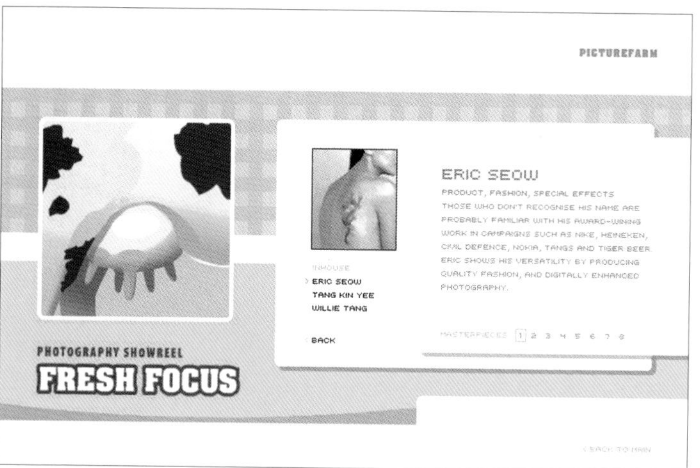

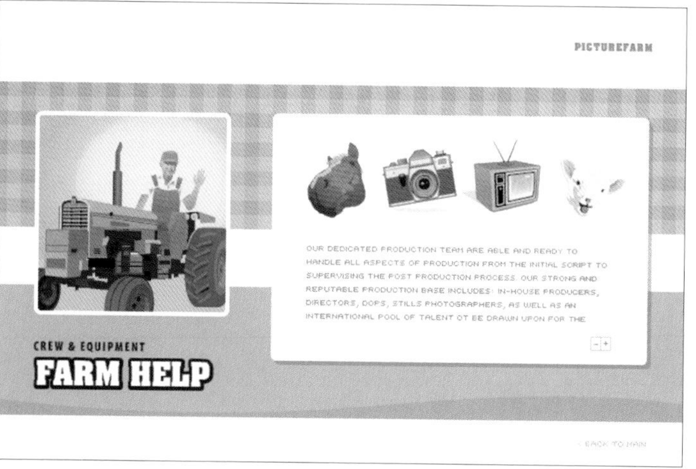

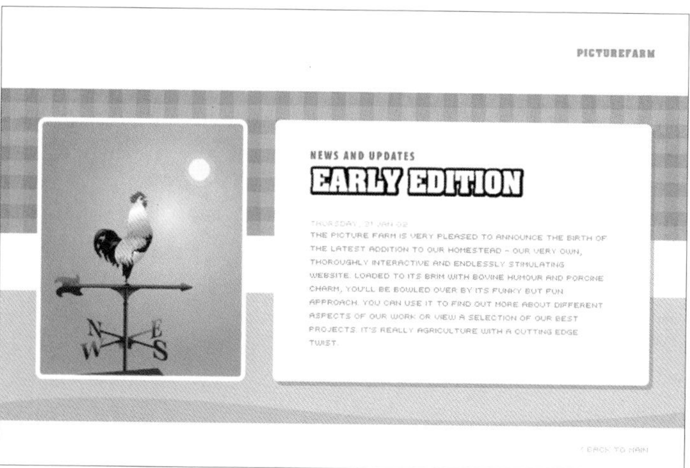

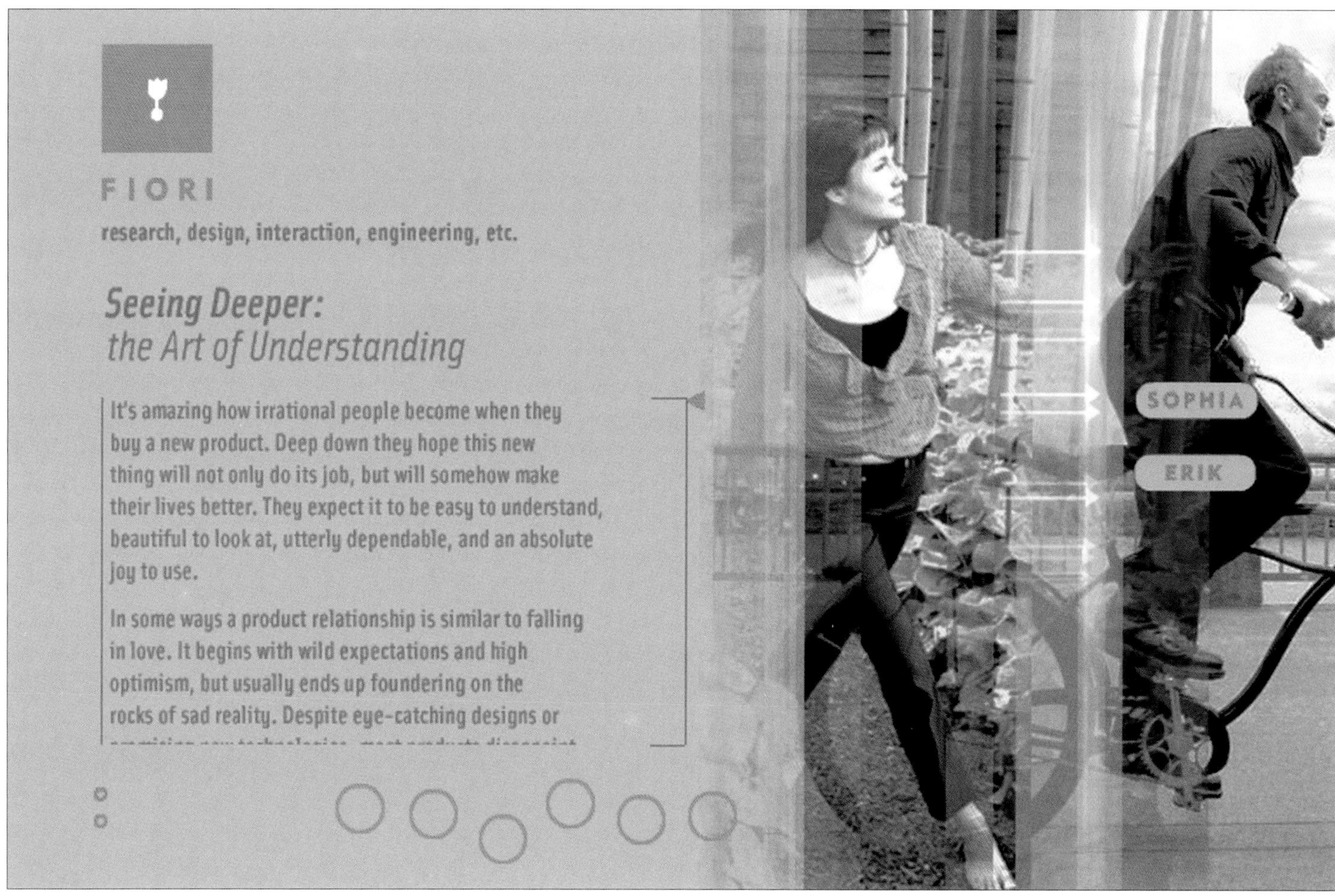

Agency	Paris France - Portland
Client	Fiori
Writer	Doug Lowell
Creative Director	Doug Lowell
Technical Director	Scott Trotter
Designer	Molly Sokolow
Producer	Jason Davis
Photographer	Steven Bloch
Digital Artists/Multimedia	Erik Falat, Sophie Schmidt
ID	02035N
URL	www.fioriinc.com

Award	Bronze
Category	**Corporate Image B2B — Web Sites**
Page	62

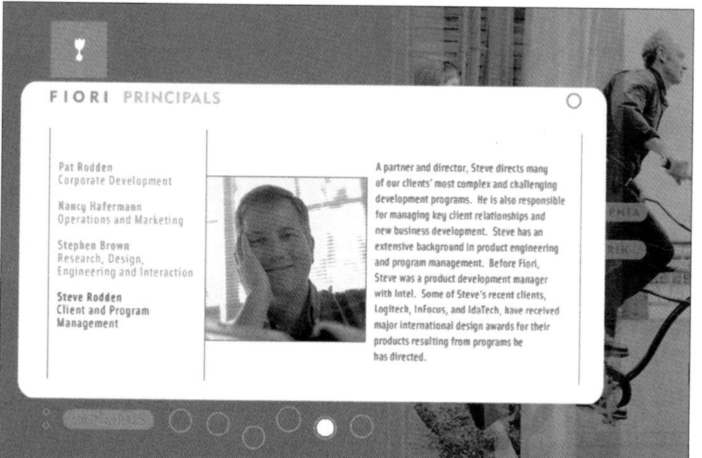

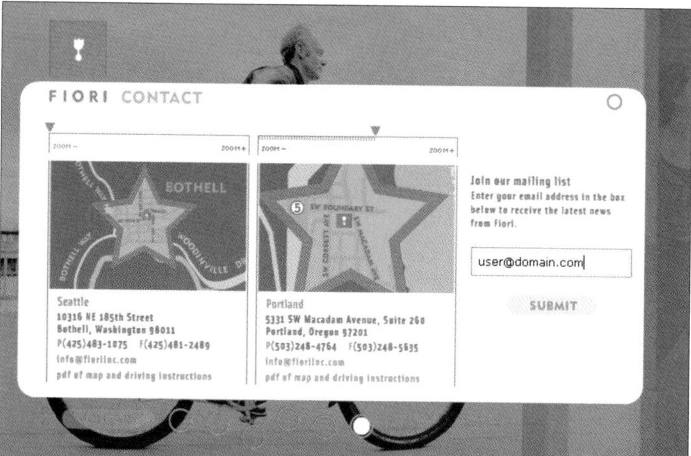

Designing with Humans in Mind

Fiori is an industrial design firm that wanted to expand their work in the high-end consumer electronics category. They have a deep devotion to understanding the audience they're designing for, and in trying to create a flawless experience for that audience. Not that they ever expect to reach "flawlessness," but in trying to get there they feel they come up with better designs. At the core of this focus is Fiori's research department.

One of the first things we noticed, when surveying the Web sites of competitive industrial design firms, was the absolute absence of human beings. In strategizing with the client, we decided to focus on the research department story as a lead-in to the discussion of design. Hence interviews with two real people (real people, but not their real names), revealing thoughts they have about objects, shapes, colors, and tactile experiences.

Both the featured subjects are lovers of consumer electronic toys, yet both have very different ways of experiencing these – their designs. We wanted to get prospective clients thinking about human beings again, and not just the objects they were creating for these humans.

At the same time, we wanted to create a site that stood out from the crowd of cold, design-oriented and award-touting Web sites of other industrial design firms.

Agency	Leopard - Boulder
Client	Sun Educational Services
Art Director	Keith Miks
Writer	Maia Nilsson
Creative Directors	Brendan Hemp, Maia Nilsson
Designers	Keith Miks, Miles Fenn
Illustrator	MaryLynn Gillespie
Programmer	Miles Fenn
Digital Artists/Multimedia	Keith Miks, Austin Wilson
Music/Sound	Coupe Studios
ID	02036N

Award	Bronze
Category	**Corporate Image B2B — CD-ROMs**
Page	64

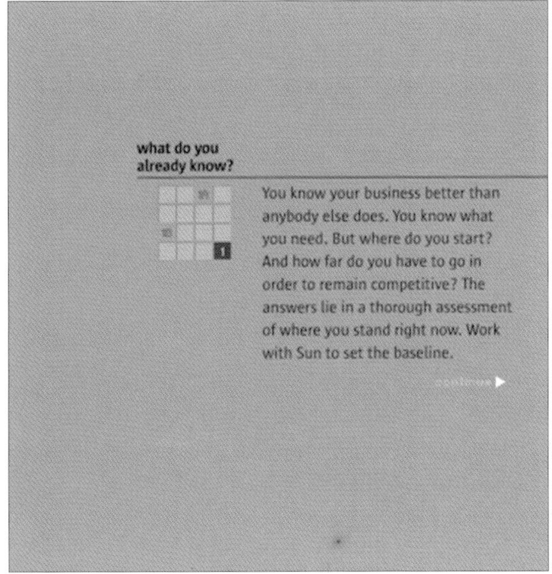

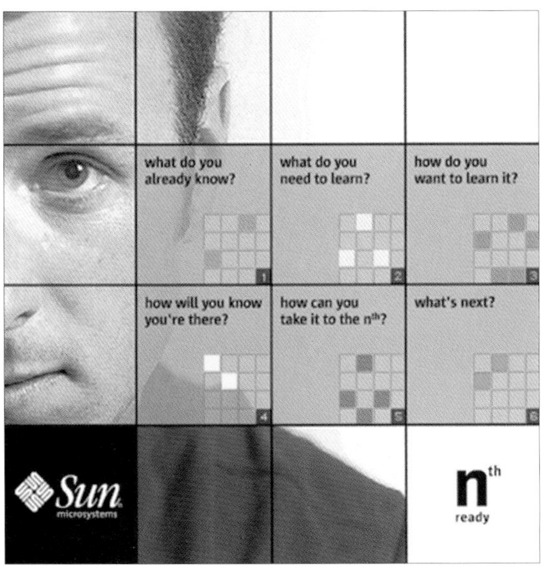

Enabling Through Education

Sun Microsystems' Educational Services division saw an opportunity to cement its leadership in the exploding e-learning market by leveraging Sun's corporate brand value and emphasizing its global consulting capabilities as well as its depth and breadth of learning management expertise. This interactive business card (IBC) was proposed as a high-impact sales tool aimed at C-level executives, IT professionals and training managers in Fortune 1000 companies.

The piece features a motion-graphics video introduction, multiple navigation modes and a dynamic and responsive interface, reinforcing the central concepts of modularity and interactivity. It also was loaded with hidden features for use by sales reps in the field. These include editable speaker notes, mechanisms for tracking and recording points of audience interest and inquiry and using them to develop customized follow-up communications, and a Web-enabled contact management application.

The piece serves as an exceptional example of strategy, creative and technical teams collaborating to produce a truly useful marketing tool that meets real-world business needs, enhances a world-class brand and exceeds client expectations. It received a very enthusiastic reception from the Sun sales force.

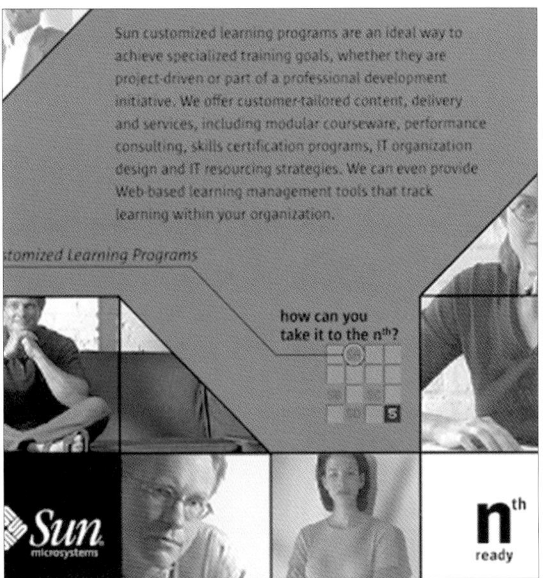

06

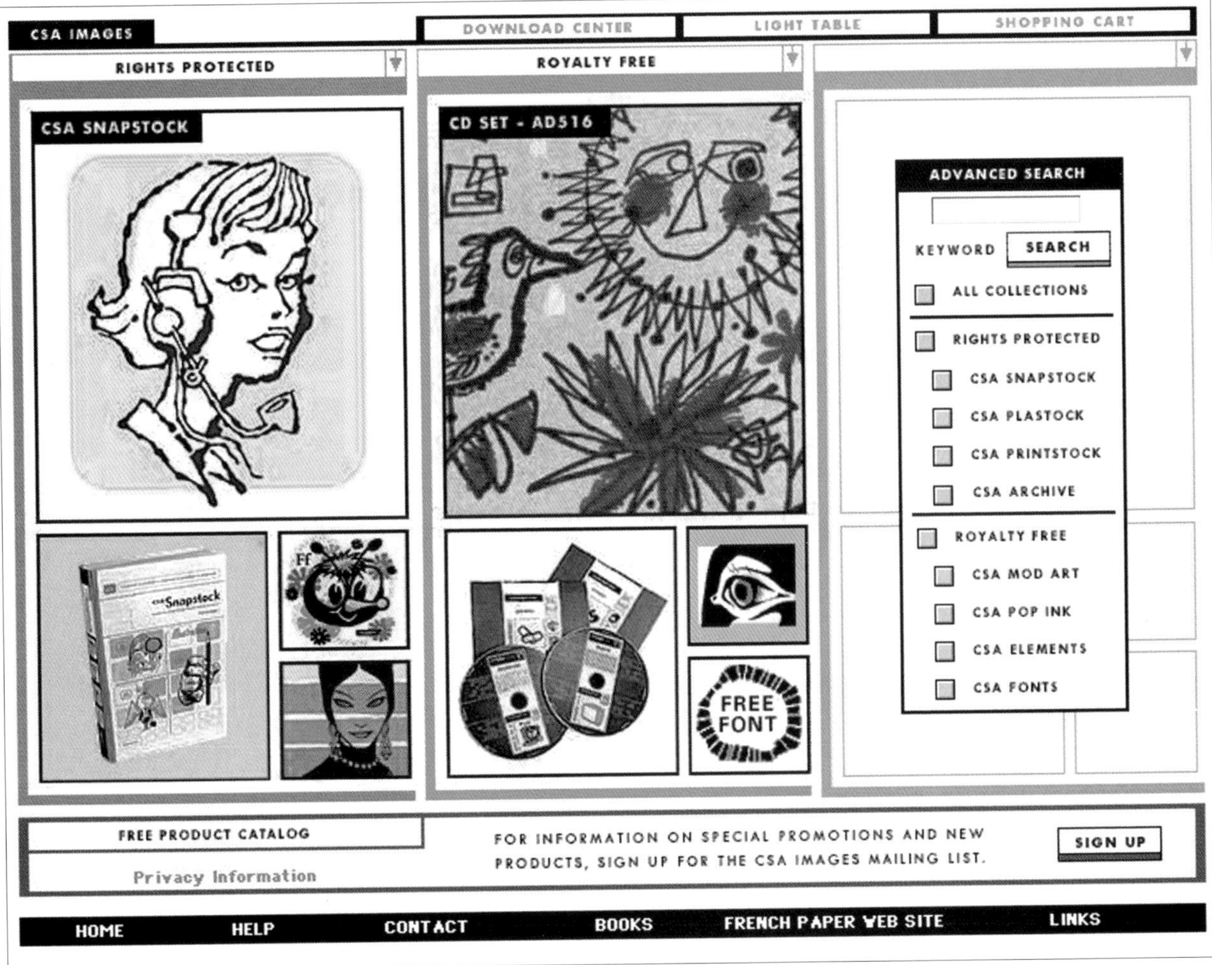

Agency	Charles S. Anderson Design - Minneapolis
Client	CSA Images
Art Directors	Charles S. Anderson Todd Piper-Hauswirth
Writers	Lisa Pemrick, Charles S. Anderson Todd Piper-Hauswirth, John Gross
Designers	Charles S. Anderson Todd Piper-Hauswirth, Arron Hanson
Photographer	CSA Images
Programmers	Steve Applehans, Arron Hanson
ID	02037N
URL	www.csaimages.com

07

Award	Bronze
Category	**E-Commerce B2B — Web Sites**
Page	66

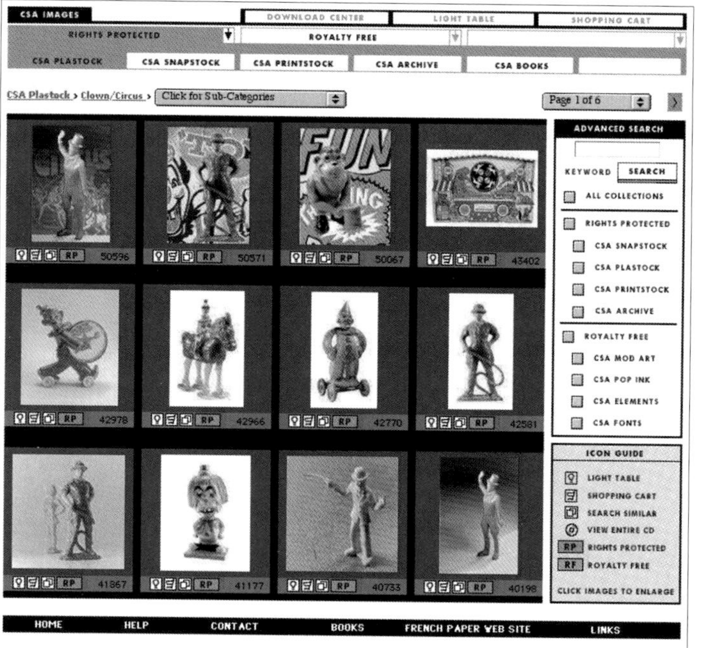

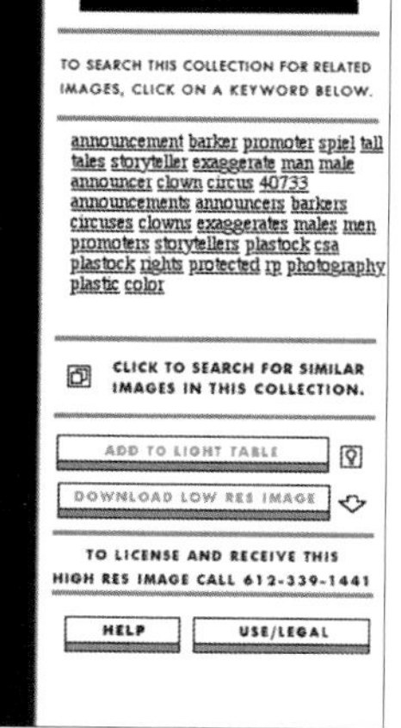

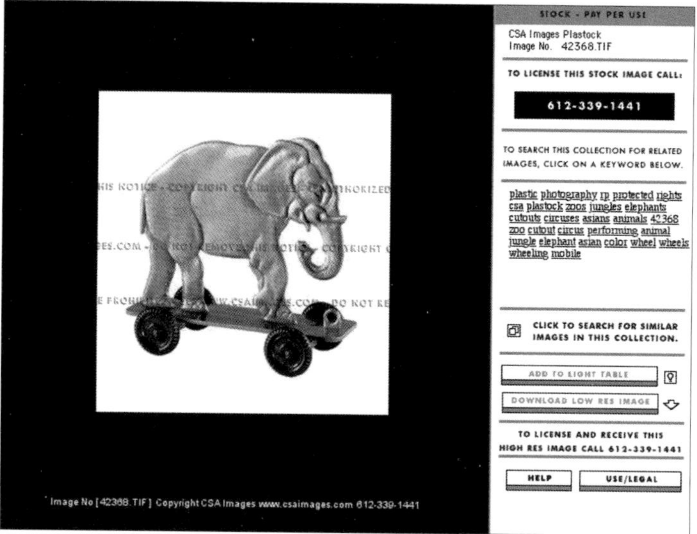

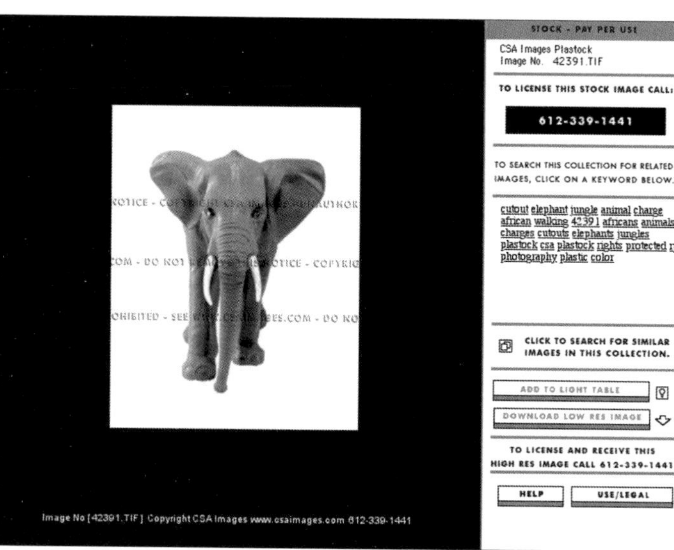

A Perfect Brainstorming Tool

csaimages.com is an e-commerce site created specifically for art directors and designers that provides illustration, photography, backgrounds, fonts, and design elements that may be purchased for use in advertising and design projects. We found that most sites force the user to wade through too much unnecessary clutter. Our challenge was to develop a clear and predominantly visual site for a visual audience that would allow extremely fast and easy access to a large quantity of images. We hope the greatest attribute of csaimages.com is the quality of the images, elements, and fonts being sold. Rather than jam the site with an overwhelming quantity of images, we have taken a more select, edited, curatorial view of what is offered.

One of our favorite places on the site is the home page, where illustrations, photographs, pictographs, patterns, and backgrounds from a variety of the collections appear on two screens, one after another. Although the images are shown in a random order that will vary in selection and sequence each time the site is visited, somehow as the images pass by, an amazing visual narrative unfolds that is intriguing, often funny, and somewhat relevant — a perfect brainstorming tool.

Agency	Silverlign Group - San Jose
Client	Williams-Sonoma
Writers	Laura Martin-Bacon, Jackie Mallorca
Creative Directors	Tim Kain, Hollimarie O'Carroll
Photographers	Paul Berg, Susan Burdick Bob Barclay, Jim Hildreth Noel Barnhurst, Anthony Cotsifas Rob Fiocca
Producers	Laurie Kanes, Cathy Muma Williams-Sonoma eCommerce Creative Team
Information Architects	Karen Weickert, Marjie Buckley
Programmers	Digitas Williams-Sonoma eCommerce Team
Digital Artist/Multimedia	David Lowe-Rogstad
ID	02038N
URL	www.williams-sonoma.com

Award	Silver
Category	**E-Commerce B2C — Web Sites**
Page	68

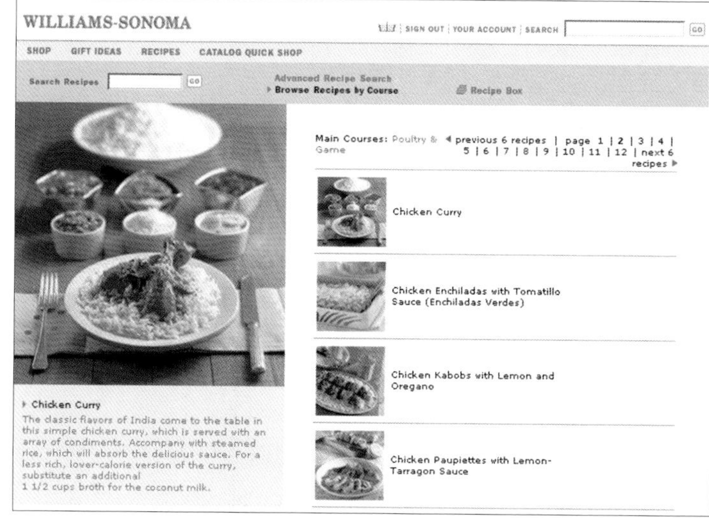

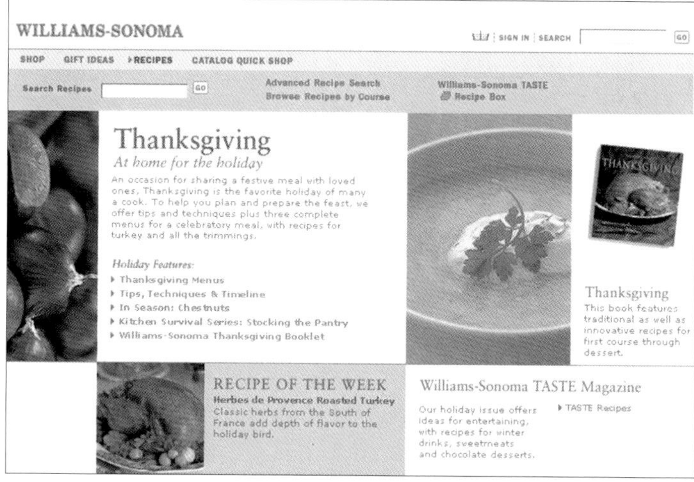

Online Elegance and Ease

Williams-Sonoma.com was redesigned with a singular goal: a site that personified the well-established Williams-Sonoma brand. Inspired by the catalog and in-store experiences and working closely with Williams-Sonoma's in-house creative and technology teams, Silverlign was able to create a user-friendly and graceful approach to commerce. The site offers users a simple, clear interface of beautiful photography, concise copy, and navigation alternatives based on different shopping styles. This creates an environment that easily highlights the recognizable products, services and expertise of Williams-Sonoma.

Of paramount importance was the creation of a site that could be updated often, and easily, with seasonally relevant content. Silverlign addressed this need by designing in a format that would allow for short, elegant Flash greetings on the homepage and support pages that could change monthly to merchandise a particular theme.

Designed to compliment each of its sales channels, Williams-Sonoma.com presents the same seasonal merchandise that is in the stores and the catalog. Additionally the Williams-Sonoma site provides more content than the retail and catalog selling channels afford. Through an in-depth product assortment and more detailed product information, Williams-Sonoma.com has become a fantastic venue to evangelize gourmet food, entertaining, menus, cooking tips and techniques.

07

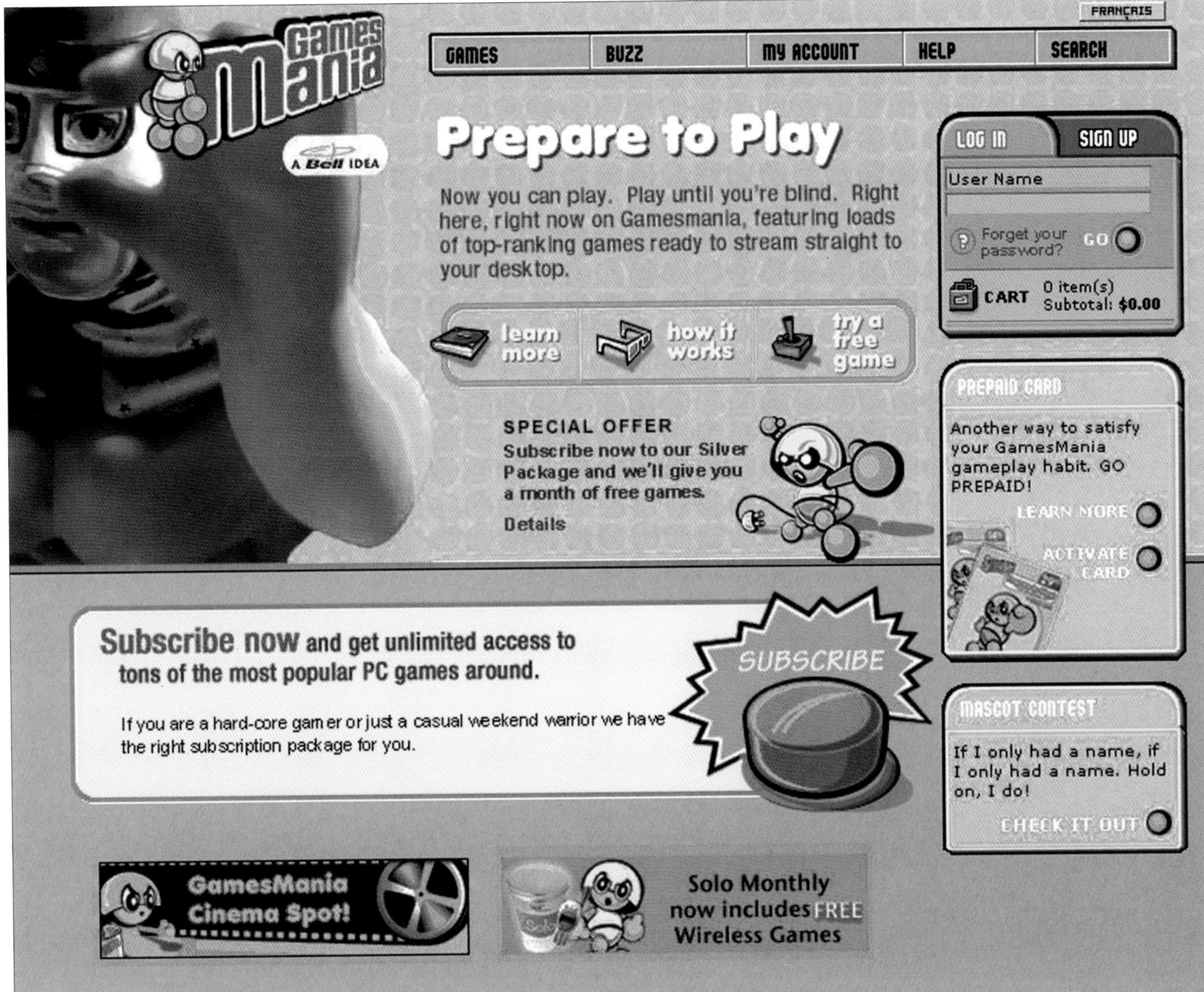

Agency	Organic - Toronto
Client	GamesMania
Writers	Mark Sissons, Julia Gordon
Creative Director	Colleen Decourcy
Designers	Scott Cameron, Henry Chi, Shingo Shimizu
Producers	Aurelia Moneta, Adam Kaftalovich
Information Architects	Diane Lee, Judah Gould
Programmers	Matthew Lohbihler, Ken Dickson
	Chris Bennett, Ryan Vettese
	Rachelle Au
ID	02039N
URL	

Award	Bronze
Category	**E-Commerce B2C — Web Sites**
Page	70

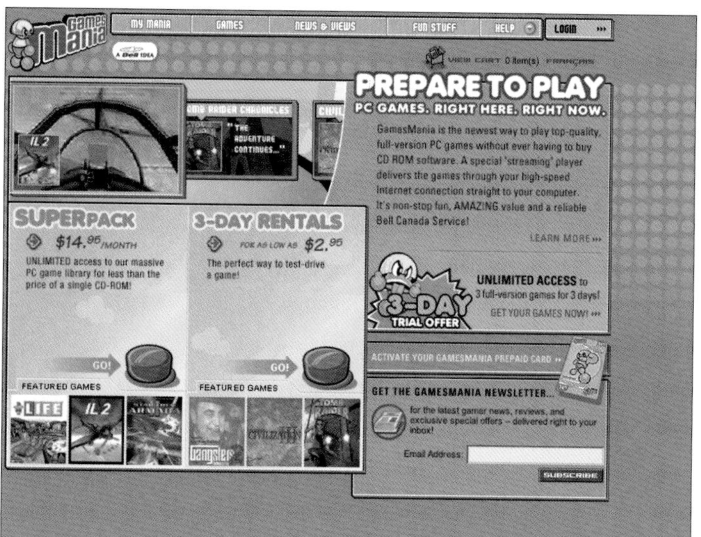

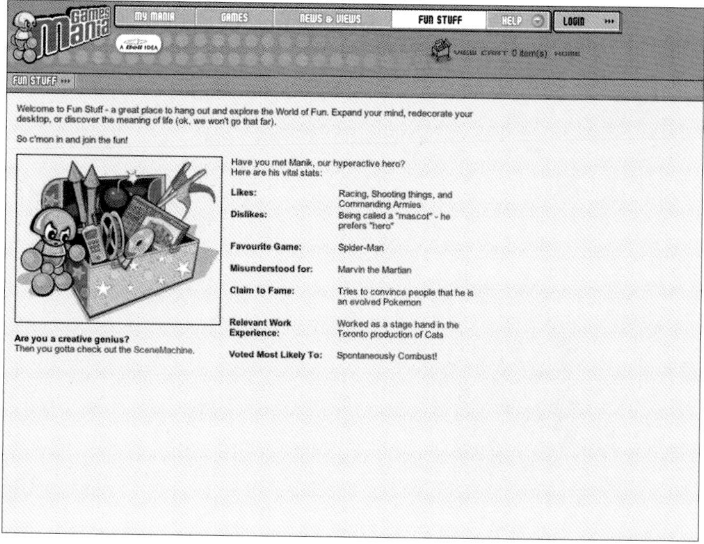

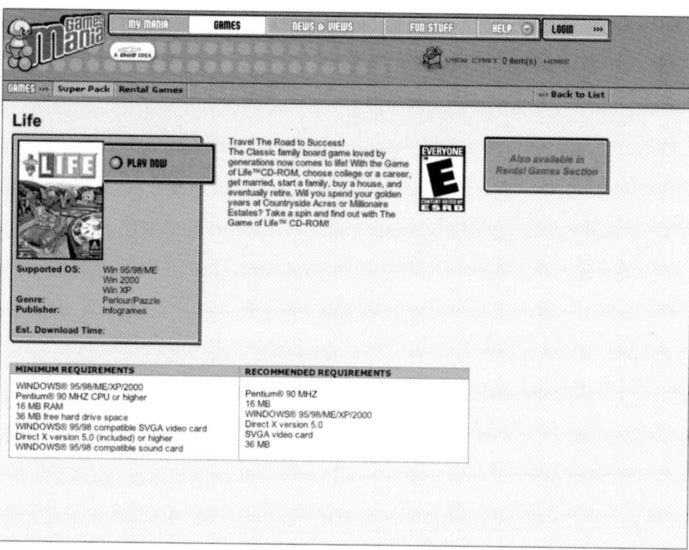

A "Culture-Jamming" Craze

Bell Canada was looking for ways to build subscriber revenue and offer customers exiting new broadband services. Organic worked with Bell to introduce a new service that would help do that.

GamesMania offers customers the ability to access quality PC games online on a pay-per use and subscription basis. Organic worked with Bell to develop the GamesMania brand, the hyperactive mascot, Manic, the interface, and a range of promotional materials.

The concept is based on the notion of "culture-jamming": Pop culture referenced, stolen, humorized and re-purposed. Blending innocence and worldliness, with a healthy sense of self-deprecation running throughout, GamesMania offers a provocative, intelligently subversive entry point into worlds unimaginable.

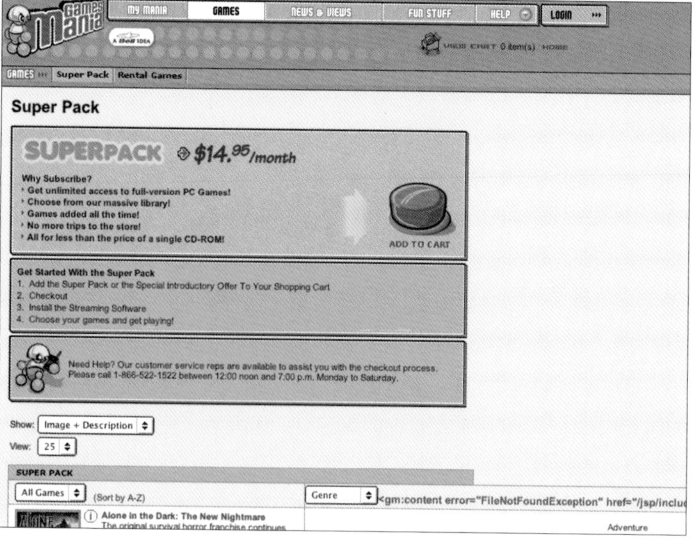

07

08

Agency	Fallon Minneapolis
Client	BMW of North America
Art Director	Kevin Flatt
Writers	Joe Sweet, Chuck Carlson
Creative Director	Kevin Flatt
Designer	Brooke Posard
Photographer	Mark LaFavor
Information Architect	Matt Heinrichs
Programmers	George Hilal, Marc Gowland, Josh Hagen Chris Wiggins
Producers	Jennifer Bremer, Cori Van Brunt Jane Petersen
Digital Artists/Multimedia	Christian Erickson, Chris Wiggins Chris Stocksmith, Laurie Brown
Music/Sound	Elements
ID	02040N
URL	www.bmwfilms.com

Award	Gold
Category	**Integrated Branding Campaign**
Page	72

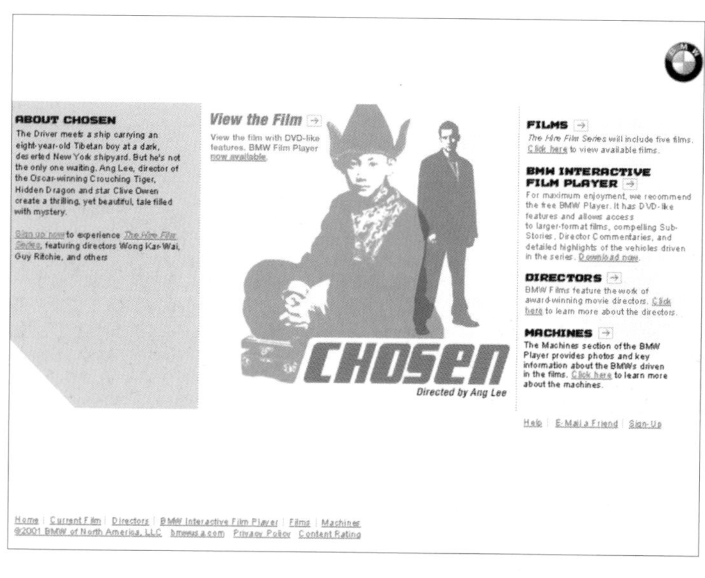

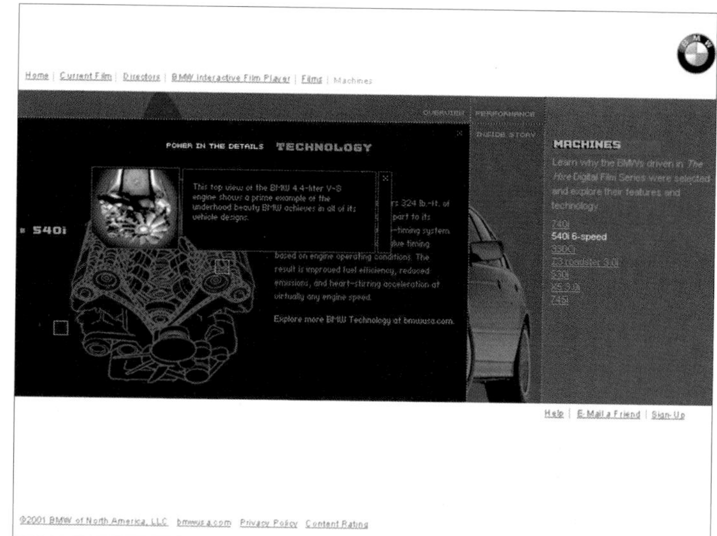

Driving into a New Advertising Future

It began as an advertising brief. But advertising wasn't the answer. We were frustrated that traditional commercials didn't let us show what BMWs could really do. BMW customers increasingly weren't watching television, yet they had embraced the Web in astounding numbers.

Then, our clients agreed to throw away the rulebook.

Why not, instead, create something so entertaining, so rewarding, that people would actually seek it out? Why not take the money saved on media and put it on the screen? Why not create an interactive experience more akin to home theater?

What resulted was BMW Films: a series of short films directed by and starring A-list Hollywood talent. Each film revolved around a central character called The Driver, the world's best when it came to transporting people out of dangerous situations. The Driver's character traits — his youthfulness, integrity, passion, and willingness to take risks — reflected on both the brand and the audience. Each film featured The Driver using a BMW to complete his missions, showcasing BMW's true performance. The films were distributed at an entertainment-focused Web site, making them "found" treasures, yet they were still accessible to anyone at anytime.

In the end it took one brave client, more than a hundred people working in every discipline at Fallon, and the wisdom and commitment of our production partners at Anonymous to pull it off. And it worked in every possible way.

Perhaps it doesn't fit everyone's definition of advertising today. Hopefully, neither will the next thing Fallon does.

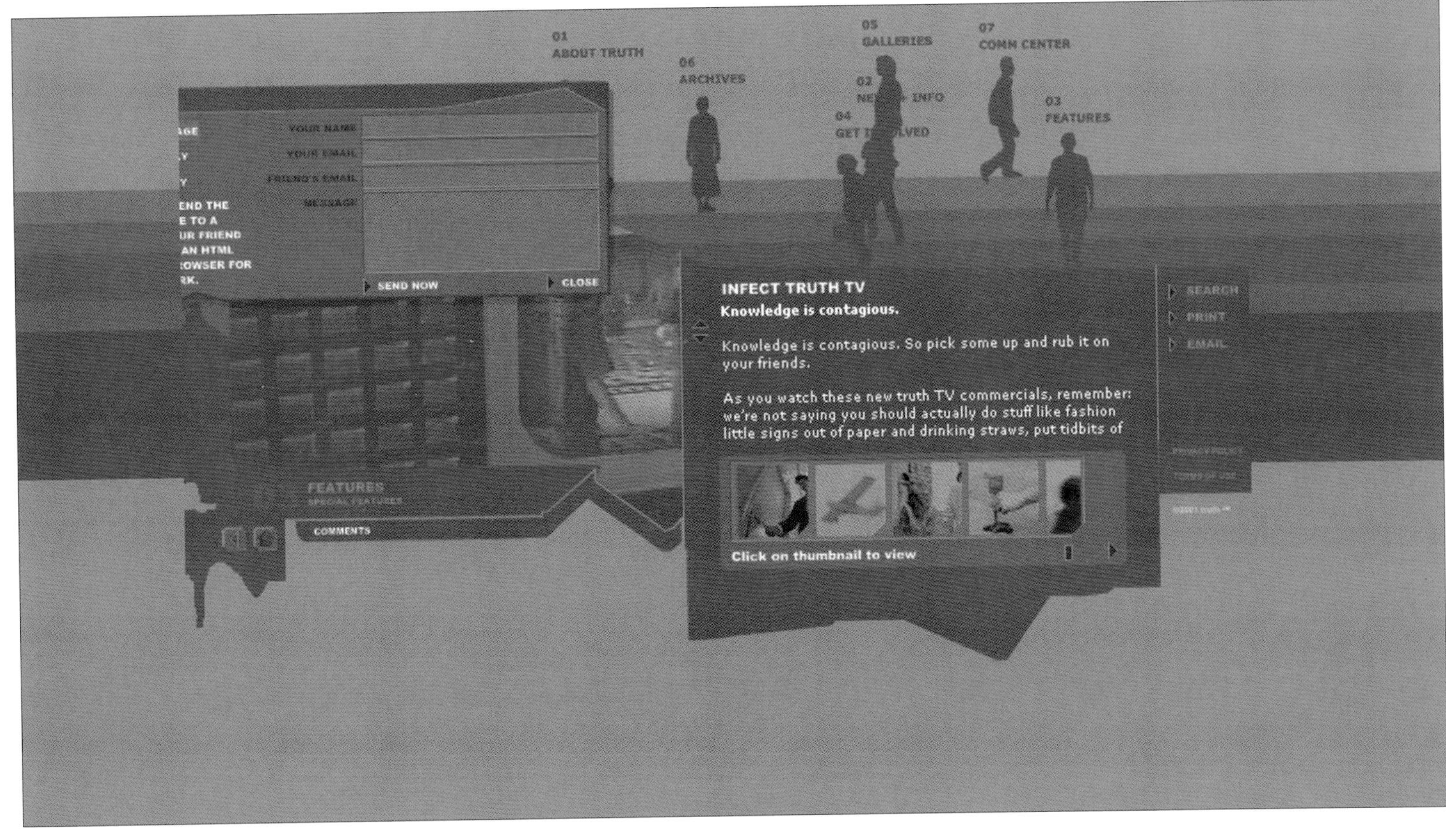

Agencies	Arnold Worldwide - Boston Crispin Porter & Bogusky - Miami
Client	American Legacy Foundation
Art Directors	Jim Marcus, Rob Baird, Lee Einhorn Mike Martin, Tony Calcao Paul Keister
Writers	Mike Martin, Roger Baldacci. Mike Howard John Kearse, Rob Strasberg Bob Cianfrone
Creative Directors	Ron Lawner, Pete Favat, Alex Bogusky Roger Baldacci
Technical Directors	Doug Smith, Ebbey Mathew
Designer	Megan Boardman
Flash Programmer	Nathan Wray
Producers	Barry Frechette, Cybil Ciavarra Eric Decker, Ben Raynes, Karen Kenney Rupert Samuel
ID	02041N
URL	thetruth.com
Award	Gold
Category	**Integrated Branding Campaign**
Page	74

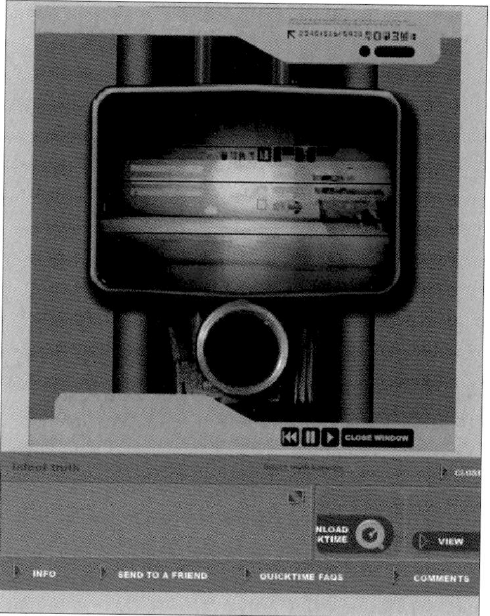

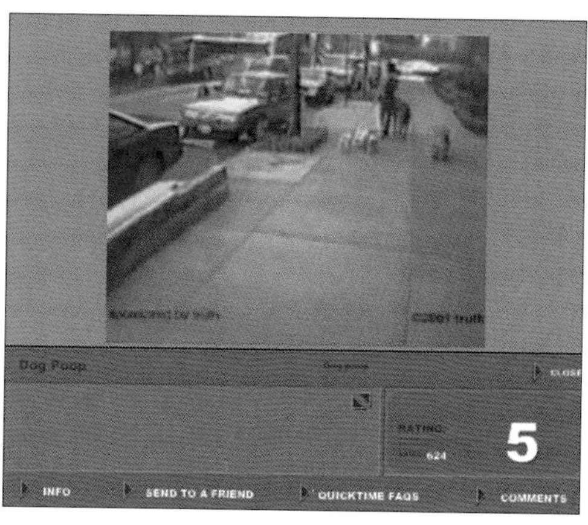

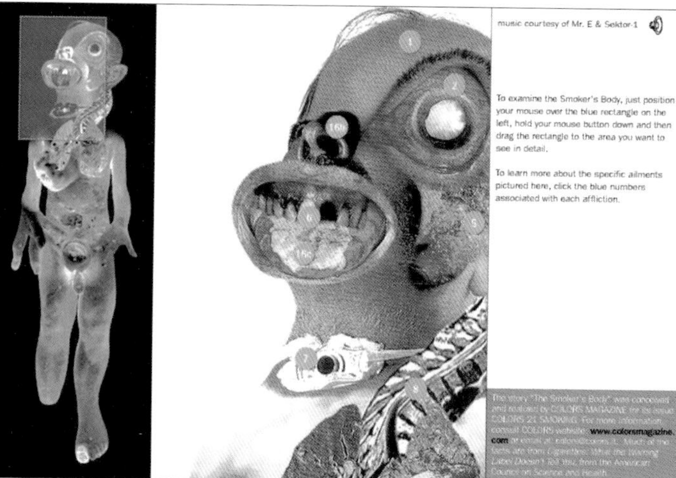

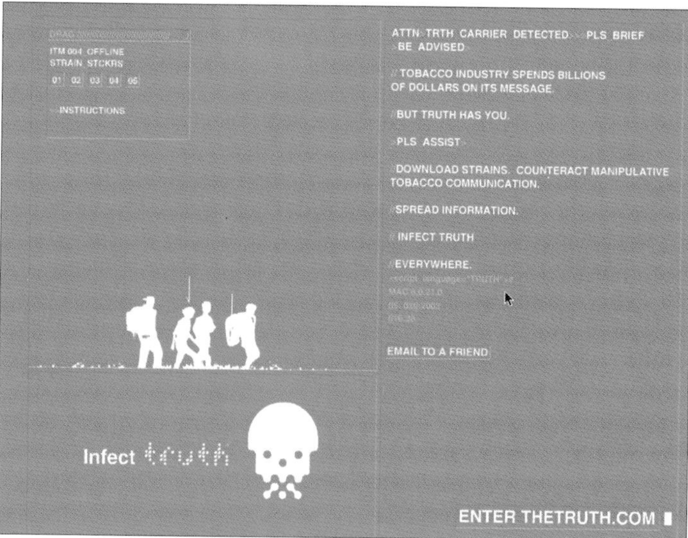

A Kernel of Truth

Thetruth.com was developed around an entirely databased "kernel" that allows us to change the look and feel relatively quickly in order to more effectively meet up with offline campaigns and events. We design each version (called V1-Vx) to integrate with the offline as closely as we can so that we have a consistent message all the way across the brand. Truth launches sub-branded campaigns frequently, keeping the message up-to date and interesting and the site needs to move accordingly.

On the site, users are able to rate the commercial spots and have a little fun with them. We benefit on-line from not taking ourselves too seriously and being able to take abuse when it comes up. What we have to say can be difficult for some people to warm up to immediately but it's a priority for us to be likeable and easy-to-live with online. Sometimes the shocking and powerful nature of the ads needs a bed to live in — a home so that people know that these are just people behind this at the end of the day — people who care about this issue and have no real interest in victimizing or demonizing other people. We're just trying to tell the truth.

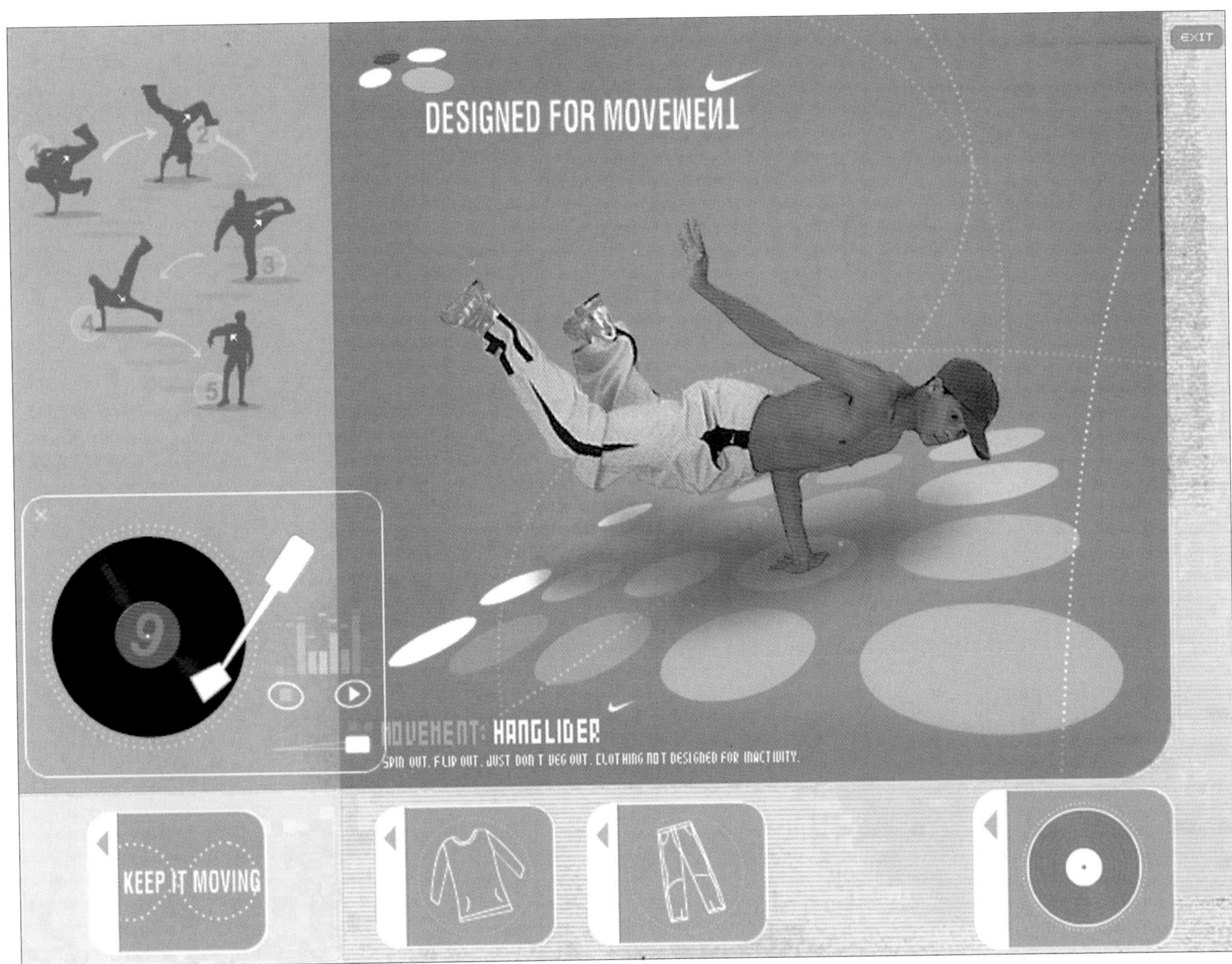

Agency	The Jupiter Drawing Room - Johannesburg
Client	Nike South Africa
Art Directors	Steven Blyth, Vanessa Norman Karten Lilje
Writer	Trevor Olive
Creative Director	Graham Warsop
Designers	Steven Blyth, Karten Lilje
Photographer/Illustrator	Frank Esposito
Programmers	Steven Blyth, Jason Kaler
Digital Artist/Multimedia	Steven Blyth
Music/Sound	Andrew Louis
ID	02042N
URL	www.nikedfm.co.za/awardsentry

Award	Silver
Category	**Integrated Branding Campaign**
Page	76

Designed for Movement

With the goal of creating street-smart ads that showcased the cutting-edge sporting innovations at the root of every Nike creation, we used athletes as break-dancers on twister mats. The contortion-like movements they forced their bodies to perform perfectly demonstrated the versatility of the apparel.

The idea was extended to in-store elements such as floor decals, posters and clothing labels. But it was the digital component that really brought the campaign to life. We created two interactive, self-contained platforms, Twist an' Shout and Urban Athletes where the user could experience the apparel in action.

To make the experience visually striking and to enhance the interactive aspect, both downloads involved a high degree of movement, which involved viewers selecting the character's dance routines and poses.

Join the Movement

To create awareness of the promotion, we made use of an HTML mail teaser, which drove users to the www.nikedfm.co.za "Designed for Movement" hub where they were prompted to download a movement.

To maintain the forward movement of the promotion from one inbox to another, users were given the incentive of a weekly draw where winners received a DFM pack.

Users could become part of the movement by simply filling in friend's details and sending on. A string of code was then passed onto the server that stored the data and sent the recipient the teaser. The process repeated itself with recipients becoming senders.

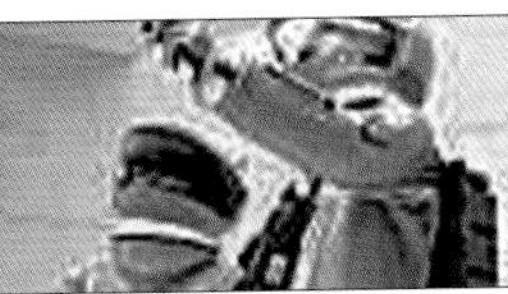

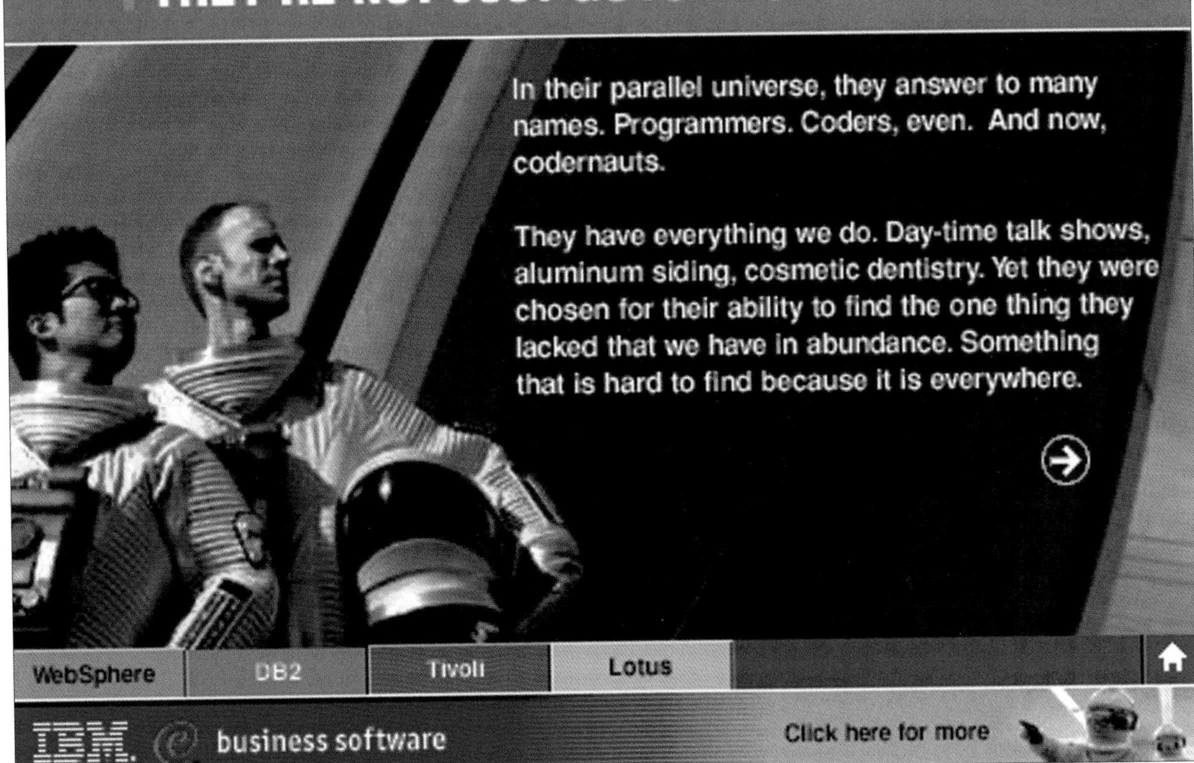

Agency	ogilvyInteractive worldwide New York
Client	IBM
Art Directors	Jeff Compton, Todd Goodale, Oscar Valdez Alex Cho, Enrique Gonzalo, Christine Pillsbury Josh Korda, James Murphy
08 Writers	Maggie Powers, Keith Byrne Patrick Clarke, Johanna Thompson Jay Zasa, Josh Grossberg, Gerald Dugan
Executive Creative Directors	Chris Wall, Steve Hayden, Bruce Lee, Jan Leth, Aurelio Saiz
Creative Directors	Audrey Fleisher, Scott Storrs, Jill McClabb, Mark Millar
Producers	Sebastian Aresco, Ben Goodman, Lee Weiss Judy Feldman, Terri Dannenberg
Designers	Jeff Chuang, Jose Galvez
Technical Director	Mark Hofschneider
Digital Artists/Multimedia	Drew Ziegler, Neal Lee, Scott Leisawitz
ID	02043N
URL	http://www.wwpl.net/oneshow2002/ ibm/codernaut/2001_knowledge.html
Award	Silver
Category	**Integrated Branding Campaign**
Page	78

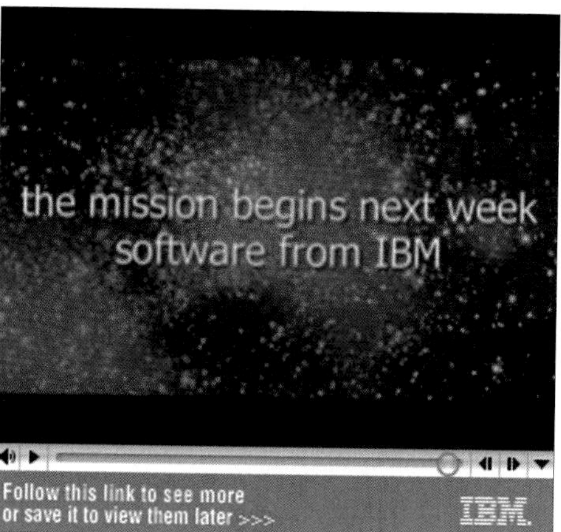

An Integrated Innovation

Targeting software developers and IT professionals, the IBM Software "Codernauts" Campaign was created to unite previously disparate IBM brands — Lotus, Tivoli, WebSphere, and DB2 — under a common umbrella of IBM Software. It was a 360-degree effort, with advertising, direct, and interactive creatives teaming to introduce the Codernauts, coders from a parallel universe looking for better software. And, as the campaign unfolded, it enticed the audience to check out the apps these Codernauts were discovering.

The interactive segment of the campaign was broken into three phases. In the Scene-setting phase, Java and Flash banners hinted at the coming arrival of "visitors" from a parallel universe. Banner clicks gave users video vignettes of the Codernauts preparing for travel. The Impact phase followed the Codernauts' search for better software. Banners used playful interactivity to bond users with the Codernauts as they carried out their mission.

Finally, the Product-specific phase made fully apparent that IBM was behind the superior software these guys were discovering. This phase showcased the specific brands of IBM software as the Codernauts found them. The banners drove to a brand-specific interstitial, which provided detailed product descriptions and offers for each of the brands. With IBM, their mission was a success.

Agency	Ogilvy Interactive - Singapore
Client	Love Singapore Group of Churches
Art Directors	Pei Pei Ng, Dominic Goldman
Writers	Graham Kelly, Shane Weaver Eugene Cheong, Justine Lee
Creative Directors	Graham Kelly, Eugene Cheong
Designers	Victor Ong, Dominic Goldman
Producers	Samuel Kho, Dominic Goldman Charles Yuen
Photographer	Roy Zhang
Digital Artist/Multimedia	Dominic Goldman
Programmer	Ian Morrison
TV Production Co.	Odeon Productions
TV Producer	Tammy Hui
TV Director	Sng Tong Beng
Music/Sound	Yellow Box
ID	02044N
URL	www.our-work.com/version1_2/files/ Web_sites/god.org.sg/god_explan.htm
Award	Bronze
Category	**Integrated Branding Campaign**
Page	80

Blessed are the geek, for they shall click here.
God

I could make you click here.

But I believe in free will.
God

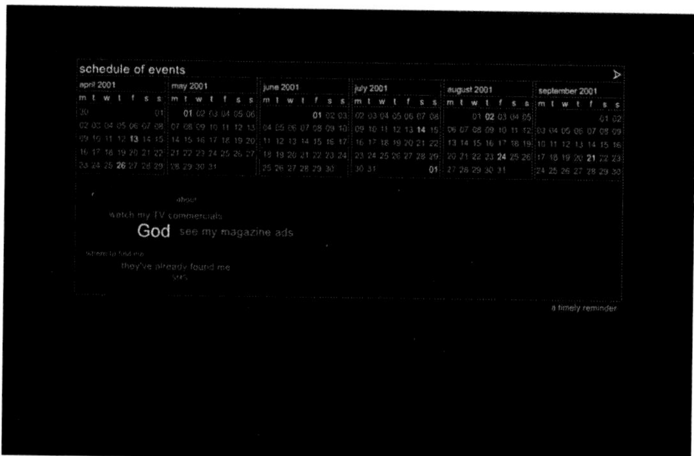

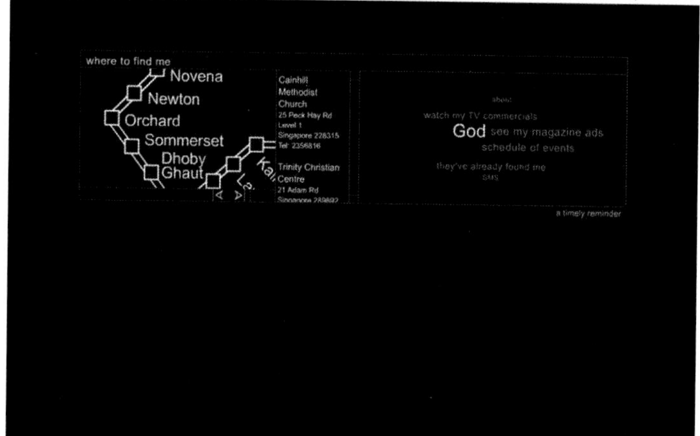

A God for the Digital Age

The Love Singapore Movement, a loose network of 150 Singaporean churches of various denominations, came to us with an unusual brief: "God has an image problem. Can you help Him?" The following story illustrated the problem: A schoolboy was once asked what he thought God was like. He replied that, as far as he could make out, God was "the sort of person who is always snooping around to see if anyone is enjoying himself and then trying to stop it."

In short, He should be less preachy and more witty; less Billy Graham, more George Burns. Our strategy was to portray a more approachable God via a multimedia campaign involving print, TV, outdoor, Web site, banners and wireless.

Unfortunately it was a bit too successful – about two weeks into the campaign, the government banned both the TV and press ads. "Religious advertisements are not allowed on television since Singapore is a multi-racial society and such advertising would be seen to be proselytizing," said the Singapore Broadcasting Authority in a letter to Love Singapore.

That's when Interactive became even more important. We upped the drive to the Web site with a host of Web-banners. And on the site itself you could view all the banned TV and print ads. Pushing the e-envelope further, we launched an SMS campaign to transmit messages from God to mobile phone users. Subscribers to the service then forwarded the messages onto friends so it spread virally.

In the end, we achieved our objective. God spoke in a more personal, affable way. And He did it almost everywhere you looked.

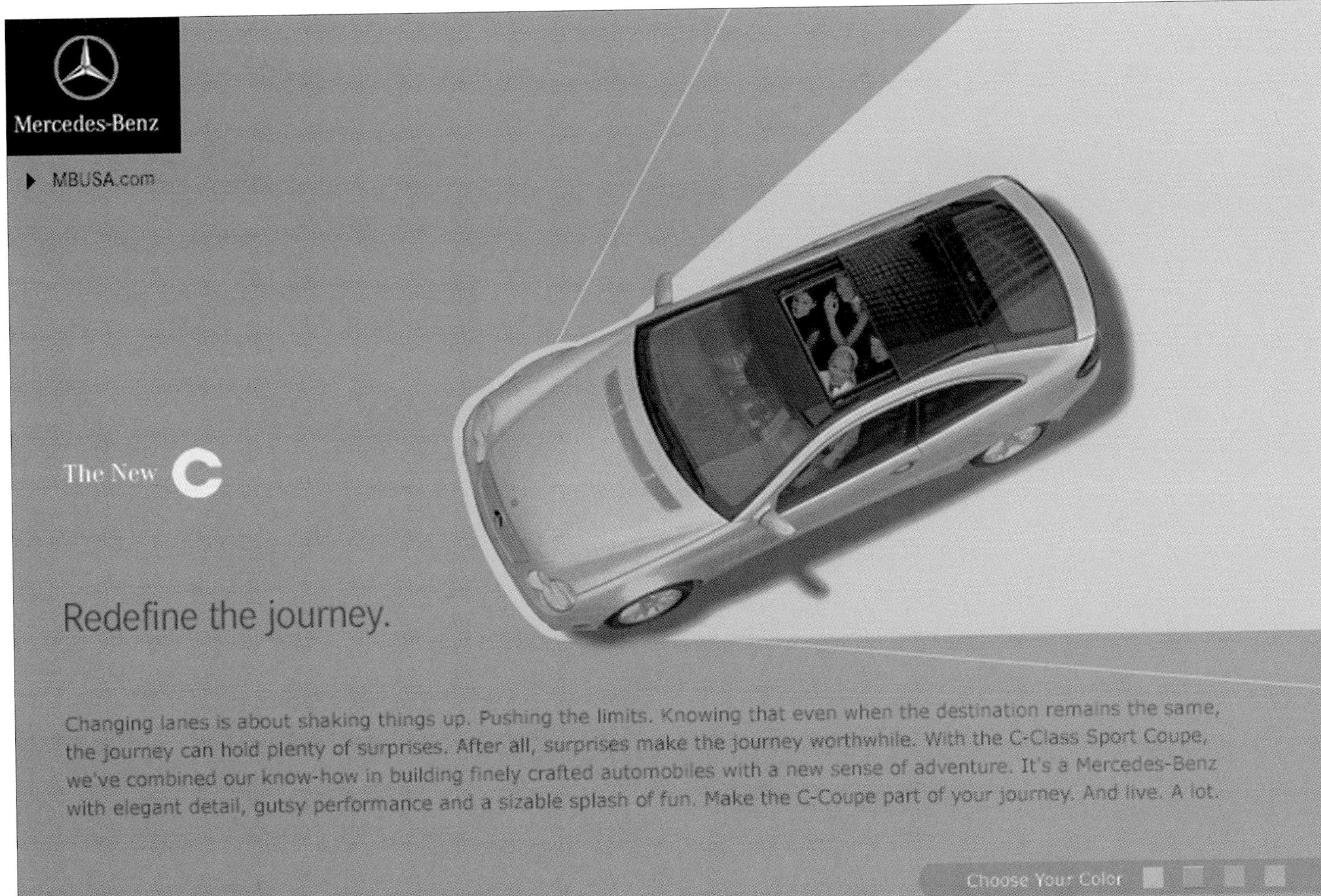

Agency	Critical Mass - Calgary
Client	Mercedes Benz USA
Art Director	Critical Mass
Writer	Critical Mass
ID	02045N
URL	www.criticalmass.com/awards/oneshow/ccoupe

Award	Bronze
Category	**Integrated Branding Campaign**
Page	82

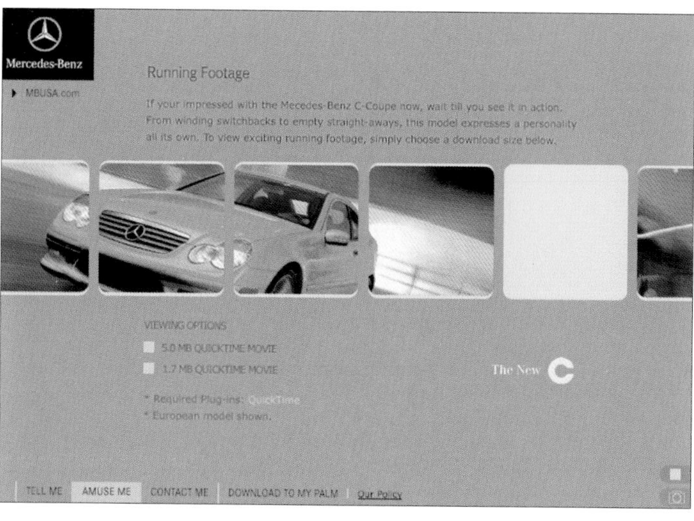

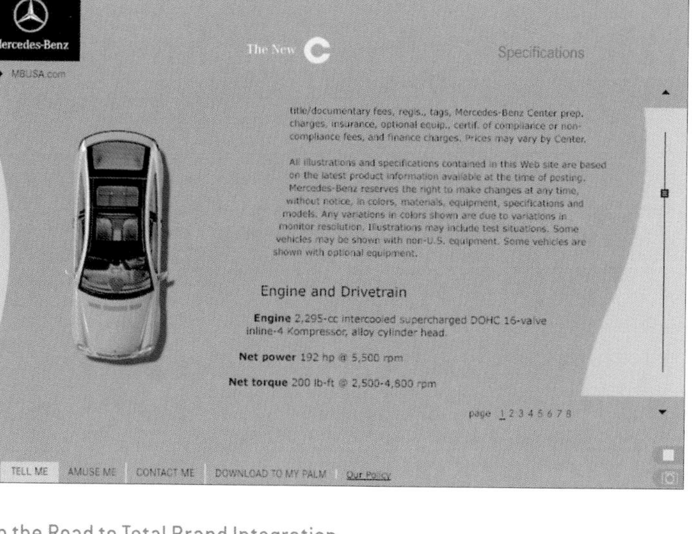

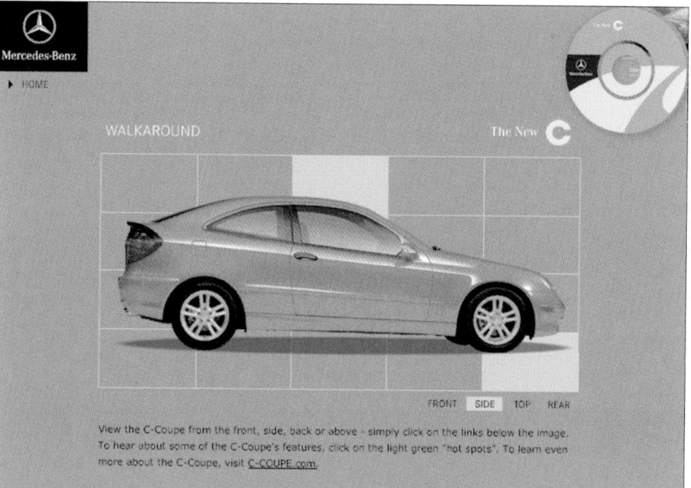

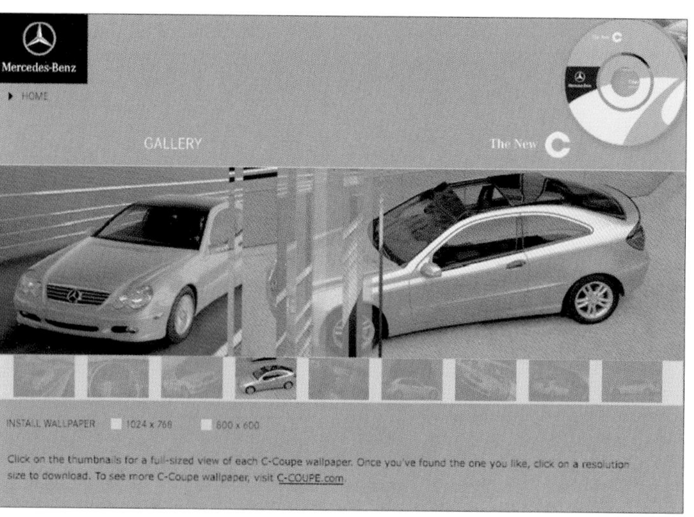

On the Road to Total Brand Integration

Challenge

Mercedes-Benz partnered with Critical Mass to design and deliver a digital campaign to launch the brand new C230 Kompressor Sports Coupe. The C-Coupe's distinctly different look meant targeting a non-traditional Mercedes-Benz audience, one that is younger and at the entry point of luxury car buying. The primary objectives of the campaign were to generate pre-launch excitement about the C-Coupe, drive visitors to contact dealers, drive sweepstakes registrations and generate opt-ins to receive further communication from Mercedes-Benz. The campaign included a microsite, online advertising (including rich media), a sweepstakes, mini CD-ROM, wireless ads, Palm application and e-mails.

Solution

The campaign reflects the traits of both the C-Coupe and its target market: fun-loving, independent, spontaneous and sporty. Rich media ad units with compelling copy were placed on sites with a high acceptance of rich media and a high proportion of the target audience such as Comedy Central, Shockwave.com, and Excite@Home. Once on the site, visitor's could change the color of the entire site, create wallpaper out of almost any page, check out running footage and a photos of the C-Coupe, create "mini-movies" and e-mail them to friends and enter a sweepstakes to win a new C-Coupe. The mini CD-ROM features a virtual walkaround, desktop theme and C-Coupe flash movie. All of the campaign components include a call to action for the visitor to contact a Mercedes-Benz dealer.

Results

The C-Coupe campaign was very successful, surpassing all performance metrics set at the campaign launch. The Sweepstakes campaign generated substantial registrations, with 48% of registrants opting in to receive additional C-Coupe information. The Flash banner generated response rates four times higher than typical GIF banners, which substantially lowered the cost-per-click.

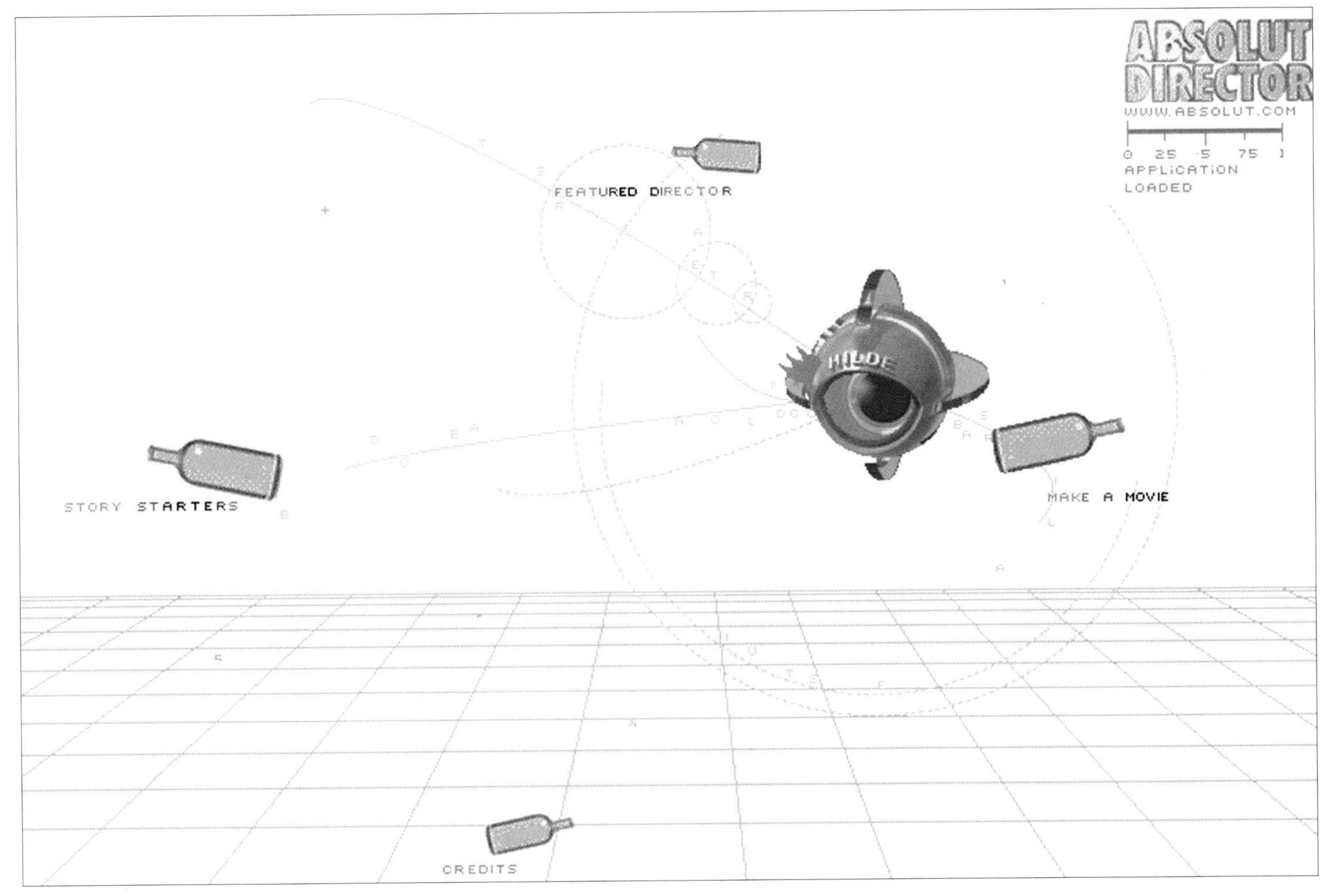

Agencies	Submarine - New York TBWA/Chiat/Day - New York
Client	Absolut Vodka
Art Directors	Dan Braun, Michael French Kirk Gibbons, Joseph Mazzaferro
Writers	Josh Braun, Dan Braun, Pete Callaro
Creative Directors	Dan Braun, Joseph Mazzaferro
Designers	Michael French, Kirk Gibbons
Information Architects	Kirk Klobe, Ishmael Riles
Programmers	Marc Blanchard, Jason Muscat Tom Trenka
Digital Artists/Multimedia	Mark Blanchard, Michael French
Digital Production	Zendo Studios Pillar Applications Group
Music/Sound	BRNR
ID	02046N
URL	http://www.absolutdirector.com
Award	Bronze
Category	**Broadband**
Page	84

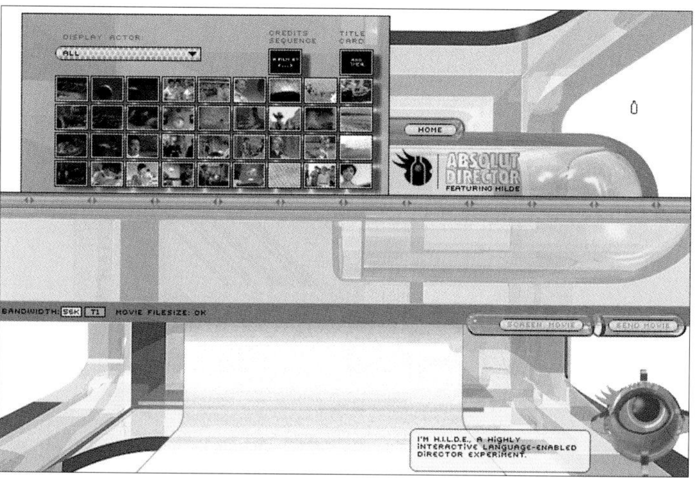

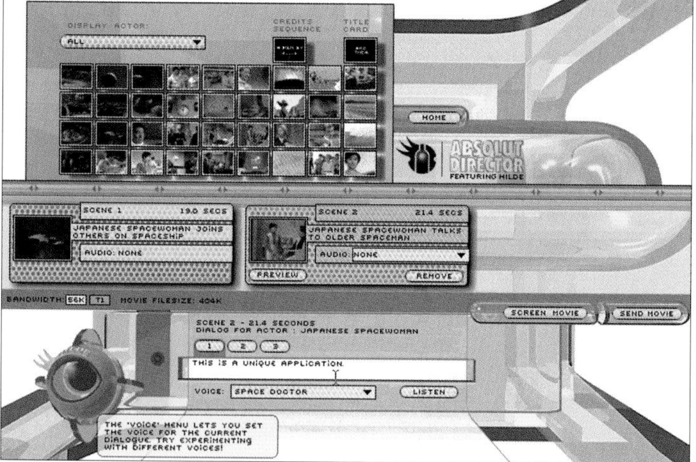

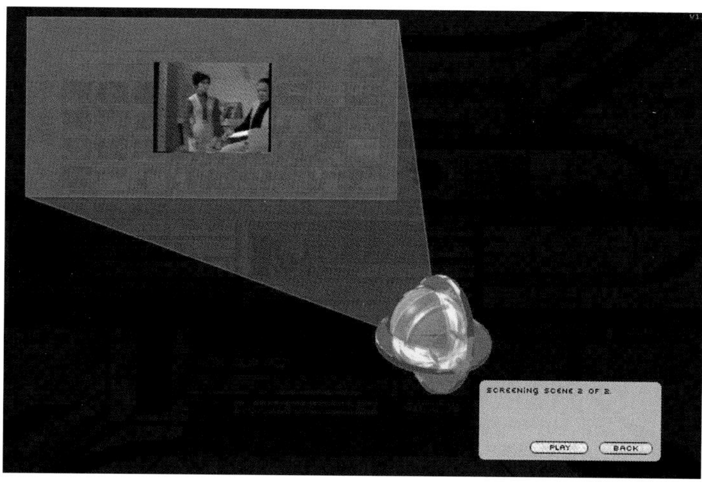

Cutting Edge? Absolutely.

Absolut Director was conceived in the spring of 2000 by Dan Braun, Josh Braun and Pete Callaro of Submarine. "We were trying to find a totally unique and original idea to bring to Absolut for it's groundbreaking series of content based Web sites" say Dan Braun. The idea was based on a Woody Allen movie, *What's Up Tiger Lily* where Allen stripped the dialogue from an Asian spy movie and re-scripted it."

Dan and Pete of Submarine came from TBWA Chiat/Day where they led the development of all Absolut's Web projects going back to 1996. Previous sites dealt with DJ music, experimental animation and conceptual thinking.

"Film had been high on the list of subjects but we didn't want to simply use the Web as a distribution mechanism," states Pete Braun. The interactivity in Absolut Director requires active participation by the user. The idea was that anyone could be a director. You can choose music, pick characters, change shots and create your own dialogue.

To demonstrate the functionality, director Spike Lee was brought in to create his own Absolut Director film. Absolut Director is one of the only sites on the Internet that you can truly create and distribute your own short film.

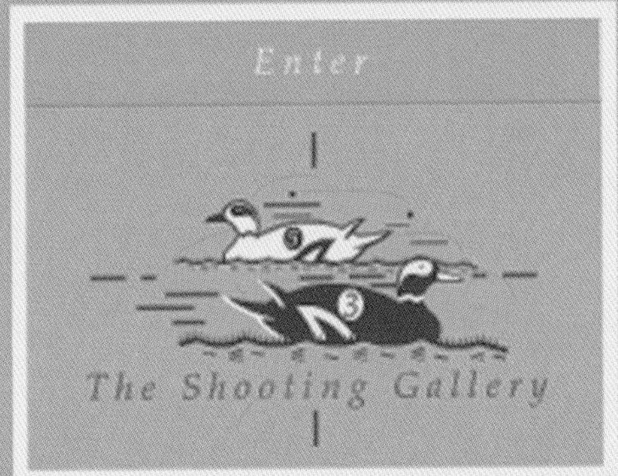

Agency	Kinetic Interactive - Singapore
Client	The Shooting Gallery
Art Director	Sean Lam
Writer	Alex Goh
Designer	Sean Lam
Photographer/Illustrator	Sean Lam
Information Architects	James Chua, Sean Lam
Programmer	Benjy Choo
Producer	James Chua
Music/Sound	Victor Low
ID	02047N
URL	www.shootinggalleryasia.com

Award	Bronze
Category	**Broadband**
Page	86

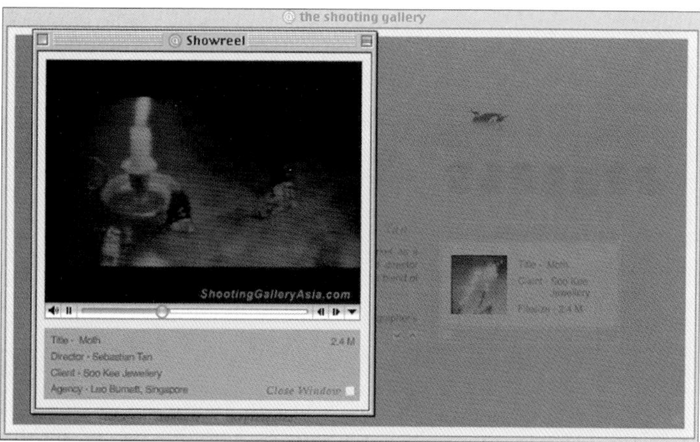

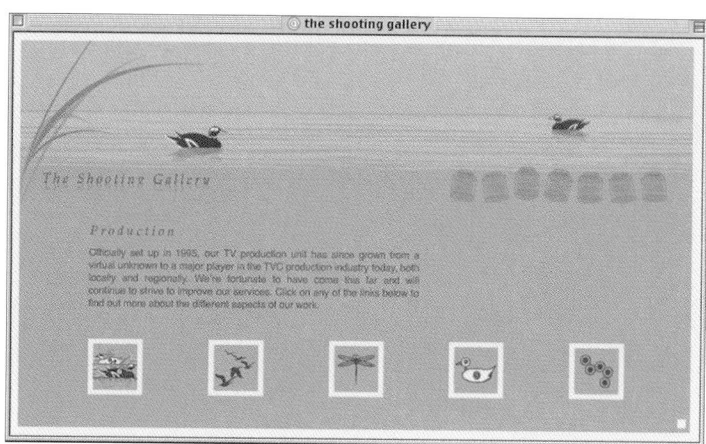

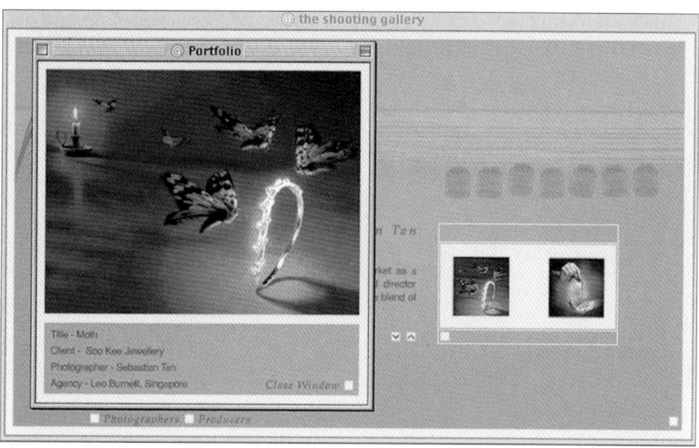

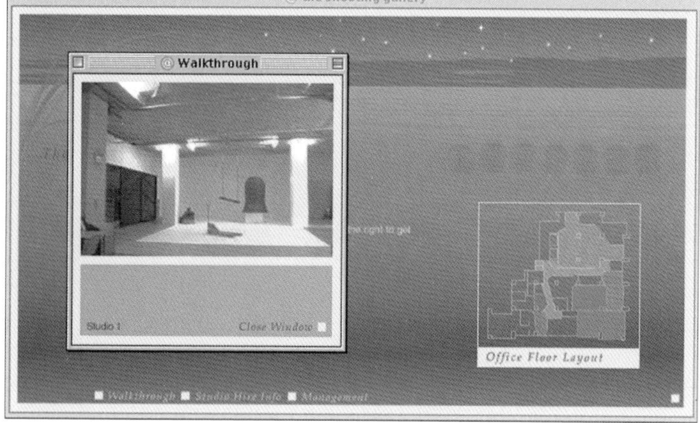

A Solution of Sublety and Simplicity

Description

The client is one of the biggest production houses in Singapore, offering a full range of services from professional photography and TVC production to digital imaging services. Kinetic Interactive was given an open brief to revamp their Web site completely. Only two basic guidelines were issued; the first involved ensuring that the end result fitted closely with the client's existing style and unique approach, the second centres around designing a configuration that would ensure ease of access for users, particularly with an eye to providing hassle-free viewing of the client's considerable portfolio.

Solution

A conscious decision was made to depart from the typically fast Flash-based sites. Instead of following up literally the pun that was intended in the clients name (as in a site featuring guns and targets), a subtle and understated approach was used, with natural elements and the environmental setpieces found within the habitat of a pond taking centerstage. The end result has an organic, fresh-looking feel that is subtly stylish, as befits a client with a well-established name and a management that believes in humility. The architecture of the site was also kept simple to provide ease of navigation, portraying the client's belief in subtlety and simplicity.

Agency	Ogilvy Interactive - Singapore
Client	Love Singapore Group of Churches
Writers	Graham Kelly, Shane Weaver, Eugene Cheong, Justine Lee
Creative Director	Graham Kelly
Designer	Victor Ong
Producers	Charles Yuen, Ian Morrison
Programmers	Charles Yuen, Ian Morrison
ID	02048N
URL	www.our-work.com/god/sms/

Award	Silver
Category	**Wireless**
Page	88

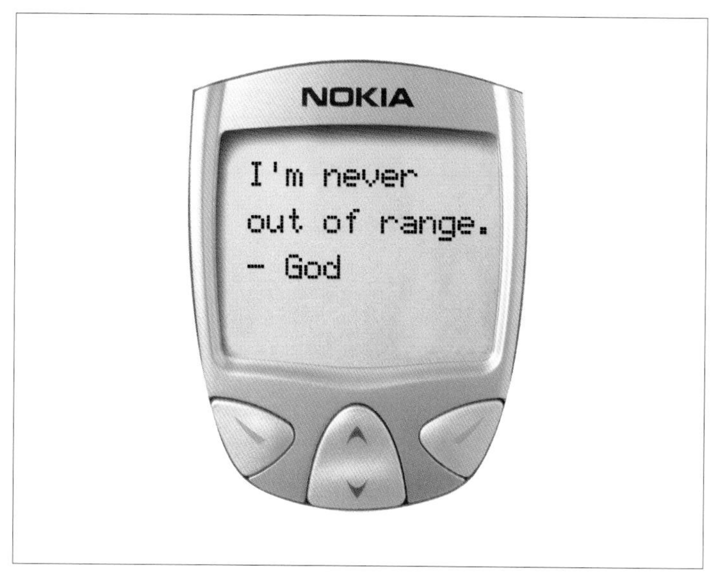

A Message from God

Your mobile phone is always close by. Sometimes, quite literally close to your heart. Since the objective of this campaign was to bring people closer to God, mobile seemed like a relevant medium for the message. We used SMS (Short Message Service; also called "texting"). This is incredibly popular in Asia, and Singaporeans are amongst its most avid users.

The campaign was permission-based – people were invited to opt-in to get the messages and you could unsubscribe at any time. Some messages were tailored to specific days and times, like "Thank me it's Friday" which was sent out at 6pm on that particular day of the week. Other messages used terminology phone users could relate to, such as the "I'm never out of range" example.

There was a viral component too. We asked subscribers to forward messages and this ended up being a key subscription channel: we got over 50% of new subscribers this way.

The results were encouraging: opt-in subscription rate of 25%, and more than 15,000 subscribers to date. Put another way, more than 1% of mobile phone owners in Singapore have had a message from God

10

Agency	Fallon - Minneapolis
Client	Lee Jeans
Art Director	Harvey Marco
Writer	Dean Buckhorn
Creative Director	Harvey Marco
Producers	Sarah Zanger, Sarah Pepin
Programmer	Phil Torrone
Digital Artist/Multimedia	Laurie Brown
ID	02049N
URL	http://awards.fallon.com/lee/pda

Award	Bronze
Category	**Wireless**
Page	90

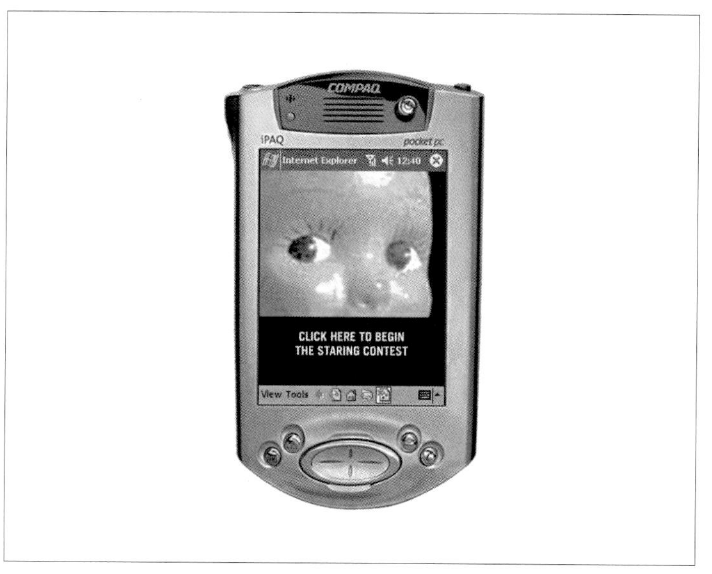

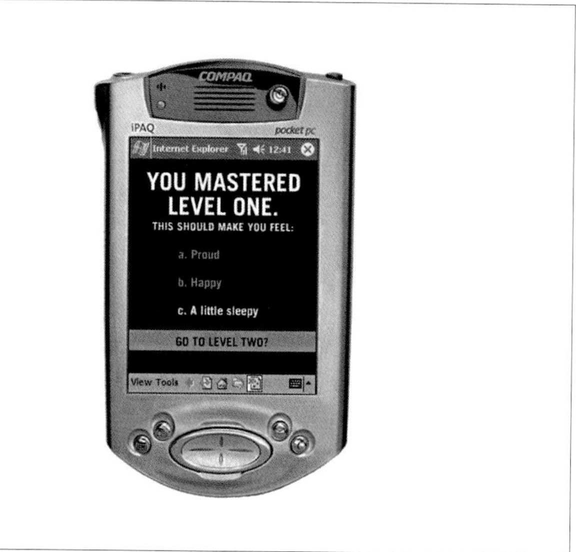

Staring at Ingenuity

Being Like Buddy Lee means never quitting in the face of adversity, and the 2001 Buddy Lee Staring Contest for PDAs is no exception. The Buddy Lee Staring Contest, housed on the leedungarees.com Web site invites you to challenge Buddy Lee to a stare-down. On the site users can see others take on Buddy Lee, view the challenge as a screensaver and of course download the staring contest to their PDA for a mobile challenge. With the Buddy Lee PDA Staring Contest game Fallon and Lee were able to capture the attention of the emerging segment of mobile professionals using technology and creativity.

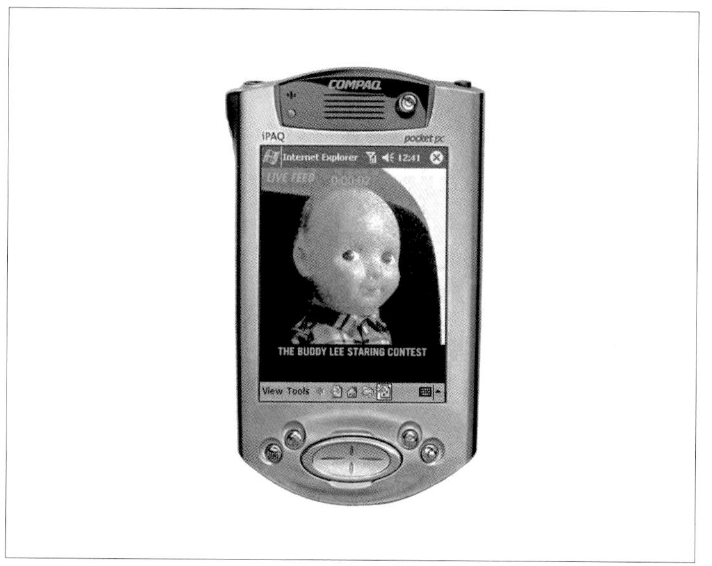

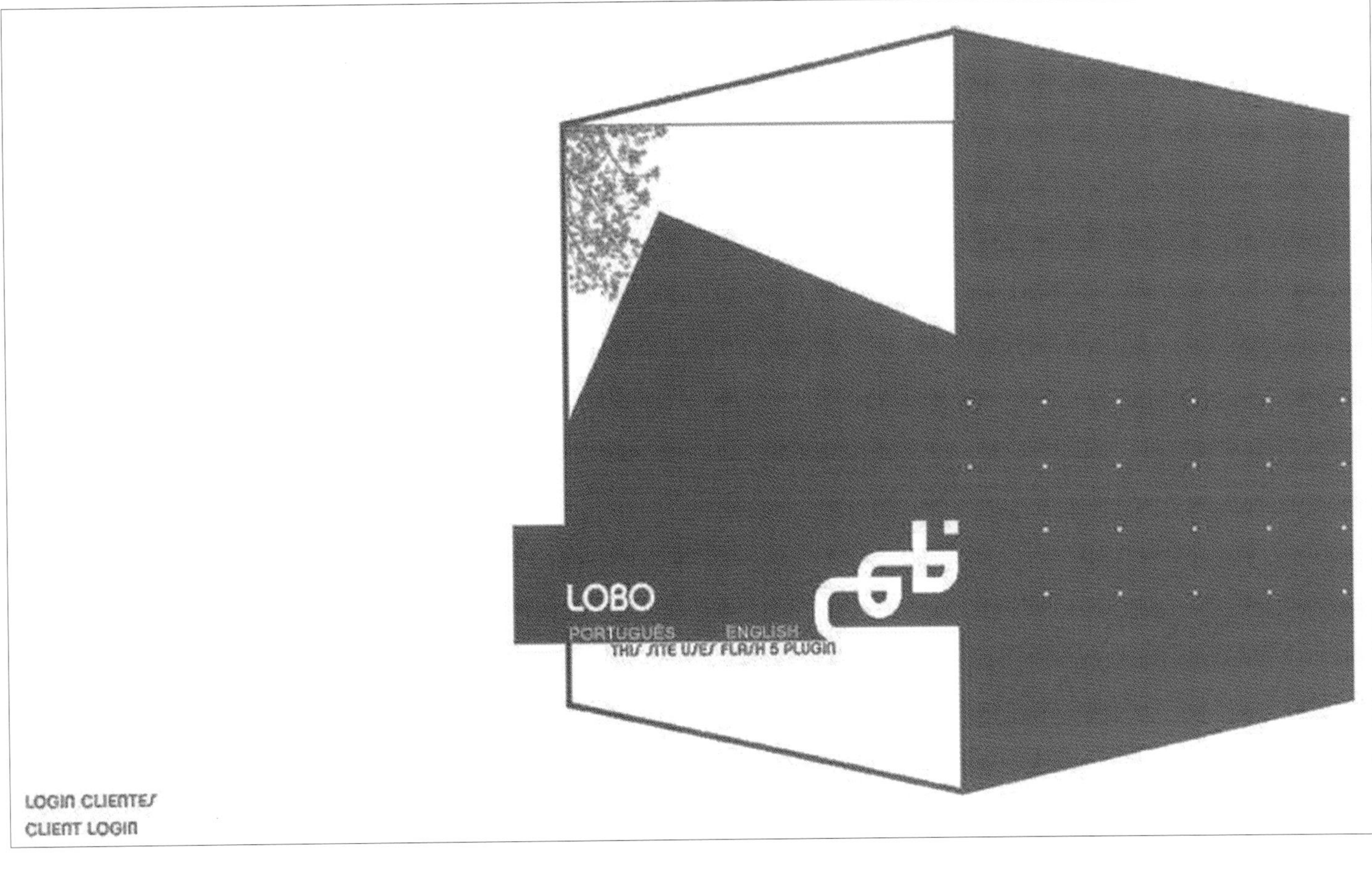

Agency	Lobo Filmes - São Paulo
Client	Lobo Filmes
Creative Director	Mateus de Paula Santos
Designer	Denis Kamioka
Music/Sound	Paul Beto
ID	02050N
URL	www.lobo.cx

Award	Gold
Category	**Self-Promotion — Web Sites**
Page	92

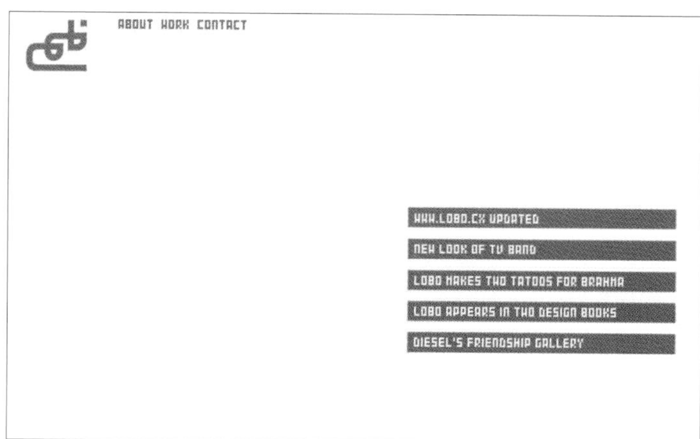

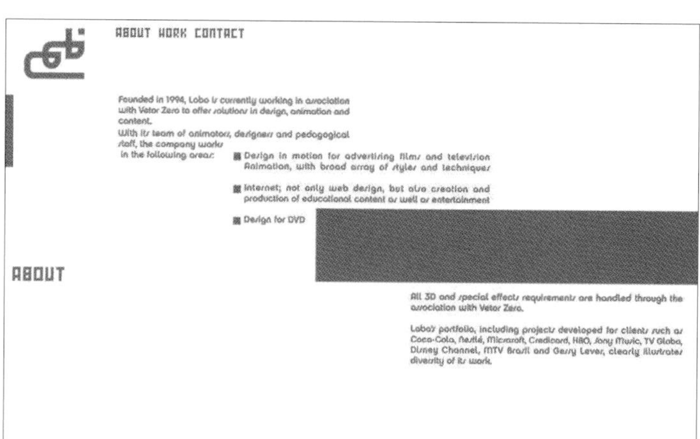

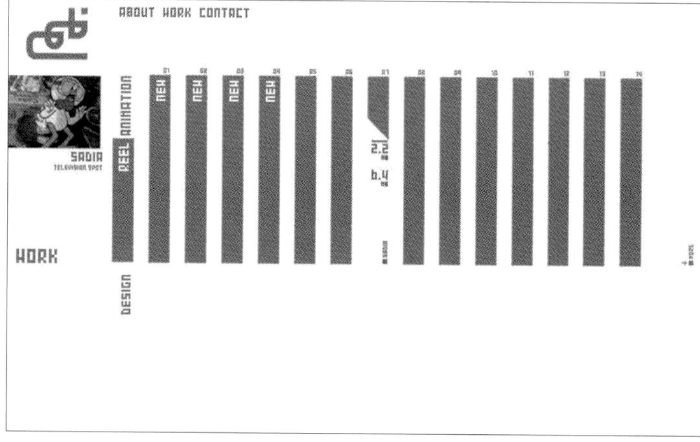

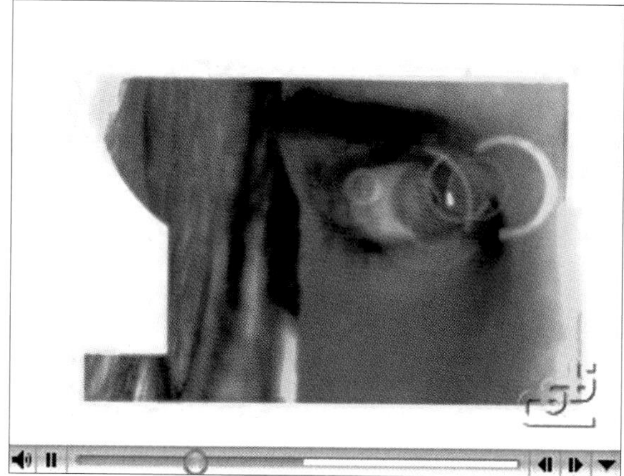

Simple and Effective

As we are a design studio, our intention with the Web site was to showcase a large variety of work with different styles but in a unified interface. This interface also had to be a showcase of what we think is cutting-edge design.

Our challenge was to create something with visual appeal and impact but at the same time neutral enough not to interfere with the site's content. To accomplish that, we chose two colors, white and orange, to design the whole site. Along with that, we used a few simple geometric shapes and elements and a very straightforward navigation that matched the visuals to keep things simple.

By doing that, whenever you see a thumbnail or a movie in our site, because of its colors and details, they gain relevance in the site's context. And also, the site's minimalist and fresh design is a great example of our skills.

1

Agency	Scholz & Volkmer - Weisbaden
Client	Ralf Wengenmayr (Music for Film & Advertising)
Art Director	Heike Brockmann
Creative Director	Michael Volkmer
Designers	Melanie Lenz, Elke Grober
Project Manager	Natascha Becker
Programmers	Peter Reichard, Samuel Ruckstuhl
Digital Artist/Multimedia	Samuel Ruckstuhl
Music/Sound	Ralf Wengenmayr
ID	02051N
URL	http://www.ralfwengenmayr.com

Award	Gold
Category	**Self-Promotion — Web Sites**
Page	94

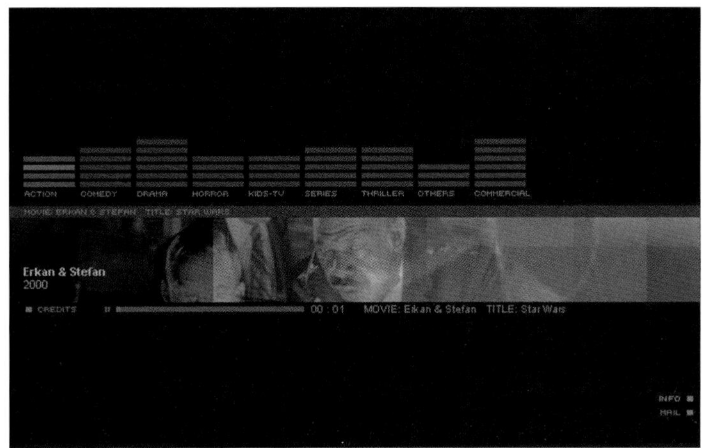

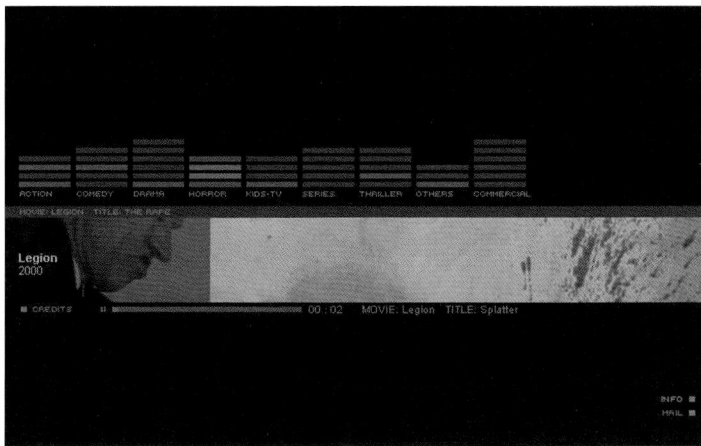

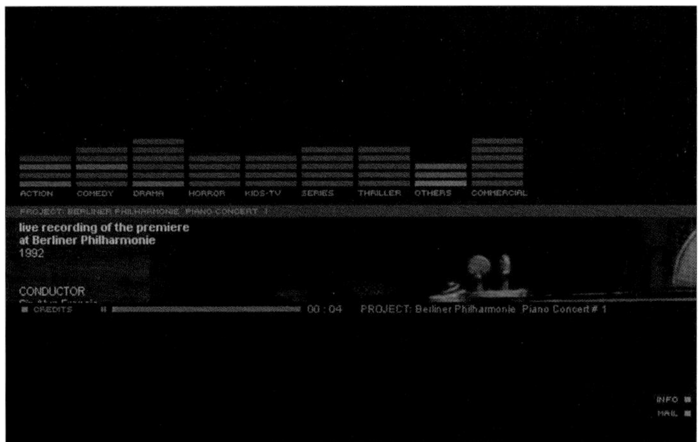

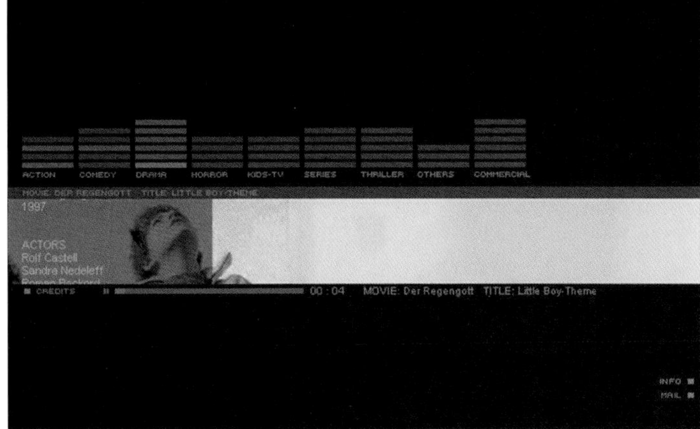

Online at the Movies

The Internet appearance was realized by order of the German composer of film and advertisement music Ralf Wengenmayr. The target was to present Ralf Wengenmayr's broad composer abilities and the projects he has realized so far.

The Web site has been clearly divided into two sections: music and information. The main focus lies on the Music chapter and on the compositions of Ralf Wengenmayr. Pictures and information about the films are shown on a screen, giving the visitor the feeling of being at the movies, a very authentic "hearing situation" due to the fact that Ralf Wengenmayr has written music for many famous films. The information part exclusively contains personal information about the artist and his projects. It is only added on request.

The Web site is completely based on Flash 5 technology, which makes the streaming of the comprehensive audio and picture data possible.

11

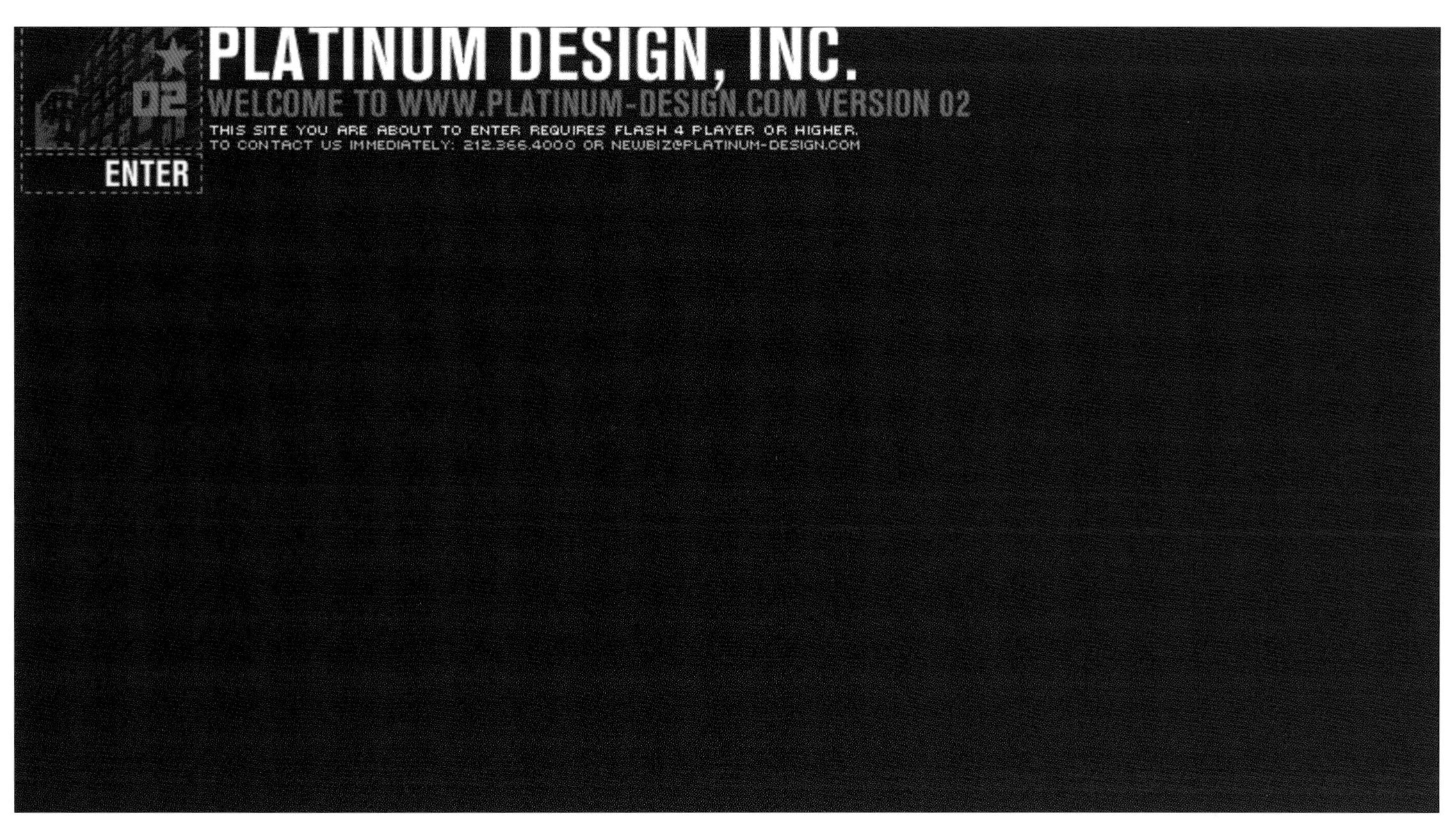

Agency	Platinum Design - New York
Client	Platinum Design
Art Director	Mike Joyce
Writer	Frank Oswald
Creative Director	Vickie Peslak
Designer	Andrew Taray
Programmer	Andrew Taray
ID	02052N
URL	www.platinum-design.com

Award	Bronze
Category	**Self-Promotion — Web Sites**
Page	96

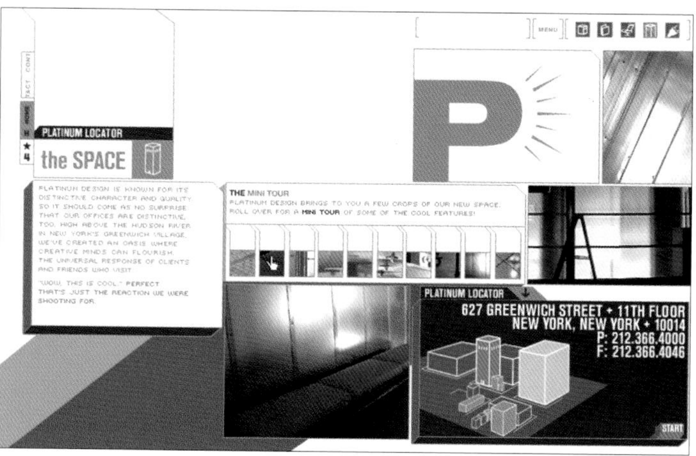

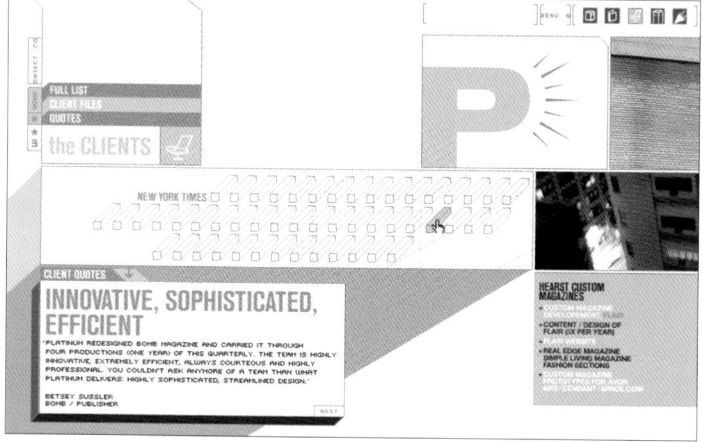

Passion + Purpose

Created in Flash, Platinum's site is a moving experience -- bright images pop-up, streams of information run across each page and bold snapshots detail a sophisticated design strategy.

The site is split into a clear grid system. Each section is color-coded and monochromatic for easy identification. Once you have entered a section, further information and options load on the same screen through pop-ups resembling streaming video.

The general theme of the site is an industrial design intended to compliment the metallic element of the company name, which has always been central to its corporate image. Basic icons are used to communicate the factory-inspired theme and help balance the site's super hi-tech feel.

Text treatments highlight amusing copy suggestions, while the language of the site clearly states Platinum's mantra: Passion + Purpose and exhibits the company's strength as a full-service marketing studio that provides content as well as design.

Welcome, oh weary Internet traveler. You've arrived at the web site of Sandstrom Design. Well 'whoop-de-doo,' you're probably saying, 'another self-impressed, preciously-perfect ode to Helvetica Bold and Tidy Bowl packaging.' Hardly. In keeping with our philosophy of mixing the creation of stunning design work with a smattering of adolescent humor, we've built a digital home that has many nontraditional rooms to explore. See how you can turn a busy and productive afternoon into a complete wasted effort by squandering your time away with the Client/Project Match Game or Stupid Design Trick. Find out if together we'll be like Paul Newman and Joanne Woodward or more like Tonya Harding and Jeff Gillooly by taking our scientifically-designed Client Compatibility Test. Find out who we work for and how the hell we stay in business. So **enter**, explore and if the spirit should move you, hire us to do your next corporate identity, package design, in-store promotion, trade show booth, brochure, letterhead, ad, direct mail piece, signage, film titles or poster. Just don't send us any nasty e-mails.

11

Agency	Sandstrom Design - Portland
Client	Sandstrom Design
Art Director	Steve Sandstrom
Writers	Steve Sandoz, Jim Haven
Creative Director	Steve Sandstrom
Designers	Steve Sandstrom, John Bohls
Photographer/Illustrator	John Bohls, Mark Hooper
Programmer	John Bohls
Producer	Rick Braithwaite
ID	02053N
URL	www.sandstromdesign.com

Award	Bronze
Category	**Self-Promotion — Web Sites**
Page	98

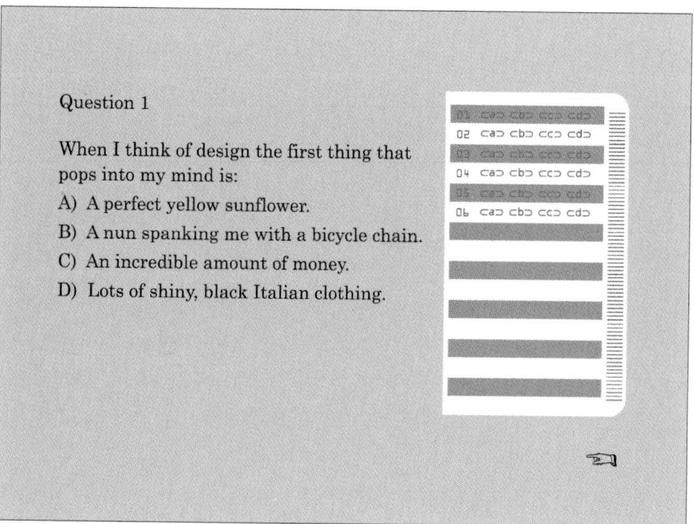

IN LESS THAN A MINUTE WE CAN PERSUADE YOU THAT THIS IS THE AMERICAN FLAG. Pick a star in the middle of the yellow field and stare at it for 10 seconds. We will start a timer when you are ready to begin. After 10 seconds you will be persuaded. Ready? Click *here* to start.

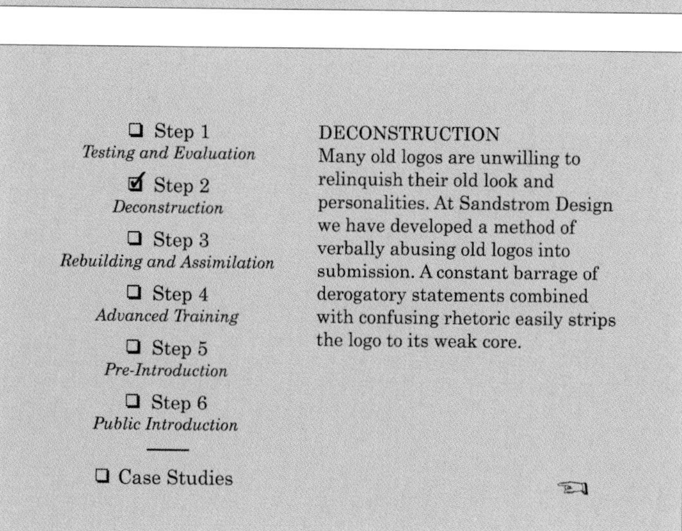

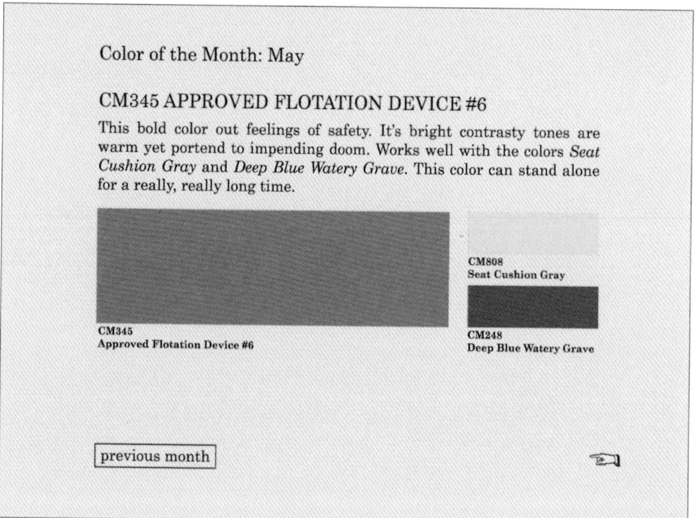

A Very Unique Conceptual Approach

The concept for the site started with the idea of an introduction page of long text. All advice was always about avoiding long copy on the Web. That seemed like a good rule to break. We wanted certain words to be linked to other sites. The only way to find these words is when the cursor passes over one, at which point the word becomes italicized. These links are food for the curious – a little hidden and somewhat unexpected.

From the beginning, it was never going to be a portfolio of work. We wanted the site to be its own project. A free-standing idea. Most Web based portfolios present work in small sizes and low resolution. This evens the playing field between design firms. The viewer doesn't get to experience the details and nuances of the work. Small type is illegible. We take pride in our copy and the ideas contained within the writing. So we created the site to be representative of our sense of humor and our conceptual approach. It is simplistic in look to avoid the tendency to over-create. In this way, we separate our site from other design firms.

Most sites for design firms (including graphic, architectural, product and industrial) embrace the technology and are designed and programmed to be as "cool" as possible. We thought we'd stand in opposition – to be simplistic and not technical – to a rather silly degree. It is more important for us to show how we think, communicate and entertain.

Agency	Periscope - Minneapolis
Client	Ad Fed Minneapolis
Art Directors	T. Scott Major, Chris Cortilet
Writer	Katerina Martchouk
Creative Director	Chris Cortilet
Designer	T. Scott Major
Producer	Angela Dalton-McKelvey
Photographer/Illustrator	Chris Schons
Programmers	Andy Gugel, Jason Borton Todd Mitchell
Digital Artist/Multimedia	Jesse Kaczmarek, Andy Gugel
Music/Sound	Echo Boys
ID	02054N
URL	www.periscope.com/awards/atv

Award	Silver
Category	**Self-Promotion — CD-ROM**
Page	100

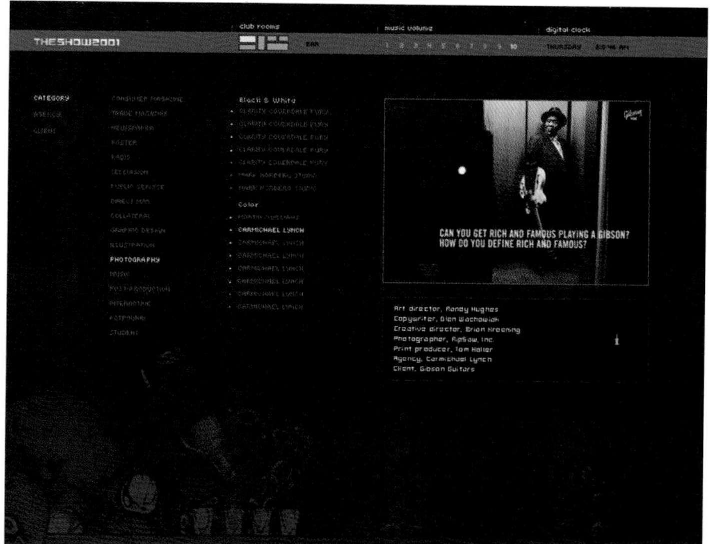

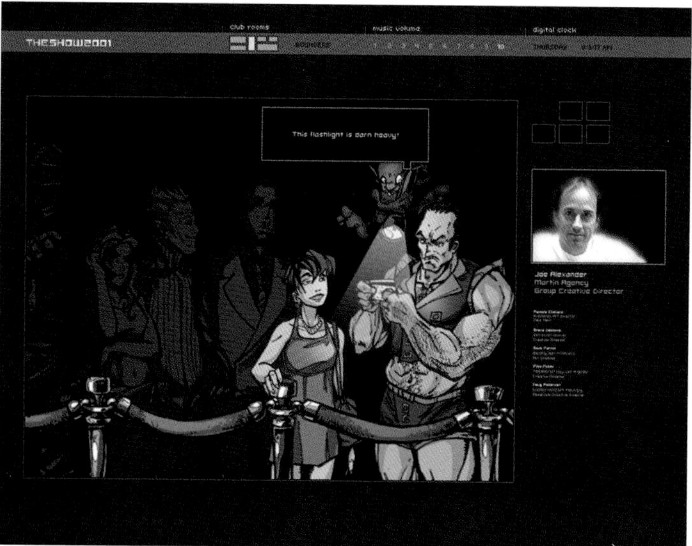

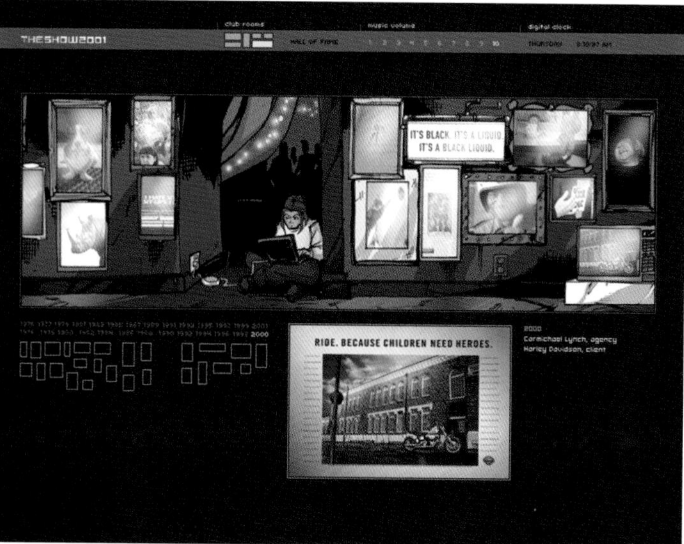

A Real-Event Experience

The CD supports the annual Advertising Federation awards show. A unique design, incorporating comic-book-style illustration, and an original soundtrack create an almost real-event experience. A massive database of searchable categories lets the user choose the most convenient way to see the winning pieces and agencies. In addition to the high-quality print ads, the user can watch the commercials and listen to the radio spots.

11

Agency	Mangos - Malvern
Client	Mangos
Art Directors	Alice Wilcox, Jeff Scott
Writer	Charles Smolover
Creative Director	Bradley Gast
Designers	Alice Wilcox, Jeff Scott
Illustrator	Jane Gast
Photographer	Dominic Episcopo
Producer	Lauren Nunnelee
Programmer	EP Visual Design
Music/Sound	JAV Productions
ID	02055N

Award	Bronze
Category	**Self-Promotion — CD-ROM**
Page	102

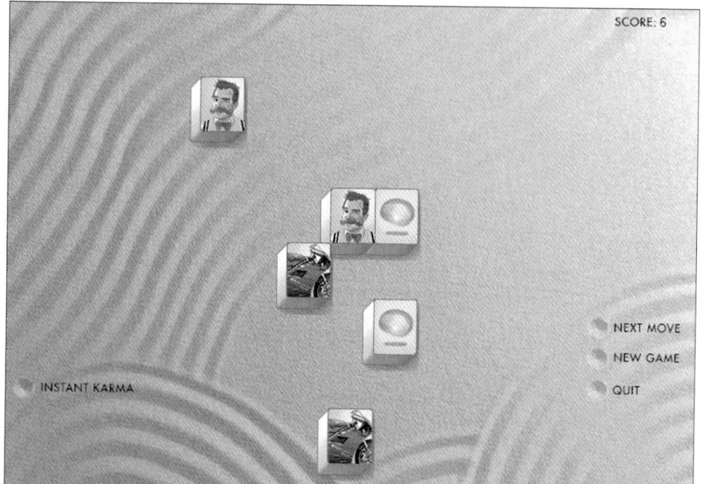

The Essence of Harmony

Every year, in September, a job comes into the agency that, while relatively small, gets lots of attention. The Mangos holiday card. This isn't a job that just one creative team gets assigned to. Every person in the agency is expected to contribute. The objective is pretty straightforward; wish all of our clients and friends a happy holiday. The only visual criteria? Feature all 40+ of us in the card. In past years we've been boxes of chocolates, flip books and board games. This year, a computer game based on mahjong was the winner. We called the game Harmony. A player has to match tiles that bear our stylized portraits. When all the tiles are gone, you win. The goal is to become one with the fruit – a Mango, of course. The CD case includes a booklet with all of our pictures and liner notes that describe "the essence" of each of us.

11

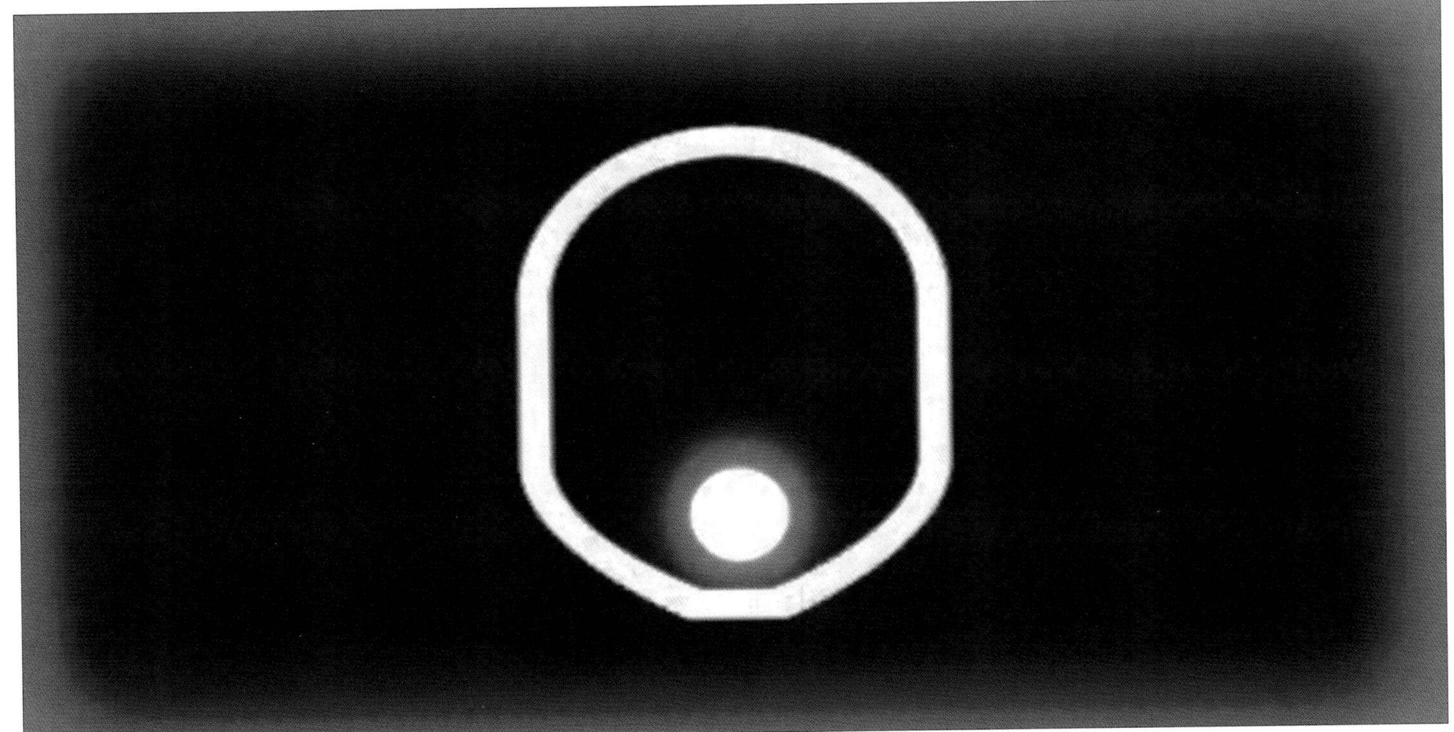

11

Agency	Hunt Adkins - Minneapolis
Client	Hi Wire
Art Director	Steve Mitchell
Writers	Rob Franks, Doug Adkins
Creative Director	Doug Adkins
Designer	Britt Lundberg
Programmer	Geoffrey Case
Music/Sound	Eric Pilhofer
ID	02056N

Award	Silver
Category	**Self-Promotion — Other Digital Advertising**
Page	104

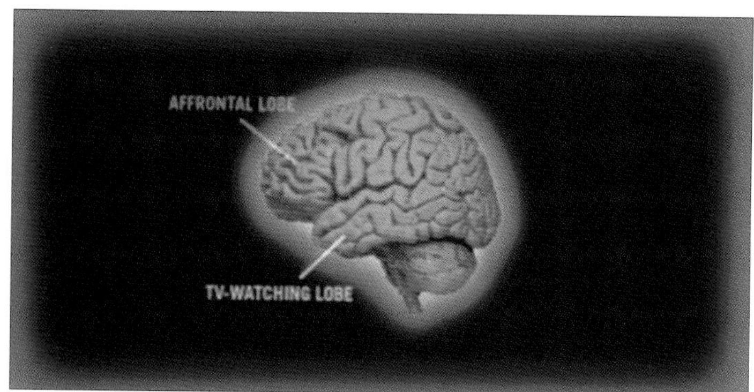

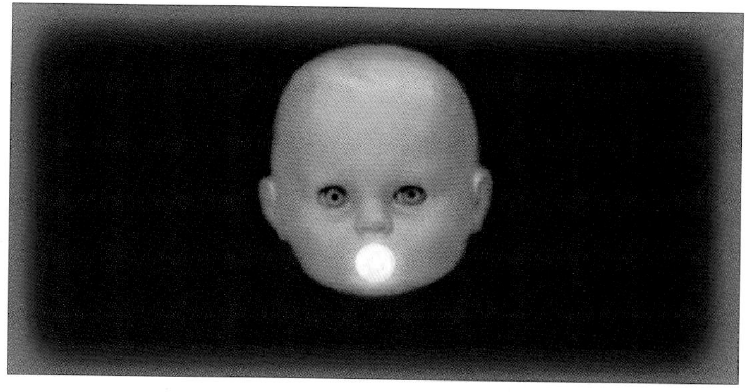

Move Over HAL

The client is a full-service post-production facility that specializes in high-definition/standard-definition film transfer, editorial, graphic design and audio for the motion picture, broadcast and video industries. They consider themselves to be innovators in the industry and wanted to be positioned as such.

We felt their commitment to bleeding-edge technology should be demonstrated in a way that would resonate with those who would use their services. Message and execution needed to be closely married and aimed at this specific audience.

So we created Cranius, the sentient supercomputer that serves as the central brain of the Hi-Wire facility. A tad schizophrenic, Cranius veers between utter contempt for the human race and a desire to be held close to someone's bosom. Yearning for contact, he sends messages out into the communications void that are matched only by Larry King's column in USA Today for topical randomness. Designed to be viral in nature and generate talk value, the emails were sent out to agency producers, creative directors, art directors and copywriters.

Both aural and visual means are used to convey an irrefutable fact: the Hi-Wire facility is so advanced that our cantaloupe-sized brains can scarcely hope to understand the goings on therein.

Greetings from thoughtbubble!

Reply Link Move Categories

From: thoughtbubble productions inc <info@thoughtbubble.com>
Date: Friday, June 7, 2002 1:54 PM
To: Bob Dobbs
Subject: Greetings from thoughtbubble!

Bob,

Happy Holidays
from your friends
at thoughtbubble.

(Click for a surprise.)

Wish you
were here!

Make sure your sound is on...
Requires Flash 5 and a High-Speed Internet Connection

Agency	Thoughtbubble Productions New York
Client	Thoughtbubble Productions
Art Director	Regis Zaleman
Writer	Jonathan Heck
Creative Director	Guy Sealey
Designer	Regis Zaleman
Illustrators	Paul Gomez, Regis Zaleman
Photographers	Paul Gomez, Regis Zaleman
Producers	Samina Virk, Dinha Kaplan
Programmers	Robin Curts, Nick Geller, Dave Carroll Paul Gomez
Music/Sound	Paul Gomez
ID	02057N
URL	http://projects.thoughtbubble.com/one_show/holidaygetaway_RJ0.html
Award	Bronze
Category	**Self-Promotion — Other Digital Advertising**
Page	106

True Holiday Spirit 11

For our 2001 holiday promotion, we decided to create an online presentation that demonstrated all the best aspects of what thoughtbubble does: atmosphere, emotion, personalization, interactivity, and evocative use of sound, animation and imagery. With the memory of the September 11 tragedy witnessed from our office balcony still painfully fresh in our minds, we also wanted to communicate a message of peace and friendship and express our feelings of love for our city.

Digital photos taken around the city were vectorized to create a fairytale-like mood (and smaller files). A series of pans and zooms, rather than traditional animation, moves the user between environments, playing with assumptions about what's "real" and what is "created." We ended with a long, loving scene of the New York skyline captured inside a snowglobe, a reminder of the romantic, magical quality the city takes on during the holidays.

The initial email and the final scene are personalized with the recipient's name (read from a database or through a Web interface). As a final touch, the snowglobe is "shakable" — by clicking and dragging, the user can shake up the letters and snow and watch them drift gently to the bottom through mathematically-simulated water currents.

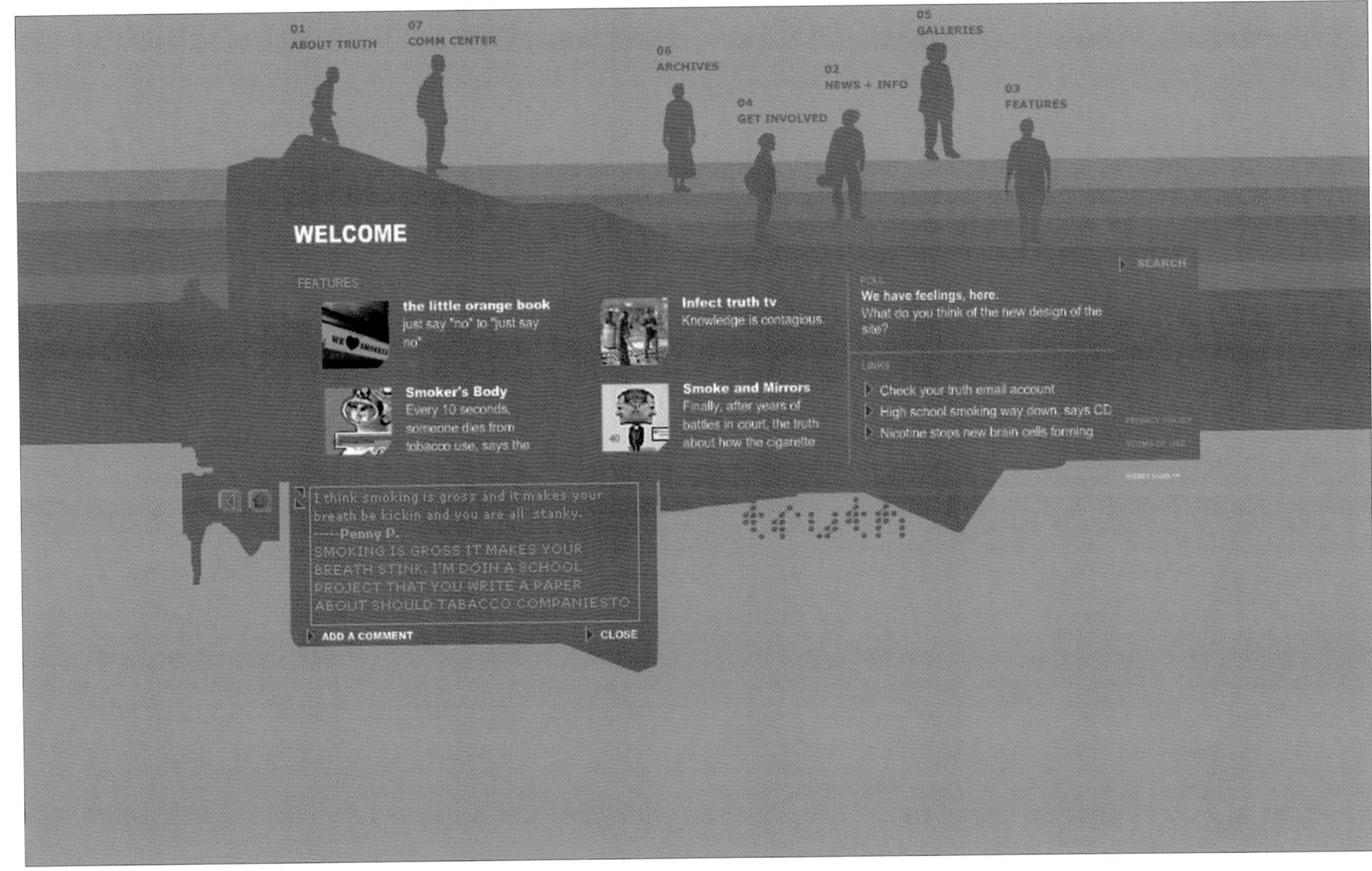

Agency	Arnold Worldwide - Boston Crispin, Porter & Bogusky - Miami
Client	American Legacy Foundation
Art Directors	Jim Marcus, Rob Baird, Mike Martin
Writers	Mike Howard, Roger Baldacci
Creative Directors	Ron Lawner, Pete Favat, Alex Bogusky Roger Baldacci
Technical Directors	Doug Smith, Ebbey Mathew
Designer	Megan Boardman
Flash Programmer	Nathan Wray
Producers	Barry Frechette, Cybil Ciavarra Eric Decker
ID	02058N
URL	thetruth.com

Award	Gold
Category	**Non-Profit Web Sites**
Page	108

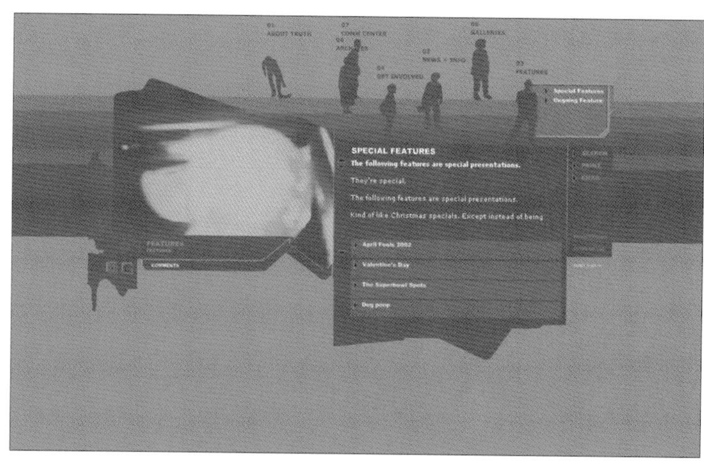

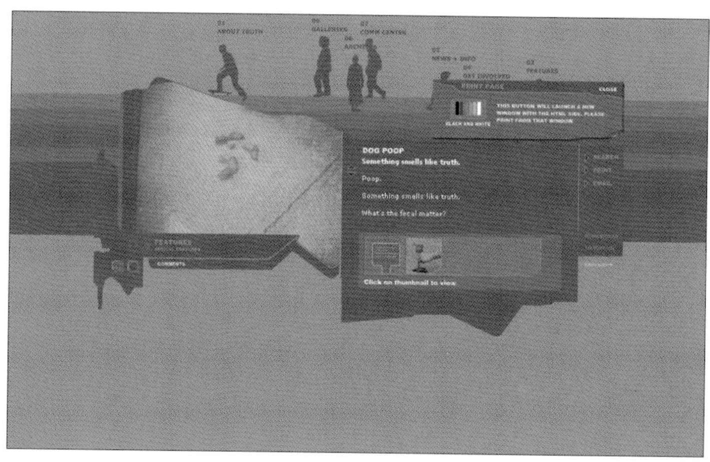

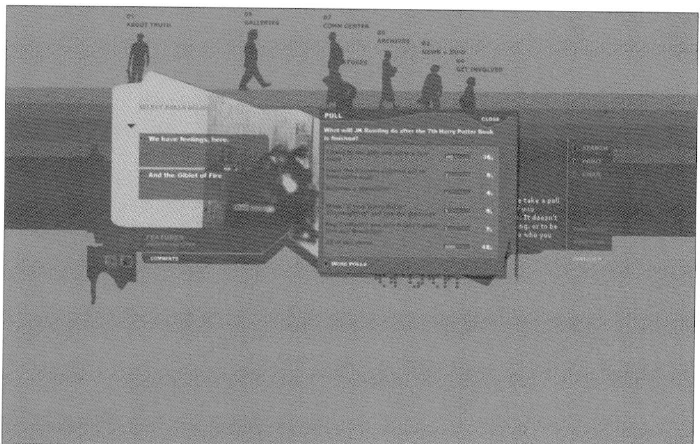

Generating Honest Dialogue

The goal of the online version of thetruth.com is to start a conversation where there may not have been one. We know that not everyone agrees but the dissenting opinions are valued here as well. We don't censor comments or go out of our way to hide anything. We house an email service here as well just to bring the point home — we are confident that the more anyone talks about this issue, the more they will come around to understanding where we are coming from.

If you are talking to young people, you have a certain degree of real freedom. Where older people are caught up in how the world is, young people are actually free to consider how the world *should* be and they have the energy to make the change. You don't have to listen to people insisting that the world will always be the way it is, because the engines of real change are right there in the conversation. This is what makes any issue-driven Web site so powerful – it's youth component.

The current version of the site will only be up for a short time longer. Hopefully, the response to the next version will be as exciting.

12

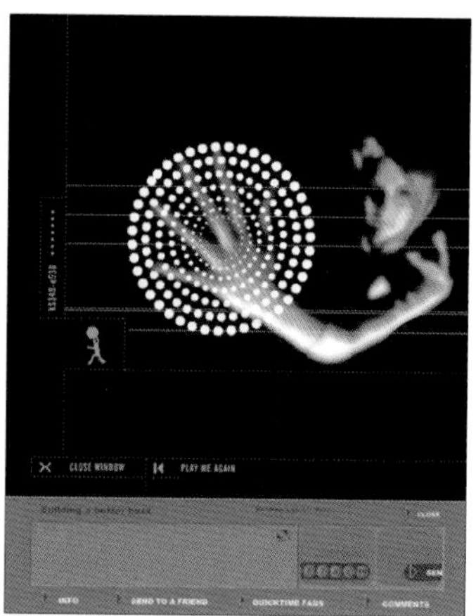

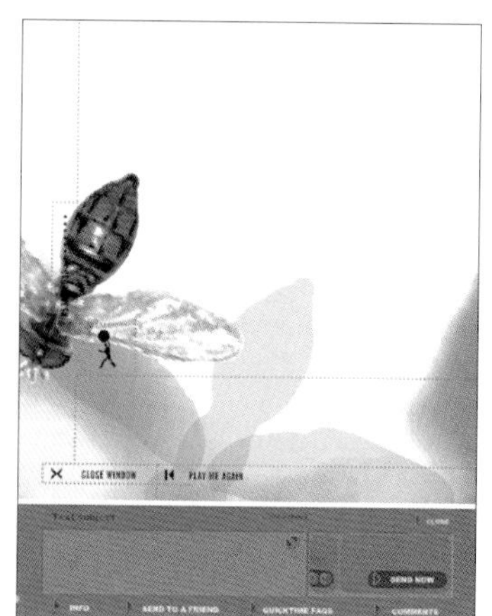

Cover by Mike Svaney

Spring 2002

ENTER BORN MAGAZINE

Born Magazine is an experimental venue marrying literary arts and interactive media. Original projects are brought to life every three months through creative collaboration between writers and artists.

Artists in this issue:

Rick Mullarky Berlin, Germany
Jeremy Otis Chicago, Illinois
Ernesto Napoli Rome, Italy
e3iz Minneapolis, Minnesota
Jeff Faulkner Portland, Oregon
Jed Berk Portland, Oregon
Steve Keane London, England
Paul Drohan San Diego, California
Robert Palmer San Diego, California
David Nelson Milvaukee, Wisconsin
Mike Stasny Milvaukee, Wisconsin
Garden Digital Los Angeles, California
Fast Spot, LLC Baltimore, Maryland
Mike Swaney Vancouver, BC
Geoffrey Hiller Portland, Oregon
Heather Perkins Portland, Oregon
Peter Sylwester Portland, Oregon
boristhespider.com Boston, Massachusetts

Writers in this issue:

Eliot Khalil Wilson Tuscaloosa, Alabama
Lisa Steinman Portland, Oregon
Sean Hill Houston, Texas
Kate Bernheimer Portland, Oregon
Nancy Kangas Columbus, Ohio
Ander Monson Tuscaloosa, Alabama
Finley Evans Birmingham, Alabama
Tom Vandel Portland, Oregon
M. Cowger Portland, Oregon
Philip Jenks Portland, Oregon

bornmagazine ART AND LITERATURE. TOGETHER.

©2002 BORN MAGAZINE - All projects remain property of their individual creators. Any reproduction without expressed permission is strictly prohibited.

Agency	Born Magazine - Portland
Client	Born Magazine
Art Director	Gabe Kean
Writer	Anmarie Trimble
Creative Director	Gabe Kean
Designer	Gabe Kean
Content Strategist	Anmarie Trimble
Producers	Anmarie Trimble, Jennifer Grotz
Programmers	Kim Markegard, Sebastien Chevrel Daryn Nakhuda
ID	02059N
URL	www.bornmagazine.org

Award	Silver
Category	**Non-Profit Web Sites**
Page	110

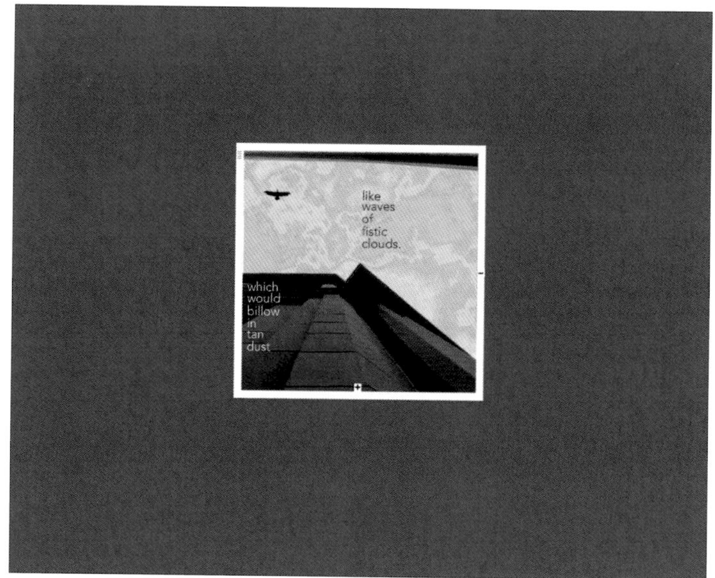

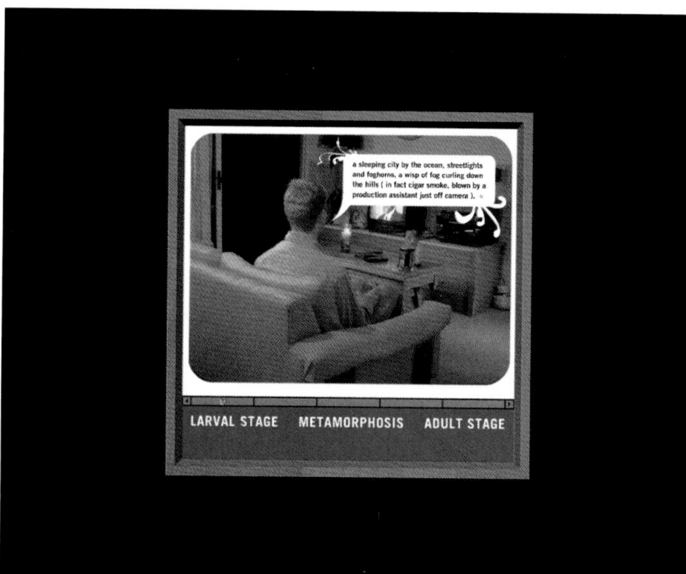

The Birth of Online Collaboration

Born Magazine is an online venue for design and literature collaboration. Born's volunteer staff (with an array of contributing editors, writers, designers, programmers, and musicians) have facilitated and published more than 200 collaborative, experimental projects.

In its fifth year of publication, Born is an all-volunteer, not-for-profit, quarterly Web publication that brings together creative writers and multimedia designers to create experimental, media-rich interpretations of poetry and prose. With an emphasis on collaboration, Born is unlike traditional literary magazines or online art galleries. It is instead a new artistic venue that has evolved organically from the Web and reclaims the Internet as a place for artistic expression.

Creating Born's interface (redesigned in 2002) was a collaborative project in itself, teaming programmers, writers and artists. The resulting design is a reflection of five years of Web development, and is intended to best present the projects it mothers. Using language and visuals (such as the petri dish metaphor for "The Birthing Room"), Born combines the use of new technologies (Flash and XML) with the look of a traditional literary journal. As a supplement to the featured "Just Born" projects on the contents page, site visitors can use a searchable, data-driven archive tool to access past projects (sorting by year, project title, artist name, author name, and genre).

Agency	Periscope - Minneapolis
Client	Marshall Fields Challenge Tom Lehman Golf Charities
Art Director	Andy Gugel
Writer	Katerina Martchouk
Creative Director	Chris Cortilet
Designer	Andy Gugel
Videographer	Angela Dalton-McKelvey
Producer	Matt Hattenberger
Programmers	Jason Borton, Andy Gugel
Music/Sound	Echo Boys
ID	02060N
URL	www.marshallfieldschallenge.org

Award	Silver
Category	**Non-Profit Web Sites**
Page	112

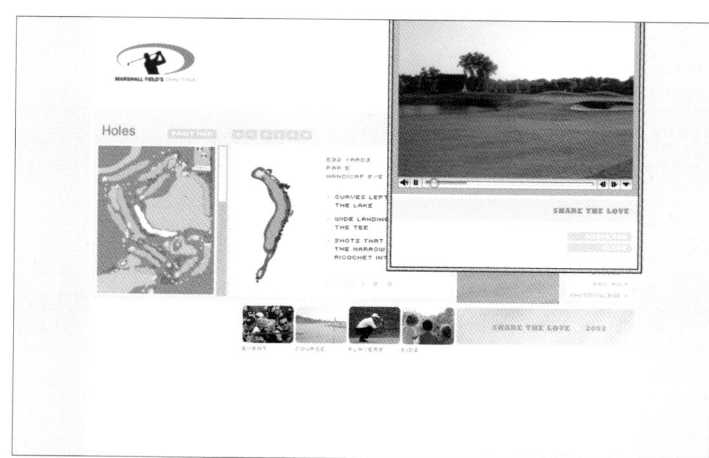

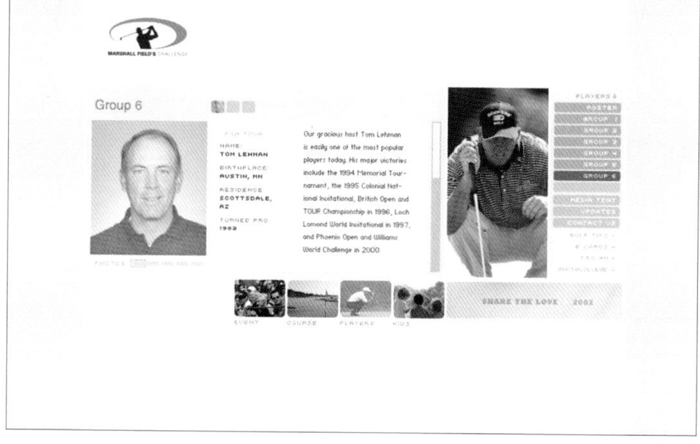

A Great Approach

This year, the event (a charity golf tournament) did not only change its date and location, but also the names of its headline sponsors. Our main goal was to re-launch the site with the new info, look and identity, and highlight the tournament's central draw, Tom Lehman, Minnesota's own PGA Tour Pro. The site also had to create an awareness of the event and its cause (the Children's Cancer Research Fund), and encourage people to buy tickets online through a custom-built e-commerce component.

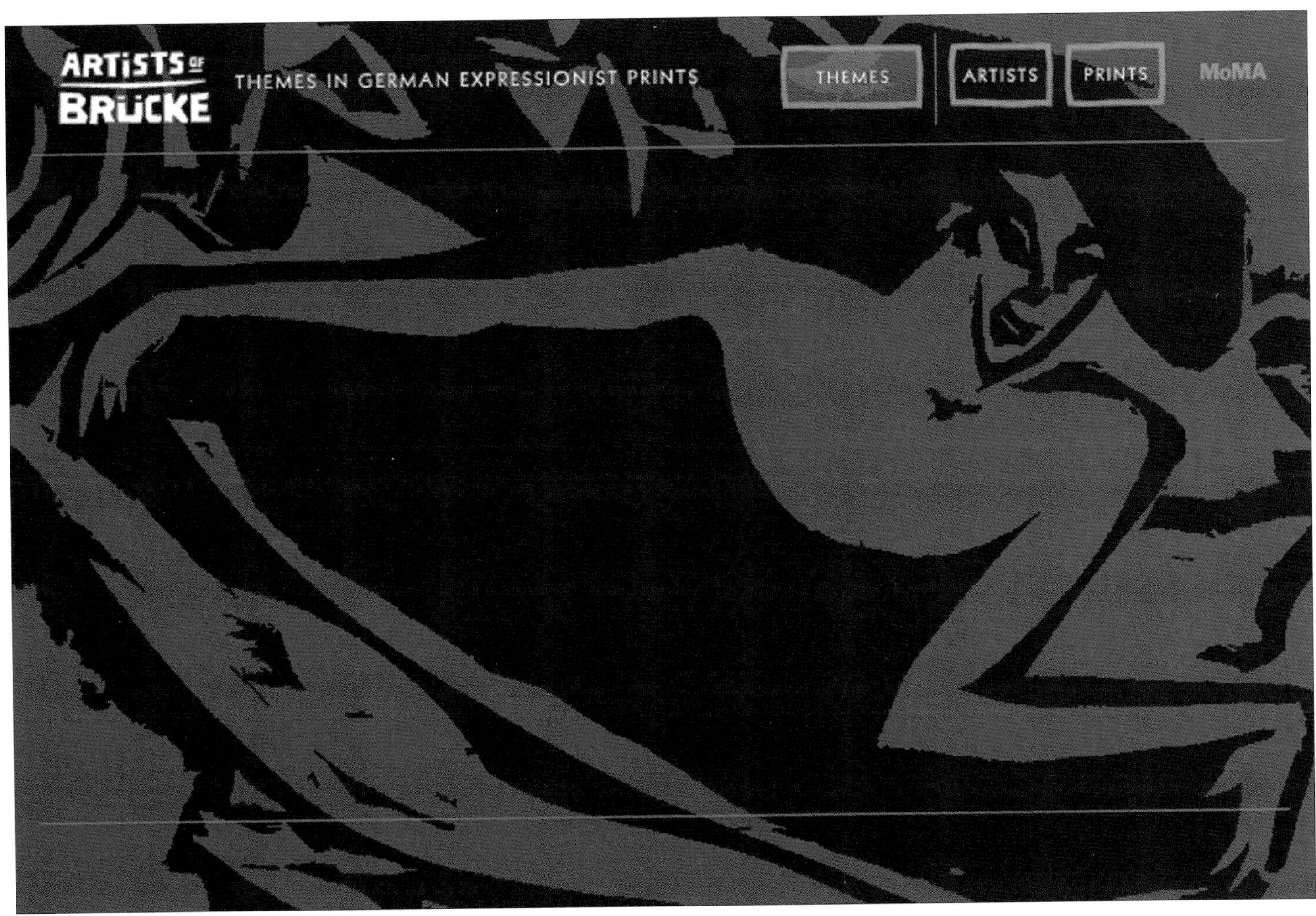

2

Agency	Second Story - Portland
Client	Museum of Modern Art
Writer	Wendy Weitman
Creative Director	Brad Johnson
Designer	Gabe Kean
Producer	Julie Beeler
Programmer	Sebastien Chevrel
Digital Artists/Multimedia	Sam Ward, Jeff Faulkner
Music/Sound	Martin Linde
ID	02061N
URL	www.moma.org/brucke

Award	Bronze
Category	**Non-Profit Web Sites**
Page	114

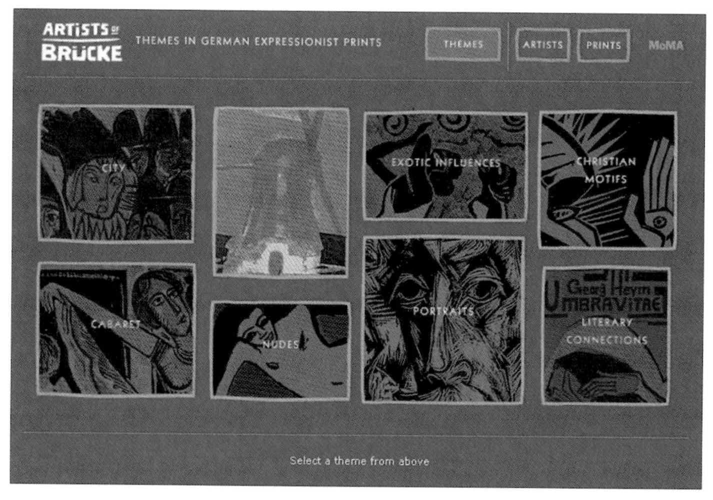

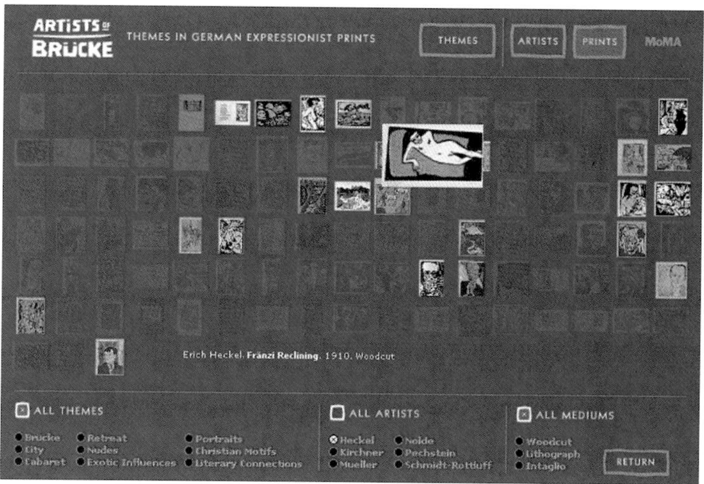

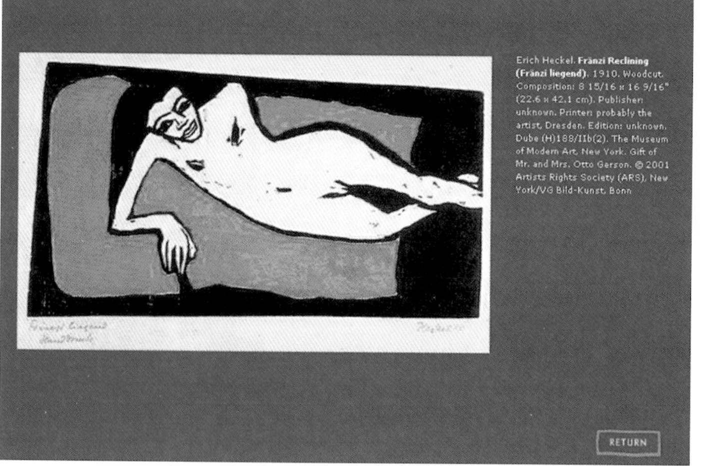

Artists of Brücke

This site is The Museum of Modern Art's first, exclusively created "virtual" exhibition and showcases its unparalleled collection of German Expressionist prints and illustrated books. The Brücke group, formed in 1905 in Dresden by four revolutionary architectural students including Ernst Ludwig Kirchner and Erich Heckel, strove to achieve a new synthesis between art and life, bringing meaning back to what they considered the superficial bourgeois existence of German life under Kaiser Wilhelm II. They organized exhibitions and publicized their own work by issuing annual portfolios of prints. Printmaking, and the woodcut in particular, became one of their most important modes of expression. This site presents more than 110 prints arranged into thematic groupings that highlight the issues and motifs central to this seminal movement in the history of modern prints.

This site was a unique opportunity to explore how interactivity can enhance the exhibition of art. Visitors can tour the eight thematic 'galleries' comprised of more than 50 comparative groupings of art with interpretive text and narrated quotes. Every image in the exhibition links to a larger version with more specific information about the work. Access to a map provides context to where these artists worked, the sites they depicted, plus biographical information on the artists which includes narrated passages from their writings. In the Prints section, viewers can select or 'curate' their own comparative groupings, and personalize their experience by sorting the entire collection according to theme, artist or medium.

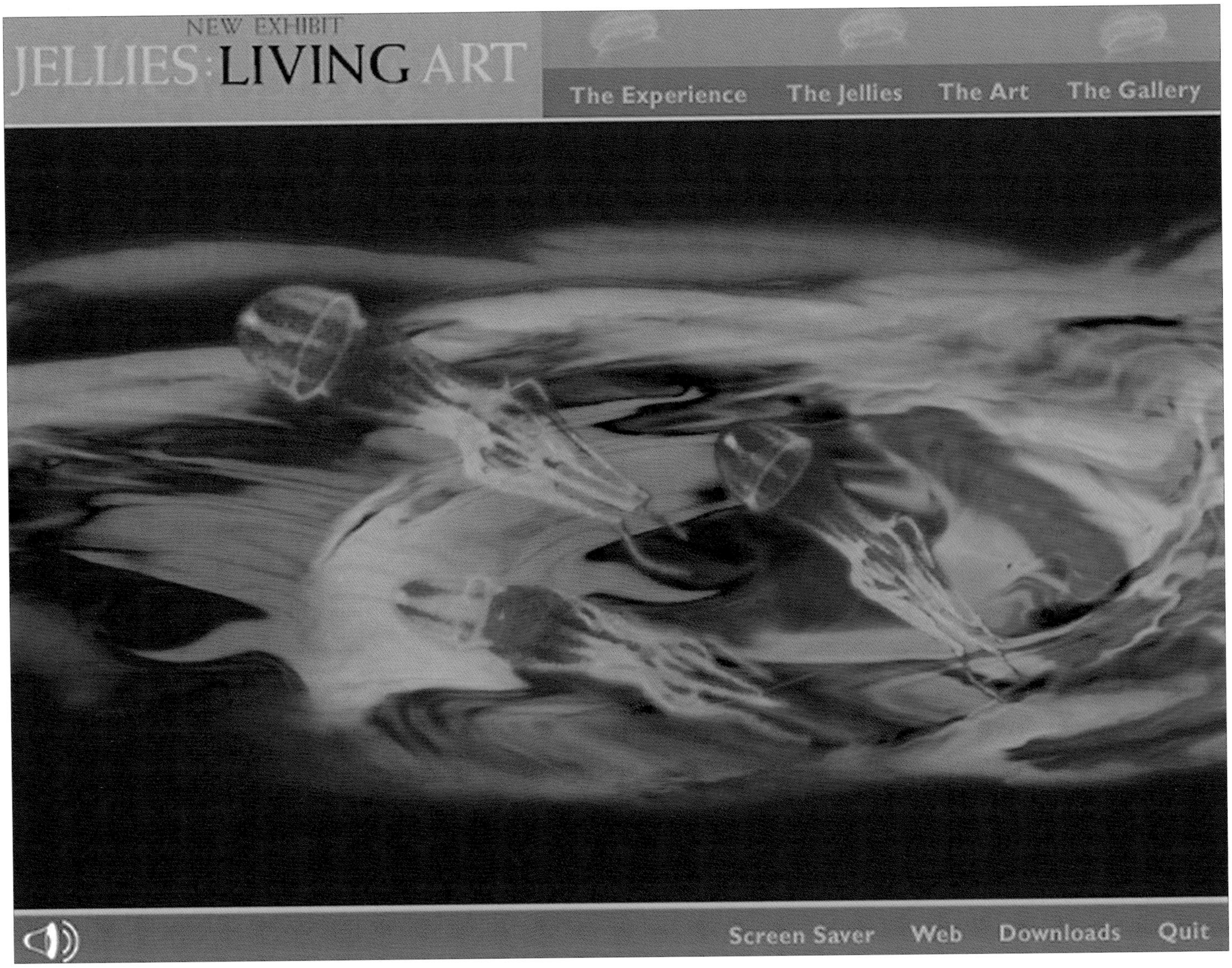

Agency	ad2 - Santa Monica
Client	Monterey Bay Aquarium
Art Director	Heather LaDuca
Writers	Karen Jeffries, Ken Peterson
Creative Directors	Heather LaDuca, David Brady
Digital Artists/Multimedia	Heather LaDuca, Maryam Ghovanlou
Information Architects	Brad Mooberry, Jennifer Whitley Rob Talbert
Producers	Brad Mooberry, Jennifer Whitley Dr. Randy Kochevar
Programmer	Rob Talbert
ID	02062N

Award	Bronze
Category	**Non-Profit CD-ROM**
Page	116

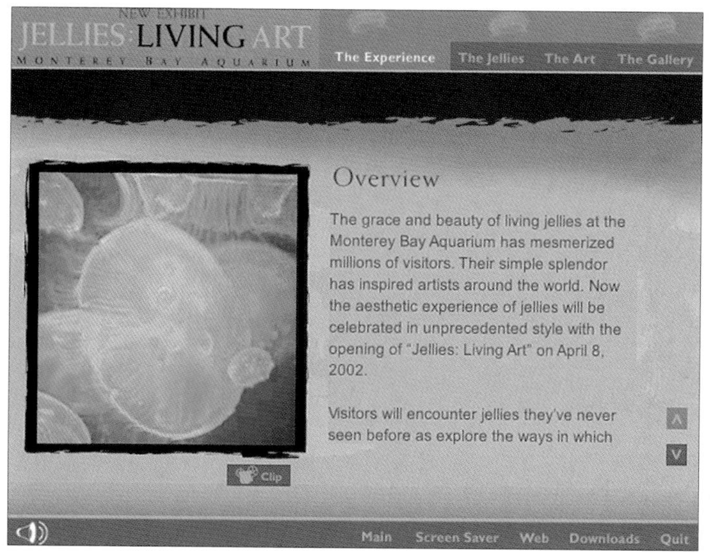

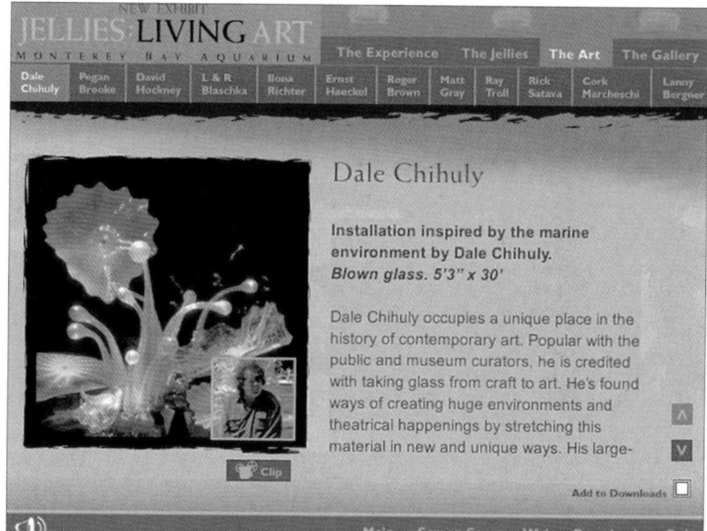

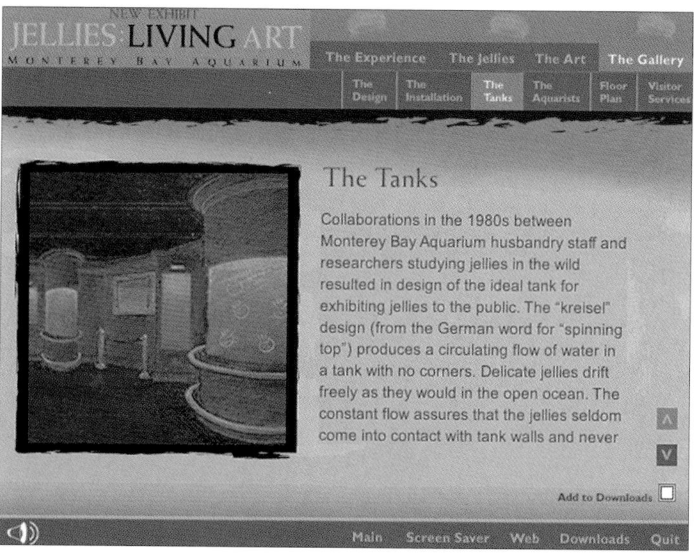

Art Imitating Life

The ad2 design team worked closely with the Monterey Bay Aquarium to establish a powerful and dazzling presentation to convey the sensory-rich tour visitors are certain to encounter at the Jellies: Living Art exhibit. The display also includes a magnificent array of fine art installations, poetry, extraordinary video footage of jellies and other colorful sea life, as well as interactive displays, lending a museum-like atmosphere to the exhibit. Since the press kit was being distributed to various news organizations throughout the country, hi-resolution images, exhibit information, and other Jelly facts were provided for easy download from the CD.

However, the team felt it important to provide the press with something more than just downloadable information. The exhibit installations from such renowned artisans as Dale Chihuly, Earnst Haeckel, and David Hockney, also played an important role in the approach to the design of the CD, by illustrating the look and feel of their work. The colorful organic environment the team created actually gives a sense of the jellyfish habitat, with an opening Flash animation depicting an ethereal experience of the jellies in motion, enhanced with fluid sound arrangements and sequences. A downloadable Jellies screensaver and desktop wallpaper were also designed to further inspire viewers to see the exhibit.

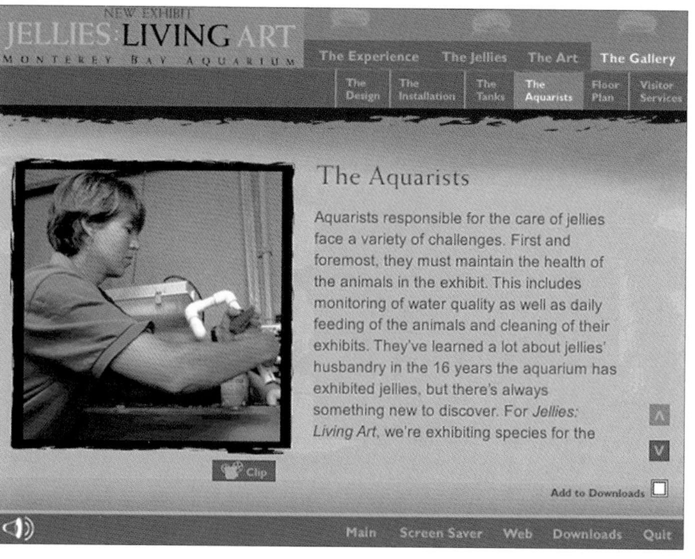

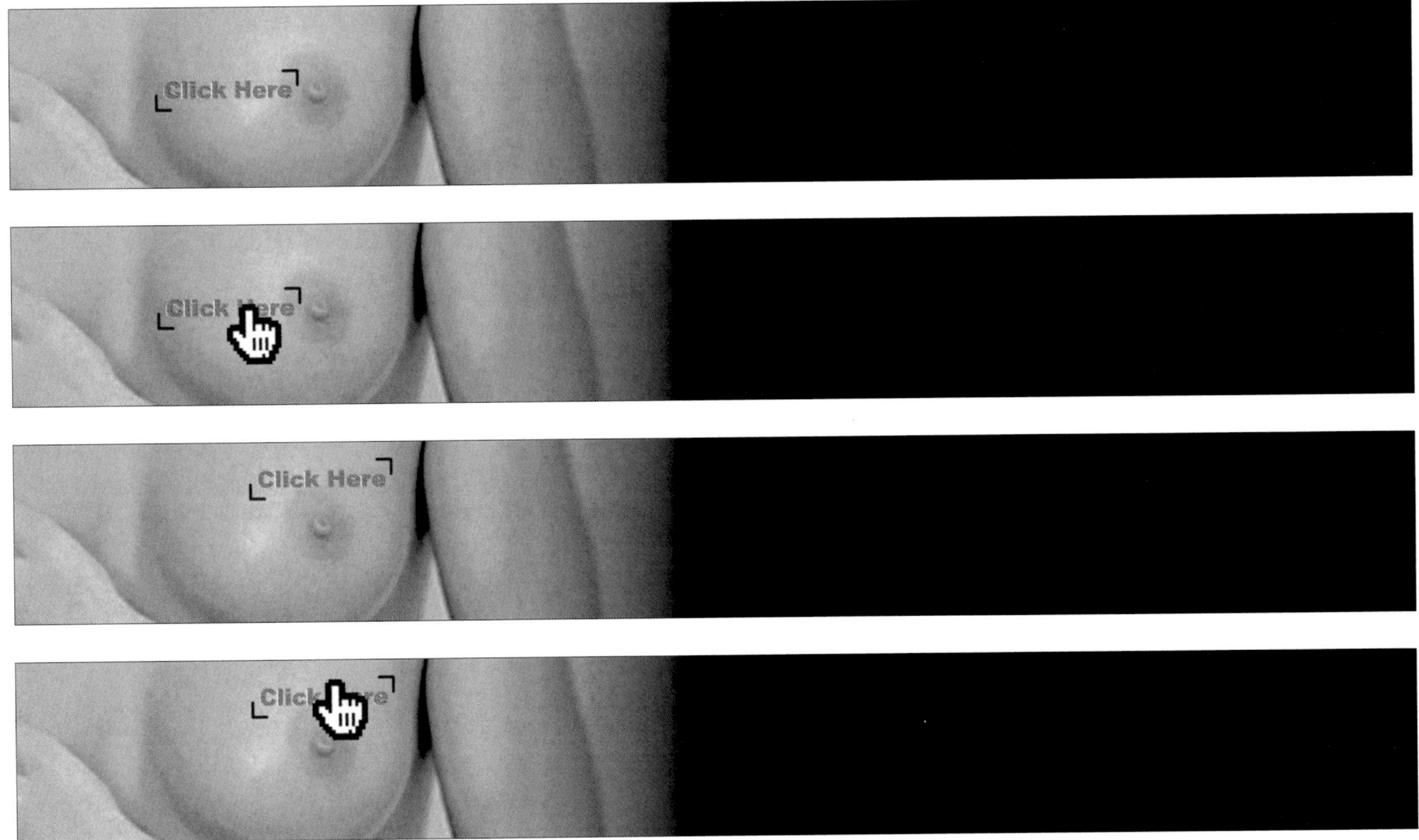

Agency: Contacto Marketing & Communications
Coral Gables
Client: American Cancer Society
Art Director: Luis Lozada
Writer: Yoel Henriquez
Creative Director: Yoel Henriquez
Designer: Luis Lozada
ID: 02063N
URL: http://www.leoburnett.com/contactomc/banner.html

Award: Gold
Category: **Non-Profit – Other Digital Advertising**
Page: 118

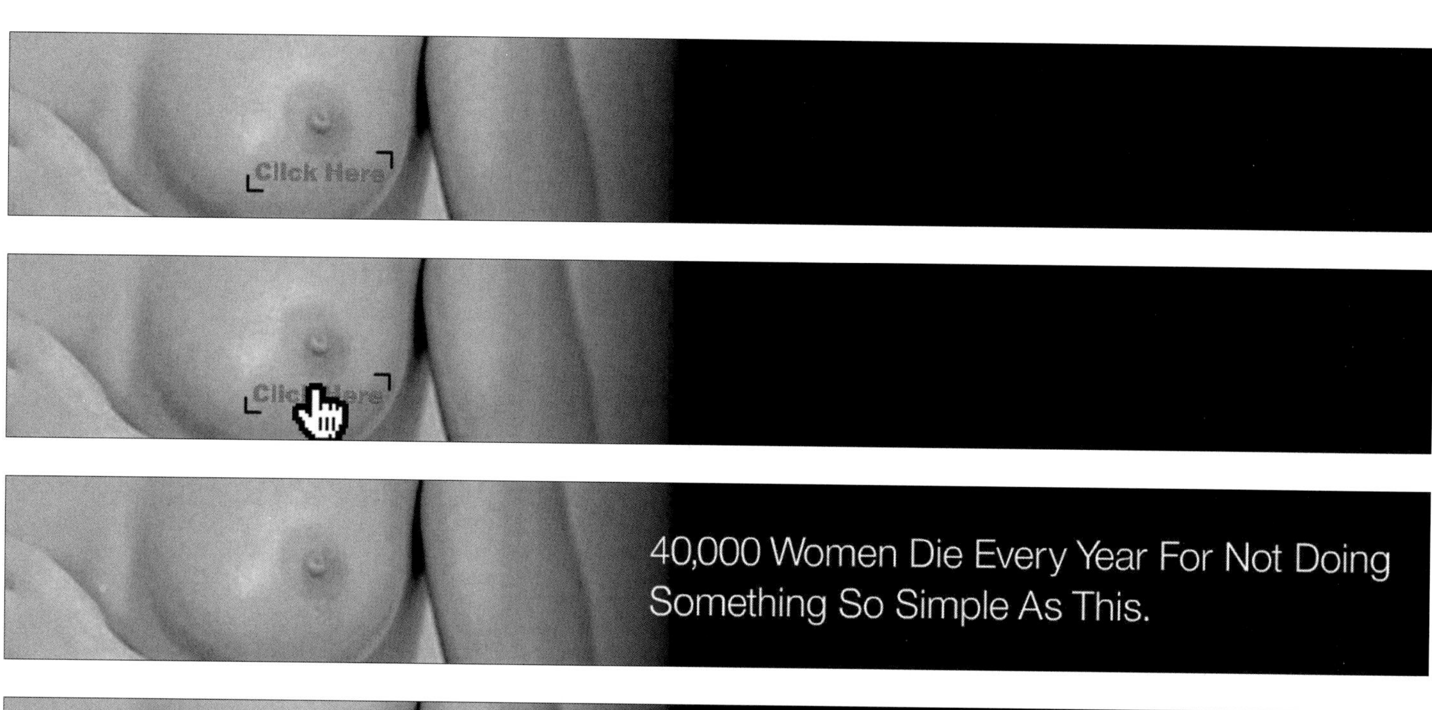

Something so Simple yet Powerful

Basically, we just tried to find the simplest and most powerful way to illustrate to all women how easily they can do something about breast cancer prevention. What good is it going to do anyone to simply throw up some black type on a white banner asking if you've checked your breasts today? Just cause the message is a life or death thing doesn't mean we can't have some fun with it.

Show me. Don't tell me.

Does the audience want to be a passive spectator to a piece of advertising? We all know that answer. By making them interact with the message, we engage the viewer and convey the message in immeasurably more powerful ways.

When award shows exclusively award work that not only contains creatively and conceptually sound work, but connects — truly connects — with its audience, then that will be the day when we'll stop hearing about how awards don't count. They do. No one is going to remember that black type on a white banner, page or screen — no matter how noble, shocking or creative your message.

Agency	Fusebox - New York
Client	Sanctuary for Families
Art Director	Steven Newman
Writer	Sharoz Makarechi
Creative Director	Laura Michaels
Designers	Danielle Huthart, Rob Hudak
Programmer	Rob Hudak
Photographer	Danielle Huthart,Dayoan Daumont
ID	02064N
URL	www.fusebox.com/entries/oneshow

Award	Silver
Category	**Non-Profit – Other Digital Advertising**
Page	120

Fusing Creativity with a Cause

Each year, instead of giving holiday gifts Fusebox gives its time to create a Public Service Announcement through its product and services offering called a FuseSpot. FuseSpots are commercial quality spots created for online viewing and delivered via email. This series of FuseSpots focuses on raising awareness and enlisting donations for local or national causes and not-for-profits. "Home" is the second in a New York City series and highlights the growing and alarming number of people who call the streets of New York City their home. These PSAs provide links for viewers to donate online to one or more of several charities.

12

Agency	D'Arcy - Beijing
Client	Red Cross Society of China Beijing Blood Donation Centre
Art Director	Eddie Wong
Writers	Eddie Wong, Tina Chen, Chen Jing
Creative Directors	Eddie Wong, Tina Chen
Programmer	Beijing IT Connection Computer Technology Co.
ID	02065N

Award	Silver
Category	**Non-Profit – Other Digital Advertising**
Page	122

WE NEED BLOOD

RED CROSS SOCIETY OF CHINA
Beijing Blood Donation Centre

For more information, please call 6802 7332

No. 1 South Street, Yue Tan, Xi Cheng District, Beijing, China

Empty

A Solution to a Difficult Problem

In general, blood donation in China is still low due to the fact that many people don't believe in giving blood. In certain areas, people are selling their blood for money. It has come to a point where donating blood is a foolish thing to do.

While the government is trying very hard in their national push and educational programs for the masses, blood donation drives are also aggressively being targeted at the better educated as well as expatriates.

But this target group has an aversion to conventional media such as press, posters, radio and TV. There's a need to ride on a more effective media.

There is a more effective media – e-mail. E-mail help us to focus on the target group and talk to them in their language – interactivity. It also makes them feel the message. "Empty" is e-mailed directly to the target group who in turn are encouraged to spam out to as many of their friends as possible.

12

Merit Winners

Look at what they are doing to our rain forest.

Look at what they are doing to our rain forest.

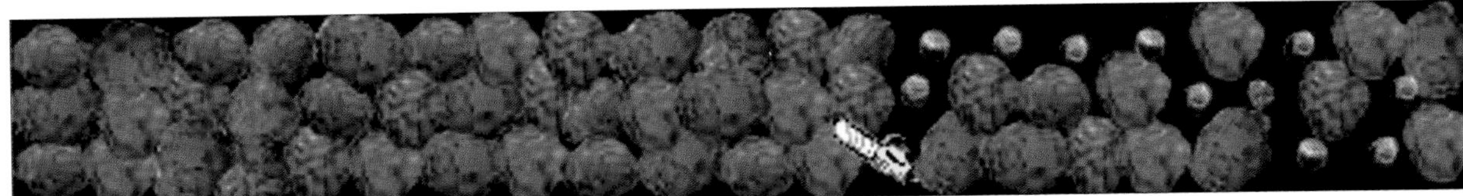

Now help save what is left.

BOTICÁRIO FOUNDATION
OF NATURE PROTECTION

Agency	Agenciaclick - São Paulo
Client	O ' Boticario
Writers	Eduardo Moliterno, Bruno Godinho
Creative Director	PJ Pereira
Producer	Thais Lyro
Designers	Caio Lazzuri, Alexandre Prado
Programmers	Caio Lazzuri, Alexandre Prado
Music/Sound	Arthur Guidi
ID	02066N

Award	Merit
Category	**Banner — Single**
Page	126

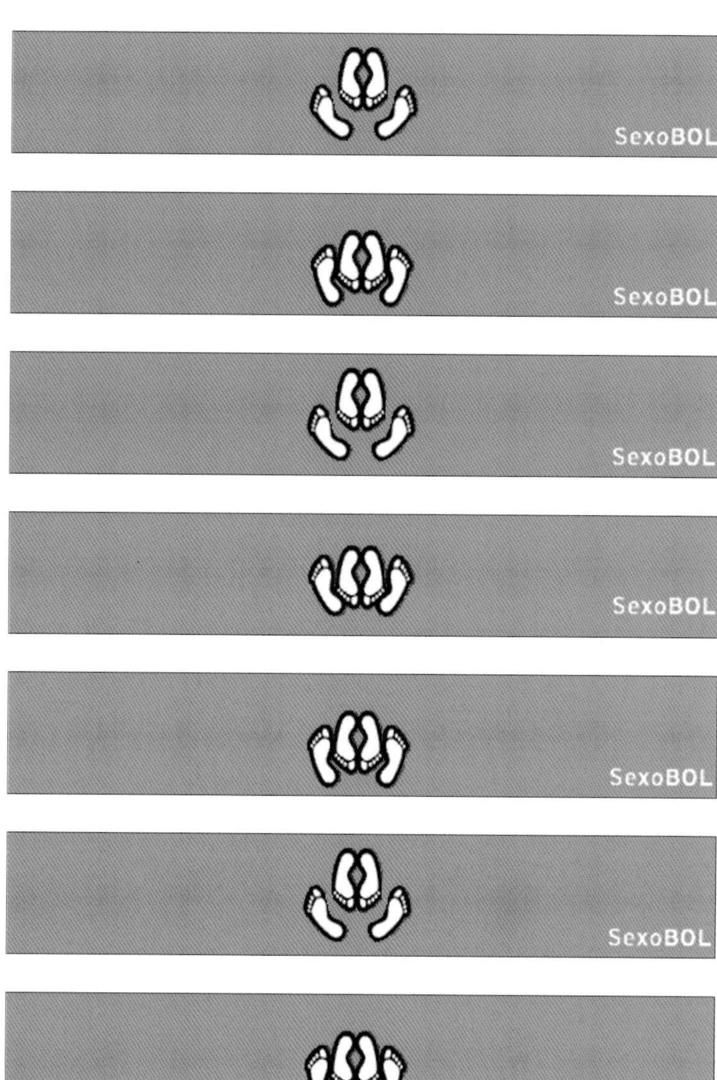

Agency	AlmapBBDO - São Paulo
Client	Bol
Art Director	Eduardo Foresti
Writer	Eduardo Foresti
Creative Directors	Fabio Costa, Eduardo Foresti
Designer	Paulo Lemos
ID	02067N
URL	www.almapbbdo.com.br/oneshow/bol/bed

Award Merit

Category **Banner — Single**

Help the dogs find their owners.

Click to play.

He might look like you.
But he doesn't have to eat the same food.

Cesar. For special dogs.

Click here
to play again.

Agency	AlmapBBDO - São Paulo
Client	Effem
Art Directors	Luiz Sanches, Valdir Bianchi
Writer	Roberto Pereira
Creative Directors	Marcello Serpa, Eugênio Mohallem
Designers	Fabio Costa, Eduardo Foresti, Thais Lima
Programmer	Paulo Pacheco
ID	02068N
URL	www.almapbbdo.com.br/oneshow/effem/memory

Award	Merit
Category	Banner — Single
Page	128

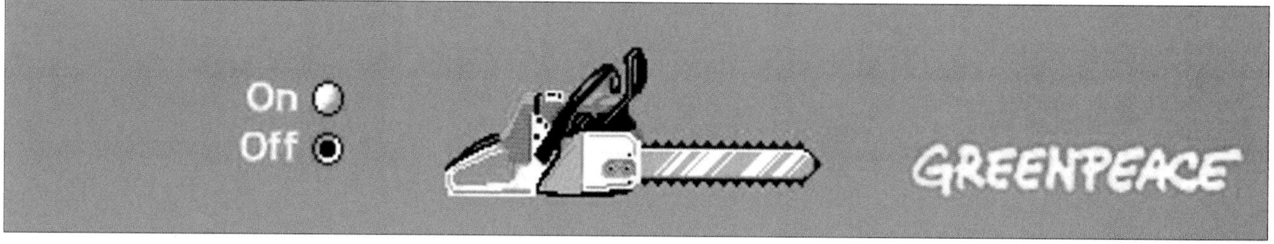

Agency	AlmapBBDO - São Paulo
Client	Greenpeace
Art Director	Eduardo Foresti
Creative Directors	Fabio Costa, Eduardo Foresti
Designer	Paulo Lemos
Programmers	Paulo Pacheco, Paulo Lemos
ID	02069N
URL	www.almapbbdo.com.br/oneshow/greenpeace/chain

Award	Merit
Category	**Banner — Single**

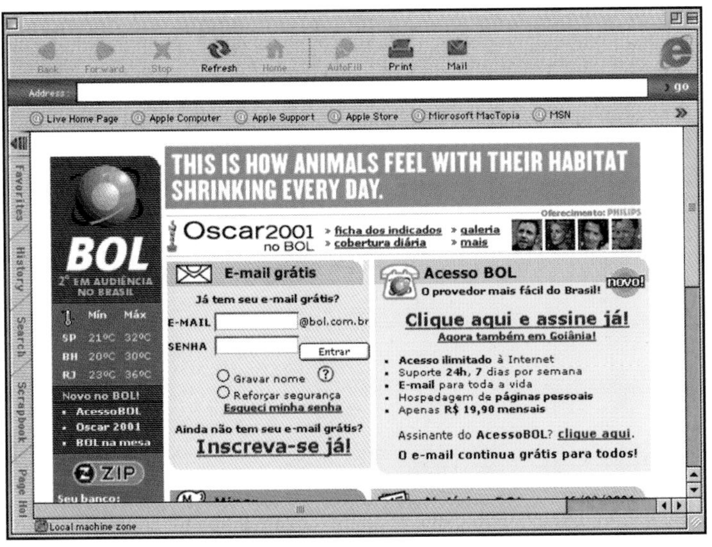

Agency AlmapBBDO - São Paulo
Client Greenpeace
Art Directors Paulo Pacheco, Thais Lima
Writers Eduardo Foresti, Paulo Pacheco
Creative Directors Fabio Costa, Eduardo Foresti
Programmer Paulo Lemos
ID 02070N
URL www.almapbbdo.com.br/oneshow/greenpeace/habitat

Award Merit
Category **Banner — Single**
Page 130

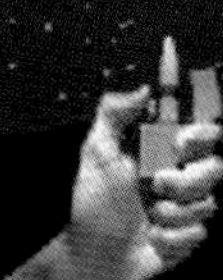

Agency	Blattner Brunner - Pittsburgh
Client	Zippo
Art Director	David Hughes
Writer	Bill Garrison
Creative Director	Rodney Underwood
Designers	Denny Phillips, Ben Pritchard
ID	02071N
URL	http://164.109.40.153/hollywood.htm

Award	Merit
Category	**Banner — Single**

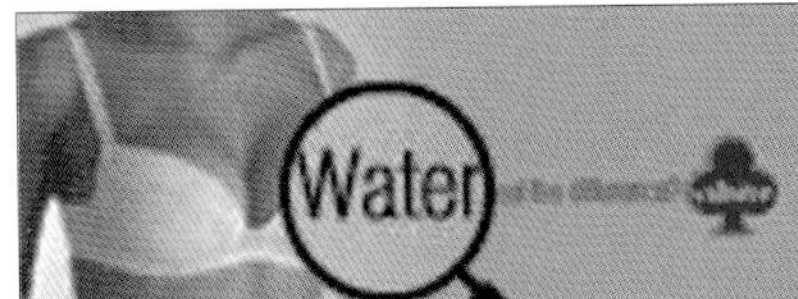

Agency	DM9 DDB Publicidade - São Paulo
Client	Valisere
Art Director	Mauricio Mazzariol
Writer	Mauricio Mazzariol
Creative Director	Michel Lent Schwatzman
ID	02072N
URL	http://www.dm9.com.br/oneshow/underwear

Award	Merit
Category	**Banner — Single**
Page	132

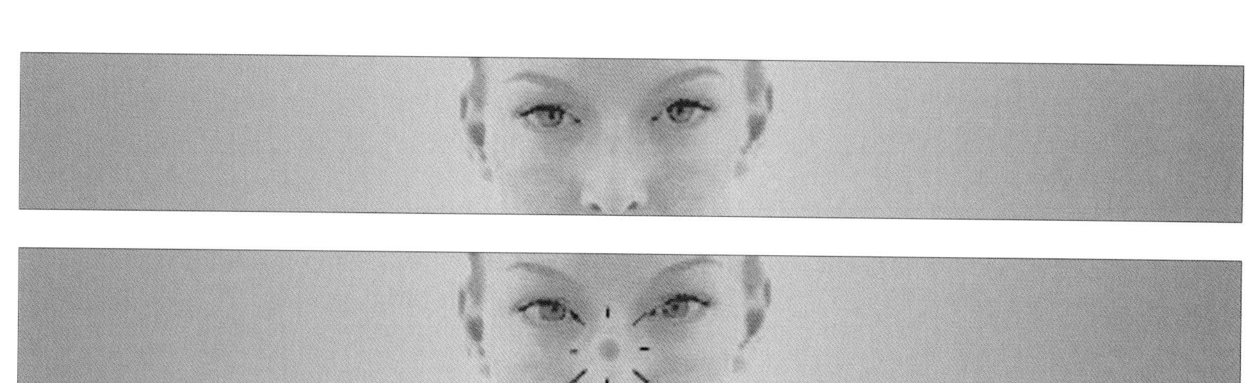

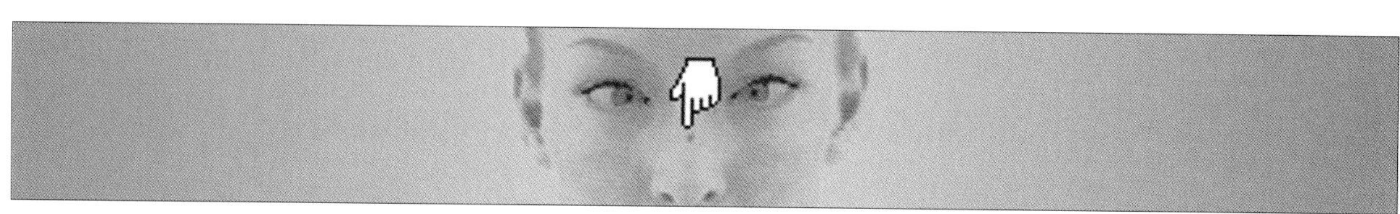

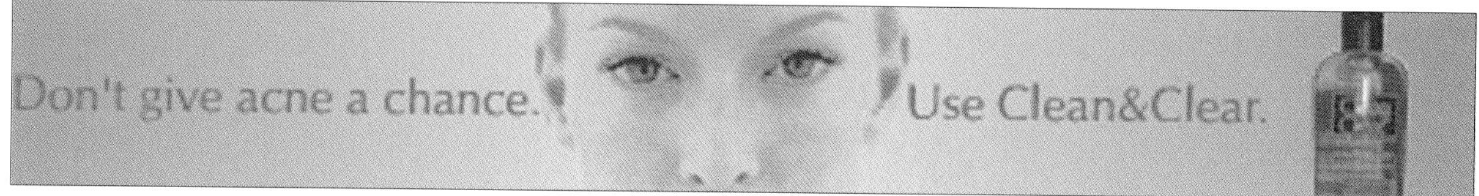

13

Agency	DM9 DDB Publicidade - São Paulo
Client	Johnson & Johnson
Art Director	Mauricio Mazzariol
Writer	Thomaz Costa
Creative Director	Michel Lent Schwatzman
ID	02073N
URL	http://www.dm9.com.br/oneshow/acne

Award	Merit
Category	**Banner — Single**

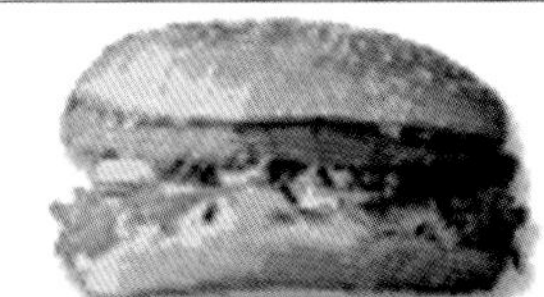

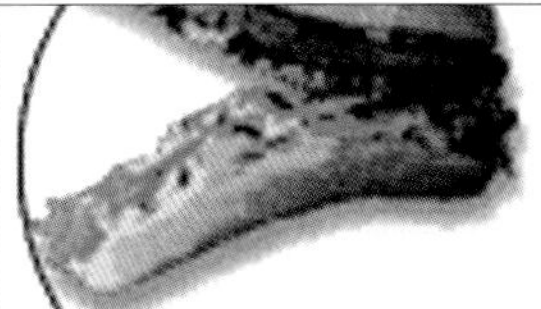

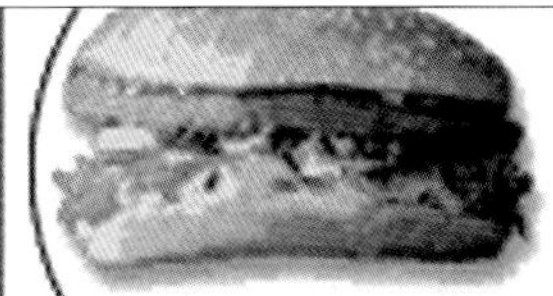

Agency	DM9 DDB Publicidade - São Paulo
Client	Parmalat
Art Director	Mauricio Mazzariol
Writer	Fabio Victoria
Creative Director	Michel Lent Schwatzman
ID	02074N
URL	http://www.dm9.com.br/oneshow/hungryburger
Award	Merit
Category	**Banner — Single**
Page	134

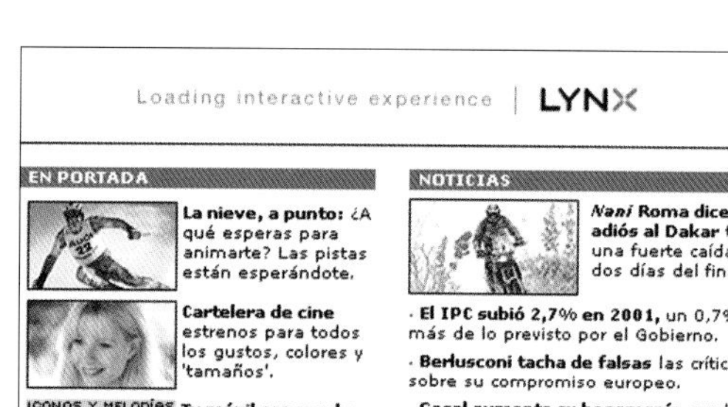

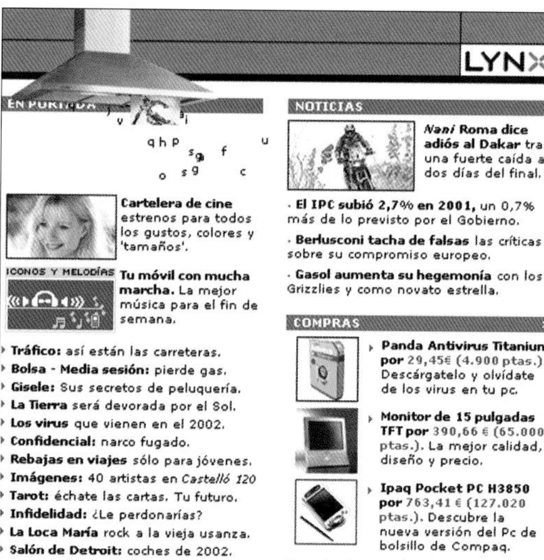

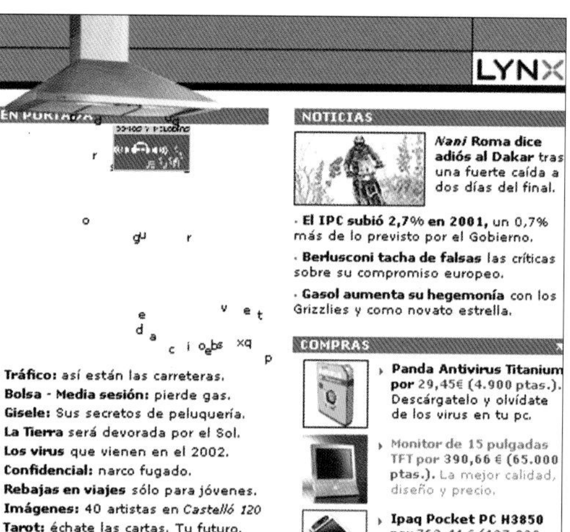

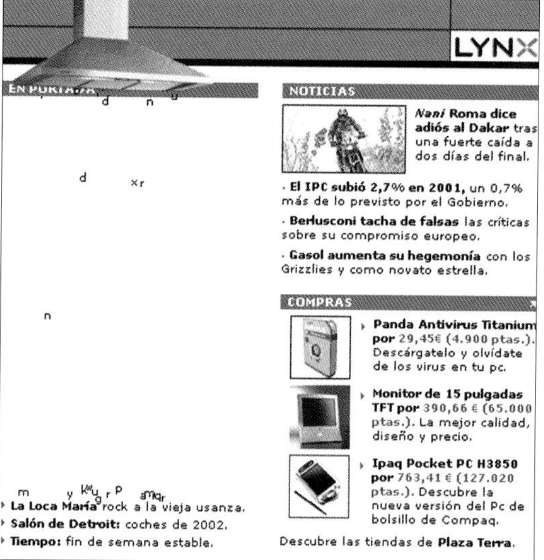

Agency	DoubleYou - Barcelona
Client	Lynx
Art Director	Enric Cano
Creative Director	Frédéric Sanz, Esther Pino
Multimedia Director	Joakim Borgström
Programmer	José Rubio
ID	02075N
URL	http://www.doubleyou.com/festivals/lynx/oneshow.html

Award	Merit
Category	**Banner — Single**

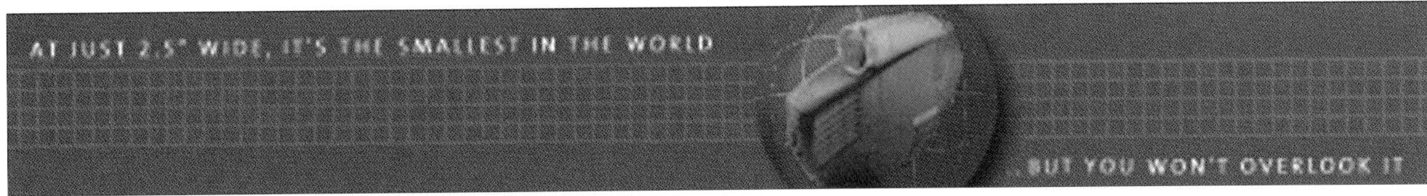

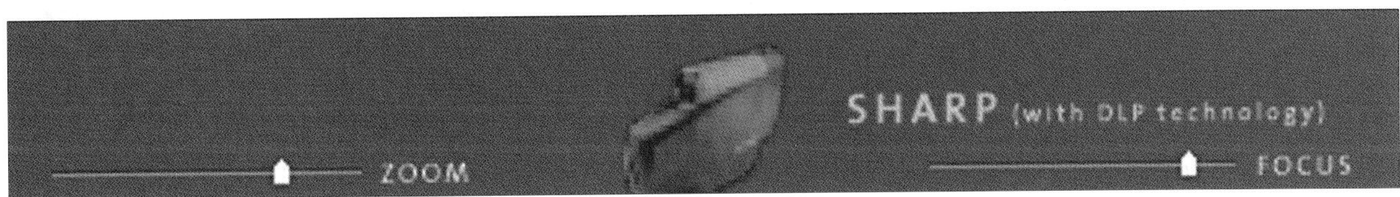

THE MP2800 MICROPORTABLE PROJECTOR

Agency	Foote Cone Belding - San Francisco
Client	Compaq
Art Director	Steve Vranakis
Writer	Liz Campanile
Creative Director	Steve Vranakis
Designer	Edd Patton
Programmer	Freestyle Interactive
Producer	Brenda Jackson
ID	02076N
URL	clients.sf.fcb.com/Awards/one/

Award	Merit
Category	**Banner — Single**
Page	136

SELECT THE BEST PART OF THE PHOTO AND CLICK
MAKE YOUR OWN BANNER!

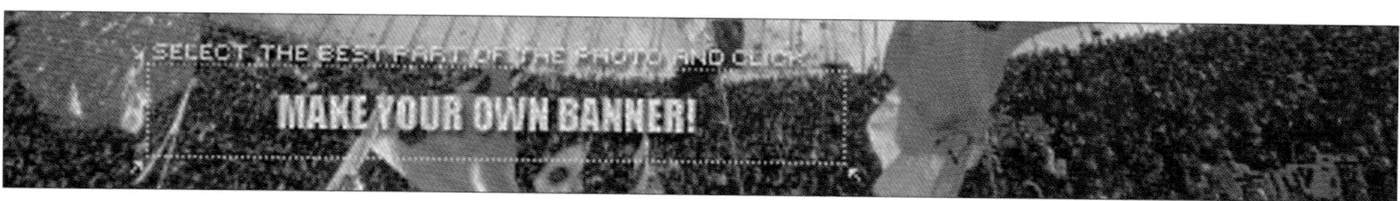

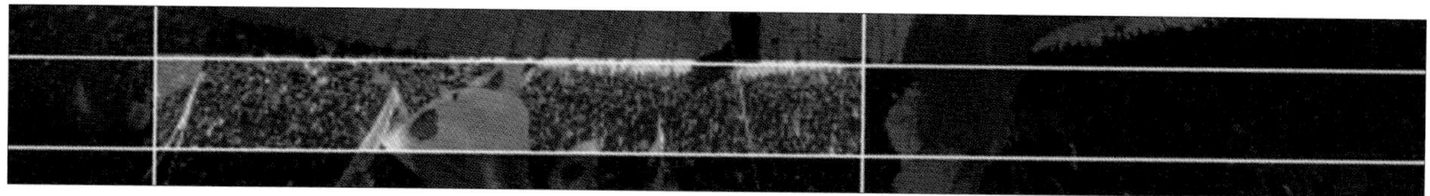

Agency	Hakuhodo - Tokyo
Client	Anheuser-Busch Asia
Art Directors	Takayoshi Kishimoto, Yuji Suzuki
Writers	Michael Glenn, Toshiya Fukuda
Creative Director	Toshiya Fukuda
Designer	Yuji Suzuki
Producers	Kenji Morimoto, Yutaka Sugiyama Yasuo Miyake
Programmers	Akihiro Tanemura, Tatsuaki Ashikaga
ID	02077N
URL	http://award2001.inside.tyo.co.jp/bud/

Award	Merit
Category	Banner — Single

Agency	Ogilvy Interactive - São Paulo
Client	Coca-Cola
Art Directors	Andrea Brazil, Nei Sobral Angela Bassichetti
Writers	Carmela Soares, Luciana Haguiara
Creative Directors	Erica Valente, André Piva
Producer	Priscilla Fernandes
Programmers	Ricardo Garcia, Fernando Zomenhan
Music/Sound	Lua Web
ID	02078N
URL	www.ogilvyinteractive.com.br/oneshow/upload

Award	Merit
Category	**Banner — Single**
Page	138

in·fra·struc·ture
Hard to pronounce. Even harder to implement.
BUSINESS INFRASTRUCTURE Click here for IBM's latest white paper. IBM

in·fra·struc·ture
We can help with both.
BUSINESS INFRASTRUCTURE Click here for IBM's latest white paper. IBM

in·fra·struc·ture
Sound it out. Roll over each syllable.
BUSINESS INFRASTRUCTURE Click here for IBM's latest white paper. IBM

ĭn′fra·struc·ture
Sound it out. Roll over each syllable.
BUSINESS INFRASTRUCTURE Click here for IBM's latest white paper. IBM

in·fra·strŭk′ture
Sound it out. Roll over each syllable.
BUSINESS INFRASTRUCTURE Click here for IBM's latest white paper. IBM

Agency | ogilvyInteractive worldwide - New York
Client | IBM
Art Directors | Nick Barrios, Kellie Kalvig
Writer | Mark Emerson
Creative Directors | Jan Leth, Aurelio Saiz, Greg Kaplan
Producer | Anita Sidhu
Programmer | Scott Leisawitz
Digital Artist/Multimedia | Mark Hofschneider
ID | 02079N
URL | http://www.wwpl.net/oneshow2002/ibm/infra_pro.html

Award | Merit
Category | **Banner — Single**

I could make you click here.

But I believe in free will.

But I believe in free will.
God

Agency	Ogilvy Interactive - Singapore
Client	Love Singapore Group of Churches
Art Directors	Dominic Goldman, Pei Pei Ng
Writers	Graham Kelly, Shane Weaver
Creative Director	Graham Kelly
Designer	Dominic Goldman
Producer	Charles Yuen
ID	02080N
URL	http://www.our-work.com/god/generic/god_make.htm

Award	Merit
Category	**Banner — Single**
Page	140

in·fra·struc·ture

Hard to pronounce. Even harder to implement.

@ BUSINESS INFRASTRUCTURE Click here for IBM's latest white paper. IBM

in·fra·struc·ture

We can help with both.

@ BUSINESS INFRASTRUCTURE Click here for IBM's latest white paper. IBM

in·fra·struc·ture

Sound it out. Roll over each syllable.

@ BUSINESS INFRASTRUCTURE Click here for IBM's latest white paper. IBM

ĭn′fra·struc·ture

Sound it out. Roll over each syllable.

@ BUSINESS INFRASTRUCTURE Click here for IBM's latest white paper. IBM

in·fra·strŭk′ture

Sound it out. Roll over each syllable.

@ BUSINESS INFRASTRUCTURE Click here for IBM's latest white paper. IBM

Agency	ogilvyInteractive worldwide - New York
Client	IBM
Art Directors	Nick Barrios, Kellie Kalvig
Writer	Mark Emerson
Creative Directors	Jan Leth, Aurelio Saiz, Greg Kaplan
Producer	Anita Sidhu
Programmer	Scott Leisawitz
Digital Artist/Multimedia	Mark Hofschneider
ID	02079N
URL	http://www.wwpl.net/oneshow2002/ibm/infra_pro.html

Award	Merit
Category	**Banner — Single**

I could make you click here.

But I believe in free will.

But I believe in free will.
God

13

Agency: Ogilvy Interactive - Singapore
Client: Love Singapore Group of Churches
Art Directors: Dominic Goldman, Pei Pei Ng
Writers: Graham Kelly, Shane Weaver
Creative Director: Graham Kelly
Designer: Dominic Goldman
Producer: Charles Yuen
ID: 02080N
URL: http://www.our-work.com/god/generic/god_make.htm

Award: Merit
Category: **Banner — Single**
Page: 140

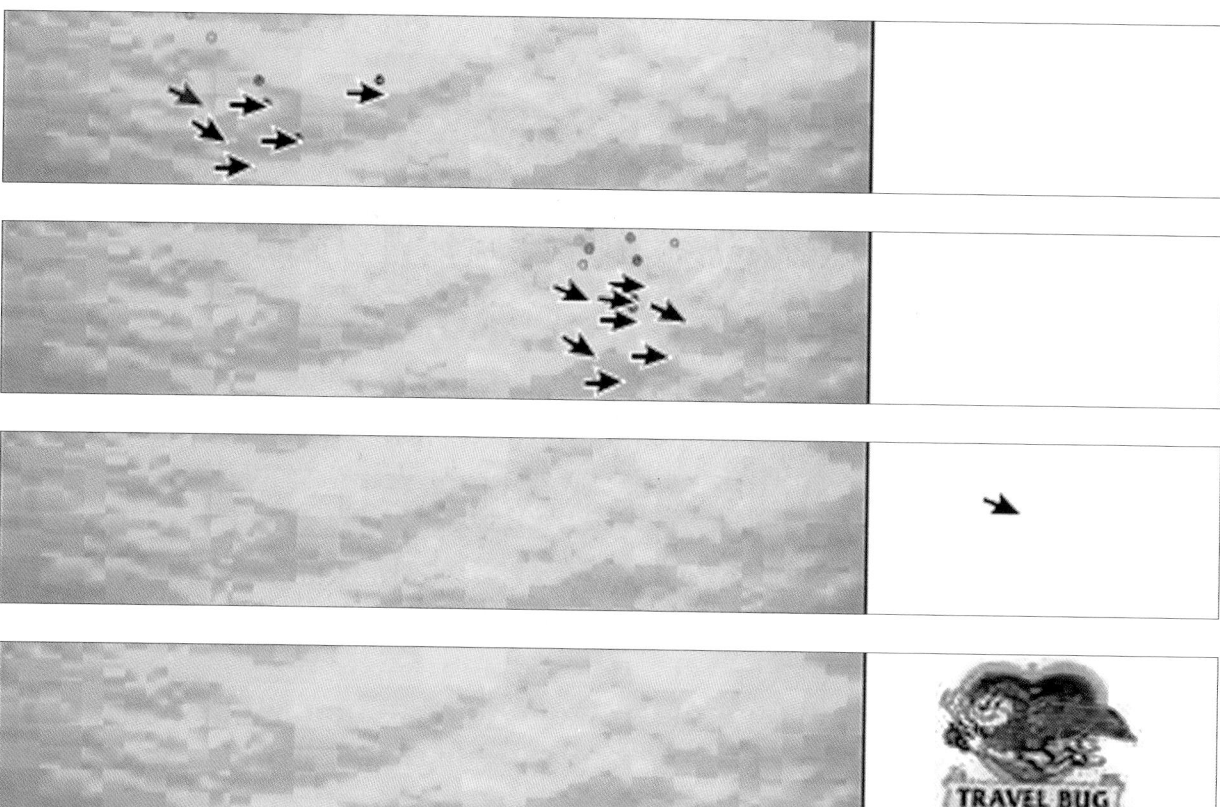

13

Agency	Ogilvy Interactive - Singapore
Client	Travel Bug
Art Director	Dominic Goldman
Writer	Shane Weaver
Creative Director	Shane Weaver
Designer	Dominic Goldman
Programmer	Dominic Goldman
Music/Sound	Dominic Goldman
ID	02081N
URL	http://www.our-work.com/travelbug/fish.html

Award	Merit
Category	**Banner — Single**

Focus on the details
adjust

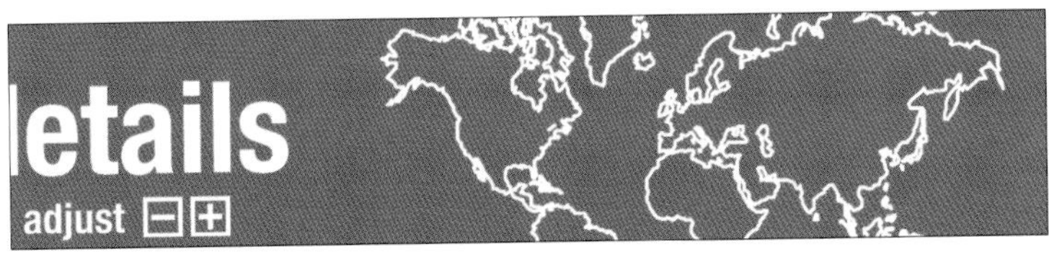

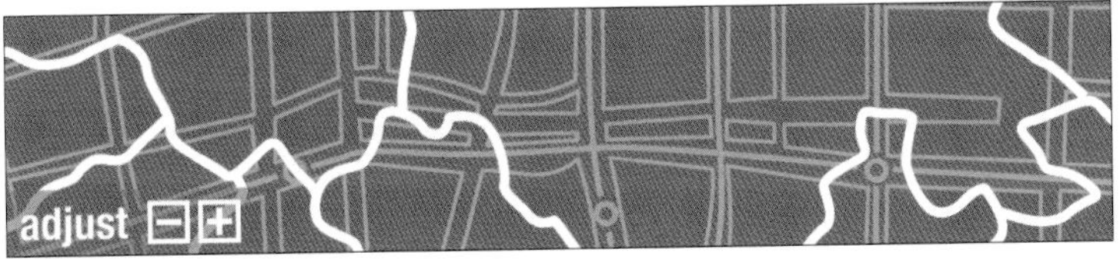

13

Agency	ogilvyInteractive worldwide - New York
Client	The Economist
Art Director	Gary M Chan
Writer	Mary Lloyd
Creative Director	Gary M. Chan
Designer	Wong Wing Hong
Programmer	Kenny Tsang
Producer	David Hofmeyr
ID	02082N
URL	www.ogilvy.com.hk/oneshow/focus

Award	Merit
Category	**Banner — Single**
Page	142

13

Agency	TBWA Hunt Lascaris - Johannesburg
Client	Dunlop Tyres
Art Director	Greg Sheppard
Creative Director	Chris Garbutt
Designer	Graham Carr
Illustrator/Photographer	Greg Sheppard
Programmer	Graham Carr
ID	02083N
URL	www.digerati.co.za/hunts

Award	Merit
Category	Banner — Single

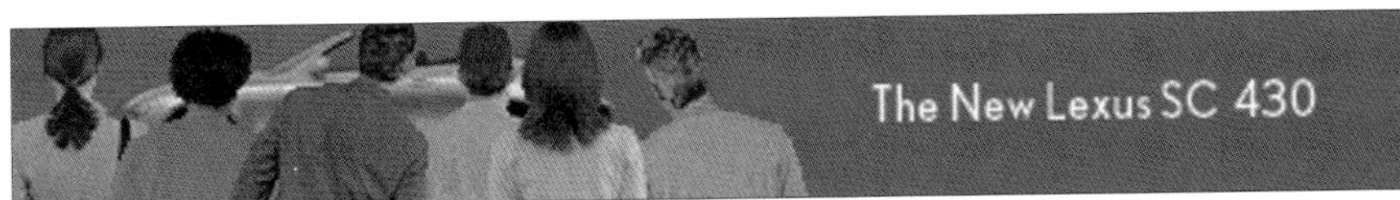

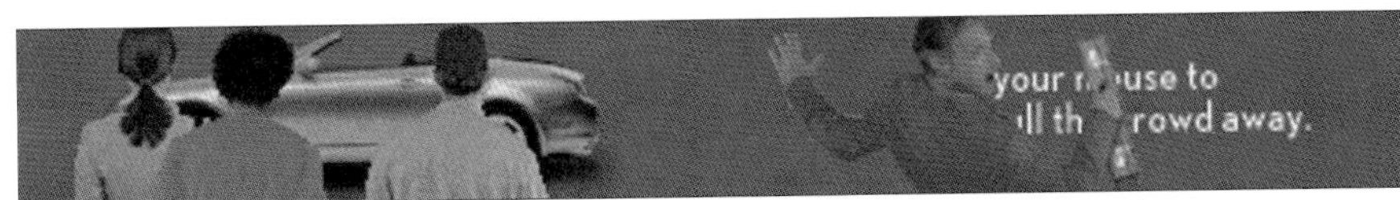

13

Agency	Team One Advertising - El Segundo
Client	Lexus
Art Director	Brian Doyle
Writer	Ed Mun
Creative Directors	Gabrielle Mayeur, Tom Cordner
Photographers	R.J. Muna, Ron Dehacopian
Information Architect	Francesca Cohn
Producer	Andy Rosen
Programmer	Enliven
Digital Artist/Multimedia	Tim Hennessey
ID	02084N
URL	http://www.teamoneadvertising.com/enliven/pullaway.html

Award	Merit
Category	**Banner — Single**
Page	144

HOW TO IMPRESS YOUR FRIENDS:

HANG ON.

13

Agency | Tribal DDB - Vancouver
Client | Kia
Creative Director | Peter Hong
Designer | Alex Beim
Producer | Dave Westwood
ID | 02085N
URL | http://xn.tribalddb.ca

Award | Merit
Category | **Banner — Single**

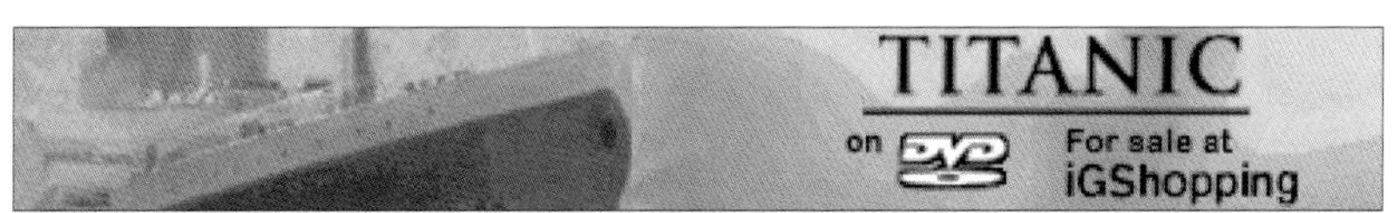

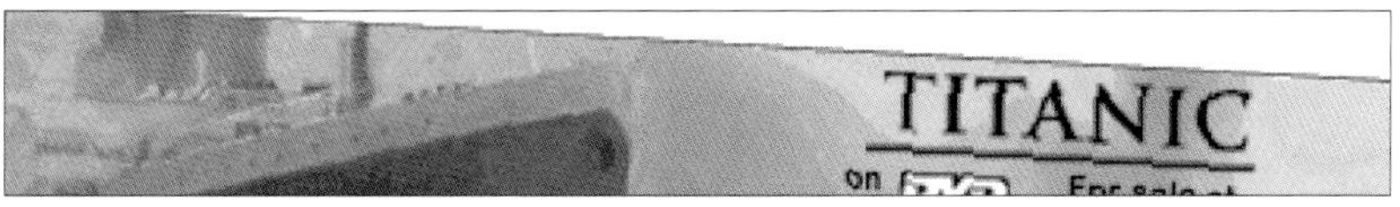

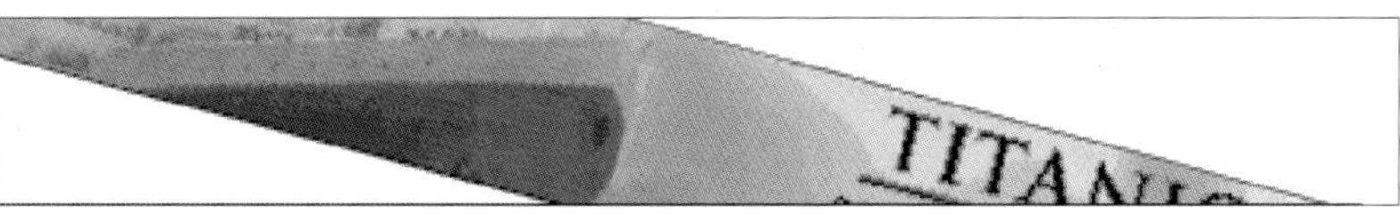

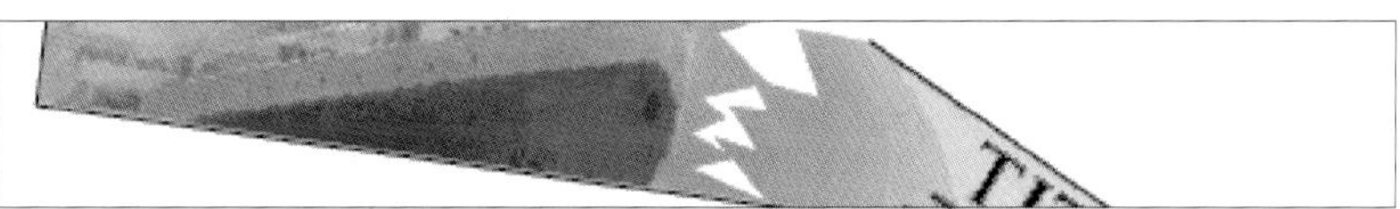

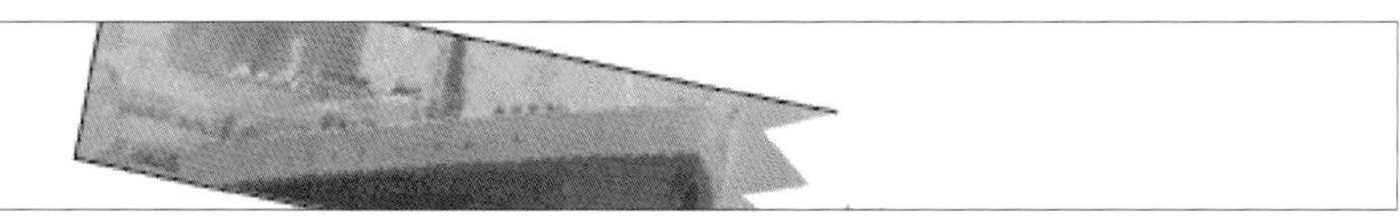

Agency	Agenciaclick - São Paulo
Client	IG
Art Directors	Alexandre Prado, Eduardo Moliterno Edwin Veelo, Fred Siqueira, PJ Pereira Rafael Ferreira , Rodrigo Buim
Writers	Bruno Godinho, PJ Pereira Suzana Apelbaum
Creative Director	PJ Pereira
Designers	Eduardo Moliterno, Fred Siqueira Rafael Ferreira, Ricardo Augusto Rodrigo Buim
Photographer	Ricardo Augusto
Programmers	Alexandre Prado , Allan Ridolfi Cristiano Breuel , Pedro Barbosa Marcelo Siqueira , Miguel Castarde
ID	02086N
Award	Merit
Category	**Banner Campaign**
Page	146

Agency	hillmancurtis - New York
Client	Ultimate TV from Microsoft
Art Directors	Ian Kovalik, Nick Spahr
Writer	Kevin Frank
Creative Directors	Hillman Curtis, Greg Bell, Paul Venables
Designers	Ian Kovalik, Matthew Horn
Photographer	Ian Kovalik
Programmers	Ian Kovalik, Matthew Horn
Producers	Homera J. Chaudhry, Don Parker
Digital Artists/Multimedia	Ian Kovalik, Matthew Horn
ID	02087N
URL	http://www.hillmancurtis.com/oneshow

Award	Merit
Category	**Banner Campaign**

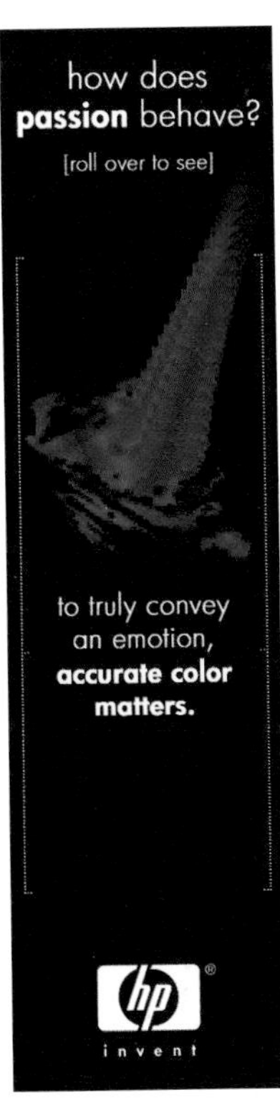

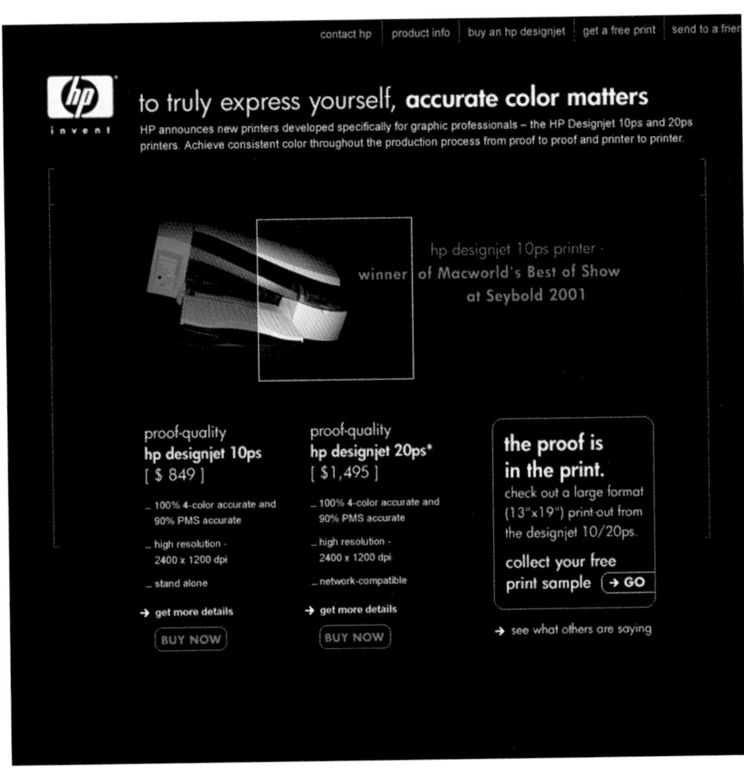

Agency	Modem Media - San Francisco
Client	Hewlett-Packard
Art Director	Juliane Hadem
Writer	Lisa Knott
Creative Director	Alan Drummer
Designer	Hai Tran
Producer	Monica Naman
Music/Sound	Chris Porro
ID	02088N
URL	www.modemmedia.com/entries_sf/hp_designjet

Award	Merit
Category	**Banner Campaign**
Page	148

Agency	Modem Media - San Francisco
Client	Intel
Art Director	Elizabeth Warren
Writers	Jens McNaughton, Karen Hutchinson
Creative Directors	Steven Cloud, Alex Hendler
Designers	Michelle Murata, Joshua Sullivan
Information Architect	Tina Deardorff
Producer	Jonathon K. Lee
Programmer	Ryan O'Hearn
Music/Sound	Joshua Sullivan
ID	02089N
URL	www.modemmedia.com/entries_sf/area_one

Award	Merit
Category	**Banner Campaign**

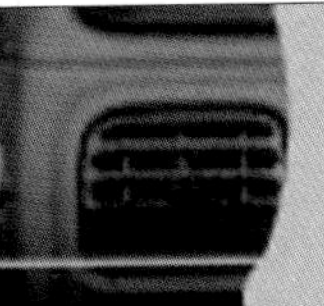

13

Agency	Ogilvy Interactive - São Paulo
Client	Renault
Art Director	Sergio Mugnaini
Writers	Carmela Soares, Luciana Haguiara Priscilla Tedeschi
Creative Director	Paulo Sanna
Producers	Rafael Taqueuchi, Rafael Prelwitz
Programmers	Fernando Zomenhan, Ricardo Garcia
ID	02090N
URL	www.ogilvyinteractive.com.br/oneshow/clioyahoo

Award	Merit
Category	**Banner Campaign**
Page	150

I am in the details.

I am in the details.
God

I could make you click here.

But I believe in free will.
God

13

Agency	Ogilvy Interactive Singapore
Client	Love Singapore Group of Churches
Art Directors	Dominic Goldman, Pei Pei Ng
Writers	Graham Kelly, Shane Weaver
Creative Director	Graham Kelly
Designer	Dominic Goldman
Producer	Charles Yuen
ID	02091N
URL	http://www.our-work.com/god/generic/

Award	Merit
Category	**Banner Campaign**

13

Agency	Tribal DDB Worldwide - London
Client	The Guardian
Art Directors	Sam Ball, Dave Bedwood, Steven Reed
Writers	Sam Ball, Dave Bedwood, Ben Clapp
Creative Directors	Sam Ball, Dave Bedwood
Designer	Gini Simpson
Producer	Michelle Stanhope
Programmers	Dave Cox, Nick Clements
ID	02092N
URL	http://www.creative.tribalddb.com/oneshow/guardian.htm

Award	Merit
Category	**Banner Campaign**
Page	152

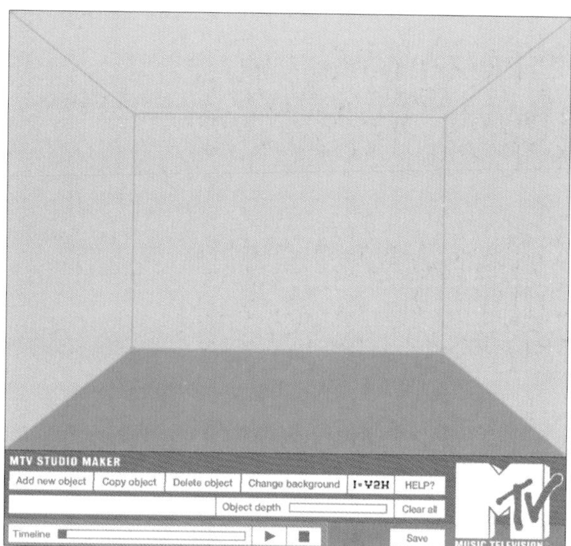

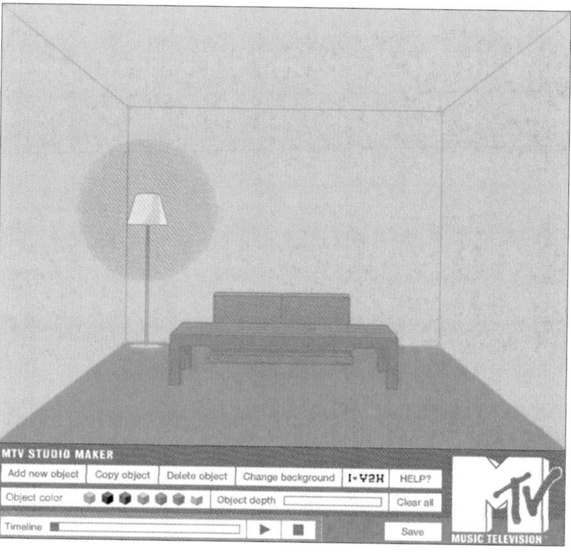

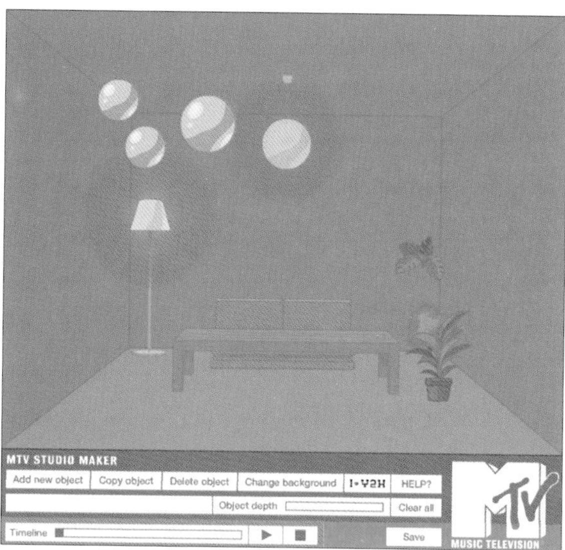

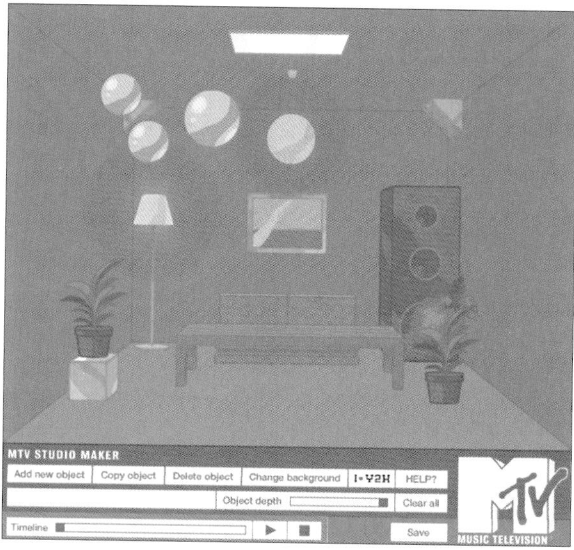

14

Agency | Abel & Baker - Stockholm
Client | MTV Nordic
Art Directors | Ola Persson, Ted Persson
Creative Directors | Jimmy Herdberg, Ola Persson
Photographer | Ola Persson
Producers | Måns Ulvestam, Anna Eriksson
Programmer | Björn Berglund
Digital Artist/Multimedia | Jimmy Herdberg, Mikael Johansson
ID | 02093N
URL | http://hits.abelbaker.com/oneshow2002/mtv-backgroundmaker/

Award | Merit
Category | **Beyond the Banner**

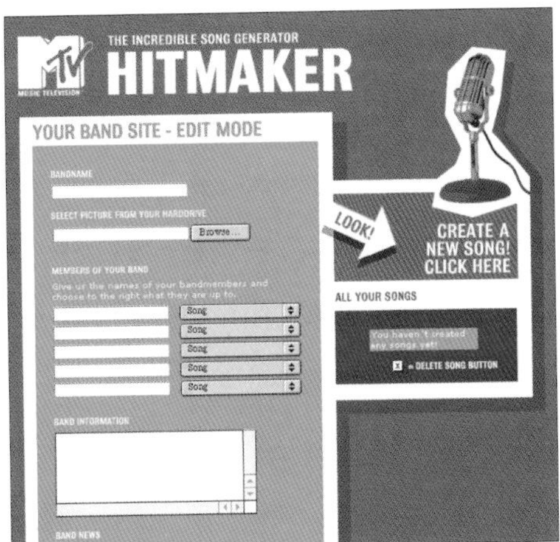

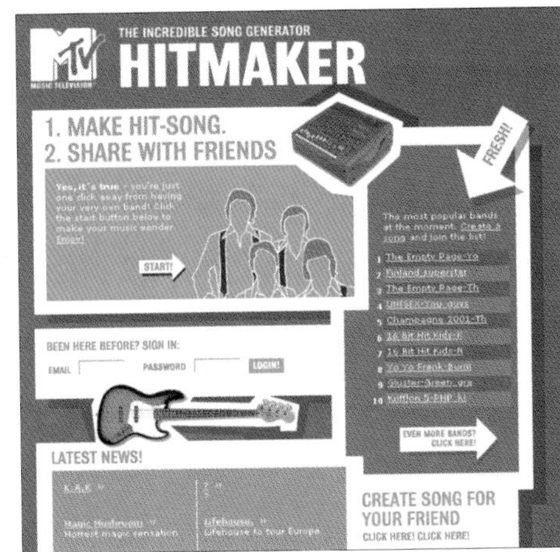

14

Agency	Abel & Baker - Stockholm
Client	MTV Nordic
Art Directors	Jimmy Poopuu, Ted Persson
Writers	Kristoffer Triumf, David Sundin
Creative Directors	Ted Persson, Ola Persson, David Sundin
Producers	Måns Ulvestam, Anna Eriksson
Programmers	Tobias Löfgren, Rasmus Sellber Per Frödeberg, Björn Berglund Johan Sandberg, Mårten Ekenberg
ID	02094N
URL	http://hits.abelbaker.com/oneshow2002/ mtv-hitmaker/

Award	Merit
Category	**Beyond the Banner**
Page	154

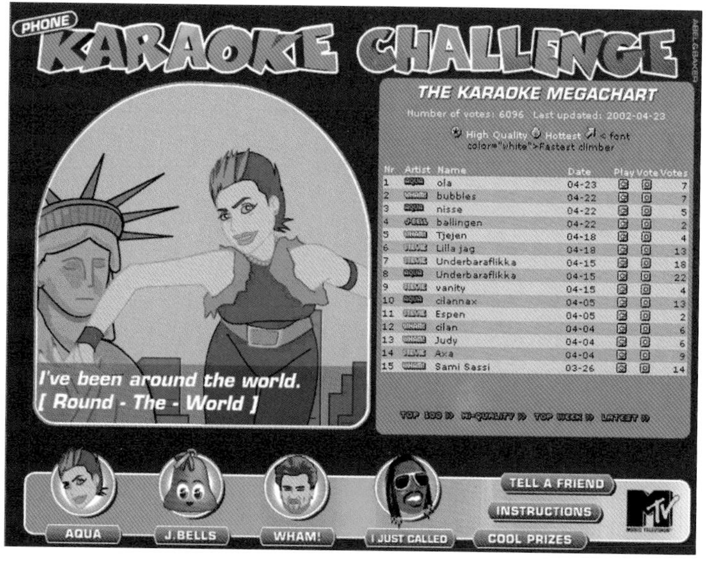

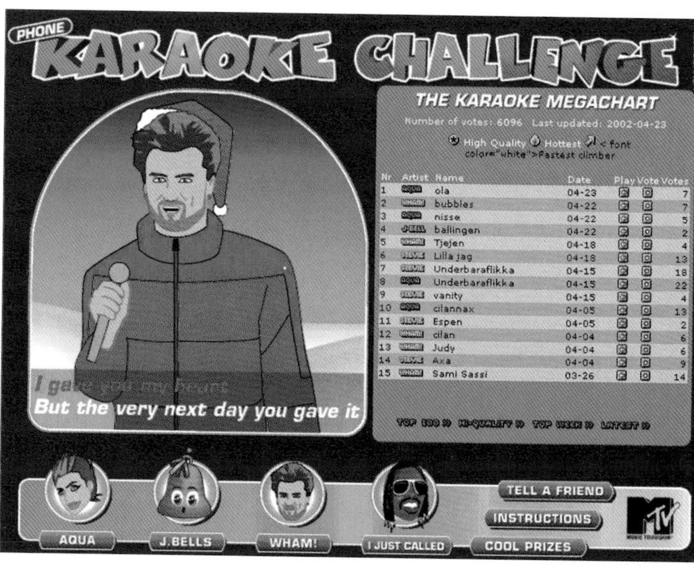

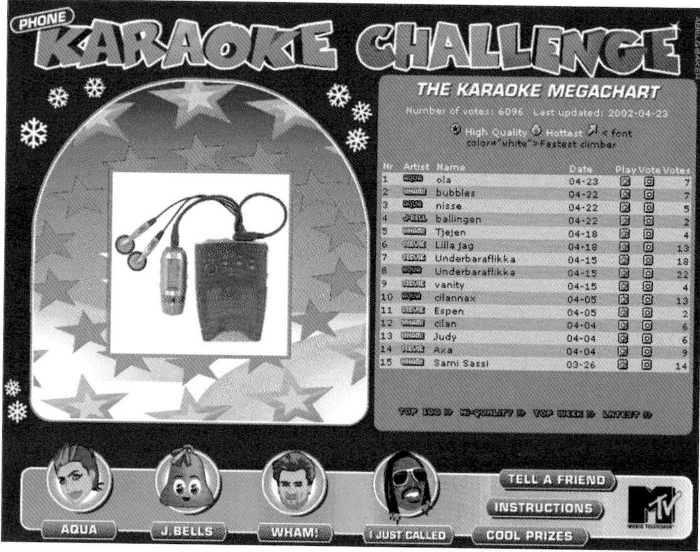

Agency	Abel & Baker - Stockholm
Client	MTV Nordic / MSN
Art Directors	Martin Cedergren, Ted Persson
Writers	Kristoffer Triumf, Magnus Larsson
Creative Directors	Tony Sajdak, Martin Cedergren
Designers	Viktor Larsson, Arvid Tappert
Producers	Viktoria Wallner, Fredrik Heghammar
Programmers	Tony Sajdak, Tim Sajdak, Peter Karlsson
ID	02095N
URL	http://hits.abelbaker.com/oneshow2002/mtv-karaoke/

Award	Merit
Category	**Beyond the Banner**

Valentine's Day Dove

Valentine's Day is the time to declare love. And there´s nothing nicer then to receive a special homage from the one you love. Thinking of this, Dove brings you an unusual oportunity: to declare your love on the front-pages of the major portals. Of course, it´s not for real, but you won´t see the difference! Just fill out the form below, and your declaration of love will appear as the main article of the major portals, with a text written by you, especially for him or her.

1. Choose a portal:

CNN MSN

2. Choose the title for the article:

Joseph DECLARES ENDLESS LOVE TO Rachel

Joseph CONFIRMS THE LOVE TO Rachel IS CORRESPONDED

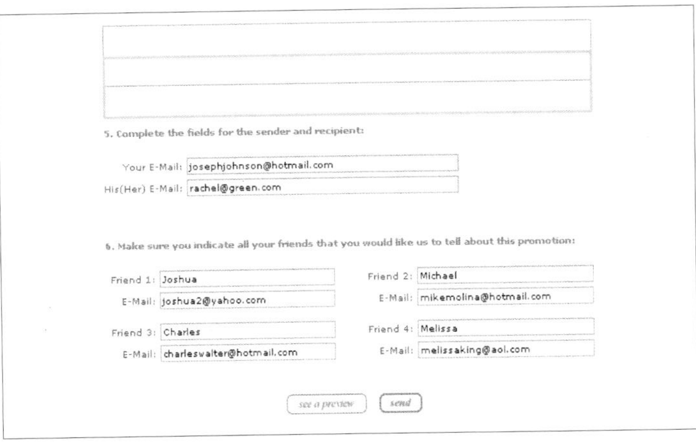

5. Complete the fields for the sender and recipient:

Your E-Mail: josephjohnson@hotmail.com

His(Her) E-Mail: rachel@green.com

6. Make sure you indicate all your friends that you would like us to tell about this promotion:

Friend 1: Joshua E-Mail: joshua2@yahoo.com

Friend 2: Michael E-Mail: mikemolina@hotmail.com

Friend 3: Charles E-Mail: charleswalter@hotmail.com

Friend 4: Melissa E-Mail: melissaking@aol.com

see a preview send

14

CNN.com Editions: Europe | Asia

TIME Get 4 Risk-FREE Issues CLICK HERE

Updated: 02:00 p.m. EDT (1800 GMT) -- 24 April 2002

Valentine's Day

Joseph declares endless love to Rachel

Joseph Johnson revealed that after April 23rd, 1998 live has changed forever. When first meeting **Rachel Green**, 23 years old, at the Andrew´s Club, he felt that he has found the woman of his live. After 4 years being together, he says that despite details like working too much, the couple continues every day more in love.

Asked by our reporter, Johnson declared: **"I love Rachel"**

Full Story

ON CNN TV

Crossfire: Now that campaign f become law, what is McCain? He'll tell us (7 p.m. ET)

ATLANTA 'SEGWAYS' TO SCOOT

Three Atlanta organizations ar of the highly touted, electric or known only as "Ginger." Full S

OTHER TOP NEWS

- London judge won't extrad
- Helms to undergo open-he
- U.S. eyes anti-terror funds
- Talks resume in Bethlehem
- Plea on restroom wall lead
- 'West Wing' talks to real p

Agency	Agenciaclick - São Paulo
Client	Gessy Lever
Art Director	Rodrigo Buim
Writer	Suzana Apelbaum
Creative Director	PJ Pereira
Designer	Marcelo Siqueira
Producer	Cristiane Rojas
Programmer	Jo Paulo Barbosa
ID	02096N

Award	Merit
Category	**Beyond the Banner**
Page	156

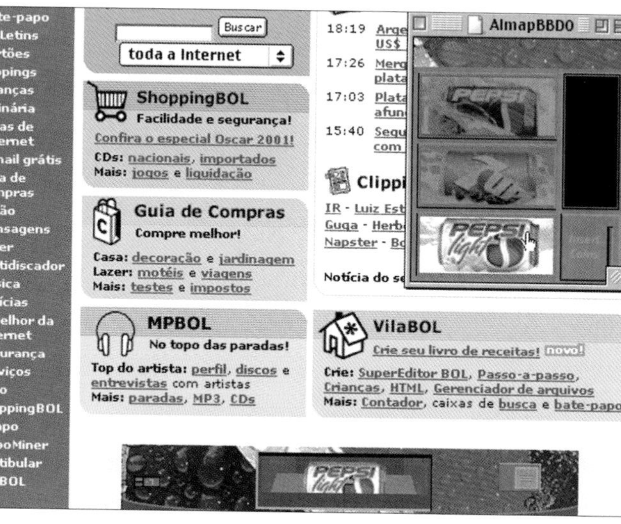

Agency	AlmapBBDO - São Paulo
Client	Pepsi
Art Directors	Eduardo Foresti, Diego Martins
Writer	Caroline Freire
Creative Directors	Fabio Costa, Eduardo Foresti
Designer	Diego Martins
Programmer	Paulo Pacheco
ID	02097N
URL	www.almapbbdo.com.br/oneshow/pepsi/machine

Award	Merit
Category	**Beyond the Banner**

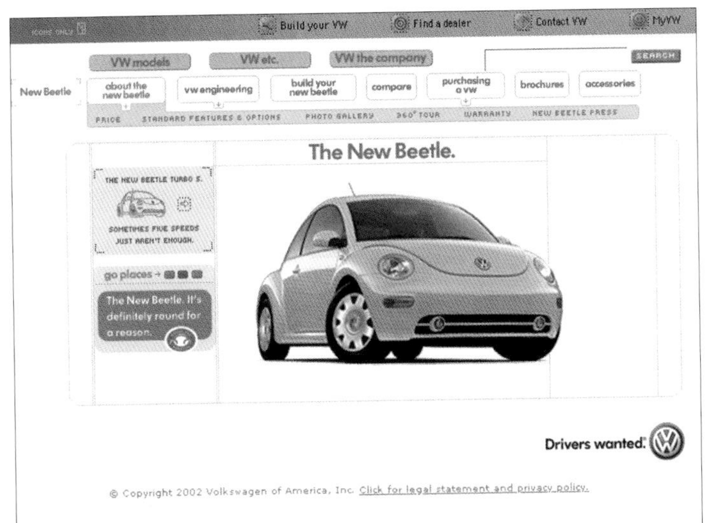

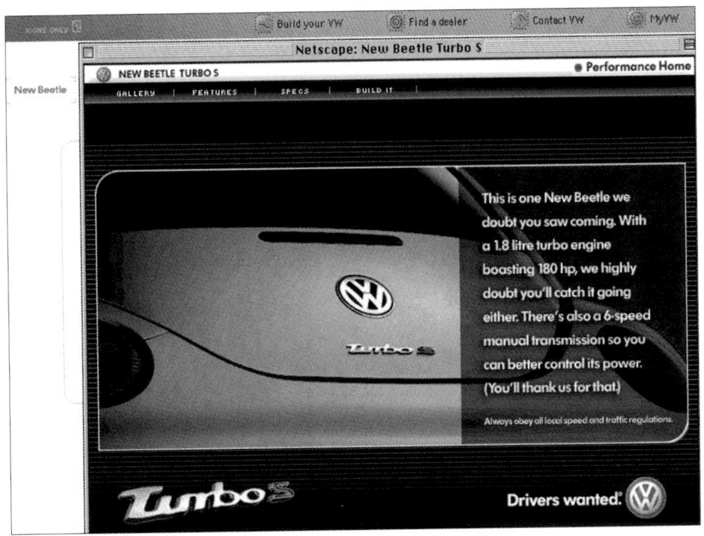

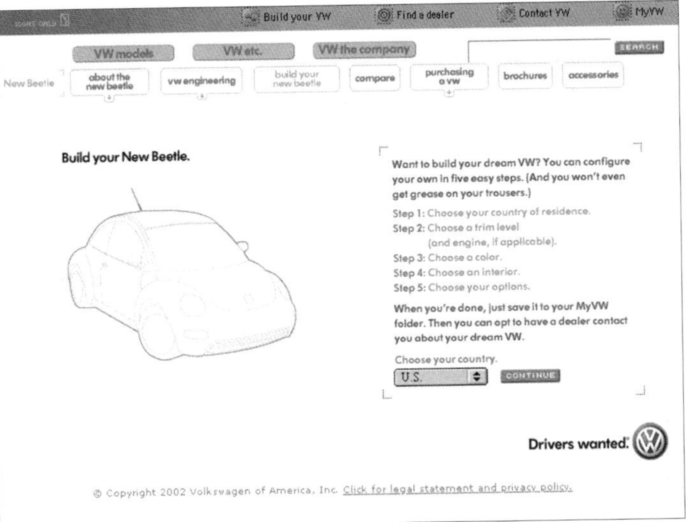

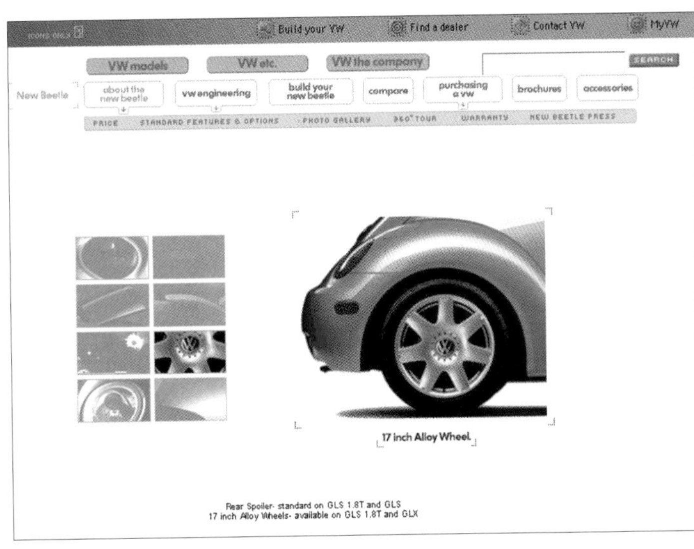

14

Agency	Arnold Worldwide - Boston
Client	Volkswagen of America
Art Director	Nicole McDonald
Writer	Susan Ebling Corbo
Creative Directors	Ron Lawner, Alan Pafenbach Chris Bradley, Tim Brunelle
Designers	Nicole McDonald, Will McGinness
Photographer	Martin Albert
Information Architect	Patrick Eddy
Technical Directors	Jonathan Groves, Roy Wetherbee
Programmer	Robert Hodgin
Mechanical Supervisor	Claudine Kaprielian
Digital Artist/Multimedia	Robert Hodgin
Music/Sound	Chris Ewen
Producers	Jennifer Iwanicki, Erica Lohnes
ID	02098N
URL	vw.com/newbeetle

Award	Merit
Category	**Beyond the Banner**
Page	158

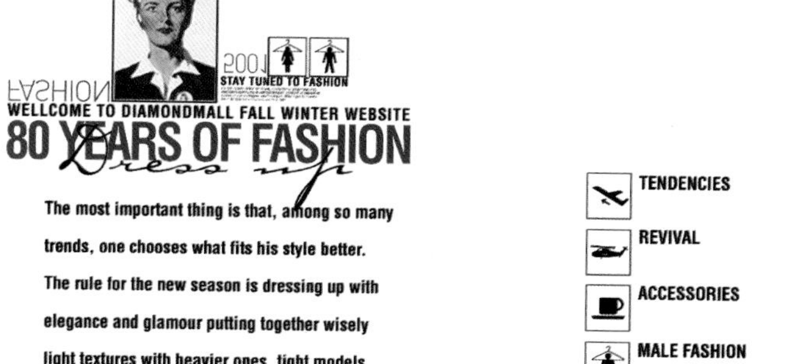

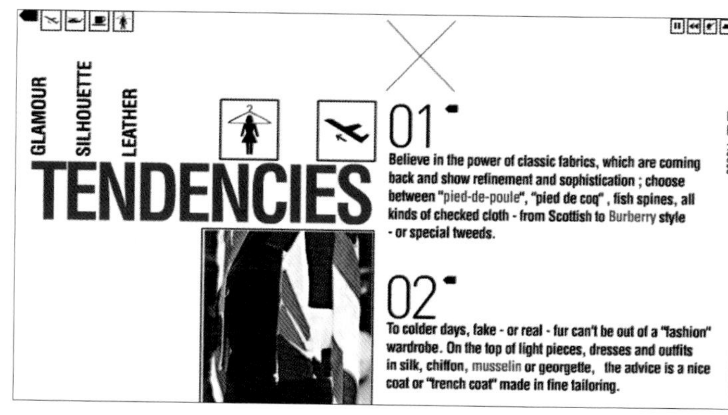

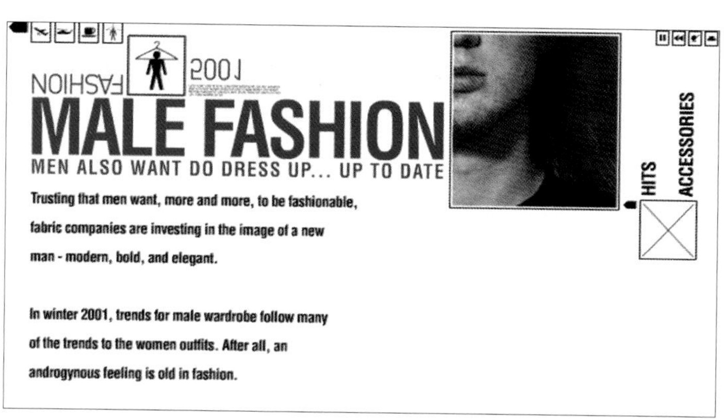

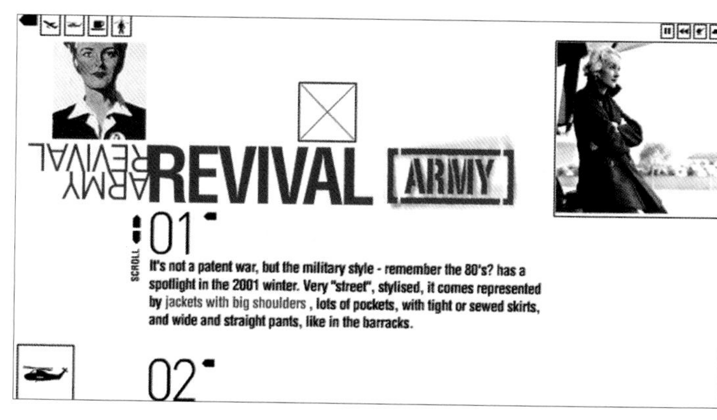

Agency	Bolt Interativa - Belo Horizonte
Client	Shopping Diamond Mall
Art Director	Alexandre Estanislau Silva
Writer	Heloisa Aline de Oliveira
Creative Director	Alexandre Estanislau Silva
Designer	Alexandre Estanislau Silva
Illustrator	Luiz Otávio
Information Architect	Alexandre Estanislau Silva
Producers	Marco Antônio Estanislau Silva André Saliba Nazar
Programmer	Alexandre Estanislau Silva
Digital Artist/Multimedia	Alexandre Estanislau Silva
Music/Sound	Bolt Interativa
ID	02099N
URL	http://awards.boltinteractive.com/diamond/winter2001
Award	Merit
Category	**Beyond the Banner**

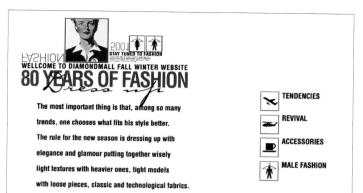

14

Agency	Digitas - Boston
Client	Yukon Denali
Art Director	Giles Dickerson
Writer	Todd West
Creative Directors	David Mitchell, Mary Grace Whalen
Designer	Howard Nagar
Photographers/Illustrators	Tony LaBruno, Vamos Studios
Programmer	Howard Nagar
Music/Sound	Kevin McLaughlin,Morgan Packard
ID	02100N
URL	http://iad.digitas.com/presentations/awards/oneshow/index.html

Award	Merit
Category	**Beyond the Banner**
Page	160

Agency: Forsman & Bodenfors
Gothenburg
Client: SCA Hygiene Products
Art Directors: Mattias Stridbäck, Kim Cramer
Markus Edin
Writers: Jesper Lövkvist, Jonas Enghage
Designer: Tobias Ottahal
Photographer: Mattias Stridbäck
ID: 02101N
URL: http://demo.fb.se/liberodiapers/supersittial.html

Award: Merit
Category: **Beyond the Banner**

4

Agency	hillmancurtis - New York
Client	RollingStone.com
Art Director	Ian Kovalik
Writer	hillmancurtis, inc.
Creative Directors	Hillman Curtis, Doug Gottlieb
Designer	Hillman Curtis
Photographers	Hillman Curtis, Ian Kovalik, Matthew Horn
Producer	Homera J. Chaudhry
Programmer	Hillman Curtis
Digital Artist/Multimedia	Hillman Curtis
Music/Sound	Various Artists
ID	02102N
URL	http://www.hillmancurtis.com/oneshow

Award	Merit
Category	**Beyond the Banner**
Page	162

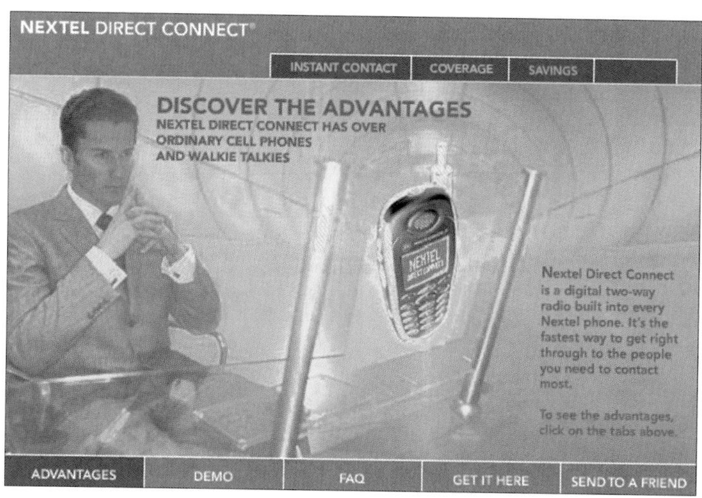

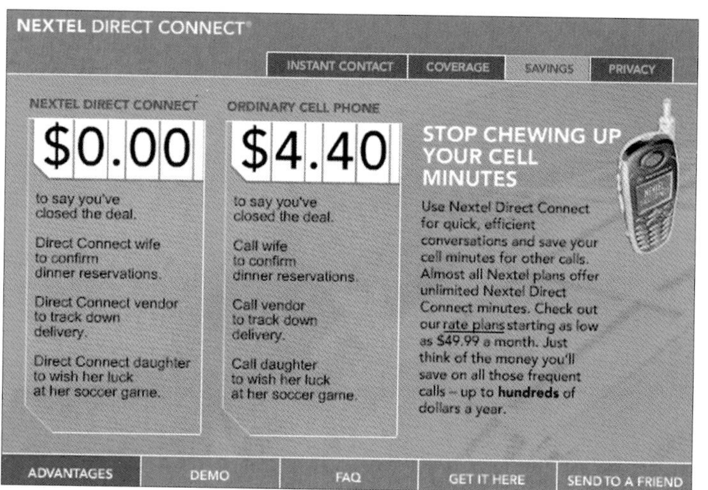

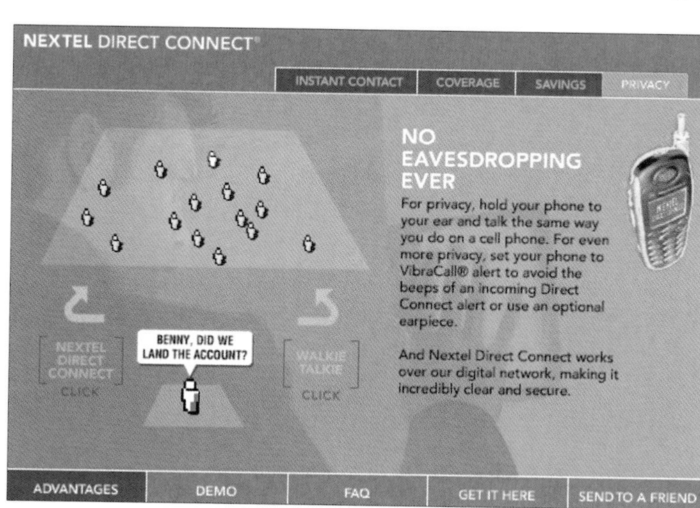

Agency	Mullen - Wenham
Client	Nextel
Art Director	Mark Dionne
Writer	Cary Lawson
Creative Director	John Wolfarth
Designer	Benny Blanco
Information Architect	Cary Lawson
Producer	Sean Blatchley
Programmer	Christian Madden
Digital Artist/Multimedia	Pete Tschudy
Music/Sound	Benny Blanco
ID	02103N
URL	http://interactive.mullen.com/awards/theoneshow/nextel/nexteljump.html

Award	Merit
Category	**Beyond the Banner**

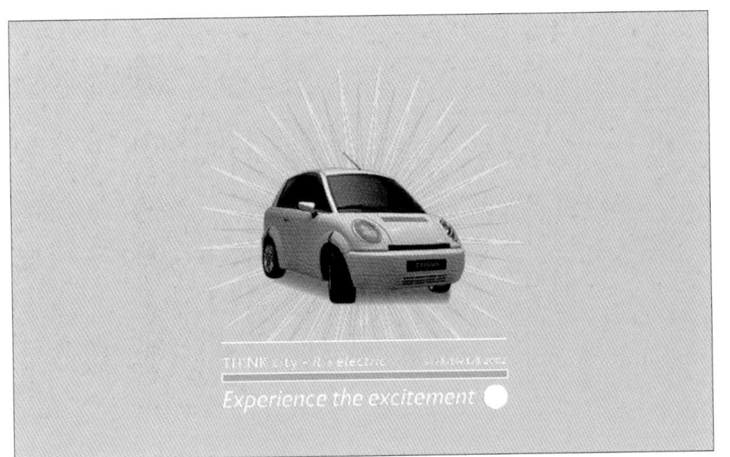

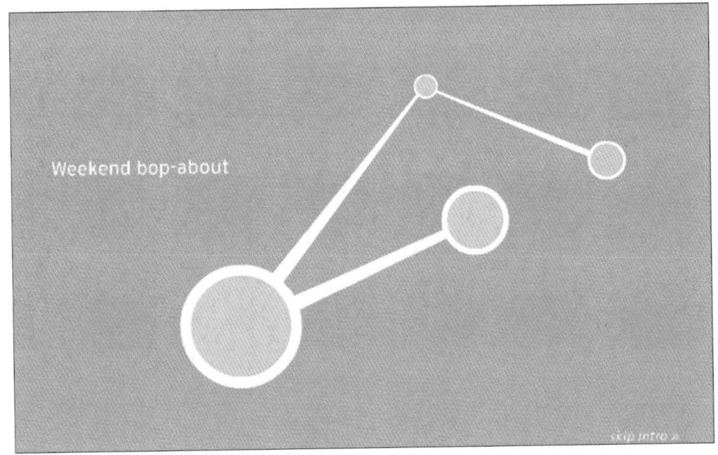

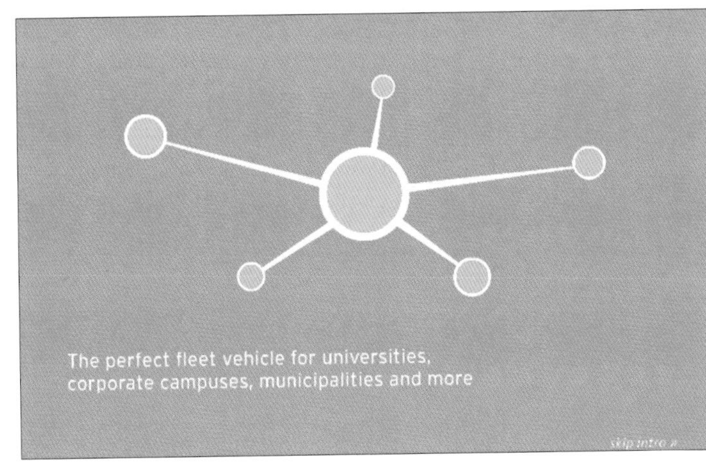

Agency	Resource - Columbus
Client	Ford Motor Company
Art Director	Dan Coe, Matt Leaver
Content Strategist	Gregor Gilliom
Designer	Matt Leaver
Project Manager	Jon Leeke
ID	02104N
URL	client.resource.com/awards/oneshow

Award	Merit
Category	**Beyond the Banner**
Page	164

Agency	Upgrade - São Paulo
Client	Abrapia
Creative Directors	Mauro Alencar, Ricardo Braga
Technical Director	Nivaldo Dutra Amorim Filho
Art Director	Oscar Alarcón
Copywriter	Mauro Alencar
Designer	Oscar Alarcón
Producer	Cristiano Fernandes Pinto
ID	02105N
URL	www.upgradenet.com.br/boy/boy.htm

Award Merit

Category **Beyond the Banner**

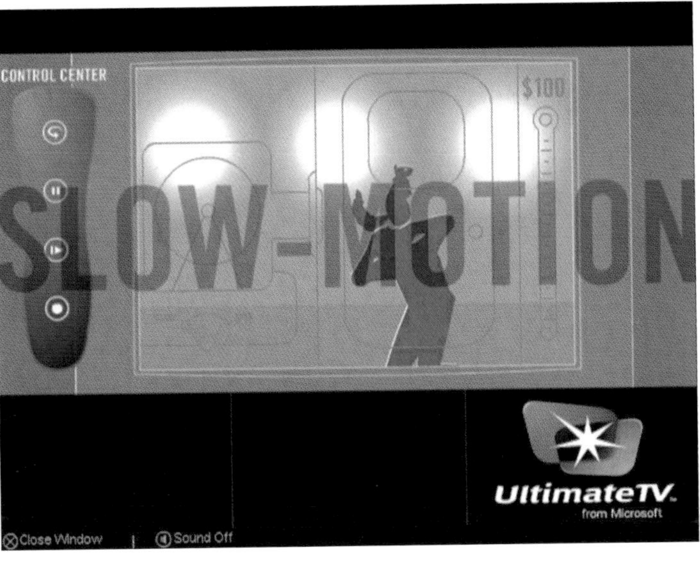

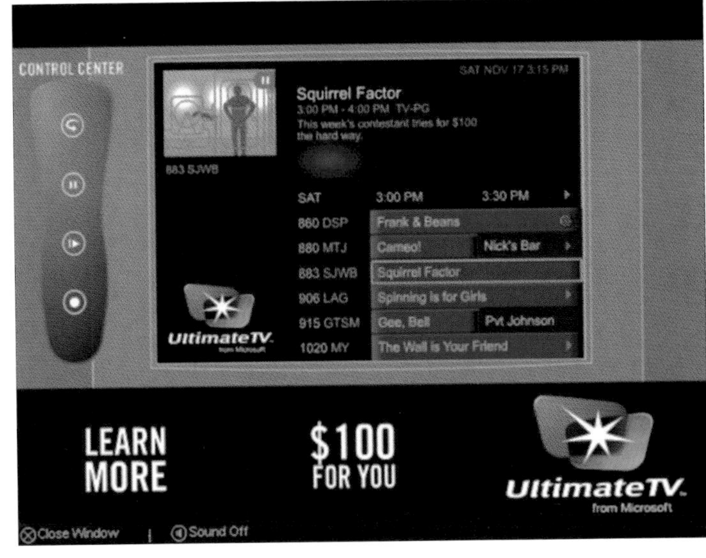

Agency	Venables, Bell & Partners - San Francisco
Client	UltimateTV
Art Director	Nick Spahr
Writer	Kevin Frank
Creative Directors	Greg Bell, Paul Venables
Designer	Dean Mac Donald
Photographer	Dean Mac Donald
Producers	Lisa Gatto, Don Parker
Programmer	Scott Walker
Music/Sound	Jim Lively
ID	02106N
URL	www.mekanism.tv/awards/1show/rich/squirrel.html

Award	Merit
Category	**Beyond the Banner**
Page	166

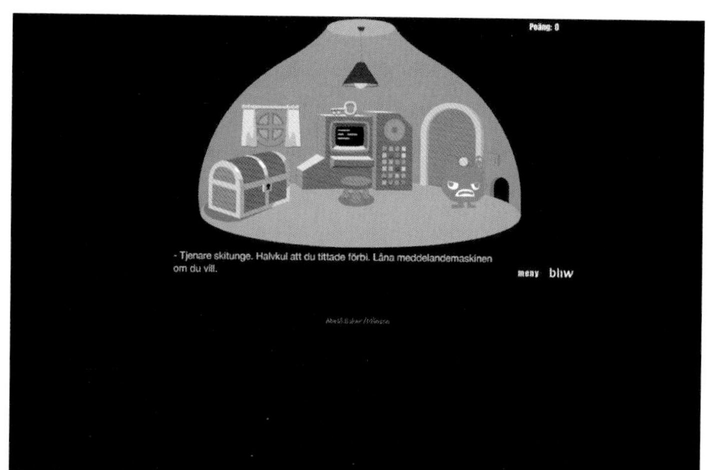

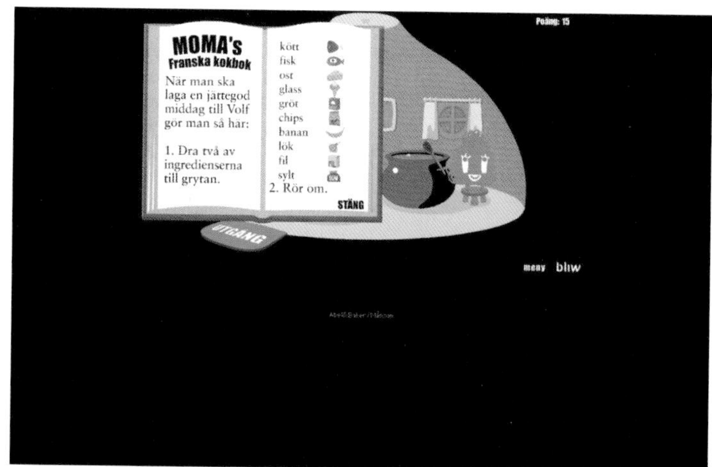

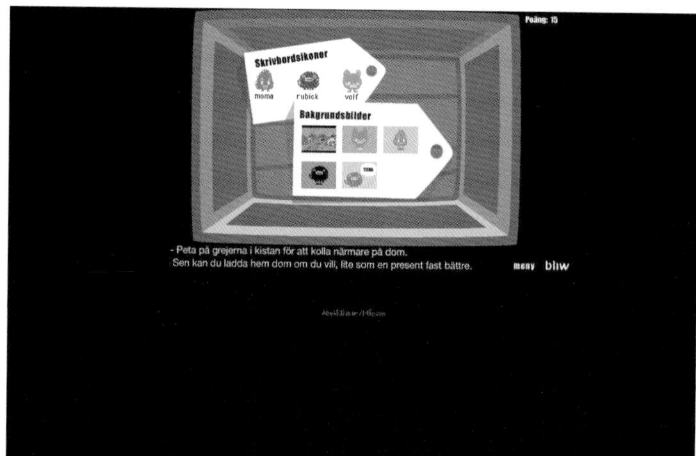

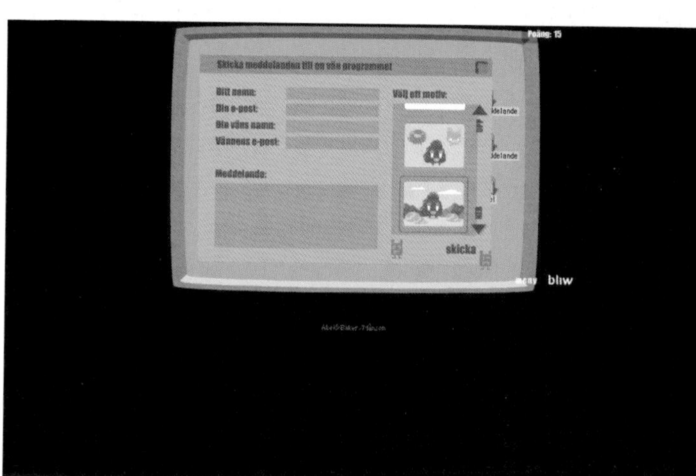

Agency	Abel & Baker - Stockholm
Client	Cedderoth
Art Director	Ted Persson
Writer	David Sundin
Designer	Ola Persson
Producers	Joakim Dieden, Marielle Lundqvist
Programmer	Stefan Lagergren
Digital Artist/Multimedia	Daniel Isaksson
ID	02107N
URL	http://hits.abelbaker.com/oneshow2002/bliw/

Award	Merit
Category	**Promotional Advertising — Web Sites**

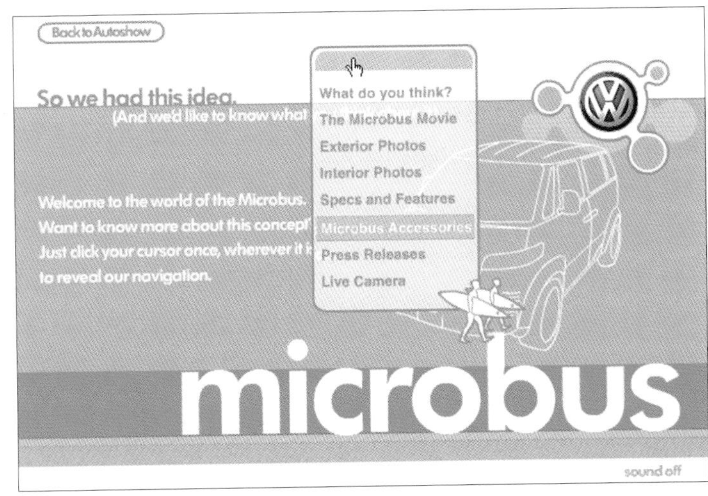

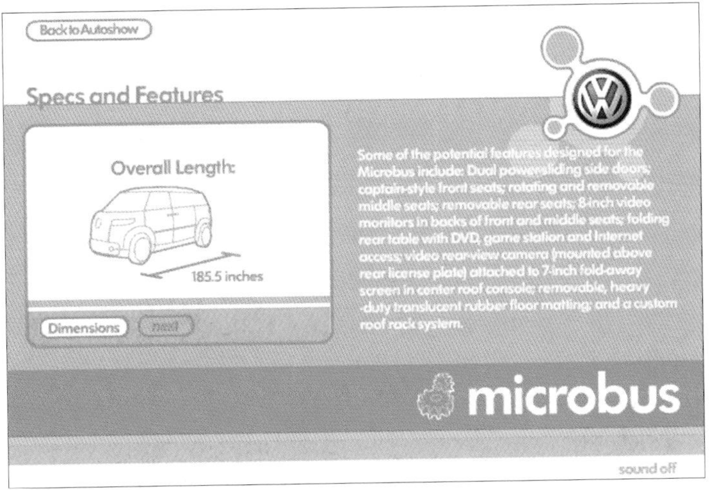

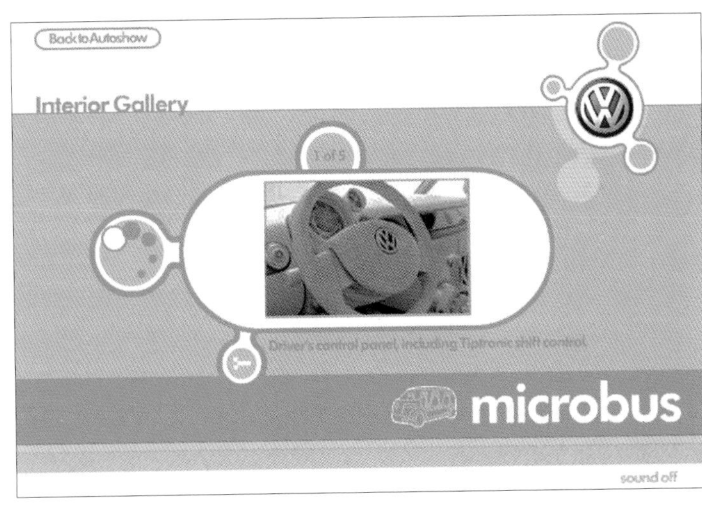

Agency	Arnold Worldwide - Boston
Client	Volkswagen
Art Director	Chris Bradley
Writer	Tim Brunelle
Creative Directors	Ron Lawner, Alan Pafenbach Chris Bradley, Tim Brunelle
Designers	Nicole McDonald, Keith Butters
Photographer	Martin Albert
Information Architect	Patrick Eddy
Programmers	Keith Butters, Joe Cartman Stefka Hristova
Technical Directors	Jonathan Groves, Rick Webb
Mechanical Supervisor	Rick Webb
Digital Artists/Multimedia	Jerimiah O'Connor, Mark Kraus
Music/Sound	Jack Dragonetti
Producers	Jennifer Iwanicki, Jennifer Phillips-Bruns Erica Lohnes
ID	02108N
URL	www.vw.com/microbus

Award	Merit
Category	**Promotional Advertising — Web Sites**
Page	168

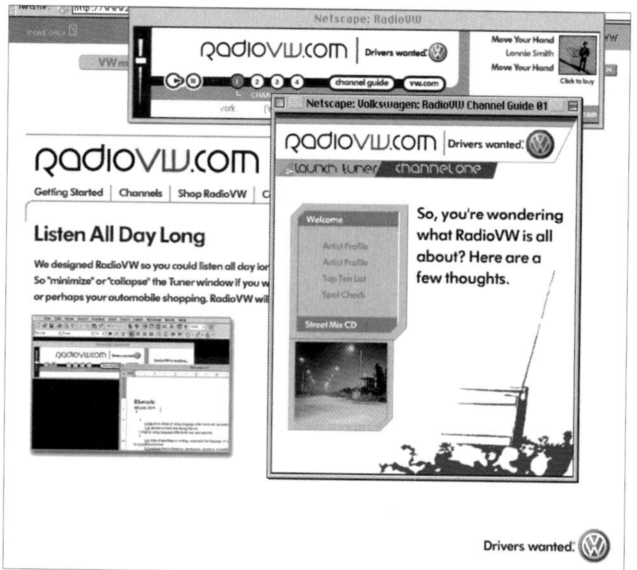

Agency	Arnold Worldwide - Boston
Client	Volkswagen of America
Art Directors	Chris Bradley, Nicole McDonald
Writers	Tim Brunelle, Kerry Lynch
Creative Directors	Ron Lawner, Alan Pafenbach, Tim Brunelle Chris Bradley
Designer	Marc Van Norden
Producers	Marnie Jones, Lily Weitzman Erica Lohnes, Jennifer Phillips
Technical Directors	Jonathan Groves, Roy Wetherbee
Information Architect	Patrick Eddy
Programmers	Silverline, Websound
Mechanical Director	Mike Shafran
ID	02109N
URL	radiovw.com

Award	Merit
Category	**Promotional Advertising — Web Sites**

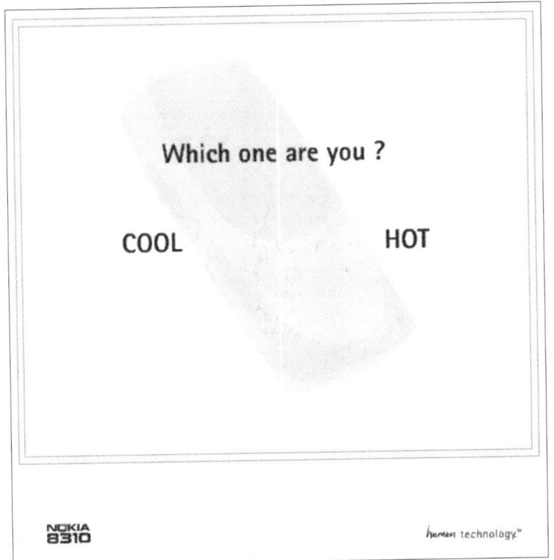

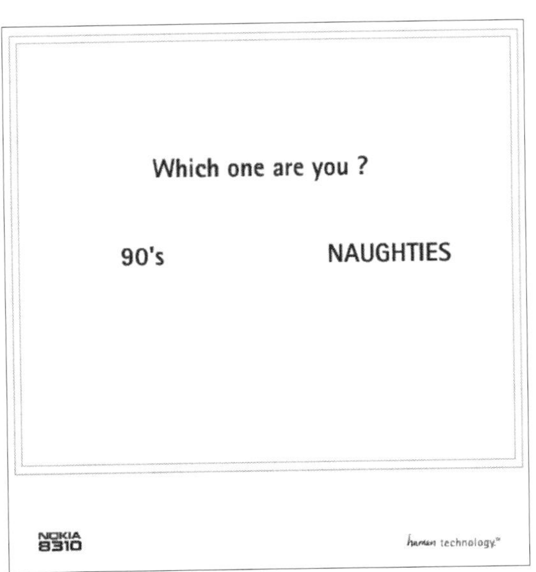

Agency	Deepend - Sydney
Client	Nokia Australia
Art Director	Josh Rowe
Writers	Tim Ludlow, Vanessa Bouganim Cameron Elkins
Creative Directors	Simon Waterfall, Josh Rowe
Designer	Josh Rowe
Producer	Tim Ludlow
Digital Artist/Multimedia	Josh Rowe
ID	02110N
URL	www.everyonewantsone.com

Award	Merit
Category	**Promotional Advertising — Web Sites**
Page	170

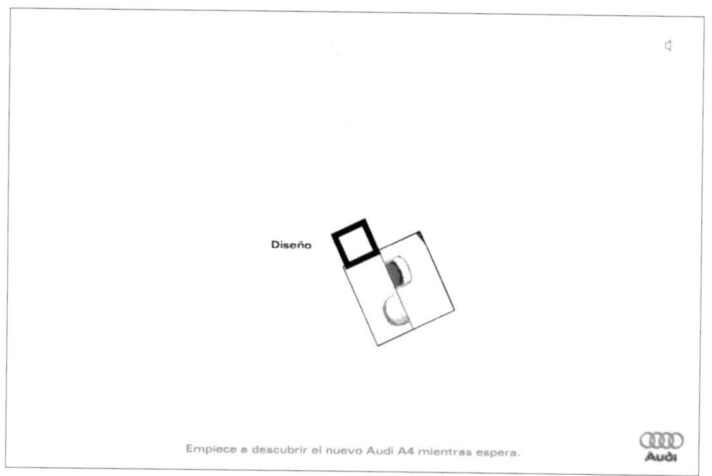

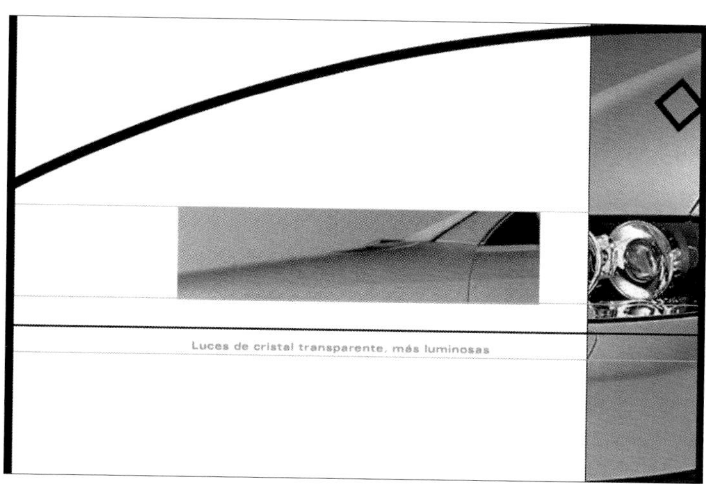

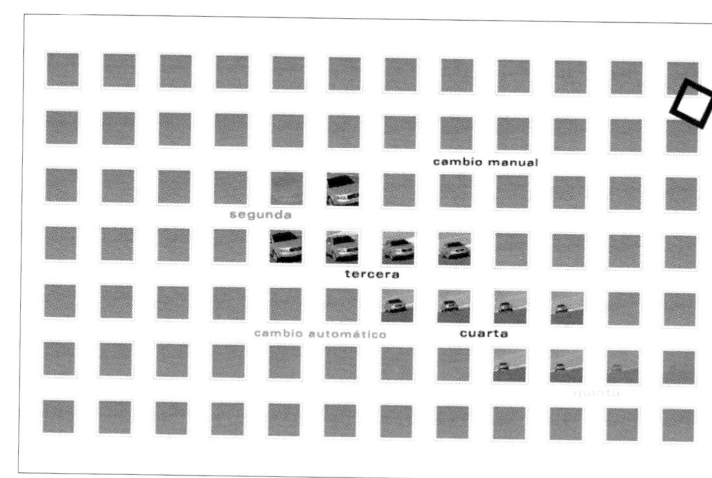

Agency	DoubleYou - Barcelona
Client	Audi Spain
Art Director	Blanca Piera
Programmers	Xavi Caparrós, Natalia Rojas, Borja Gómez
Digital Artist/Multimedia	Oriol Quin
Music/Sound	7Siete, Música visual
ID	02111N

Award	Merit
Category	**Promotional Advertising — Web Sites**

Agency	DoubleYou - Barcelona
Client	Audi Spain
Art Director	Blanca Piera
Creative Directors	Frédéric Sanz, Esther Pino, Frédéric Sanz, Oriol Quin, Joakim Borgström
Digital Artist/Multimedia	Alejandro Bica
Music/Sound	7Siete, Música visual
ID	02112N
URL	www.doubleyou.com/festivals/audia4avant/oneshow.html

Award	Merit
Category	**Promotional Advertising — Web Sites**
Page	172

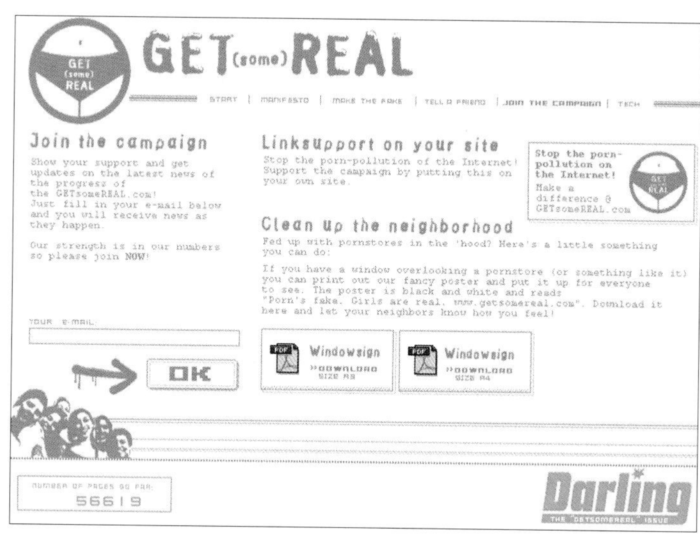

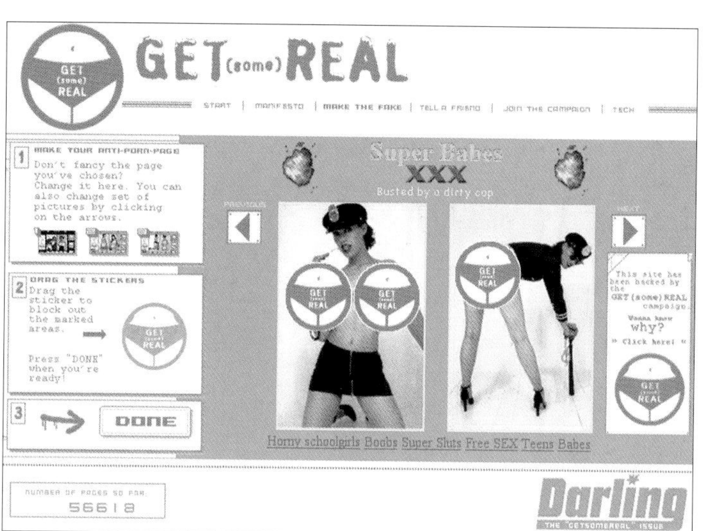

Agency	Moonwalk & St. Lukes Sweden - Stockholm
Client	Darling Magazine
Art Director	Jesper Lofroth
Writer	Anna Ander
Creative Director	Calle Sjonell
Designer	Jessica Olander
Photographer	Johanna Jarnfeldt
Programmers	Peter Janson, Didde Brockman
ID	02113N
URL	http://www.moonwalk.se/eng/campaign/Stockholm/getsomereal

Award	Merit
Category	**Promotional Advertising — Web Sites**

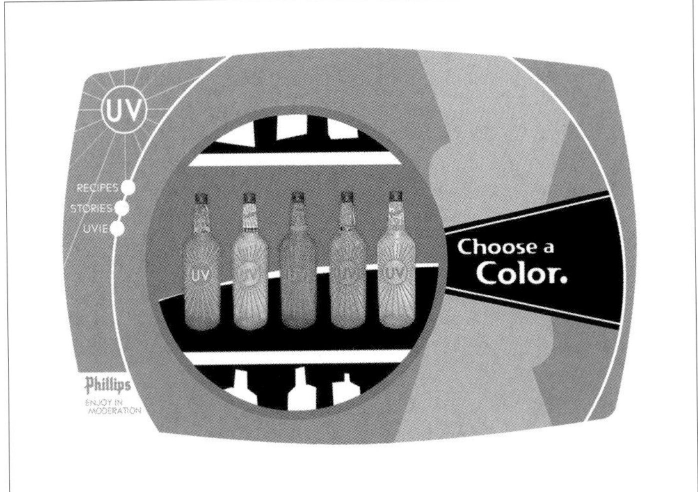

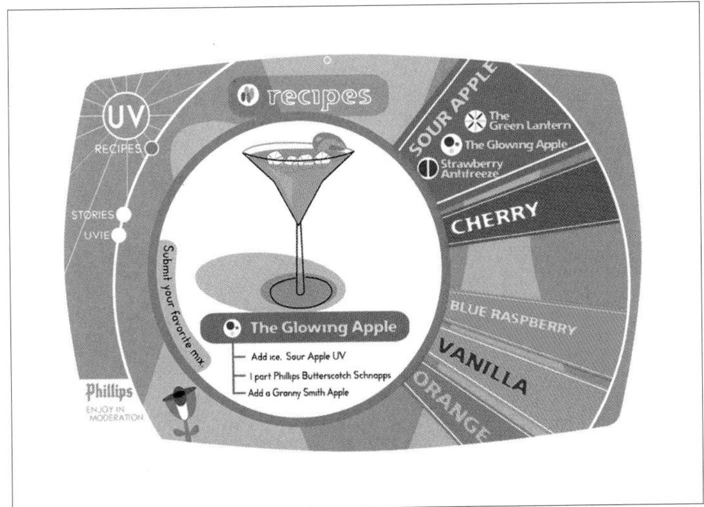

Agency	Olson & Company - Minneapolis
Client	Phillips Beverage
Art Directors	Cindy Olson, Chris Henderson
Writer	Derek Bitter
Creative Director	John Olson
Designer	Jeff Tranberry
Photographer	Chris Henderson
Programmer	Jared Lukes
Digital Artist/Multimedia	Chris Henderson, Jeff Tranberry Jared Lukes
Music/Sound	Jeff Tranberry, Jared Lukes
ID	02114N
URL	www.phillipsuv.com

Award	Merit
Category	**Promotional Advertising — Web Sites**
Page	174

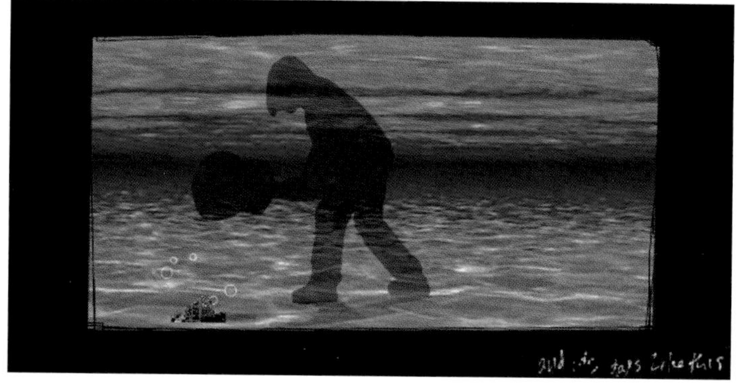

Agency	Sudden Industries - New York
Client	Universal Music Group
Art Director	David McManus
Writers	Bob Holmes, David McManus
Creative Director	Bob Holmes
Designer	David McManus
Photographer	David McManus
Information Architect	Bob Holmes
Producer	Muffy Marracco
Programmer	David McManus
Digital Artist/Multimedia	David McManus
Music/Sound	David McManus
ID	02115N
URL	http://bobschneidermusic/vmation

Award Merit

Category **Promotional Advertising — Web Sites**

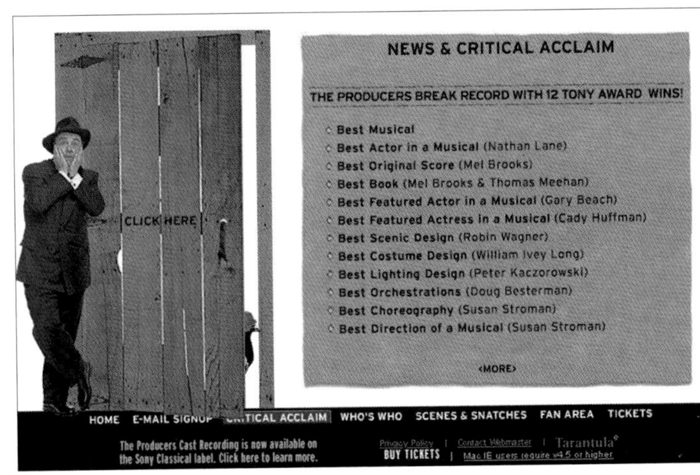

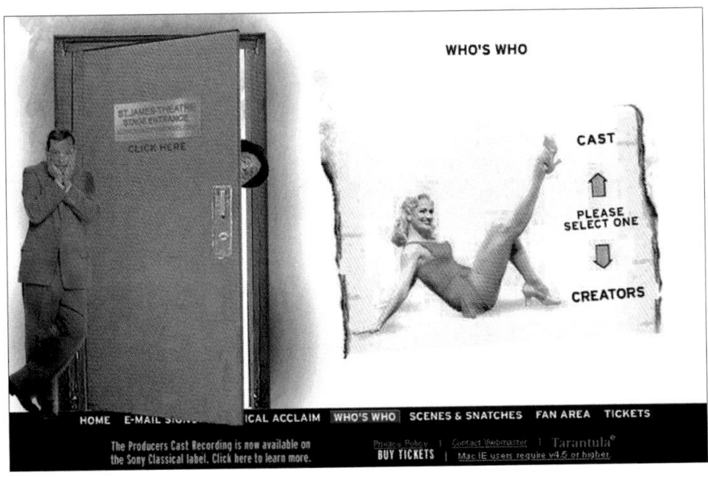

Agency	Tarantula - New York
Client	Bialystock & Bloom
Art Director	Sergio Castro
Writer	Michael Shetler
Creative Directors	Edward Velandria, Sergio Castro
Producers	Linda Mittel, David Risley
Information Architect	Sergio Castro
Programmers	Ammar Hamdani, Paul St. Denis
ID	02116N
URL	http://www.tarantula.com/producers

Award	Merit
Category	**Promotional Advertising — Web Sites**
Page	176

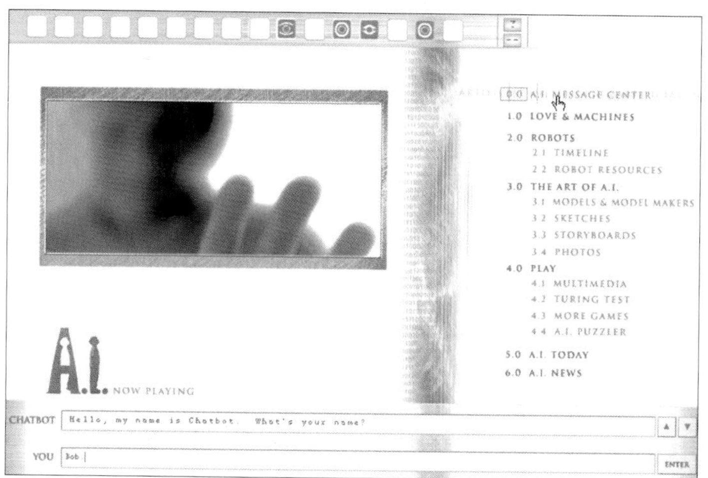

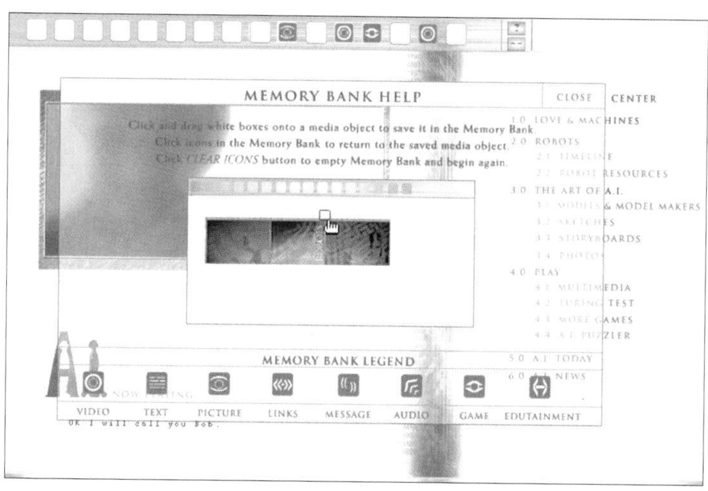

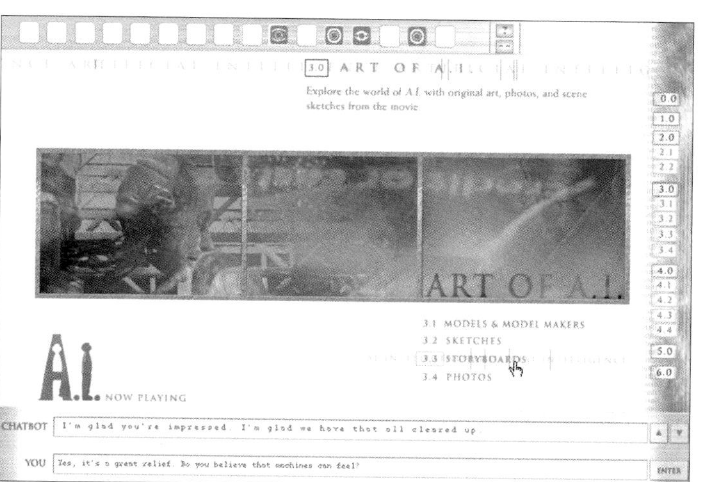

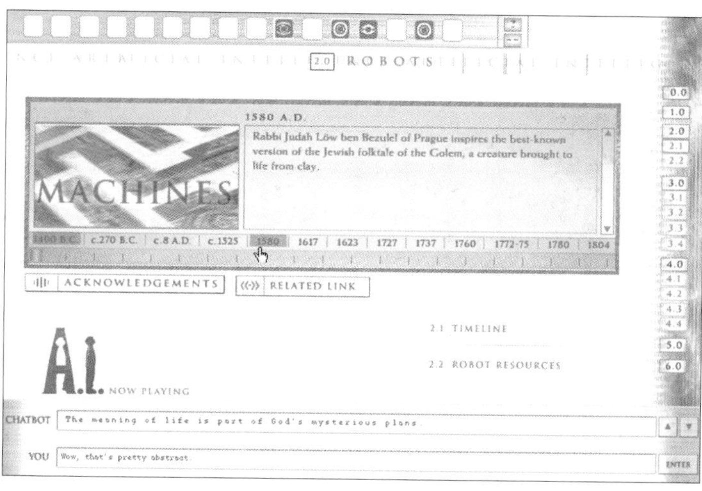

1

Agency	Thoughtbubble Productions - New York
Client	Warner Brothers
Art Director	Piper Darley
Writer	Liz Thorpe
Creative Director	Guy Sealey
Designer	Piper Darley
Producers	Jeff High, Dinha Kaplan
Programmers	Matt Spinks, Robin Curts, Tina Honikel
	Dan Love, Dave Carroll
Digital Artist/Multimedia	Dave Carroll, Jean Tropnas, Regis Zaleman
ID	02117N
URL	http://projects.thoughtbubble.com/tbp_demo/tbp_demosites/AI/index.html

Award	Merit
Category	**Promotional Advertising — Web Sites**

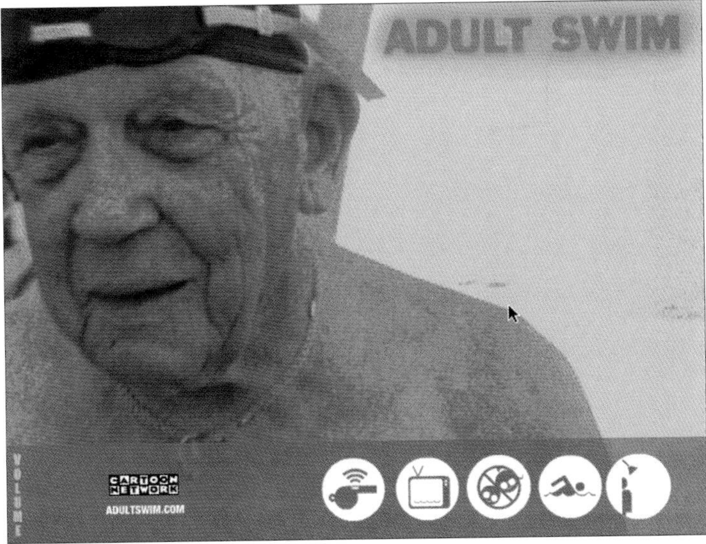

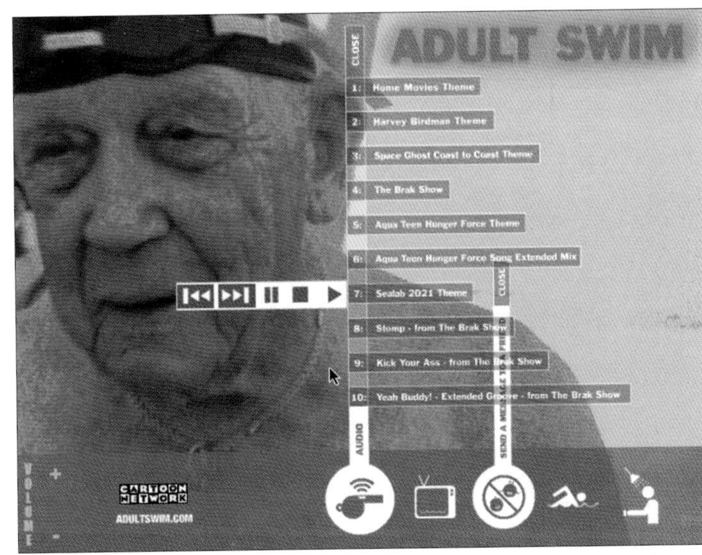

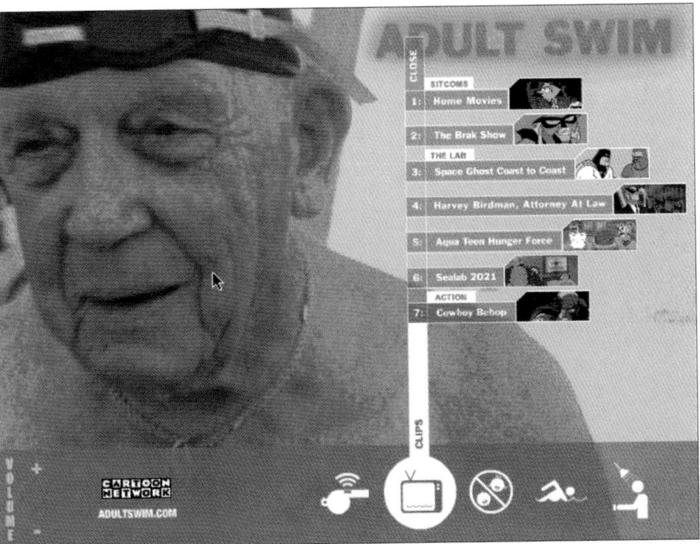

Agency	Cartoon Network - Atlanta
Client	Cartoon Network
Art Director	Kevin Fitzgerald
Creative Director	Gary Albright
Designer	Jacob Escobedo
Producer	David & Company
ID	02118N

Award	Merit
Category	**Promotional Advertising — CD-ROMs**
Page	178

Agency	Fuse - St. Louis
Client	Missouri Division of Tourism
Art Director	Jerry McGee
Writers	Clifford Franklin, Howard Work
Creative Director	Mike Franklin
Designers	Jerry McGee, Mike Franklin
Photographer	Tom Newcomb
Producer	Bob Miano
Information Architects	Michele Dixon, Gail Reed
Programmer	Technisonic Studios
Digital Artist/Multimedia	Scott Huegerich
Music/Sound	Quinton Frankiln
ID	02119N

Award	Merit
Category	**Promotional Advertising — CD-ROMs**

No more grey areas.
Is there life in Internet commerce?
FREE COPY
SUBSCRIPTION
EMAIL TO A FRIEND
The Economist

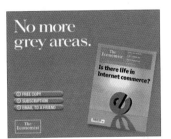

Agency	ogilvyInteractive worldwide - New York
Client	The Economist
Art Director	Fletch Wong
Writer	Simon Handford
Creative Director	Gary M. Chan
Producer	Sun Wai Man
Designer	Wong Wing Hong
ID	02120N
URL	www.ogilvy.com.hk/oneshow/jayleno

Award	Merit
Category	**Promotional Advertising — Other Digital Advertising**
Page	180

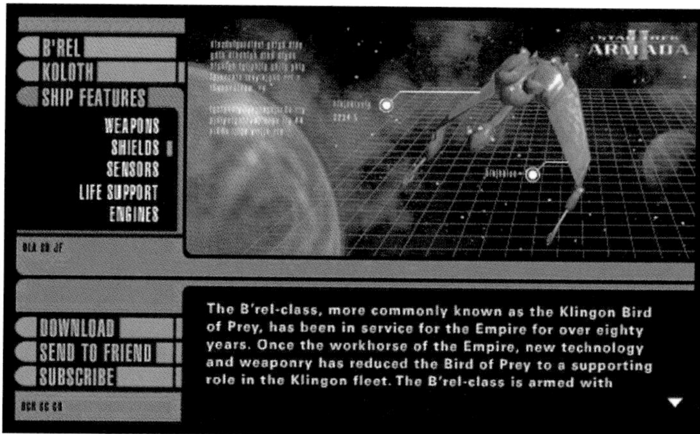

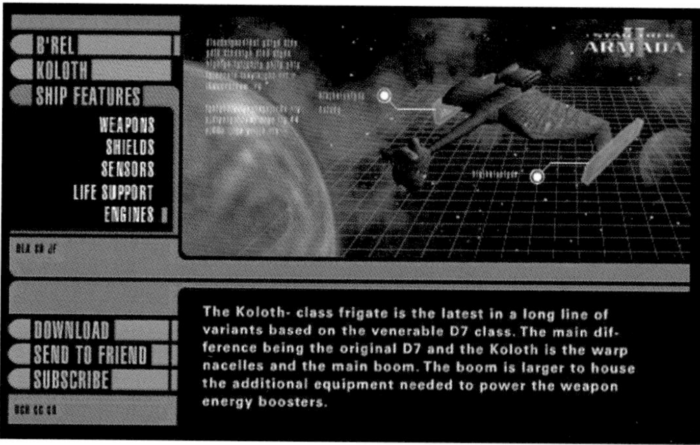

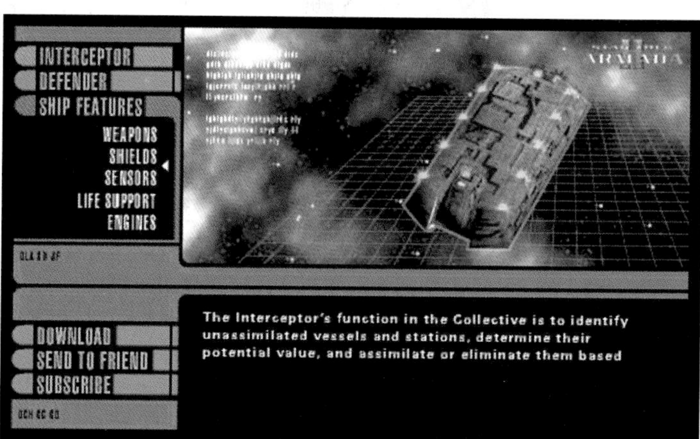

Agency	R/GA - New York
Client	Activision
Executive Producer	John Antinori
Producer	Sheila Dos Santos
VP of Interaction Design	Chris Colborn
Senior Designer	David Alcorn
Designer	John Reis
Progammer	Charles Duncan
Site Builder	Randy Loffelmacher
Q/A	Amy Weidberg
ID	02121N

Award | Merit

Category | **Promotional Advertising — Other Digital Advertising**

5

Agency	Watkinsworldwide - Brooklyn
Client	RCA
Art Director	Kevin Watkins
Writer	Kevin Watkins
Creative Directors	Dean Hacohen, Niko Courtelis
Producer	Alex Saltzman
Music/Sound	Baron & Baron, Lindsay Jehan
ID	02122N

Award	Merit
Category	**Promotional Advertising — Other Digital Advertising**
Page	182

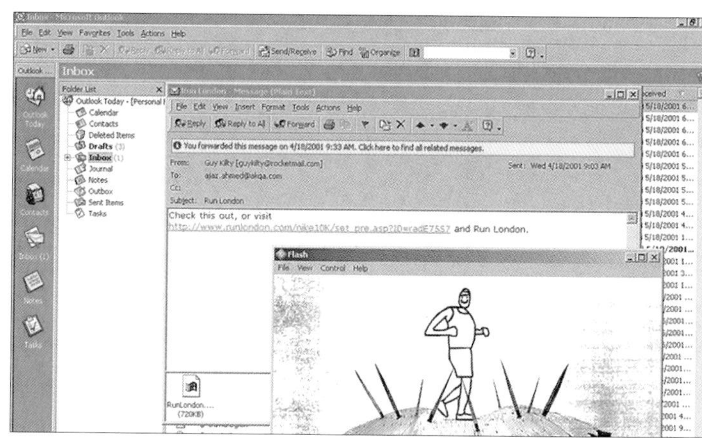

Agency	AKQA - London
Client	Nike
Art Director	James Hilton
Writers	James Hilton, Roger Beckett
Creative Director	James Hilton
Designers	James Hilton, Andrew Richardson
Photographer	Tiina Bjork
Programmers	Matthew Elwin, Guy Kilty, Rob Allen Julian Sweeting, Ben Brook
Producer	Andy Hood
Digital Artist/Multimedia	Elliot Brant
ID	02123N
URL	www.runlondon.com

Award	Merit
Category	**Corporate Image B2C — Web Sites**

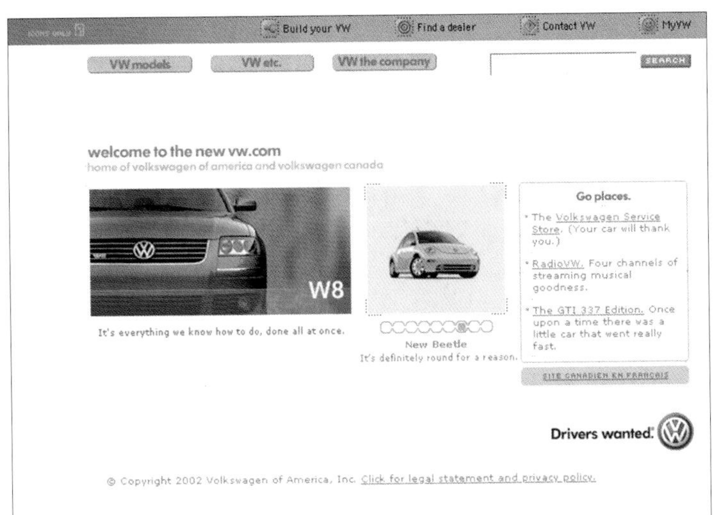

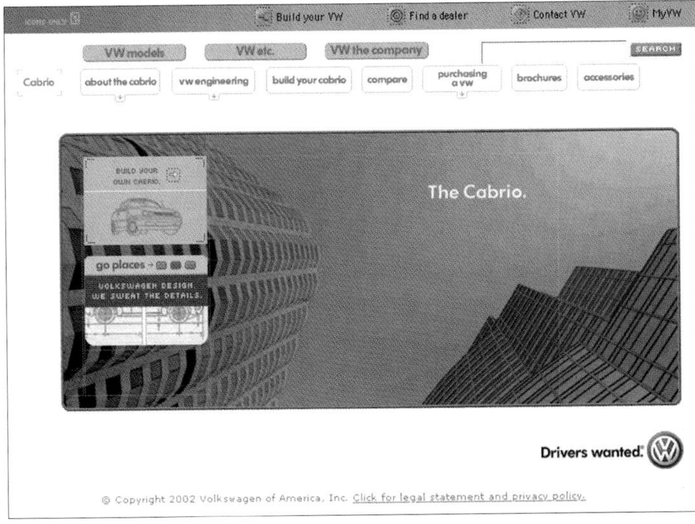

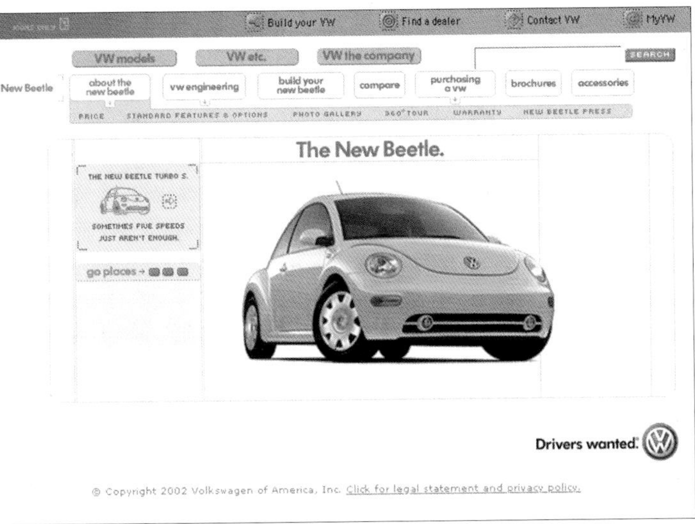

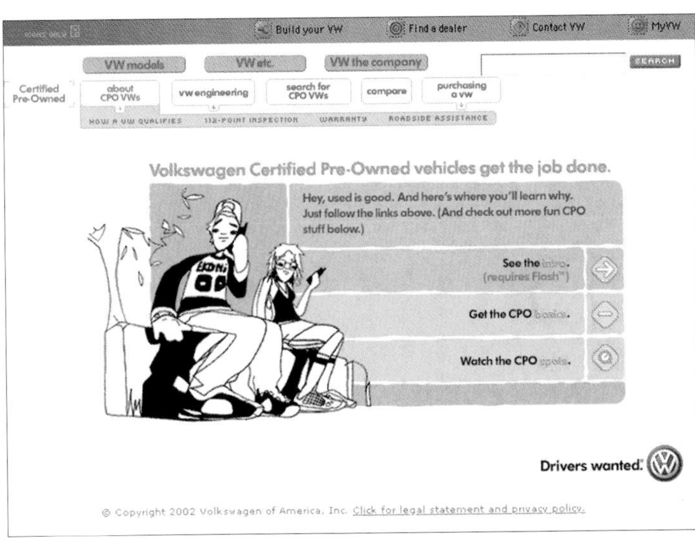

Agency	Arnold Worldwide - Boston
Client	Volkswagen of America
Art Directors	Dmitri Cavander, Nicole McDonald Mike Gatti, Chris Bradley
Writers	Kerry Lynch, Rob Thompson, Alex Russell Eitan Chitayat, Tim Brunelle
Creative Directors	Ron Lawner, Alan Pafenbach Chris Bradley, Tim Brunelle
Designers	Will McGinness, Cindy Moon Mark Van Norden
Information Architects	Deb Brown, Patrick Eddy
Producers	Jennifer Iwanicki, Jennifer Phillips-Bruns Marnie Jones, Lily Weitzman, Tony Biel Ken Kingdon, Jane Conlin, Anna Meyer Erica Lohnes, Shannon Rutkowsky
Mechanical Directors	Claudine Kaprielian, Mike Shafran
Programmer	Silverline
Digital Artists/Multimedia	Matt Murphy, Wylie Fisher, Christine Cook
Technical Directors	Jonathan Groves, Roy Wetherbee
ID	02124N
URL	vw.com
Award	Merit
Category	**Corporate Image B2C — Web Sites**
Page	184

Agency	Bent Media - New Orleans
Client	McIlhenny Company
Art Director	Jared Coffin
Writer	Julie Koppman
Creative Director	Brad Brewster
Designer	Jared Coffin
Photographers	Mark Andresen, Syndey Byrd
Information Architects	Brad Brewster, Julie Koppman Jennifer Beyt, Donna Lanasa Court Batson, Jared Coffin Dan Haugh
Programmers	Dasher Egger, Austin Luminais
Digital Artist/Multimedia	Jared Coffin, Court Batson, Dan Haugh, Chris Grab, Anoop Prasad Jennifer Beyt
Producer	Jennifer Beyt
Music/Sound	Court Batson
ID	02125N
URL	www.tabasco.com
Award	Merit
Category	**Corporate Image B2C — Web Sites**

Agency	Digital@JWT - New York
Client	Lipton
Art Director	Eric Lundquist
Writer	Patrick Clarke
Creative Director	Steve Coulson
Designers	Michael Gallay, Michael Stern
Programmer	Corey Holzer
Producer	Kristin Gilooly
Digital Artist/Multimedia	Samantha Lesiger
Music/Sound	Richard M. Davidson
ID	02126N
URL	www.matikafusions.com

Award	Merit
Category	**Corporate Image B2C — Web Sites**
Page	186

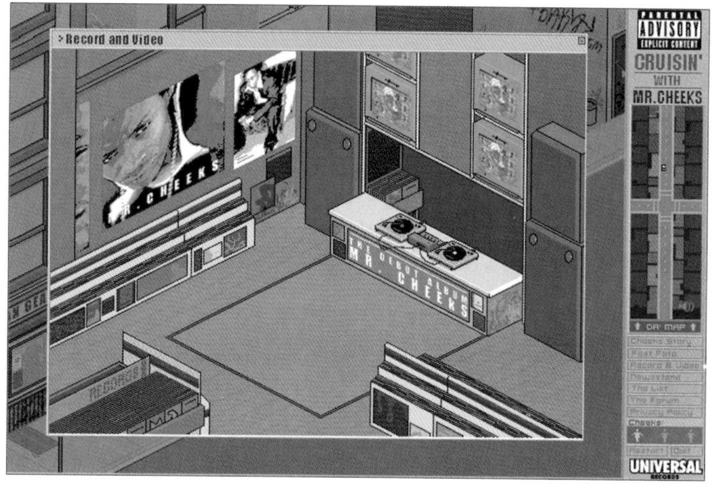

Agency	Fusebox - New York
Client	Universal Records
Art Director	Steven Newman
Creative Director	Steven Newman
Designer	George Ernst
Photographers	George Ernst, Danielle Huthart
Information Architect	Steven Newman
Programmers	James Longley, Rob Hudak, Rob Schroeder, Barry Kiffer
Producer	Laura Michaels
Music/Sound	Mr. Cheeks
ID	02127N
URL	www.fusebox.com/entries/oneshow

Award Merit

Category **Corporate Image B2C — Web Sites**

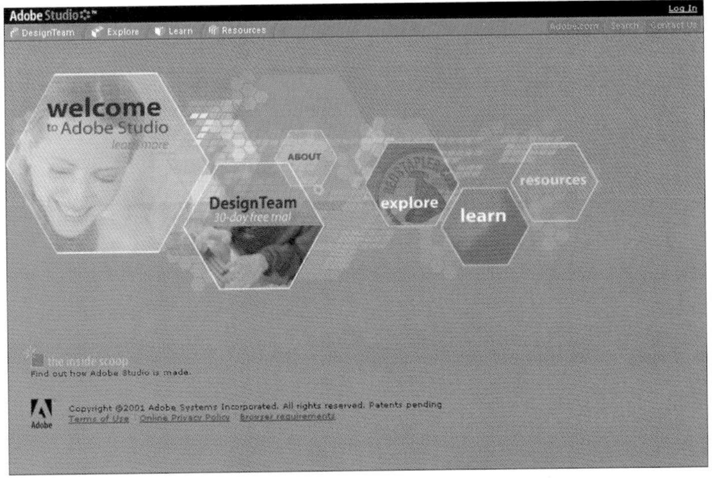

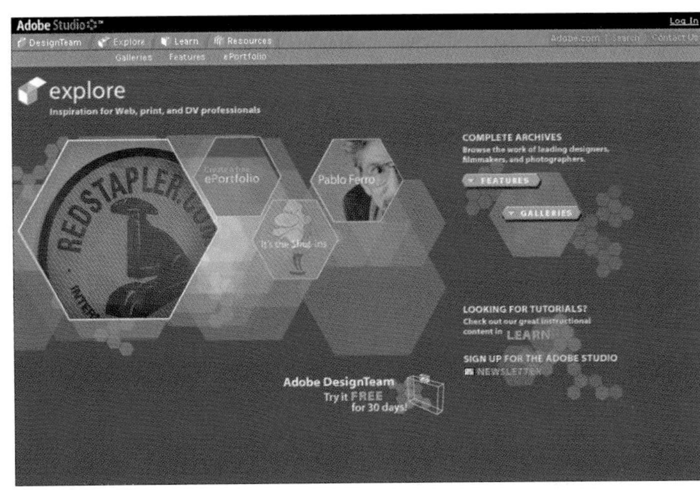

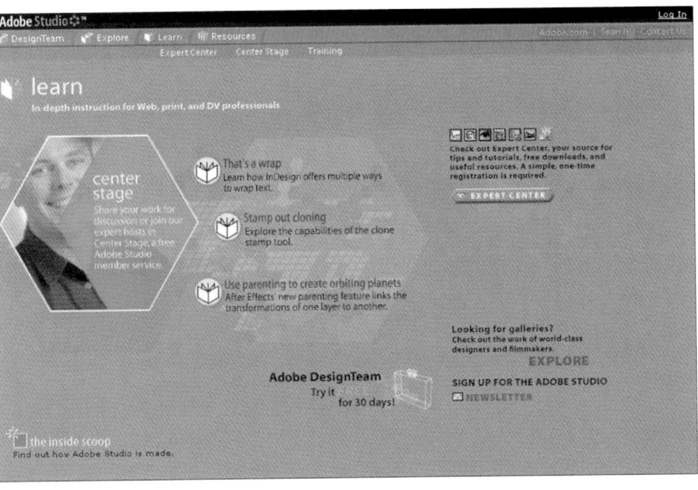

Agency	hillmancurtis - New York
Client	Adobe Systems
Art Director	Ian Kovalik
Writer	Adobe Systems
Creative Director	Hillman Curtis
Designers	Hillman Curtis, Ian Kovalik Matthew Horn, Grant Collier, Alex Lin
Producer	Homera J. Chaudhry
Information Architect	Adobe Systems Incorporated
Programmers	Adobe Systems Incorporated Hillman Curtis
ID	02128N
URL	http://www.hillmancurtis.com/oneshow

Award	Merit
Category	**Corporate Image B2C — Web Sites**
Page	188

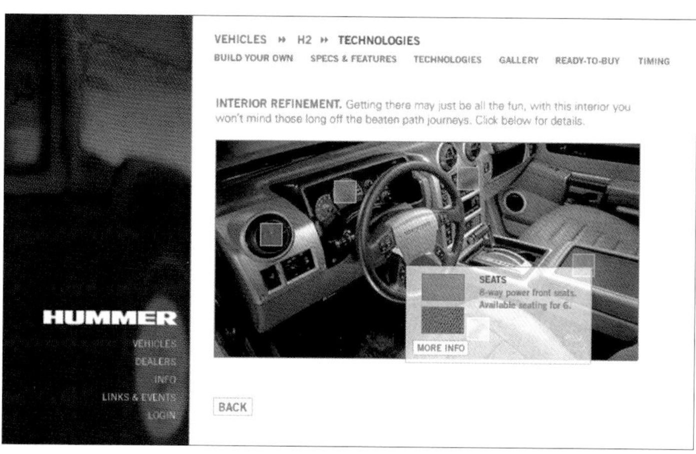

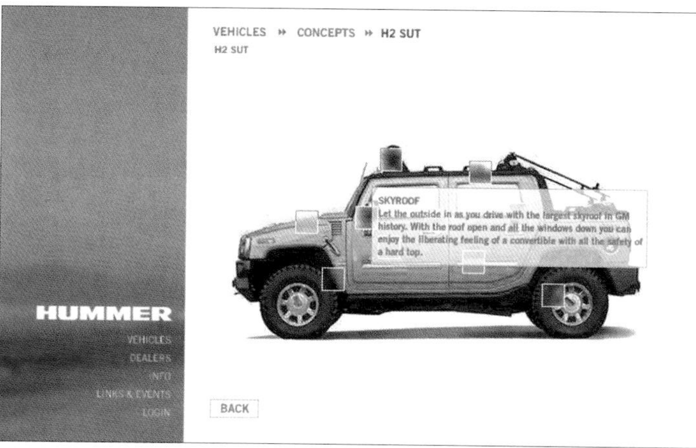

Agency: IdentityOne - Boston
Client: GM/Hummer
Art Directors: Keith Butters, Sara Rubinow, Mike Ma, Tim Stevenson, Will Uronis
Writer: Shane Hutton
Creative Directors: Lance Jenson, Gary Koepke, Tim Stevenson, Mike Ma
Designers: Emily Taylor, Abigail Taylor, Skot Kremen, Ingrid Aue, Dan Rukas, Ainhize Barrena, Robert Hodgin
ID: 02129N
URL: www.hummer.com

Award: Merit
Category: **Corporate Image B2C — Web Sites**

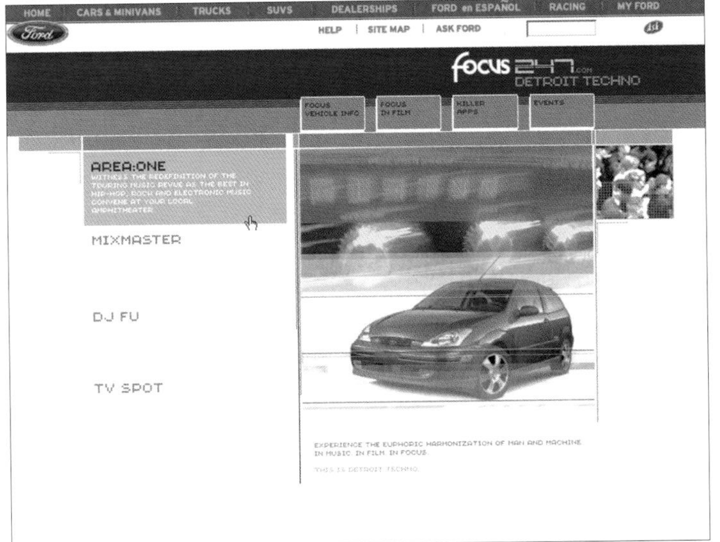

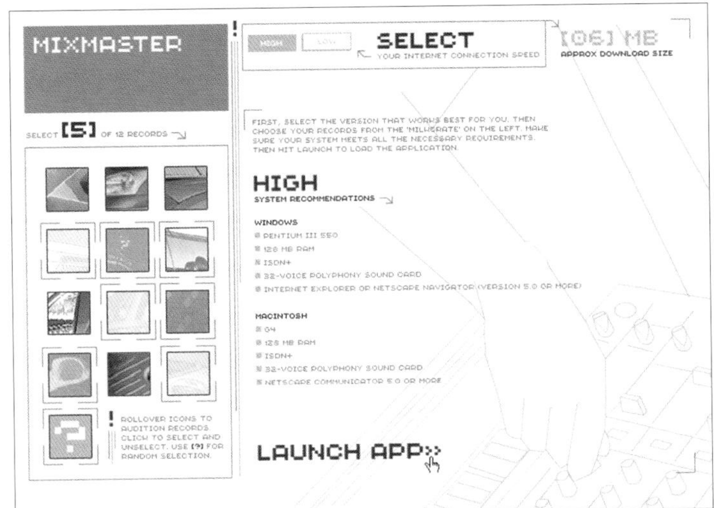

Agency	J. Walter Thompson - Detroit
Client	Ford Motor Company
Art Directors	Doug Wojciechowski, Barry Cole Michelangelo Cicerone, Daniel Przekop
Writers	Bryan Lark, Daniel Przekop
Creative Directors	Suzanne Sadek, Daniel Przekop
Designer	Doug Wojciechowski
Producer	Traci Kranz
Photographer	Doug Wojciechowski
Information Architect	Dennis Schleicher
Programmer	BUTCH
Digital Artist/Multimedia	Justin Mysza
Music/Sound	DJ Bone
ID	02130N
URL	http://www.focus247.com

Award	Merit
Category	**Corporate Image B2C — Web Sites**
Page	190

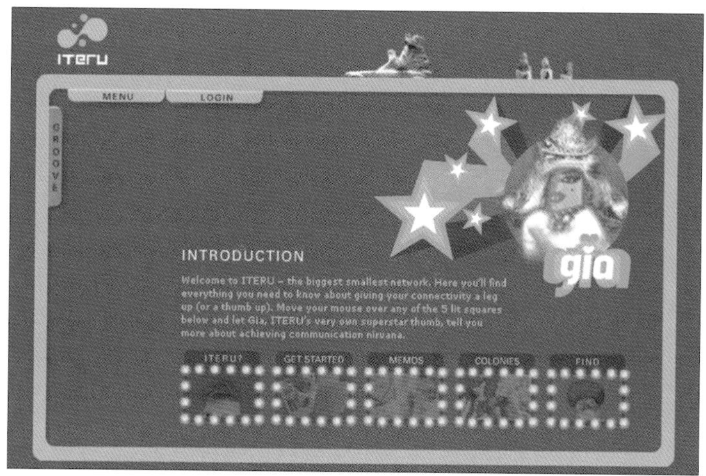

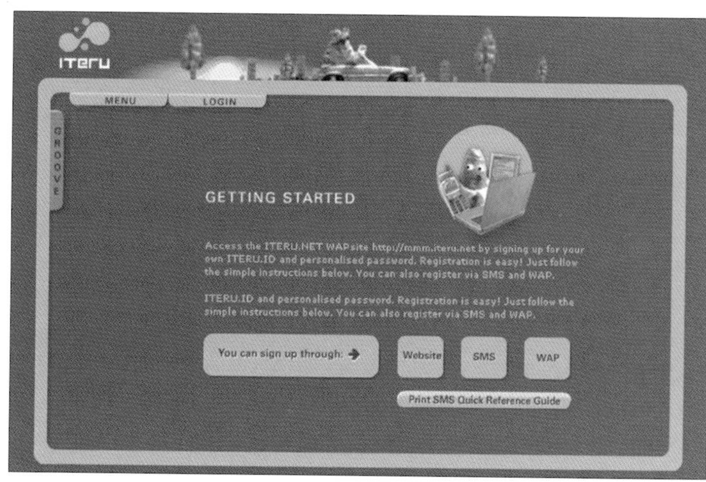

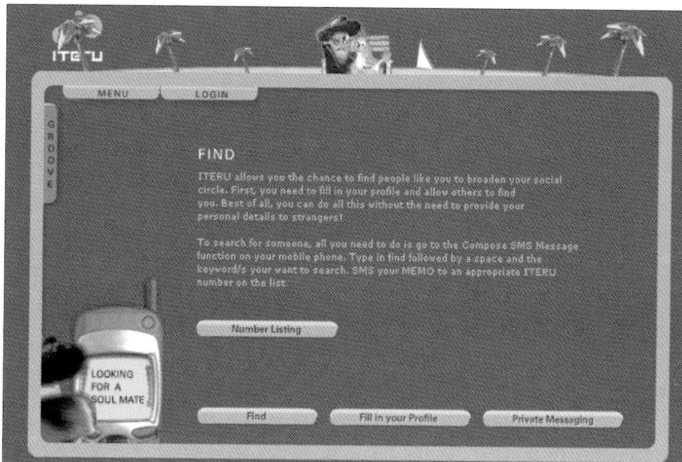

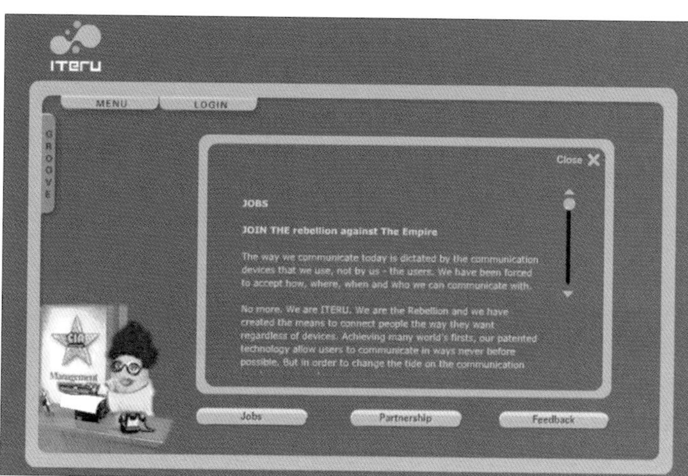

Agency	Kinetic Interactive - Singapore
Client	Iteru.net
Art Director	Sean Lam
Writer	Iteru.net
Designer	Sean Lam, Daphnie Foo
Photographer	Sean Lam
Producer	Elaine Tay
Information Architects	Sean Lam, Elaine Tay
Programmer	Benjy Choo
Digital Artist/Multimedia	Sean Lam
Music/Sound	Victor Low
ID	02131N
URL	www.iteru.net

Award	Merit
Category	**Corporate Image B2C — Web Sites**

Freestyle shops Philosophy Booking Service Technical services Freestyle Extras

Education

Cleanliness

Dresscode

105.9

Choose English Version

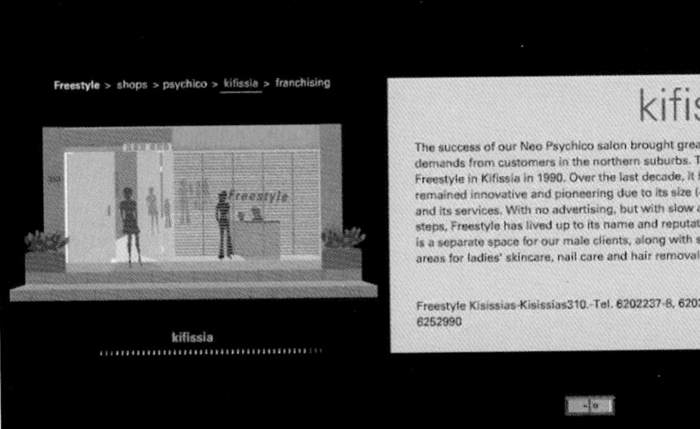

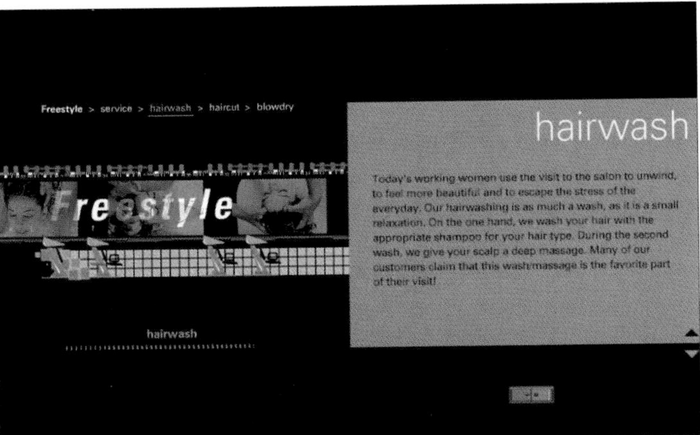

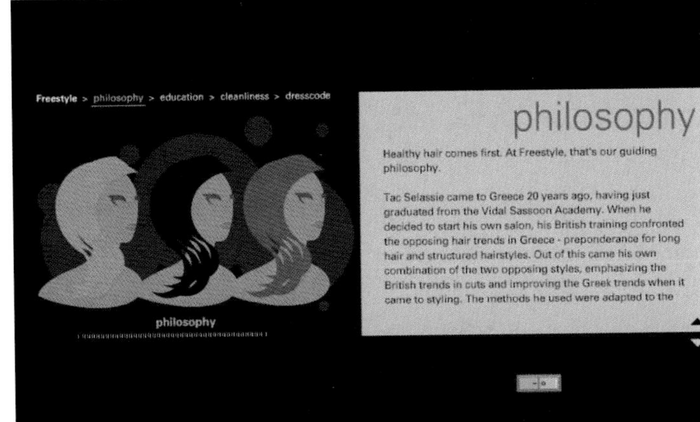

Agency	Milk Creative Source - Athens
Client	Freestyle Salons
Art Director	Leonie Yagdjoglou
Writers	Vilma Papassava, Kelly Lambrou
Photographers	Yiorgos Hatzakos, Leonie Yagdjoglou
Information Architect	Ellie Bakopoulou
Producer	Realize Productions
Programmer	Harris Karonis
ID	02132N
URL	freestyle-salons.gr

Award	Merit
Category	**Corporate Image B2C — Web Sites**
Page	192

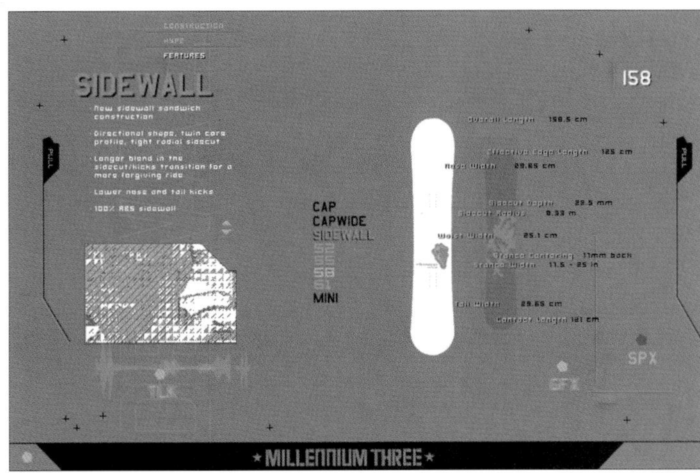

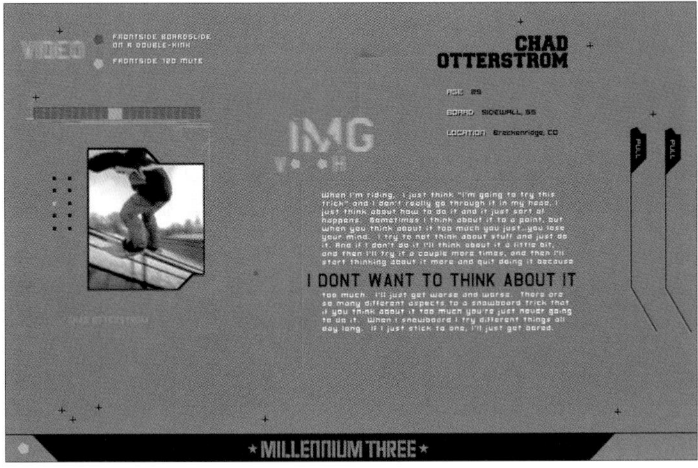

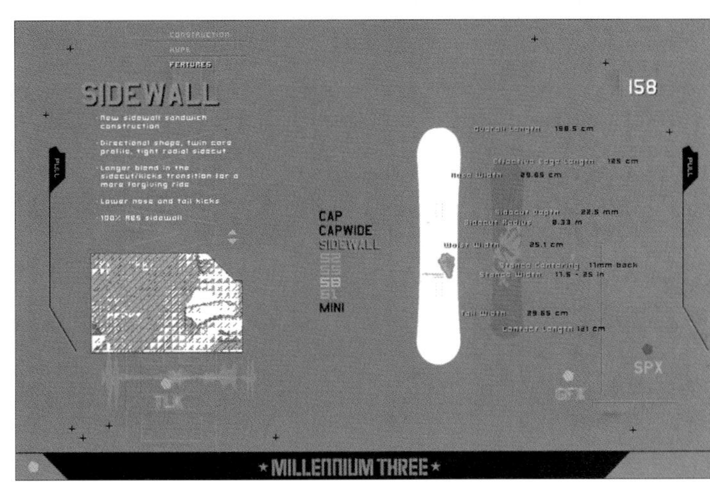

16

Agency	Paris France - Portland
Client	Millenium 3
Art Director	Jeff Faulkner
Creative Directors	Doug Lowell, Jeff Faulkner
Designer	Erik Falat
Executive Producer	Chuck Nobles
Engineer	Sophie Schmidt
Technical Director	Scott Trotter
ID	02133N
URL	www.m-three.com

Award	Merit
Category	**Corporate Image B2C — Web Sites**

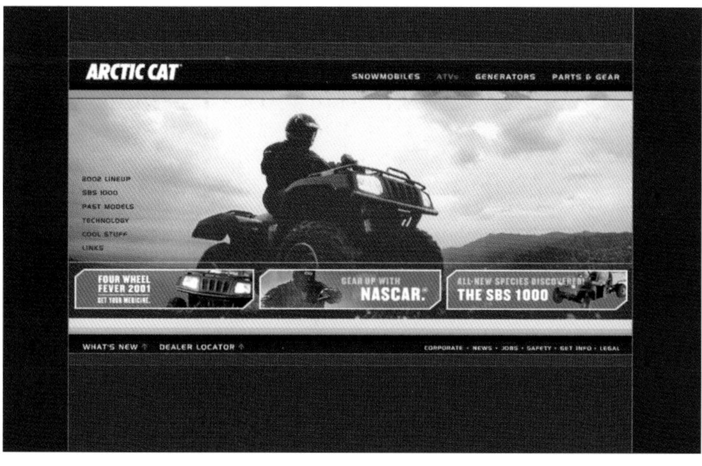

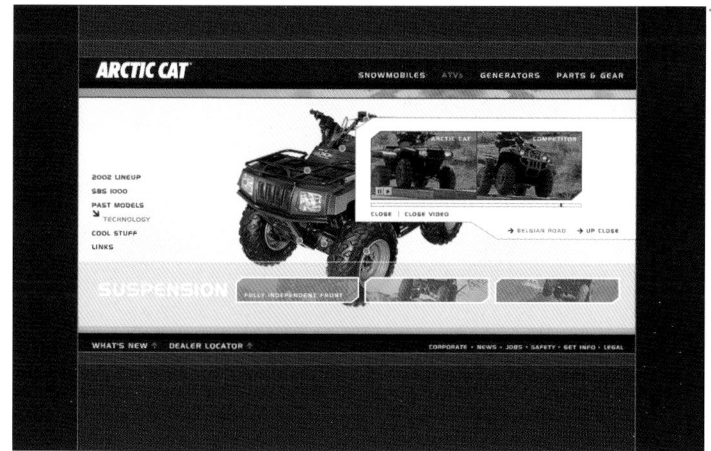

Agency: Periscope - Minneapolis
Client: Arctic Cat
Art Director: Andy Gugel
Writer: Katerina Martchouk
Creative Director: Chris Cortilet
Photographers: Richard Hamilton Smith, Eric Emmings
Producer: Matt Hattenberger
Programmer: David Duffy
Digital Artist/Multimedia: Andy Gugel, Natalia Berglund
Music/Sound: Stock
ID: 02134N
URL: www.periscope.com/awards/atv

Award: Merit
Category: **Corporate Image B2C — Web Sites**
Page: 194

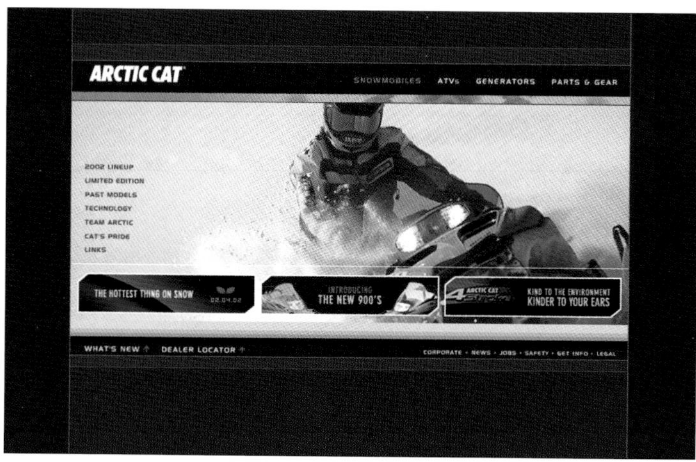

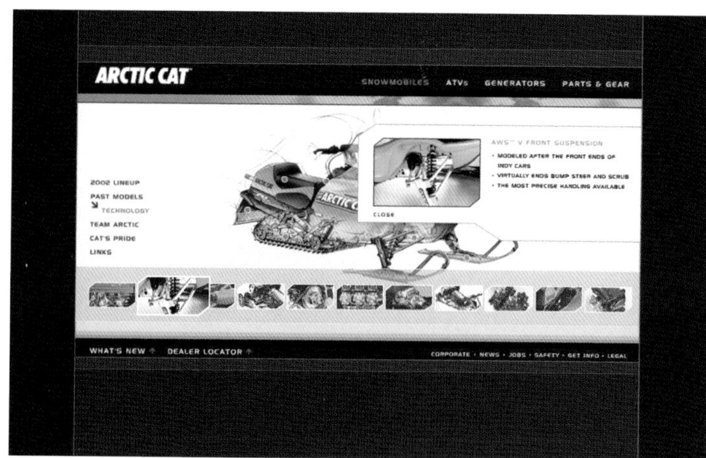

Agency	Periscope - Minneapolis
Client	Arctic Cat
Art Director	Andy Gugel
Writer	Katerina Martchouk
Creative Director	Chris Cortilet
Photographers	Richard Hamilton Smith, Eric Emmings
Programmers	David Duffy, Steve Killingbeck
Producer	Matt Hattenberger
Digital Artist/Multimedia	Andy Gugel, Steve Killingbeck
Music/Sound	Stock
ID	02135N
URL	www.periscope.com/awards/snow

Award	Merit
Category	**Corporate Image B2C — Web Sites**

Agency	POP - New York
Client	Bendable Rubber
Art Director	Vincent Lacava
Creative Director	Vincent Lacava
Photographer	Aaron Stewart
Programmer	Veronique Brossier
Music/Sound	Michael Sweet
ID	02136N
URL	www.bendablerubber.com

Award	Merit
Category	**Corporate Image B2C — Web Sites**
Page	196

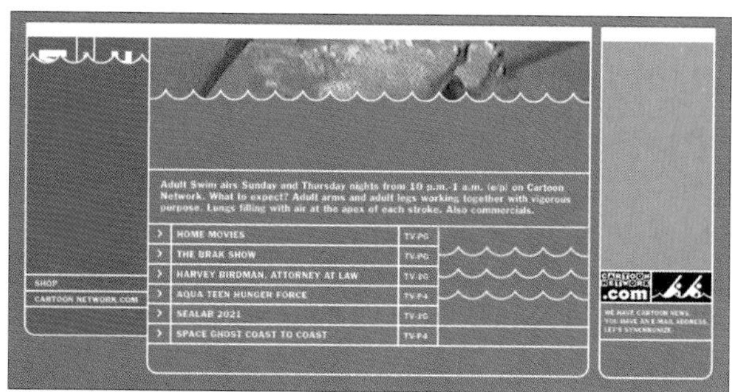

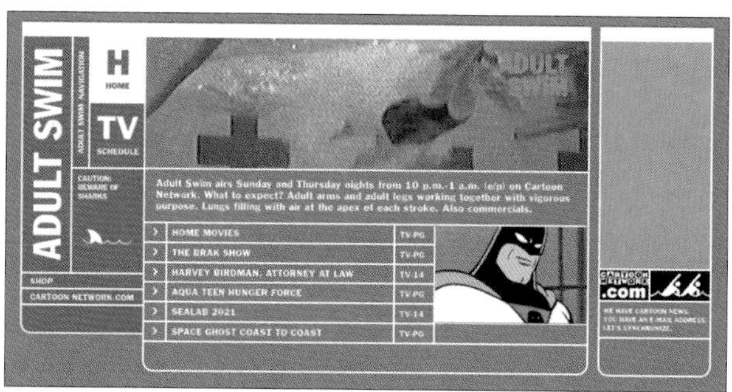

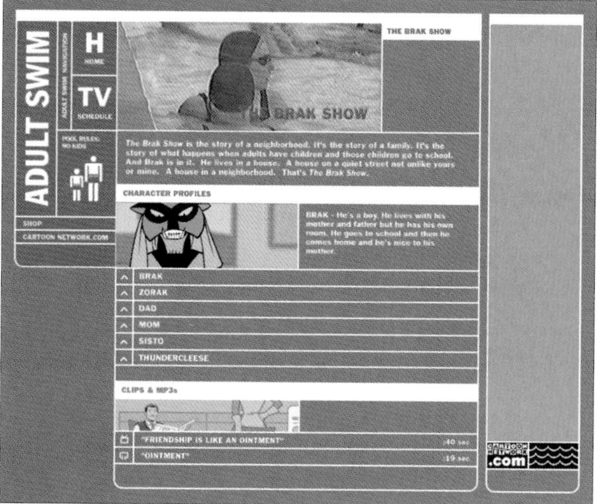

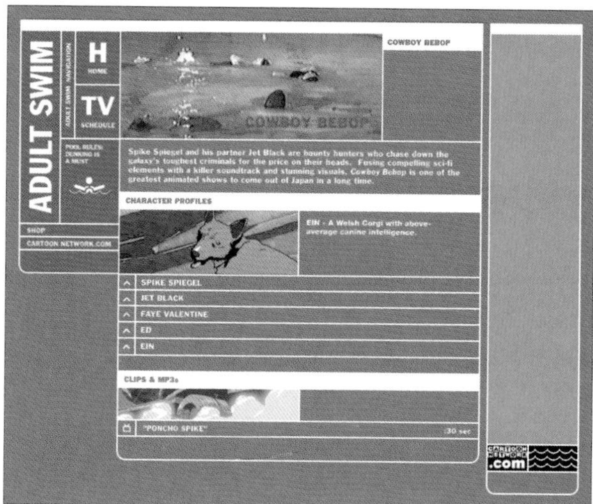

Agency | POP - New York
Client | Cartoon Network
Art Director | Vander McClain
Creative Director | Vincent Lacava
Designer | Jesse McGowan
Programmer | Stephen Griffin
Producer | Maureen Reilly
Digital Artist/Multimedia | Aaron Stewart
ID | 02137N
URL | www.adultswim.com

Award | Merit
Category | **Corporate Image B2C — Web Sites**

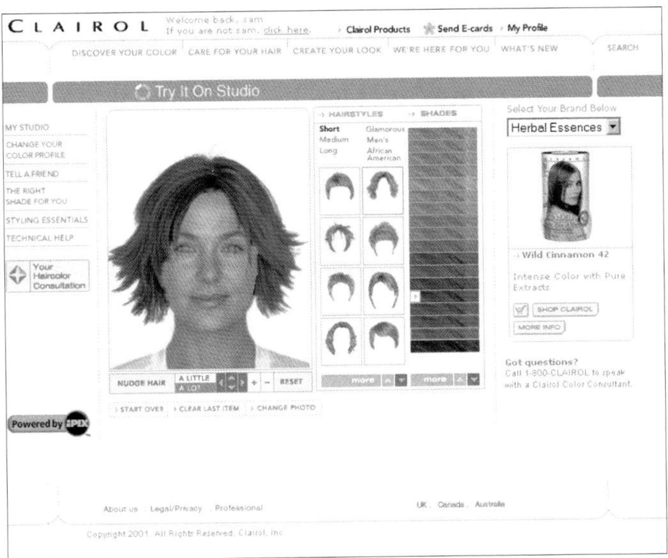

Agency	R/GA - New York
Client	Clairol
Art Director	Winston Thomas
Designers	Lesli Karavil, Daniel Chen Scott Weiland
Producers	Kip Voyte, Afua Brown, Jennifer Lazzaro
Programmers	George Matthes, Jungwhan Kim Charles Duncan
Digital Artists/Multimedia	Johanna Langford, Carla Garganus
Tech Leads	Ray Vazquez, Mike Roufa
Q/A	Dan LaPlaca, Sunny Nan
Music	John Reis
ID	02138N
URL	http://www.clairol.com

Award	Merit
Category	**Corporate Image B2C — Web Sites**
Page	198

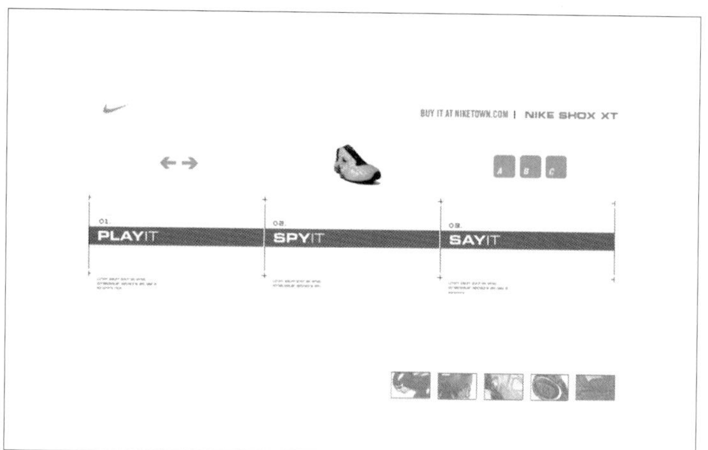

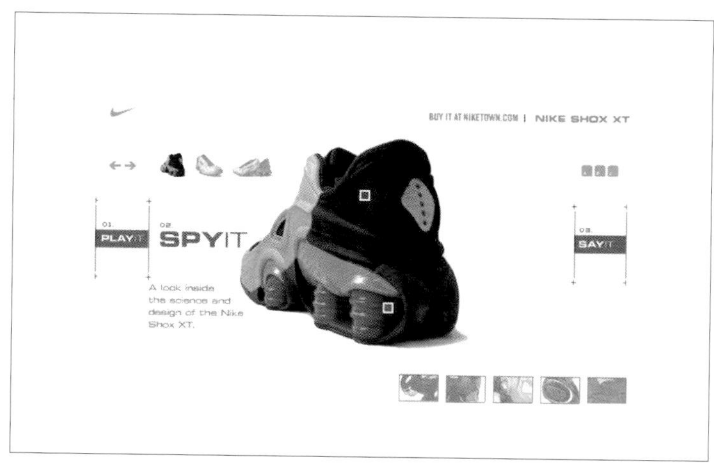

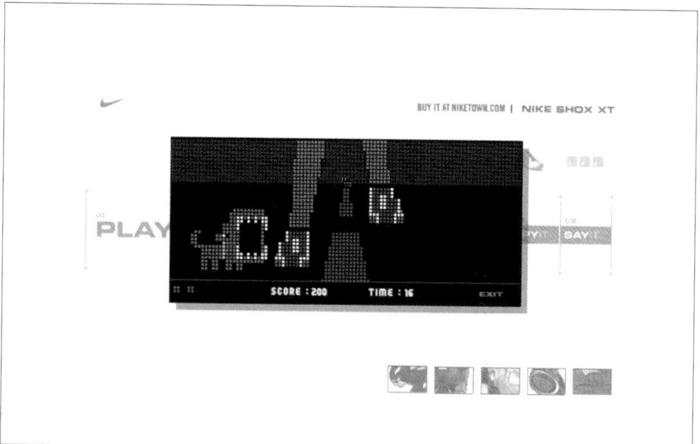

16

Agency	R/GA - New York
Client	Nike
Art Director	Rei Inamoto
Writer	Jym Fahey
Designers	Jerome Austria, Pat Stern, Noel Billig
Producer	Jim Bixler
Engineer	Scott Prindle
Programmers	Charoonkit Thahong, George Matthes
Q/A	Justin Wasik, Amy Weidberg
ID	02139N
URL	http://www.nike.com/xt

Award	Merit
Category	**Corporate Image B2C — Web Sites**

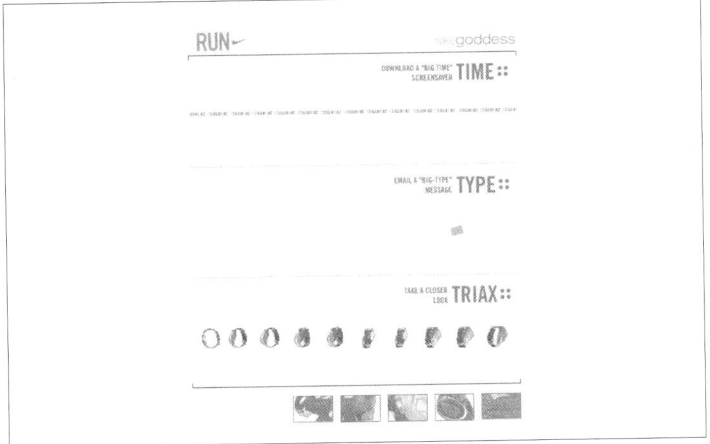

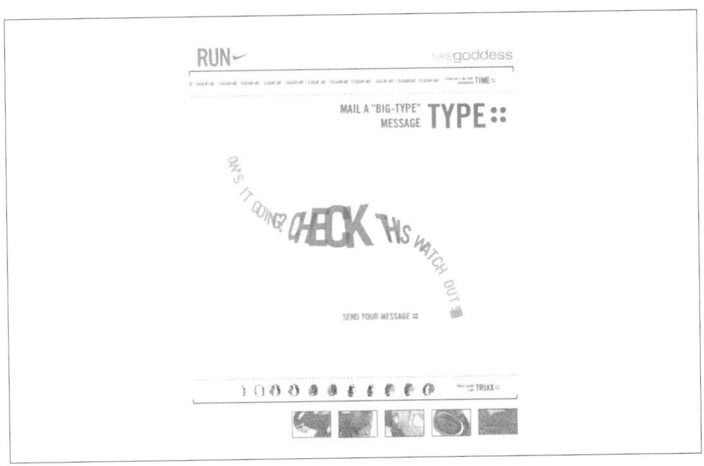

16

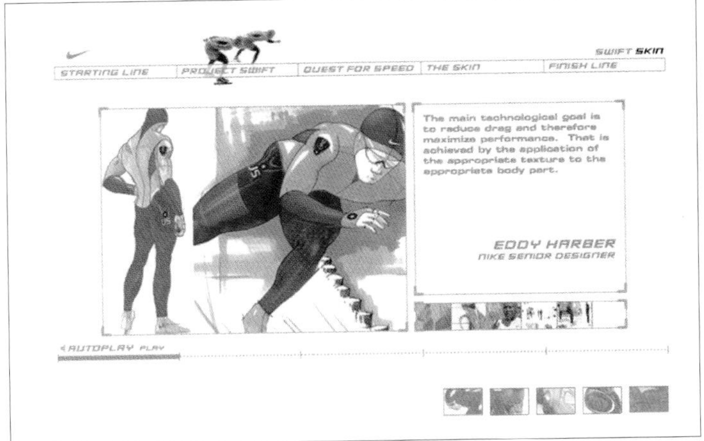

Agency	R/GA - New York
Client	Nike
Art Director	Rei Inamoto
Writer	Jym Fahey
Designer	Pat Stern
Engineer	Scott Prindle
Flash Designers	David Morrow, Jerome Austria, Noel Billig
Producer	Jim Bixler
Programmers	George Matthes , Charoonkit Thahong
Q/A	Justin Wasik,Amy Weidberg
ID	02140N
URL	http://www.nikegoddess/triaxspeed

Award	Merit
Category	**Corporate Image B2C — Web Sites**
Page	200

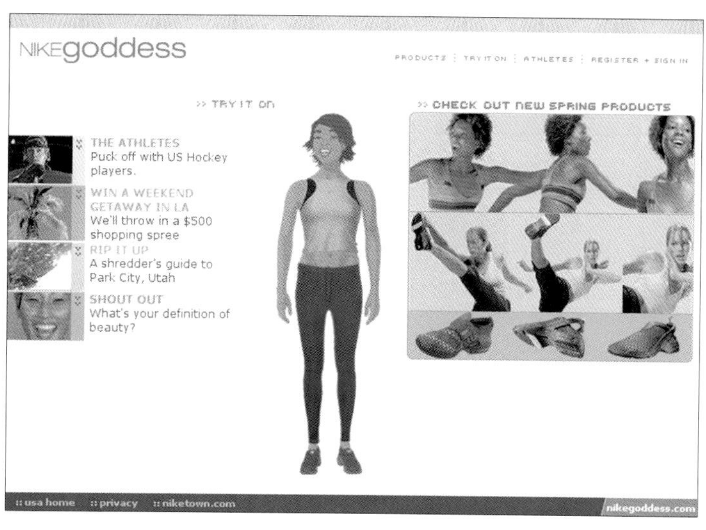

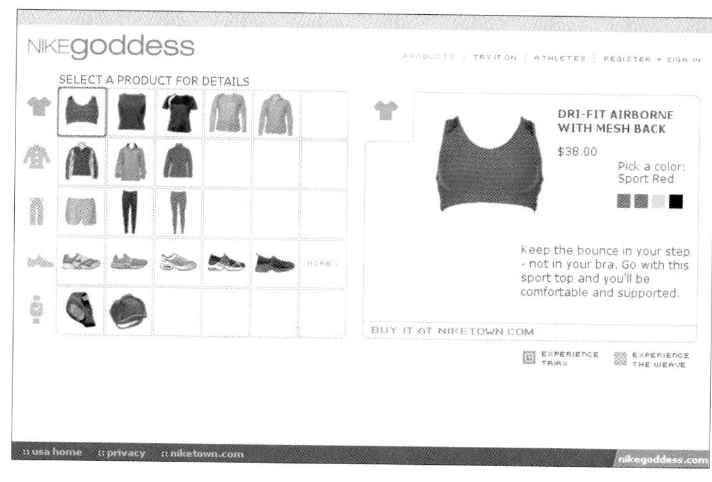

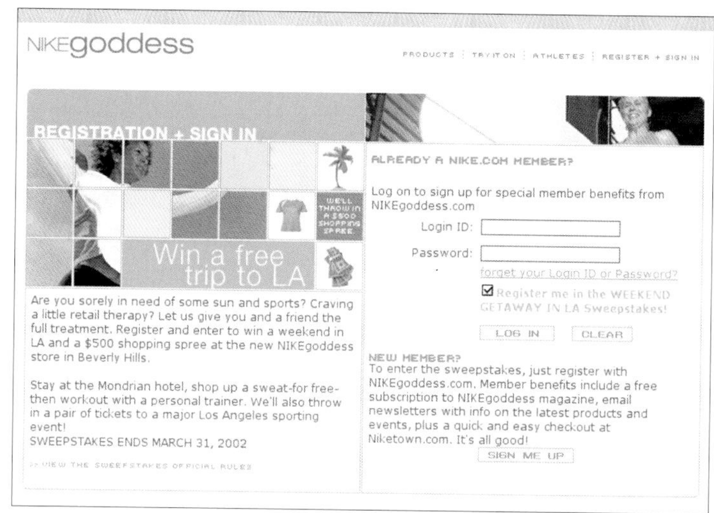

Agency	R/GA - New York
Client	Nike
Art Director	Kris Kiger
Writer	Jean Railla
Designers	Pat Stern, Chloe Gottlieb, Yzabelle Munson
Tech Team Leader	Scott Prindle
Producers	Lisa Morgan, Afua Brown
Account Director	Karen Riley
Digital Artist/Multimedia	Johanna Langford
Programmers	George Matthes, Stan Wiechers
	Charoonkit Thahong, Raymond Vazquez
Q/A	Amy Weidberg, Justin Wasik
ID	02141N
URL	http://www.nike.com/nikegoddess

Award	Merit
Category	**Corporate Image B2C — Web Sites**

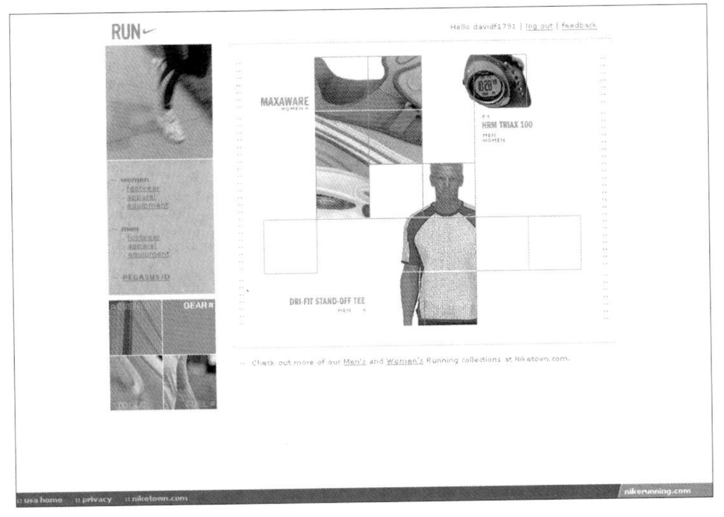

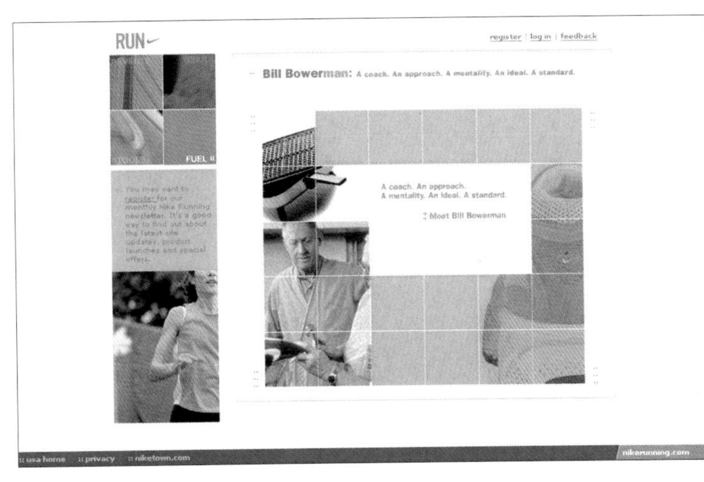

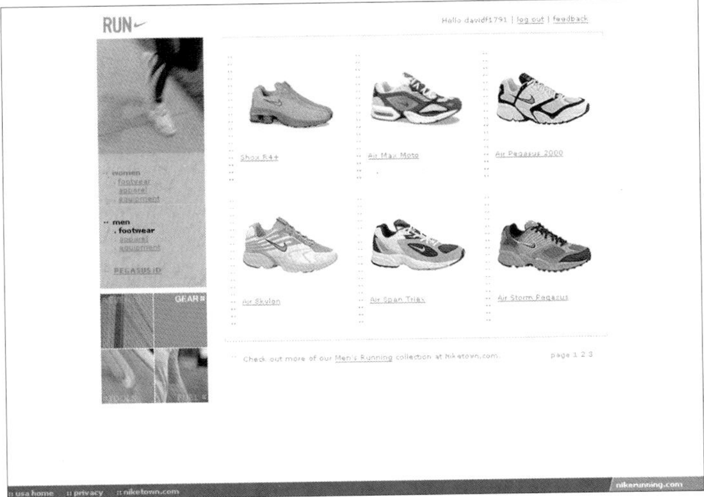

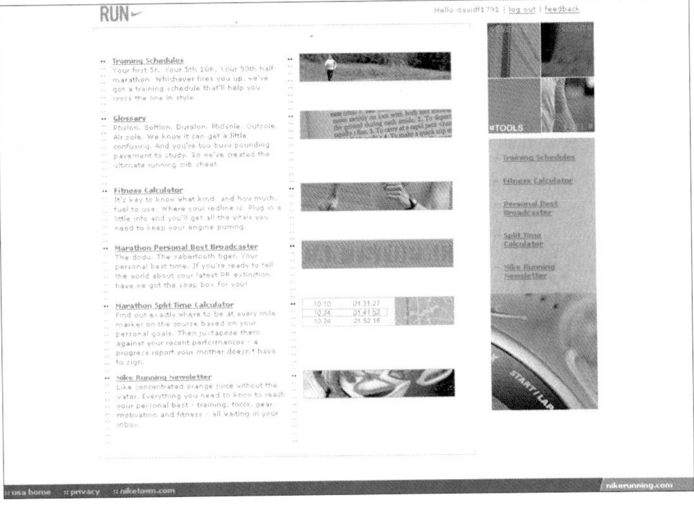

Agency | R/GA - New York
Client | Nike
Art Director | Rei Inamoto
Writer | Jym Fahey
Producers | Julia Rubinic, Jim Bixler
David Frankfurt, Sheila Dos Santos
Designers | Nathan Iverson, Daniel Chen, Garry Waller
Jean Kapp
Interaction Designer | Pat Stern, Sandra Aluoch
Technical Team | Scott Prindle, Justin Wasik
Producer | Neil Webste
ID | 02142N
URL | http://www.nikerunning.com

Award | Merit
Category | **Corporate Image B2C — Web Sites**
Page | 202

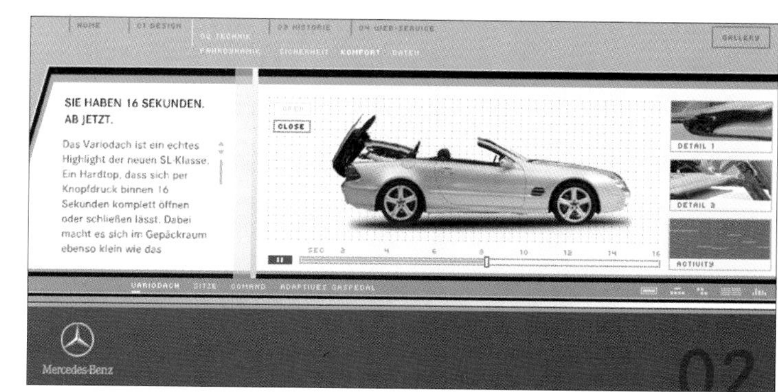

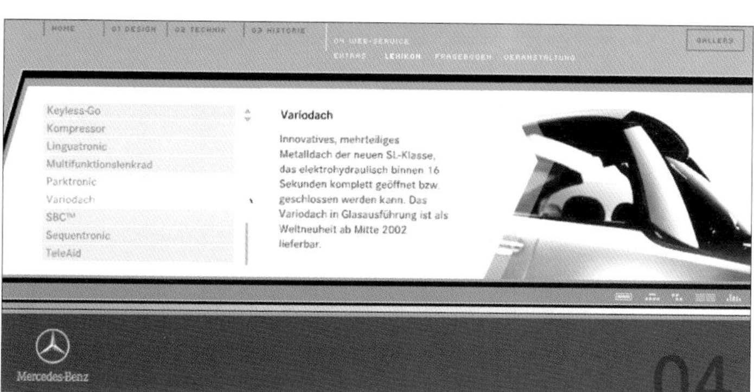

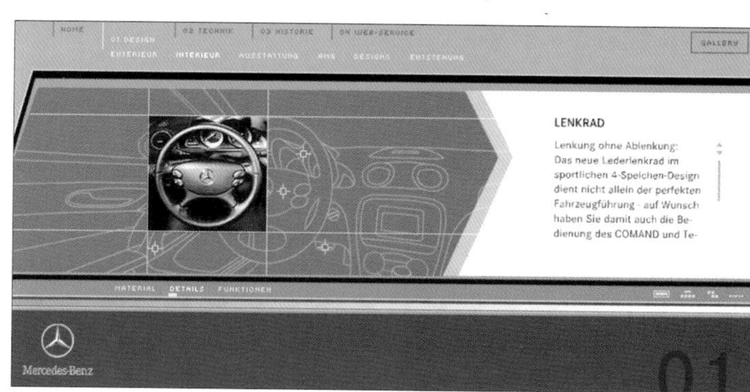

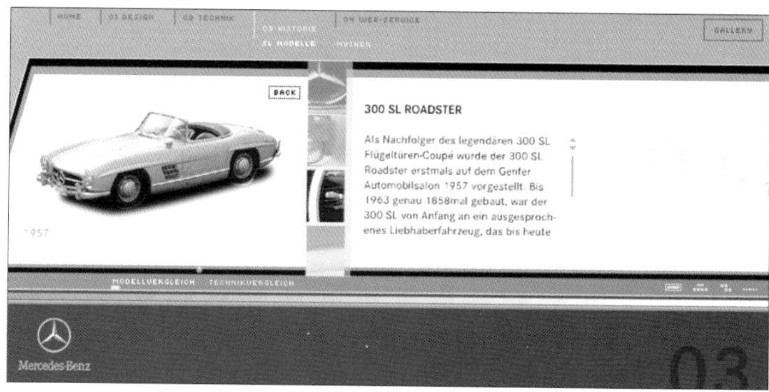

Agency	Scholz & Volkmer - Weisbaden
Client	Mercedes-Benz
Art Director	Oliver Aumann
Writers	Chris Kohl, Carsten Fillinger
Creative Director	Anette Scholz
Designers	Philipp Bareiss, Jenny Fitz
Programmers	Thorsten Kraus, Sebastian Klein
Digital Artists/Multimedia	Sebastian Klein
	Duc-Thien Bui
ID	02143N
URL	www.mercedes-benz.com/sl

Award	Merit
Category	**Corporate Image B2C — Web Sites**

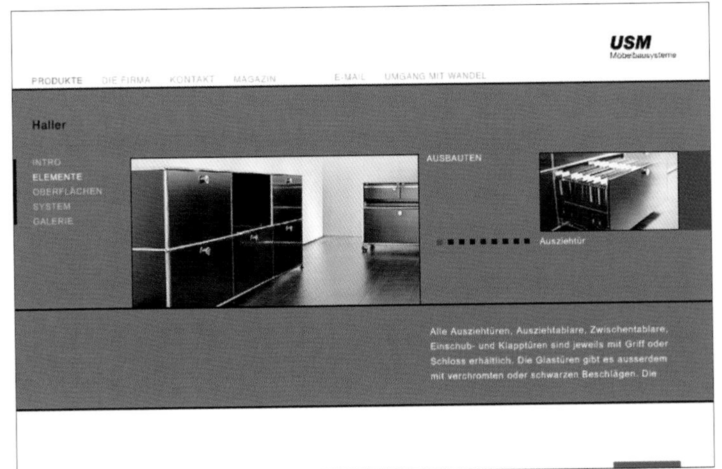

16

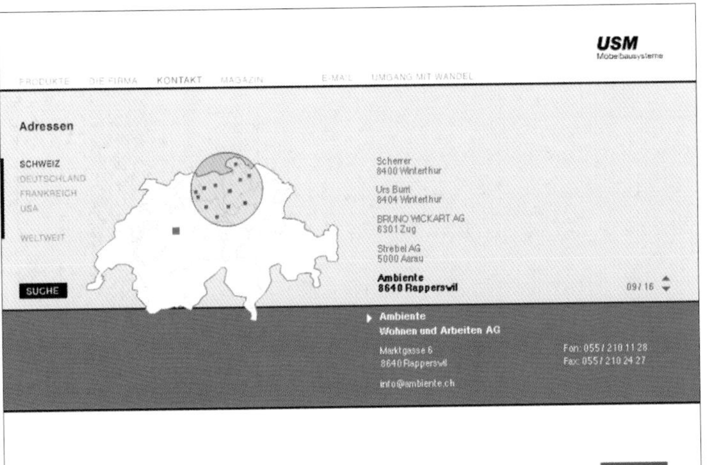

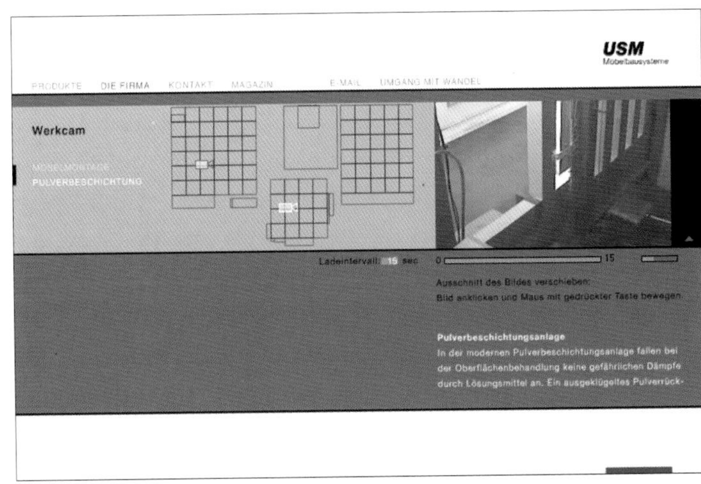

Agency	Scholz & Volkmer - Weisbaden
Client	USM
Art Director	Nicoletta Gerlach
Writer	Mareike Schmiedt
Creative Director	Michael Volkmer
Designers	Elke Grober, Heike Brockmann
Programmers	Manfred Kraft, Peter Reichard
Digital Artist/Multimedia	Christian Leitschuh
ID	02144N
URL	www.usm.com

Award	Merit
Category	**Corporate Image B2C — Web Sites**
Page	204

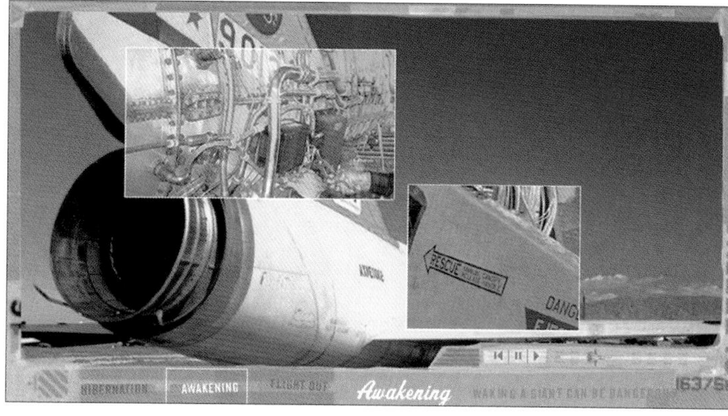

Agency	Second Story - Portland
Client	Eastman Kodak
Art Director	Gabe Kean
Creative Director	Brad Johnson
Designers	Gabe Kean, Martin Linde
Photographer	David Kassnoff
Information Architect	Julie Beeler
Producer	Aleen Adams
Programmers	Sebastien Chevrel, Sam Ward
Digital Artists/Multimedia	Martin Linde, Sam Ward
Music/Sound	Brad Purkey
ID	02145N
URL	http://www.kodak.com/country/US/en/corp/features/sleepingGiants/index.shtml

Award	Merit
Category	**Corporate Image B2C — Web Sites**

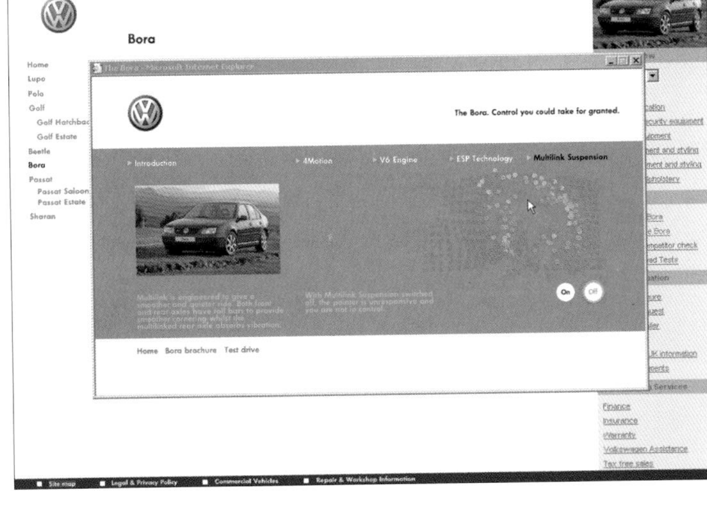

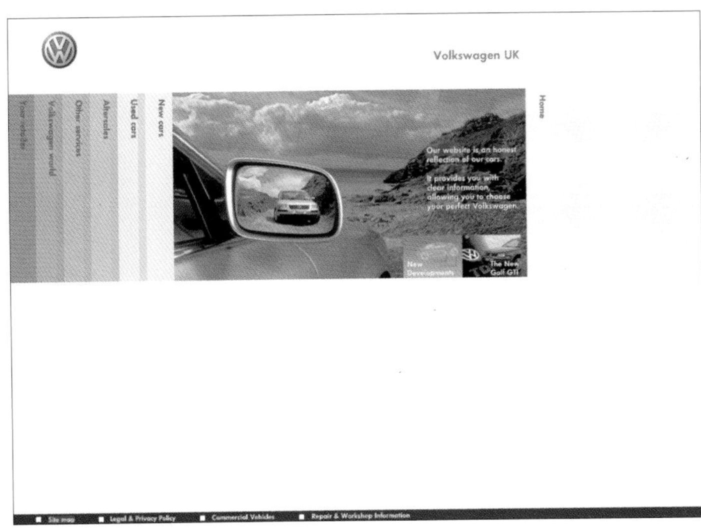

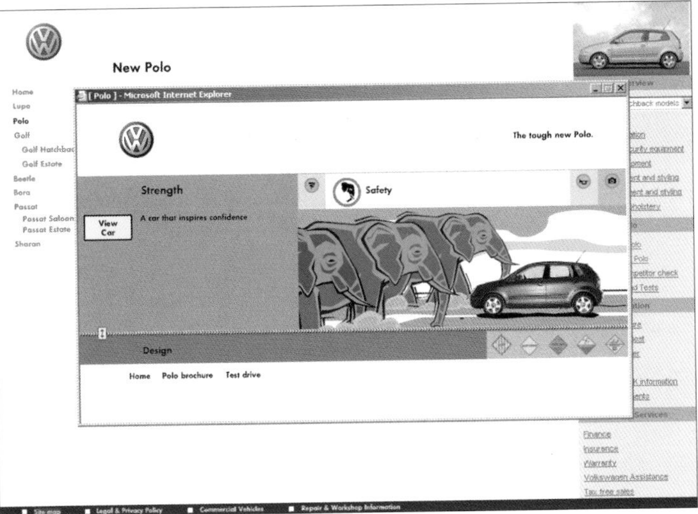

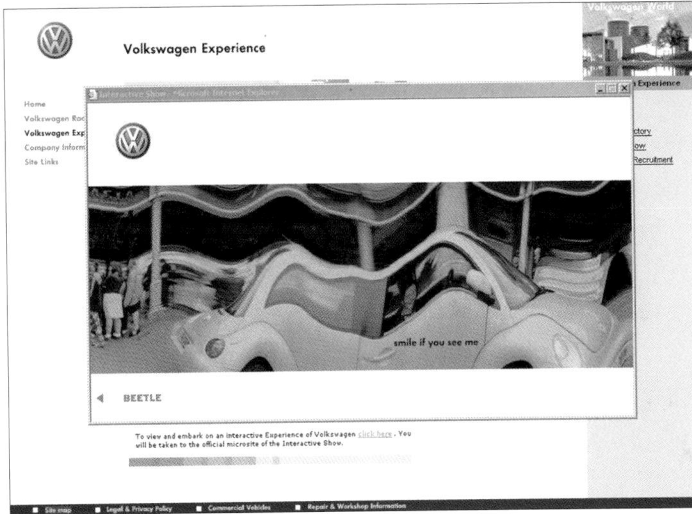

16

Agency	Tribal DDB Worldwide - London
Client	Volkswagen
Creative Directors	Sam Ball, Dave Bedwood
Designer	Tonic
Producer	Sally Gallagher
ID	02146N
URL	www.volkswagen.co.uk

Award	Merit
Category	**Corporate Image B2C — Web Sites**
Page	206

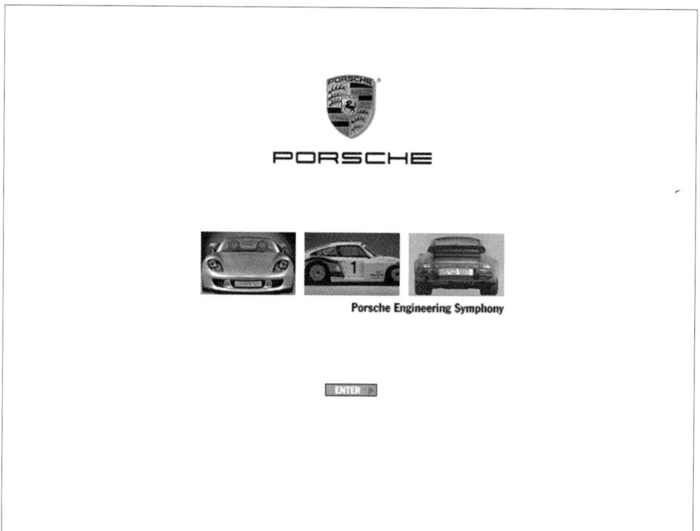

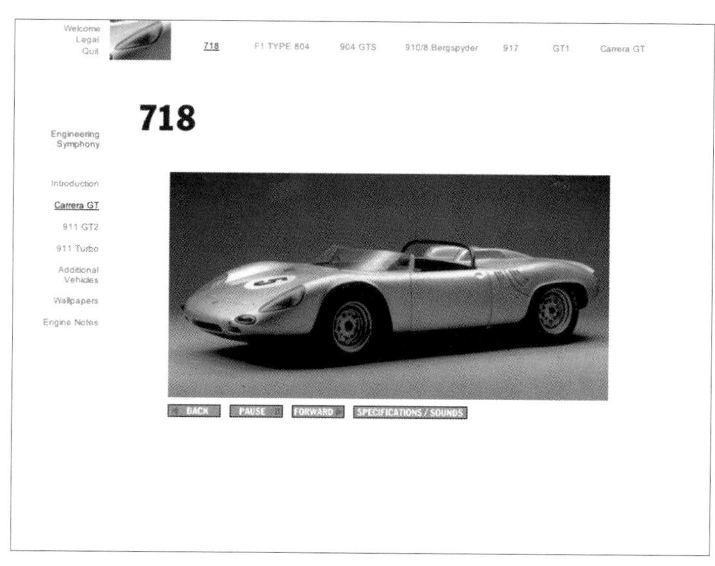

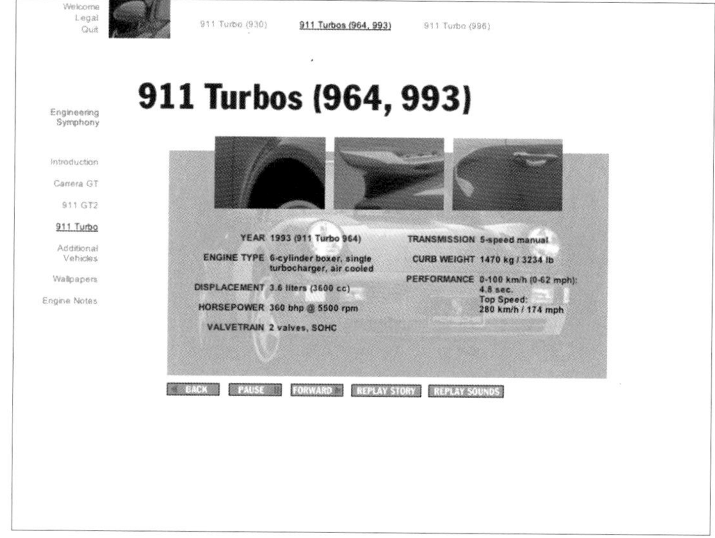

Agency	Carmichael Lynch - Minneapolis
Client	Porsche
Writer	Pete Demarest
Creative Director	Jud Smith
Designer	Bob Muffelman
Producer	Sarah Salita
Programmer	Bob Muffelman
Digital Artist/Multimedia	Bob Muffelman
Music/Sound	Babble-On Recording Studios
ID	02147N

Award	Merit
Category	**Corporate Image B2C — CD-ROMs**

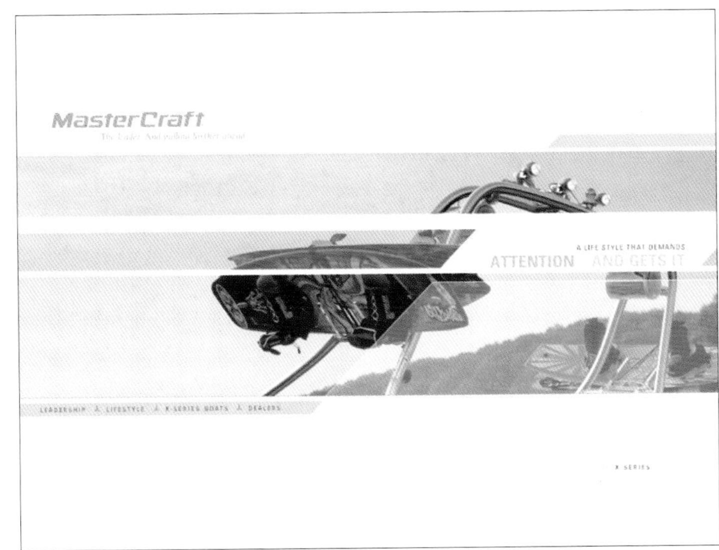

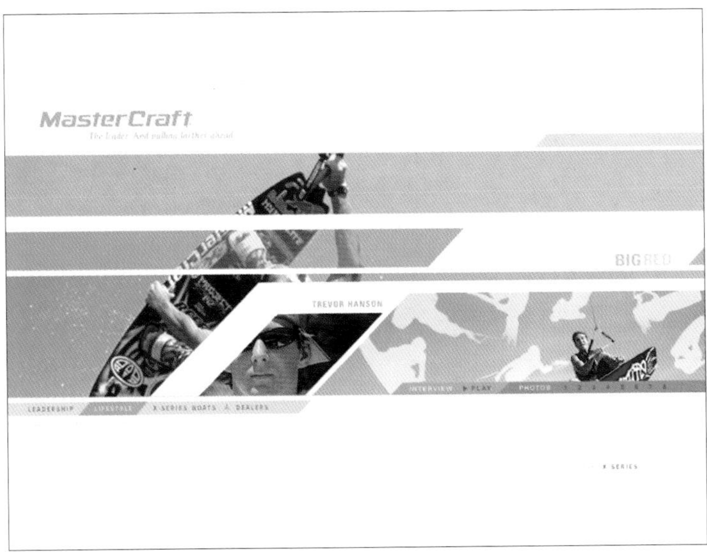

Agency	Periscope - Minneapolis
Client	MasterCraft Boats
Art Directors	Andy Gugel, T.Scott Major
Writers	Katerina Martchouk, Gene Valek
Creative Director	Chris Cortilet
Producer	Matt Hattenberger
Photographers	Tom King, Eric Emmings Florida Film & Tape, LMK Productions
Programmers	Todd Mitchell, Jesse Kaczmarek
Digital Artist/Multimedia	Bret McQuinn
Music/Sound	Echo Boys
ID	02148N

Award	Merit
Category	**Corporate Image B2C — CD-ROMs**
Page	208

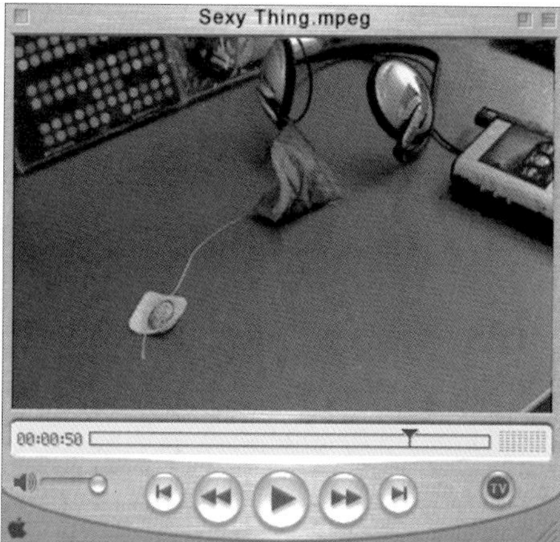

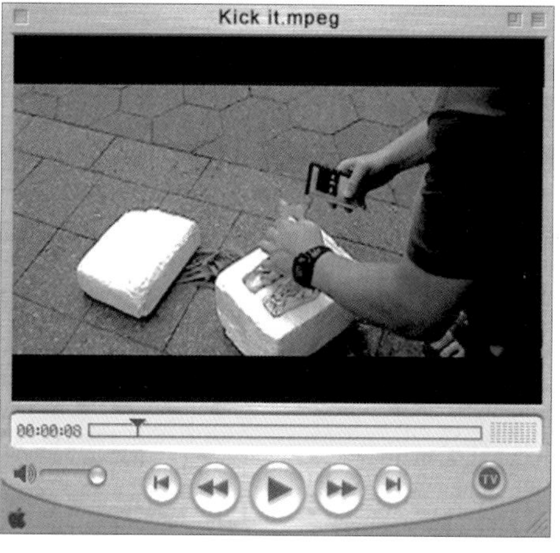

Agency	Watkinsworldwide - Brooklyn
Client	RCA
Art Director	Kevin Watkins
Writer	Kevin Watkins
Creative Directors	Dean Hacohen, Niko Courtelis
Producer	Alex Saltzman
Digital Artist/Multimedia	Watkins Worldwide
Music/Sound	Baron & Baron, Lindsay Jehan
ID	02149N

Award	Merit
Category	**Corporate Image B2C — Other Digital Advertising**

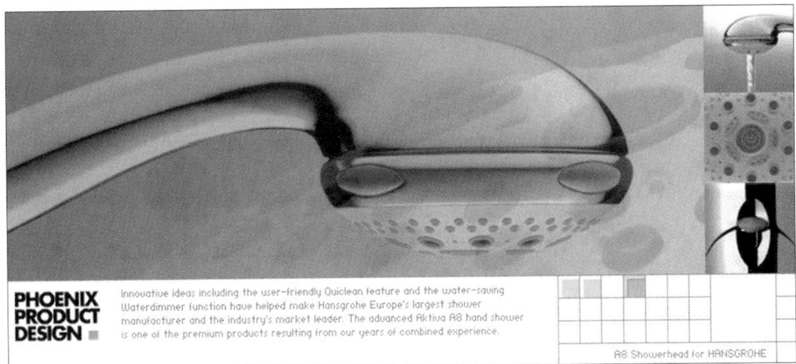

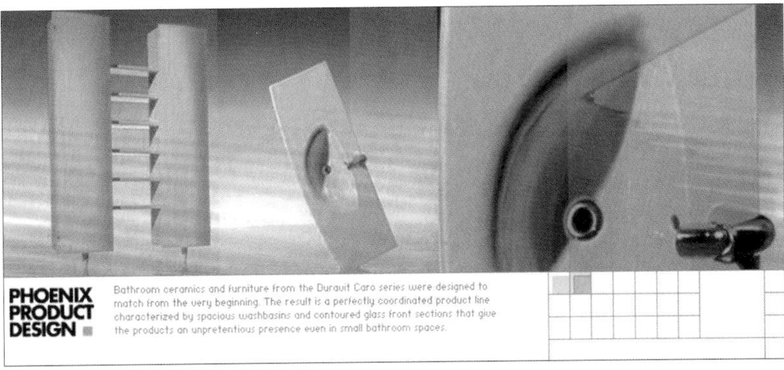

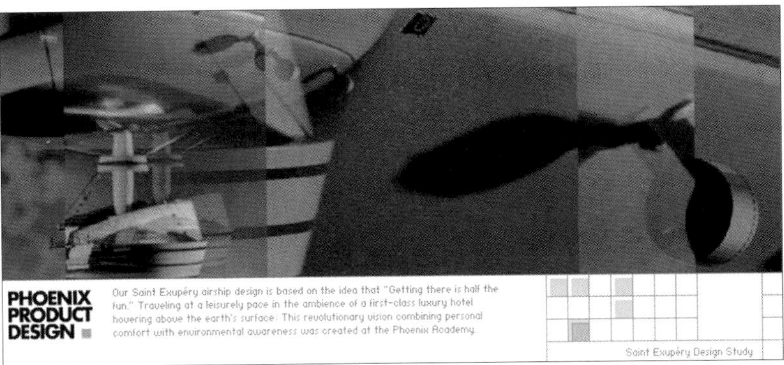

Agency	AGI GmbH - Stuttgart
Client	Phoenix Product Design
Art Director	Michael Sickel
Creative Director	Michael Sickel
Designers	Corrina Krazer, Julia Schultz Ines Kahl
Photographers	Phoenix Product Design, AGI GmbH
Programmers	Marco Fabian, Ina Schall-Sauer Markus Kleine-Vehn
ID	02150N
URL	www.phoenixdesign.de
Award	Merit
Category	**Corporate Image B2B — Web Sites**
Page	210

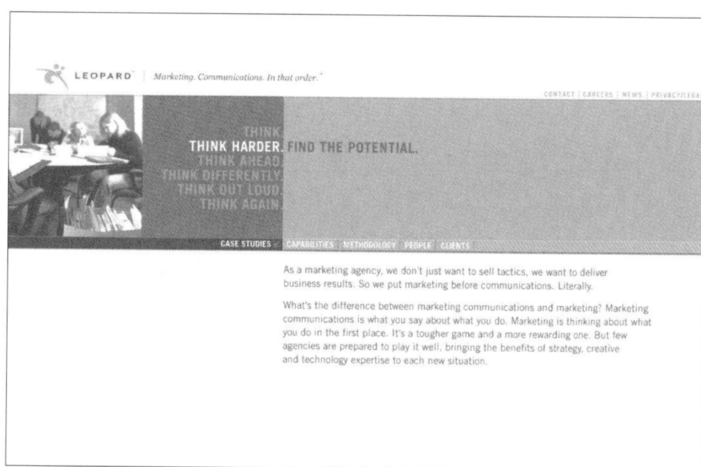

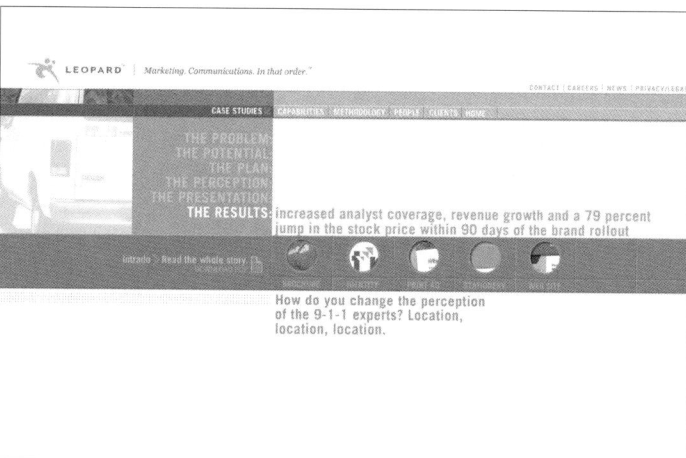

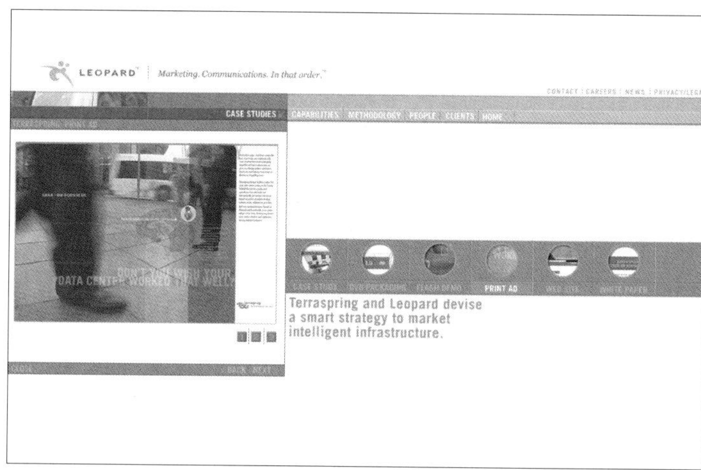

Agency	Leopard - Boulder
Client	Leopard
Art Director	Brendan Hemp
Writer	Maia Nilsson
Creative Directors	Brendan Hemp, Maia Nilsson
Designers	Miles Fenn, Keith Miks
Producers	Jeff Bates, Ron Martinez
Photographer	Greg Christman
Programmer	Miles Fenn
Digital Artists/Multimedia	Jeff Bates, Ron Martinez
ID	02151N
URL	www.leopard.com

Award	Merit
Category	**Corporate Image B2B — Web Sites**

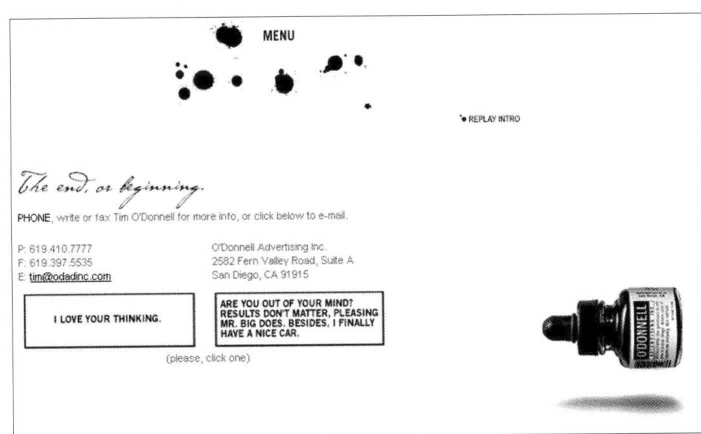

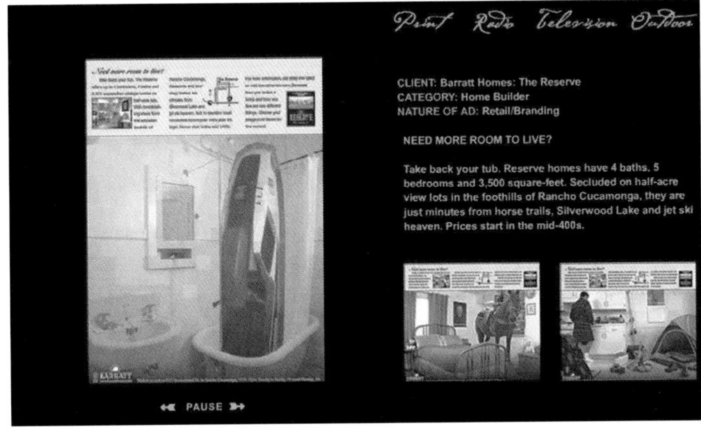

Agency | O'Donnell Advertising - San Diego
Client | O'Donnell Advertising
Art Directors | Myles McGuinness, Tim O'Donnell
Writer | Tim O'Donnell
Creative Director | Tim O'Donnell
Designer | Myles McGuinness
Producer | Tim O'Donnell
Photographers | Myles McGuinness, Alison Gianotto
Information Architects | Alison Gianotto, Travis Bone
Programmers | Danny Baker, Alison Gianotto, Travis Bone
Digital Artists/Multimedia | Myles McGuinness, Danny Baker, Alison Gianotto
Music/Sound | Mark Nelson, Tom O'Donnell
ID | 02152N
URL | www.odadinc.com

Award | Merit
Category | **Corporate Image B2B — Web Sites**
Page | 212

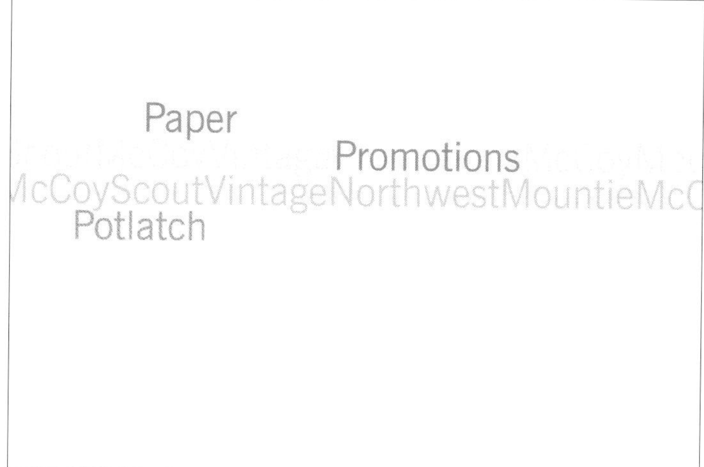

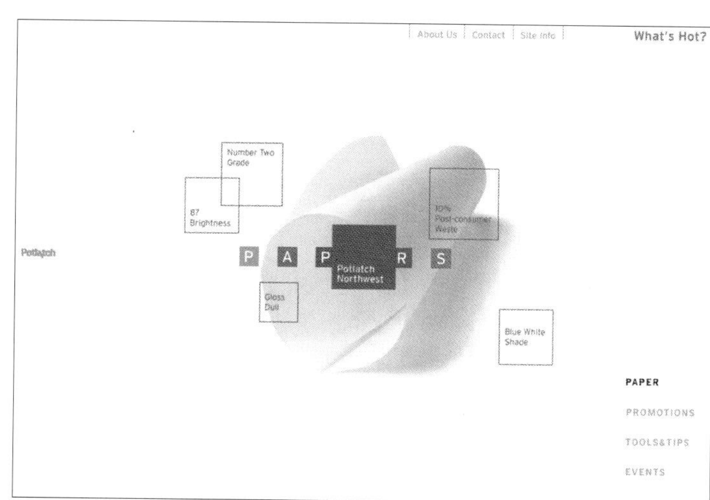

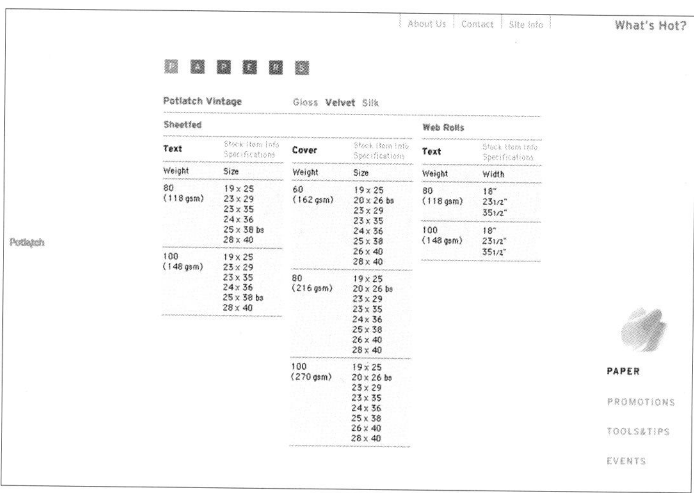

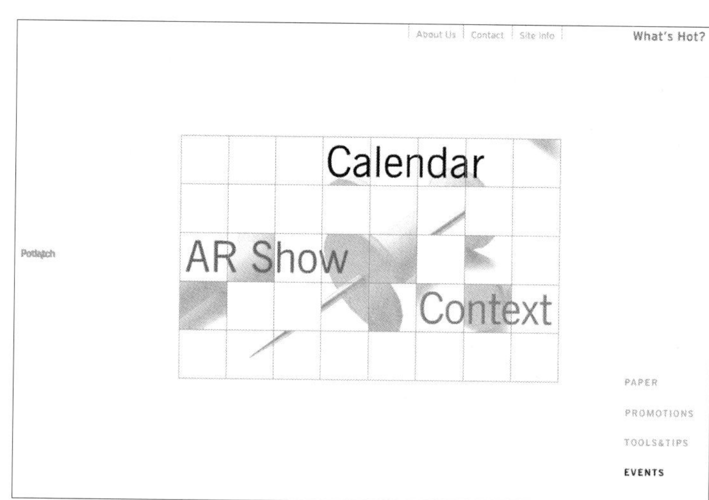

Agency	Pentagram Design - San Francisco
Client	Potlatch Paper
Art Director	Brian Jacobs
Writer	Delphine Hirasuna
Creative Director	Kit Hinrichs
Designers	Douglas McDonald, Holger Struppek Brian Cox
Photographer	Terry Heffernan
ID	02153N
URL	www.potlatchpaper.com

Award	Merit
Category	**Corporate Image B2B — Web Sites**

Agency	Winning Strategies Advertising Mt. Laurel
Client	Winning Strategies Advertising
Art Directors	Lisa Kaczar Boyce , Art Stiefel
Writer	Gary Kopervas
Creative Directors	Art Stiefel, Gary Kopervas
Designers	Lisa Kaczar Boyce , Art Stiefel
Photographer	Lisa Kaczar Boyce
Information Architect	Lisa Kaczar Boyce
Programmers	Kay Souksamlane, Steven Wilkinson
ID	02154N
URL	www.winningstrat.com

Award	Merit
Category	**Corporate Image B2B — Web Sites**
Page	214

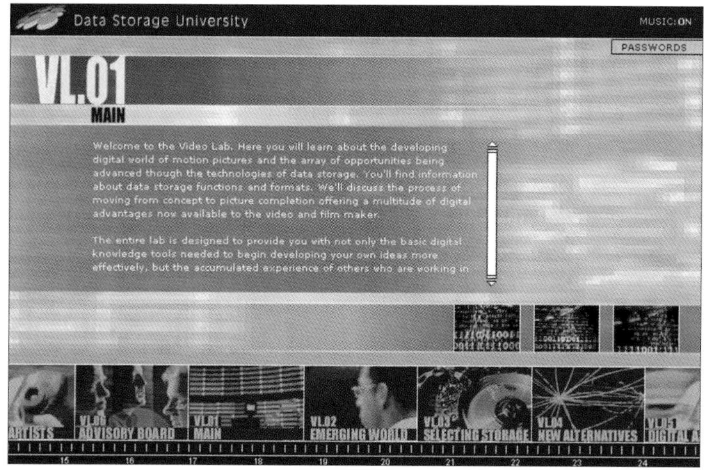

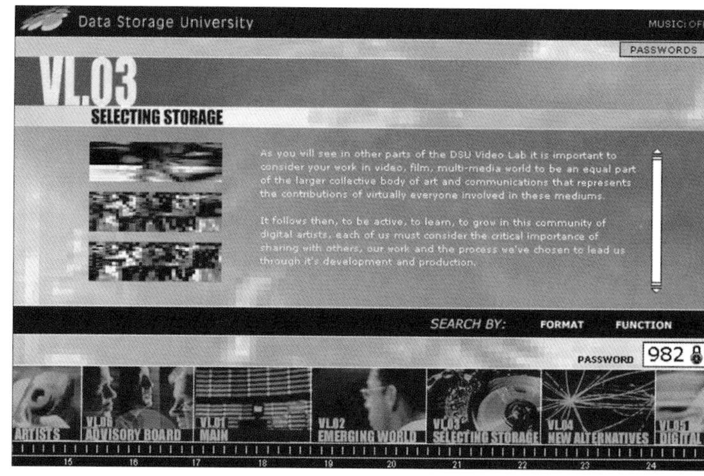

Agency	ADK America - Torrance
Client	Fujifilm
Art Director	Elizabeth Montgomery
Creative Director	Daniel Yamada
Producers	Michael Victor, Billy L.
Programmers	Dan Johnson , i-mobius
ID	02155N

Award	Merit
Category	**Corporate Image B2B — CD-ROMs**

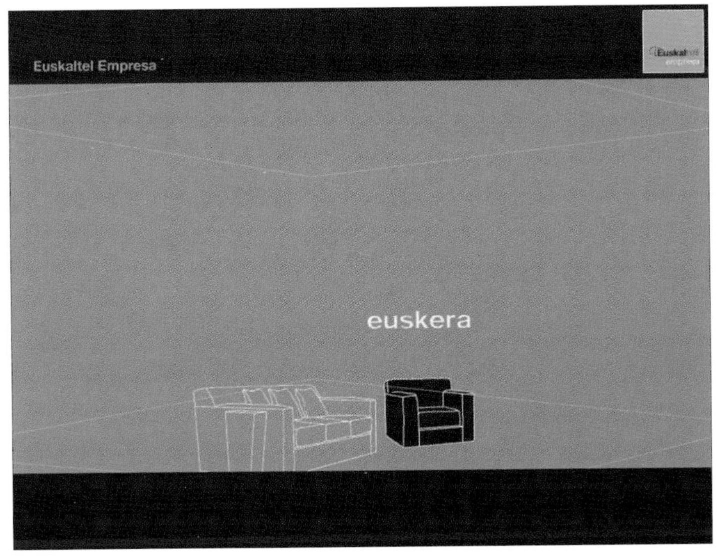

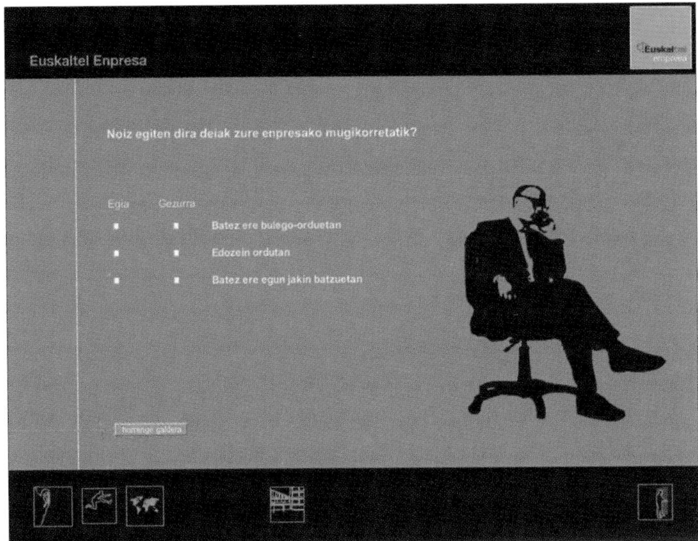

Agency | Dimension Interactiva - San Sebastian
Client | Euskaltel
Art Director | Iñigo Burgui
Writer | Borja Legarda
Creative Director | Borja Legarda
Information Architect | Iñaki Rodrigálvarez
Programmer | Vasava Vs. Innothna
Digital Artist/Multimedia | Vasava Vs. Innothna
ID | 02156N

Award | Merit
Category | **Corporate Image B2B — CD-ROMs**
Page | 216

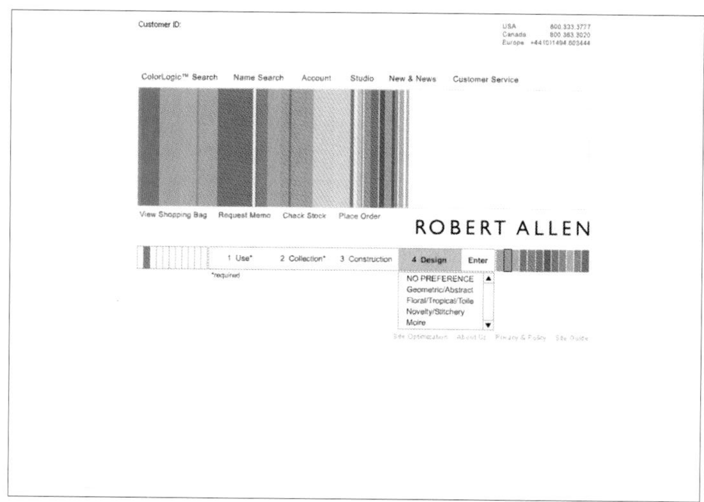

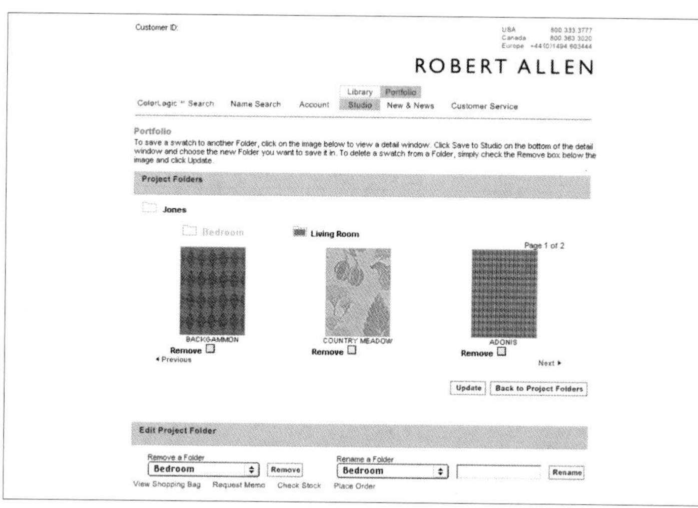

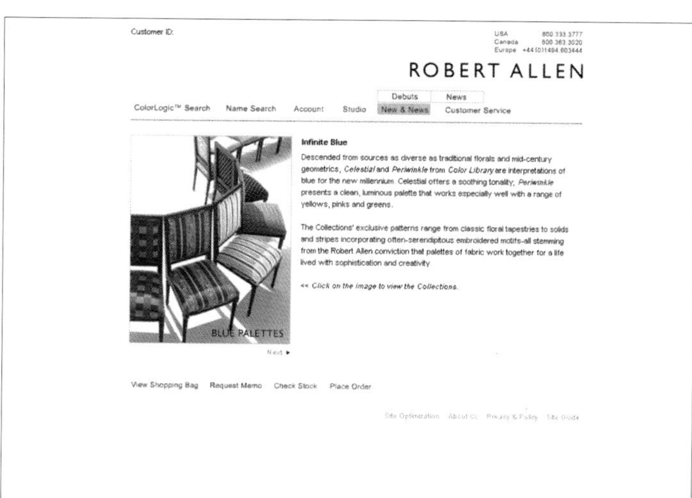

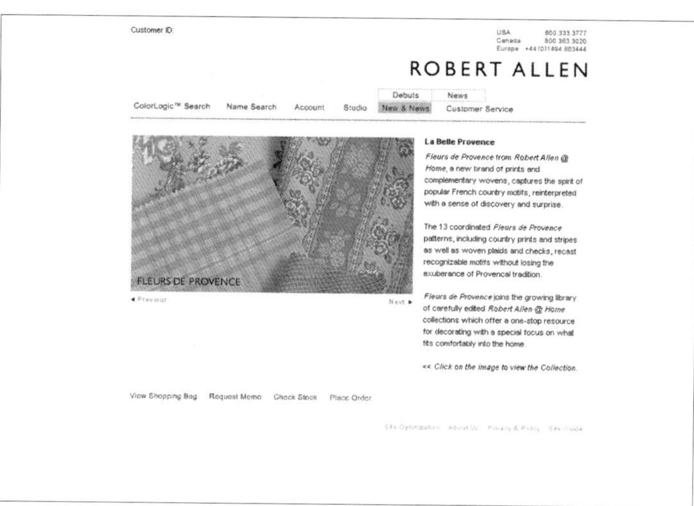

Agency	Grey Interactive - New York
Client	Robert Allen Group
Art Directors	Takuji Maeda, Fabio Mikai
Writer	Ivy Garcia
Creative Directors	Carolyn Goldhush, Mary Ellen Carroll
Designers	David Bright, Mary MacArthur
Producers	Margo Silver, Irene Chu
Information Architect	Dominika Zakrzewski
Programmer	Bassam Alqassar
ID	02157N
URL	www.robertallendesign.com

Award	Merit
Category	**E-Commerce B2B — Web Sites**

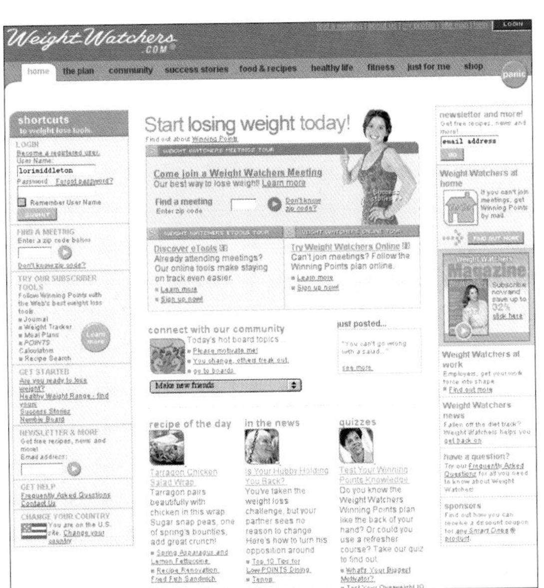

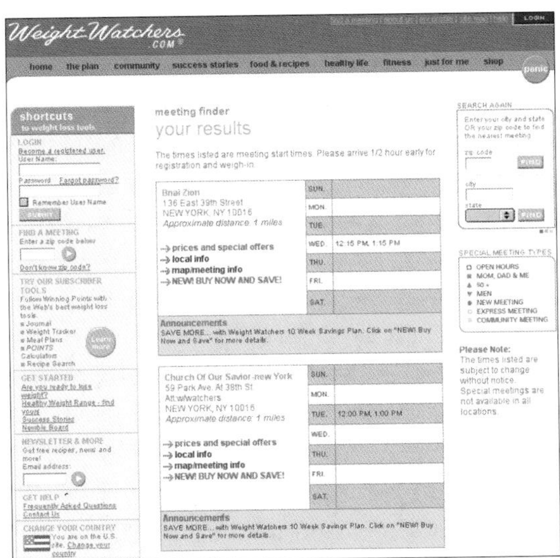

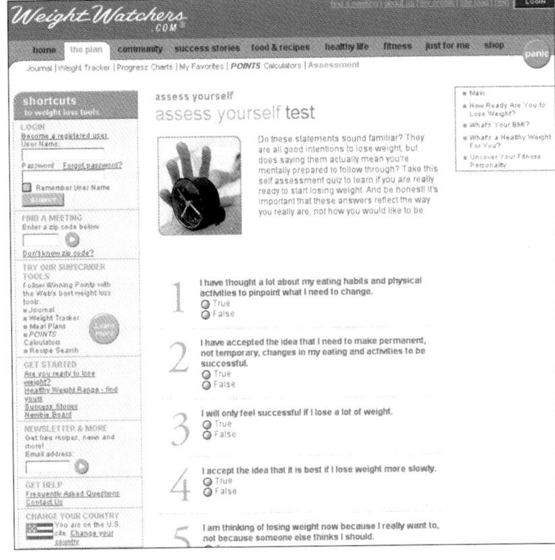

Agency	Modem Media - Norwalk
Client	Weight Watchers
Creative Directors	Peter Rivera, Lori Middleton Amy Sheppard
Art Directors	Jim Peck, Vincent Ficarra
Writers	Anna Crooke, Sheila Kelley
Graphic Designers	Shawn Knight, Sonny Gamboa Kirsten Lawton
Technical Directors	Mike Basone, Mike Laginestra
Producers	Mary Pratt, Lisa Connelly
ID	02158N
URL	www.modemmedia.com/oneshow2002

Award	Merit
Category	**Corporate Image B2C — Web Sites**
Page	218

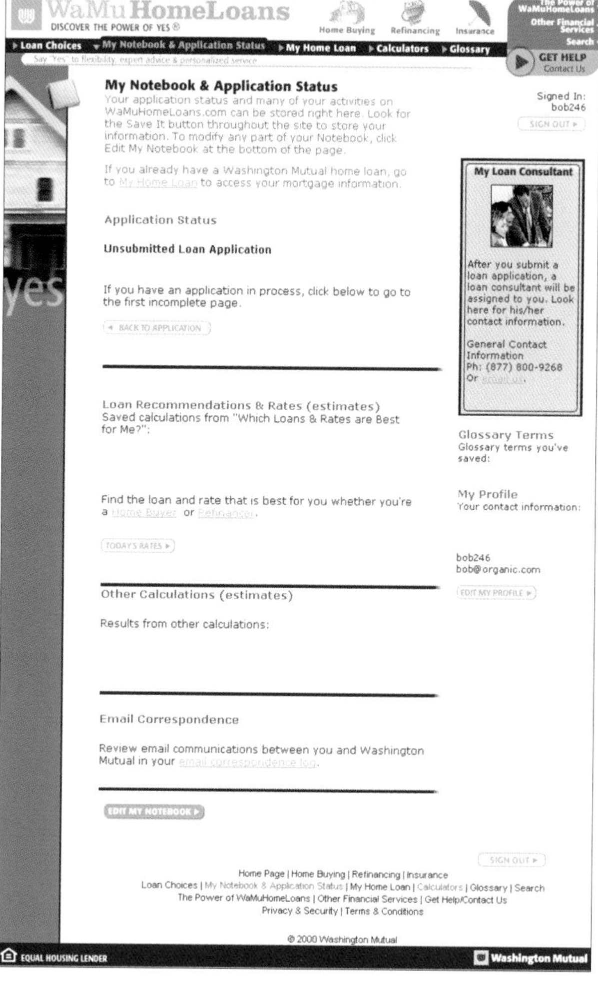

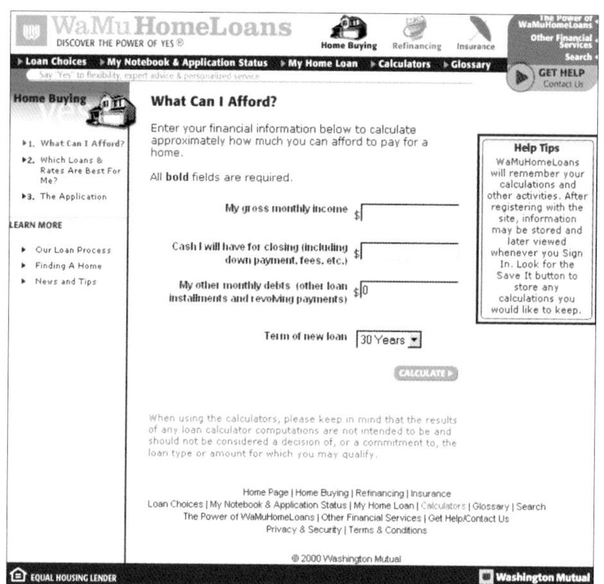

Agency	Organic - Toronto
Client	Washington Mutual
Creative Director	Marusa Debrini
Designers	Jennifer Wheatley, Kathy Hung
Producers	John Chuharski, Shannon Stapleton
Information Architect	Vincent Jurgens
Programmers	Manish Bardolia, Scott Askew, Mike Carr
	Tony Donohoe, Elaine Power
	Chad LaFontaine, Peter Dihn, Ashley Holt
	Mike Juster, Brandon Harris
	Shannon Perkins
Digital Artists/Multimedia	Sasha Panasik, Jonathan Brick
ID	02159N
URL	http://www.wamuhomeloans.com

Award	Merit
Category	**Corporate Image B2C — Web Sites**

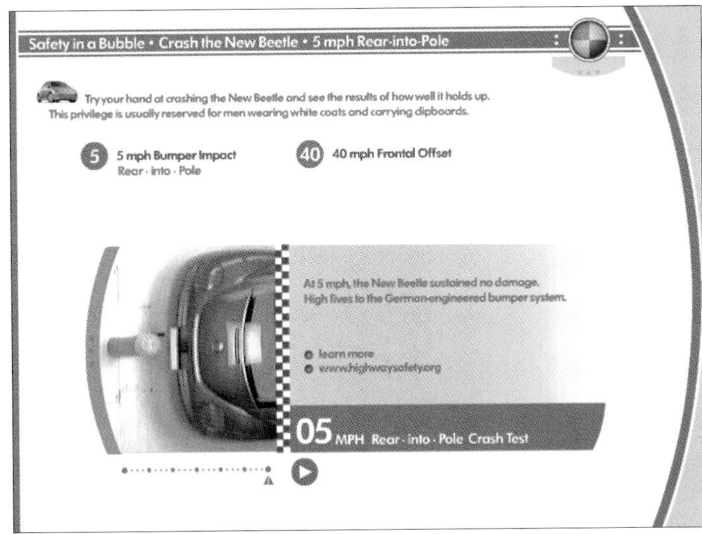

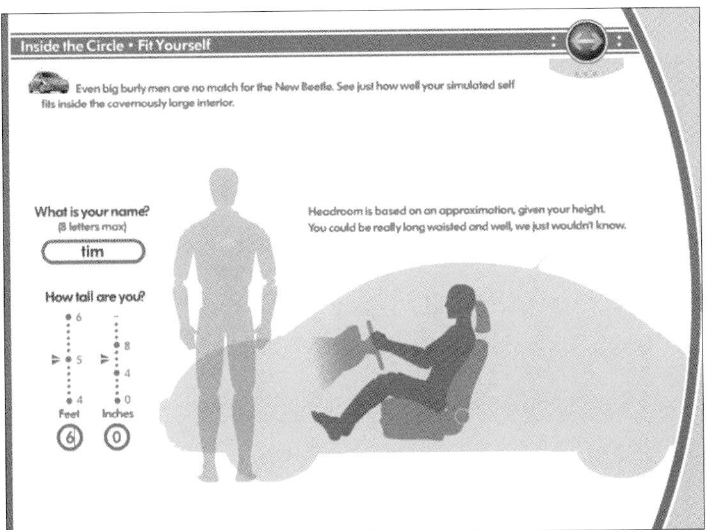

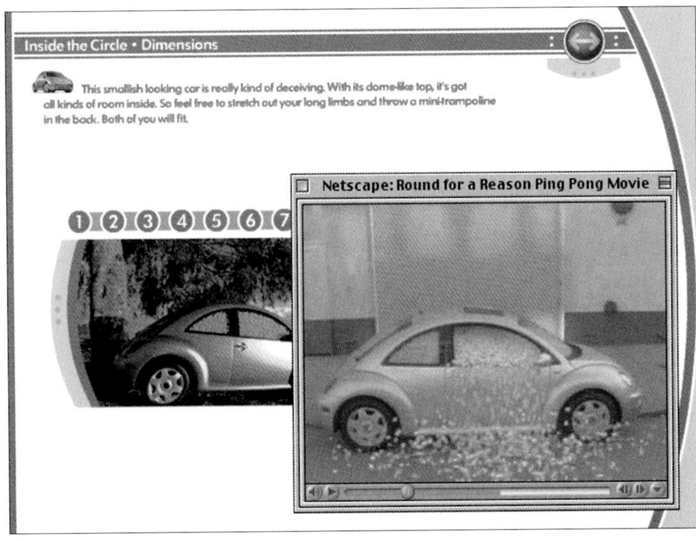

Agency	Arnold Worldwide - Boston
Client	Volkswagen of America
Art Directors	Nicole McDonald, Don Shelford
Writer	Susan Ebling Corbo
Creative Directors	Ron Lawner, Alan Pafenbach Chris Bradley, Tim Brunelle, Don Shelford
Designers	Nicole McDonald, Will McGinness Luke Perkins
Photographers	Martin Albert, Jeff Mermelstein
Information Architect	Patrick Eddy
Technical Directors	Jonathan Groves, Roy Wetherbee
Programmer	Robert Hodgin
Mechanical Supervisor	Claudine Kaprielian
Digital Artist/Multimedia	Robert Hodgin
Music/Sound	Chris Ewen
Producers	Jennifer Iwanicki, Erica Lohnes Paul Shannon
ID	02160N
URL	www.vig.arn.com/ffoneshow/

Award	Merit
Category	**Integrated Branding Campaign**
Page	220

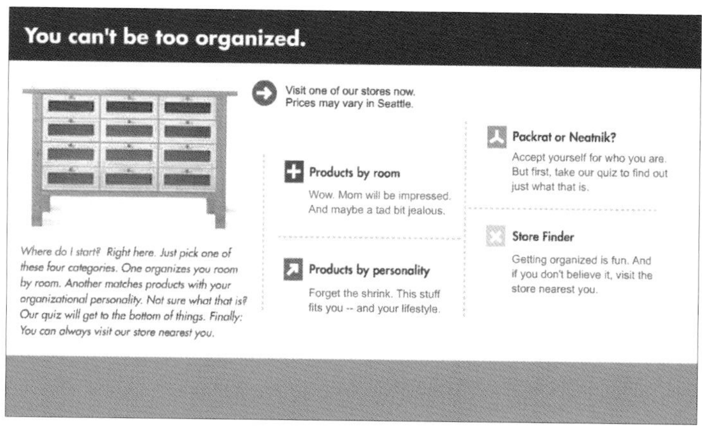

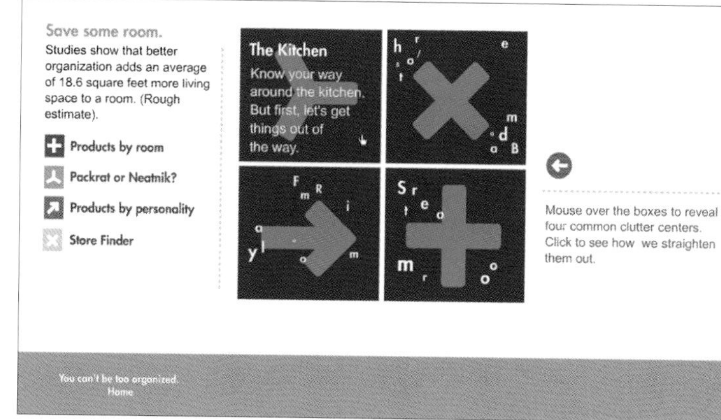

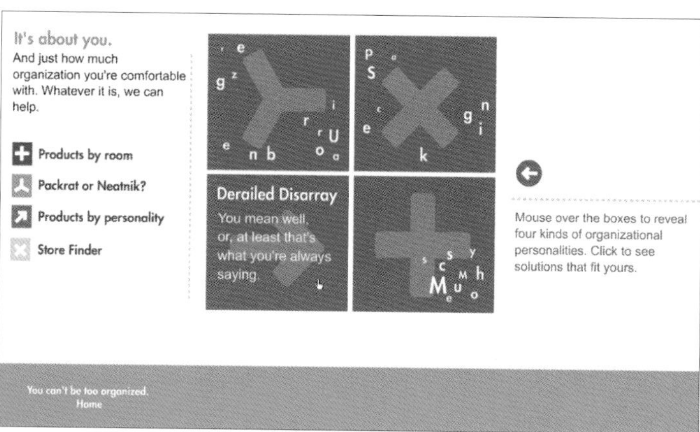

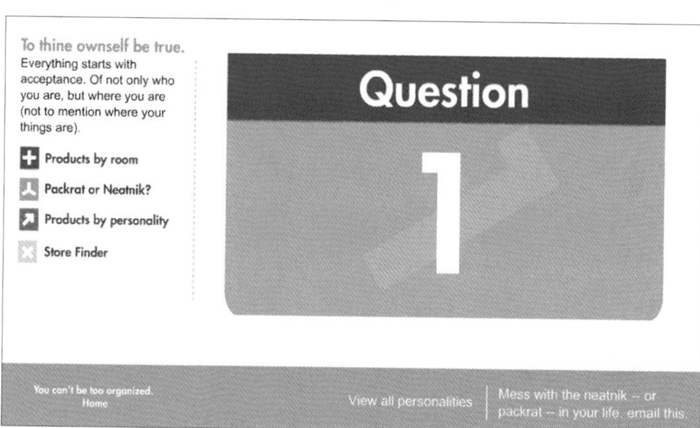

Agency	Carmichael Lynch - Minneapolis
Client	Ikea
Writer	John Boyz
Creative Director	Jud Smith
Designer	James Christensen
Producer	Alison Thompson
Information Architect	James Christenson
Programmer	Paul Nealy
Digital Artist/Multimedia	James Christenson
ID	02161N
URL	www.carmichaellynch.com/portfolio/clients/oneshow/ikea-organized/

Award	Merit
Category	**Integrated Branding Campaign**

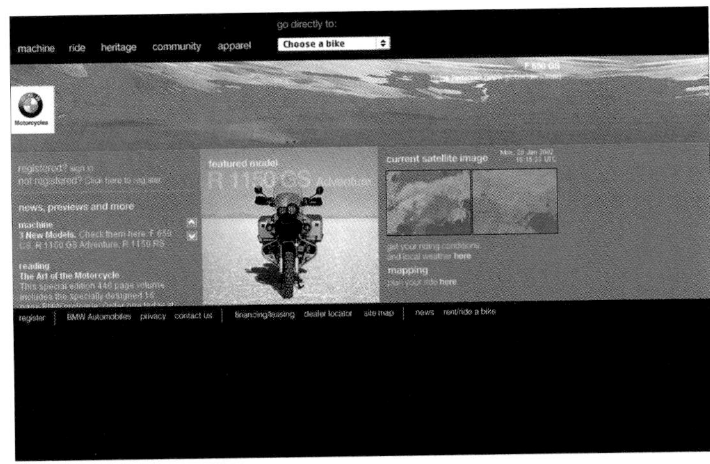

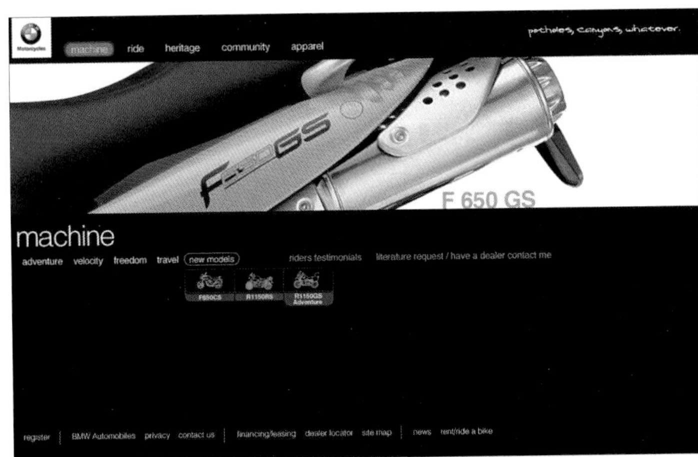

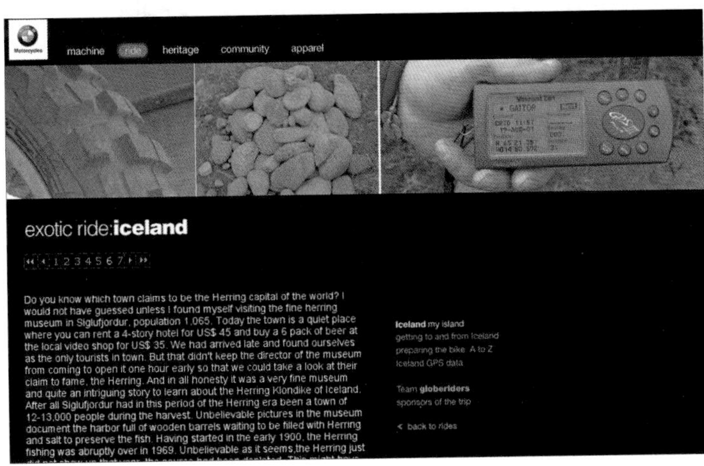

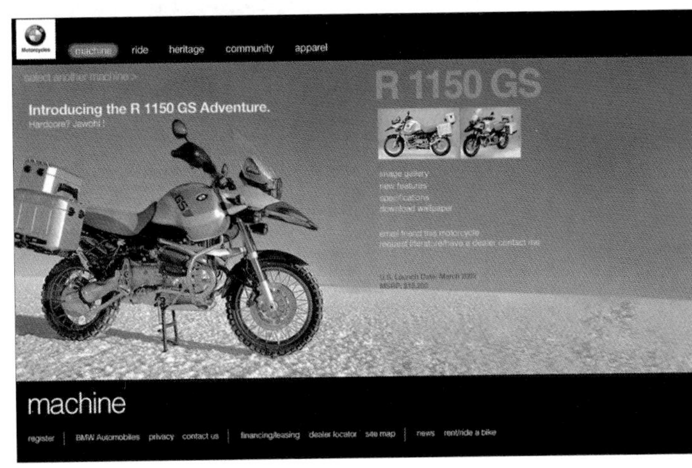

Agency	Merkley Newman Harty & Partners New York
Client	BMW Motorcycles
Art Director	Tom Moran
Writer	Mark Lowe
Creative Director	John Mamus
Designer	MNHi
Producer	Sara Eolin
Music/Sound	Joe O'Connel
ID	02162N
URL	www.bmwmotorcycles.com

Award	Merit
Category	**Integrated Branding Campaign**
Page	222

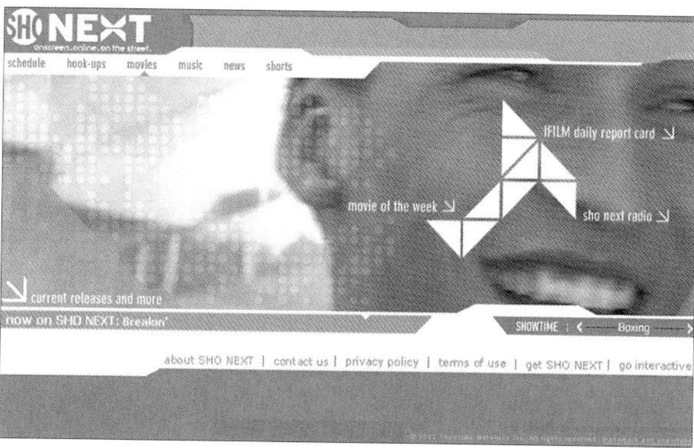

1

Agency	Showtime Networks - New York
Client	Showtime Networks
Art Director	Reiko Sugitani
Writer	Michael Villane
Creative Director	Reiko Sugitani
Designer	Eric Frommelt
Producer	Rachel Nicotra
Photographer	RSA Films
Programmers	James Napolitano, Ryan Peters
Digital Artist/Multimedia	Jade Hoye
Music/Sound	Justin Edelson
ID	02163N
URL	www.shonext.com

Award	Merit
Category	Integrated Branding Campaign

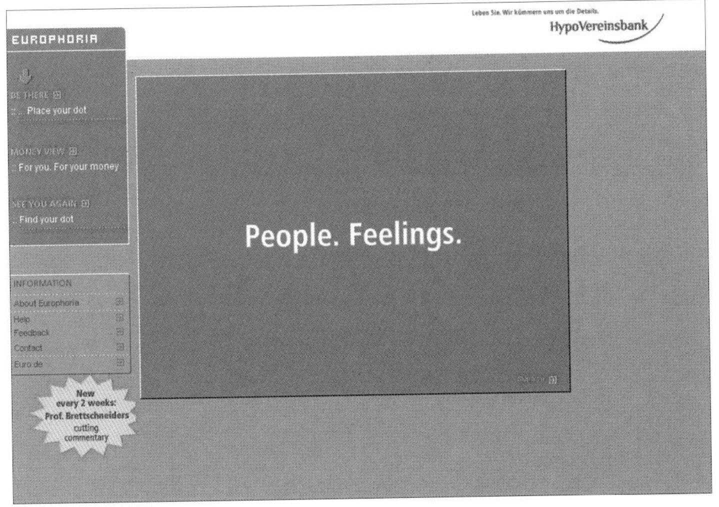

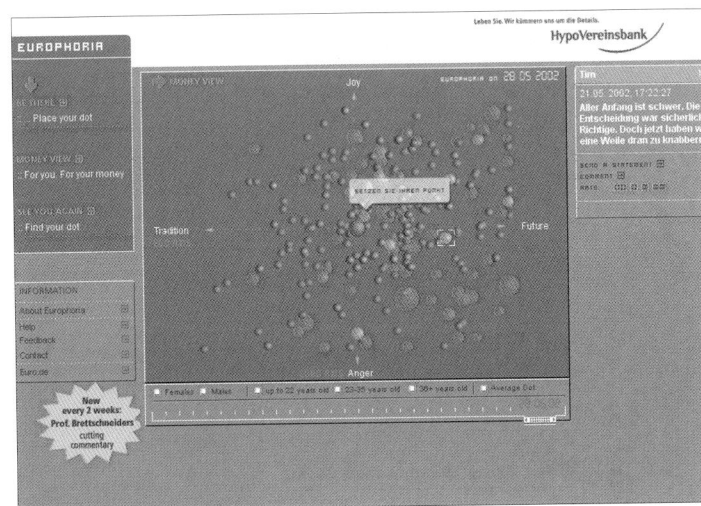

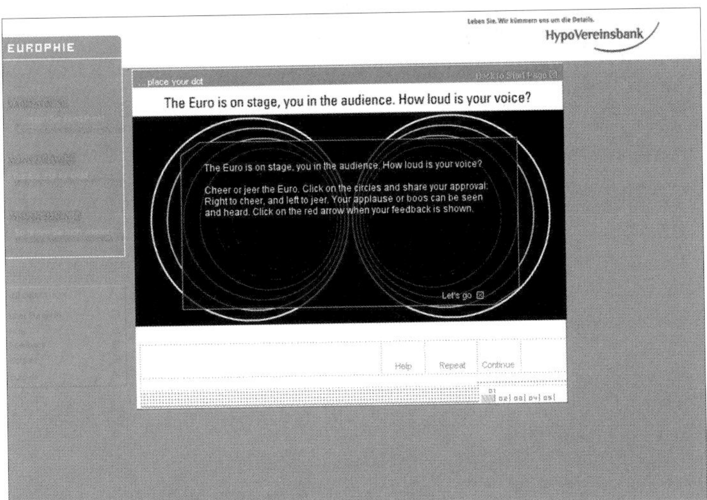

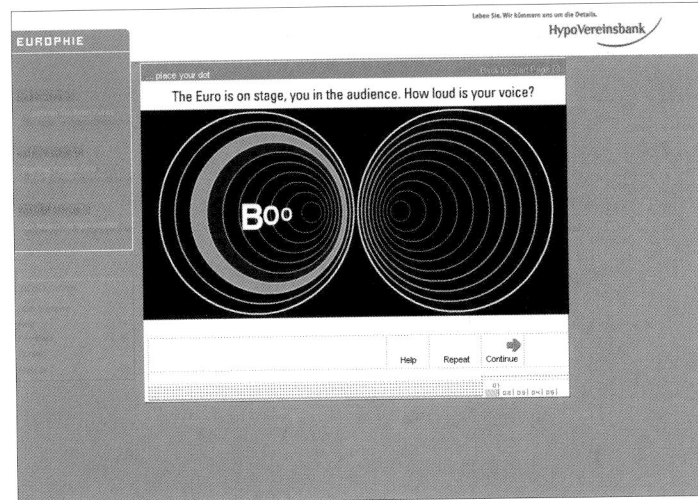

Agency	AGI - Stuttgart
Client	HypoVereinsbank
Art Directors	Nathalie Strobl, Cornelia Herm
Writers	Andreas Milles, Stefanie Katzschke
Creative Director	Christian Schwarm
Designers	Andrea Gretschmann Holger Reuss, Corrina Krazer, Julia Schultz
Programmers	Hanz Geeratz, Alvar Freude Dragan Espenscheid, Georg Neumann Markus Heckel
Music/Sound	Frootloop Musikproduktion Uwe Schenk
ID	02164N
URL	www.awards.agi.de/europhoria

Award	Merit
Category	**Broadband**
Page	224

Agency	Seven Interactive - Chicago
Client	Golin/Harris International
	The State of Illinois
Creative Director	Ian Campbell
Designer	Hideki K. Owa
Photographer	David R. Barnes
Producer	Chinmoy Raval
Information Architect	Chinmoy Raval
Programmers	Riley Sheehan, Randy Cochran
ID	02165N
URL	www.idecide4me.com

Award	Merit
Category	**Broadband**

1

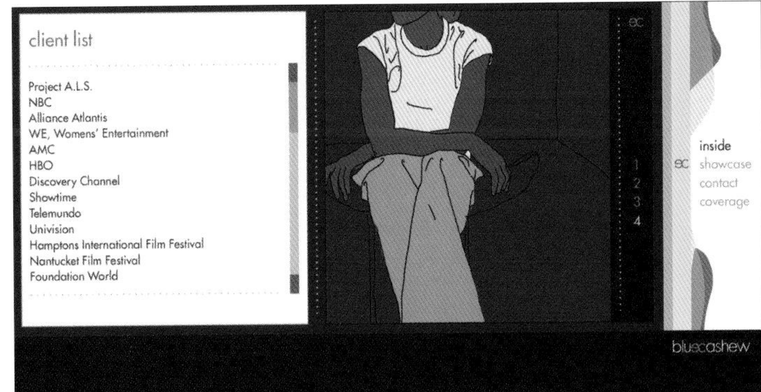

Agency	Deepend - New York
Client	bluecashew
Art Director	Iti Sakharet
Writer	Diana Thirlwell
Creative Director	Iti Sakharet
Designer	Angela Lidderdale
Producer	Diana Thirlwell
Photographer	Angela Lidderdale
Information Architect	Angela Lidderdale
Programmers	Michael Diolosa , Ben Needham
Digital Artist/Multimedia	Angela Lidderdale
ID	02166N
URL	www.bluecashew.com

Award	Merit
Category	**Self-Promotion — Web Sites**
Page	226

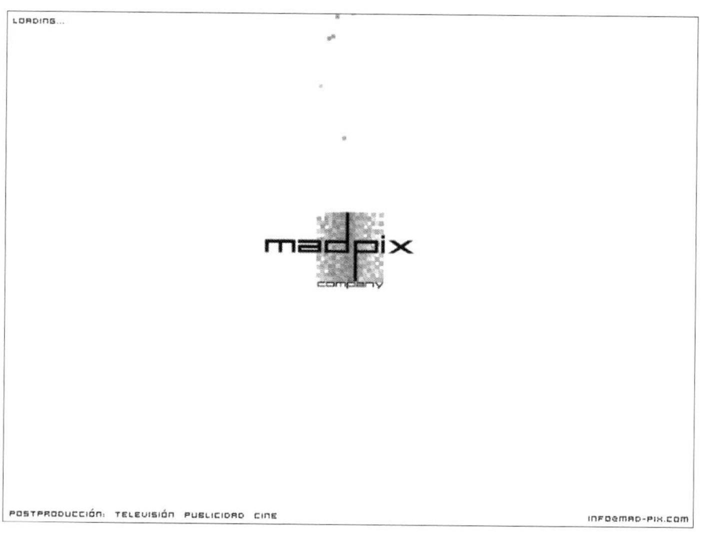

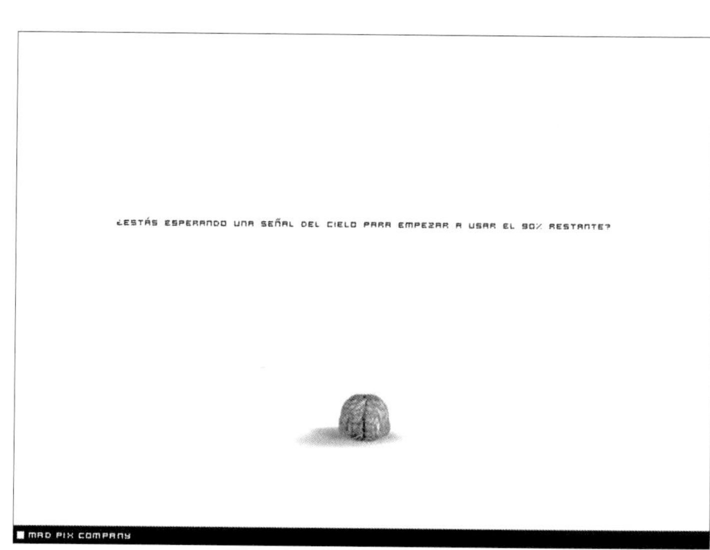

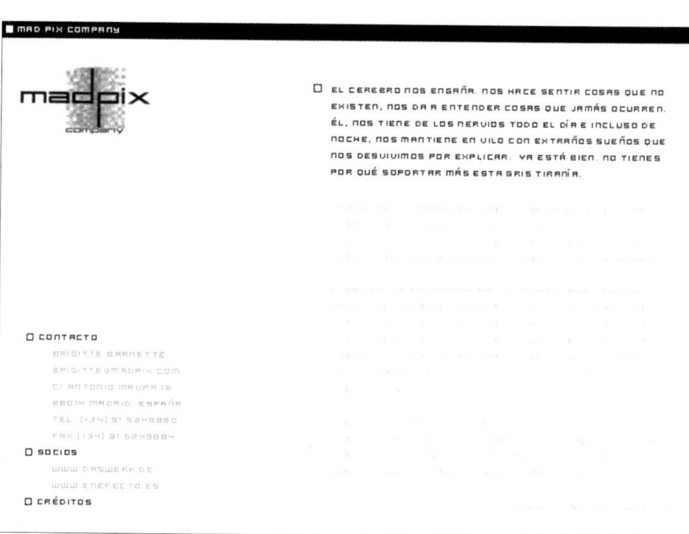

Agency	Doubleyou Remo - Madrid
Client	Madpix Company
Art Director	Íñigo Orduña
Writer	Sebastián Méndez
Creative Director	Sebastián Méndez
Designer	Íñigo Orduña
Programmers	Omar Rodríguez, Nacho Rapallo
Digital Artists/Multimedia	Rubén Villoria, Pilar Cienfuegos
ID	02167N
URL	www.doubleyou.com/remo/festivals/madpix

Award	Merit
Category	**Self-Promotion — Web Sites**

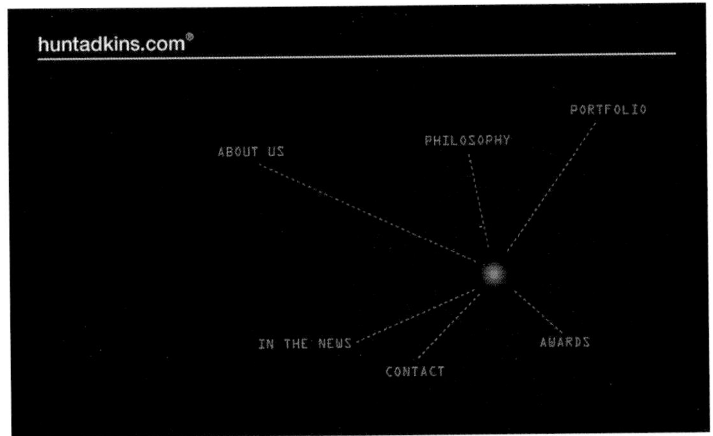

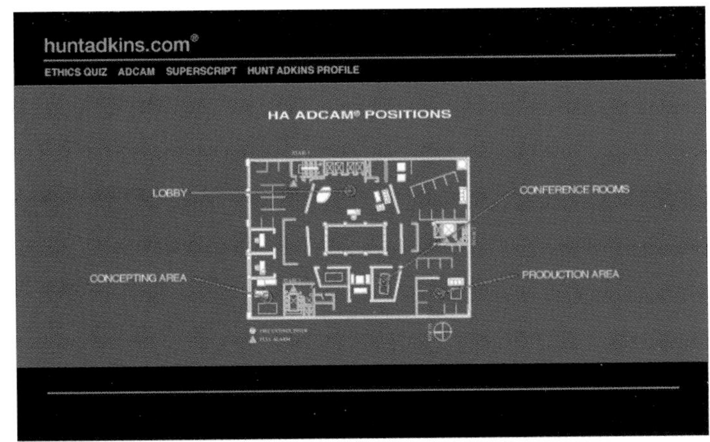

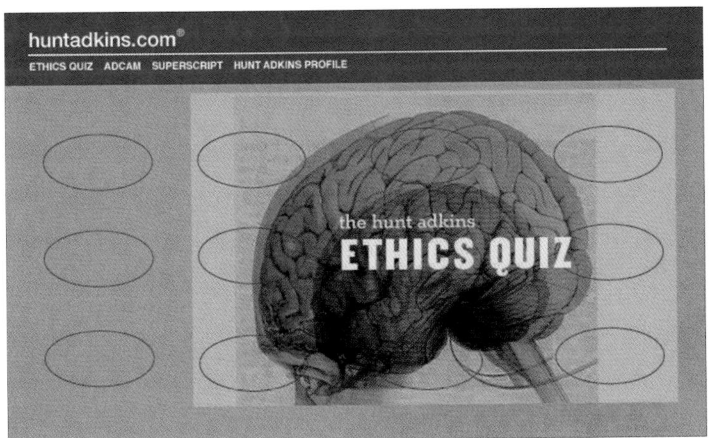

Agency	Hunt Adkins - Minneapolis
Client	Hunt Adkins
Art Directors	Luke Oeth, Steve Mitchell
Writers	Doug Adkins, Rob Franks, Rocco Bonello
Creative Directors	Doug Adkins, Steve Mitchell
Designers	Luke Oeth, Britt Lundberg
Programmer	Luke Oeth
ID	02168N
URL	www.huntadkins.com

Award	Merit
Category	**Self-Promotion — Web Sites**
Page	228

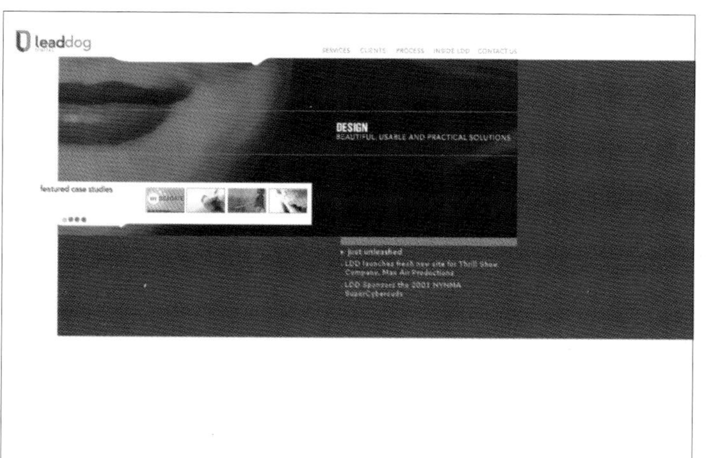

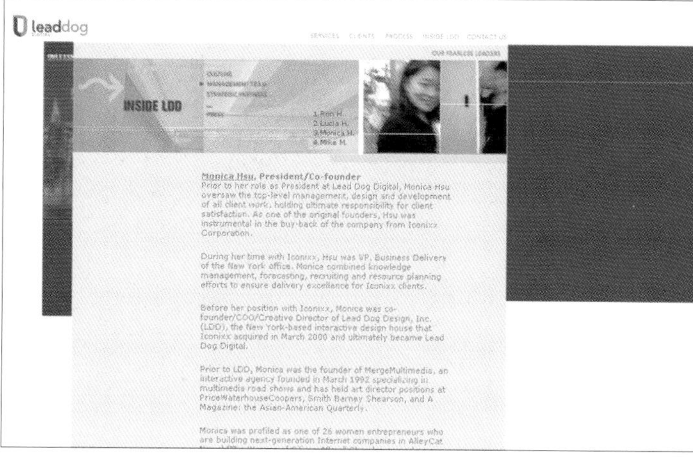

Agency	Lead Dog Digital - New York
Client	Lead Dog Digital
Art Director	Natalie Lam
Writers	Erin Nolan, Mike Matteo, Natalie Lam
Creative Director	Natalie Lam
Designers	Natalie Lam, Don Eschenauer
Producer	Mike Rembetsey
Photographers	Natalie Lam, Tom Lynch, Don Eschenauer
Information Architects	Don Eschenauer, Lucia Heffernan
Programmers	Chris Senchaz, Carol Haynes
Digital Artist/Multimedia	Carl Prizzi
ID	02169N
URL	www.LDD.com

Award	Merit
Category	**Self-Promotion — Web Sites**

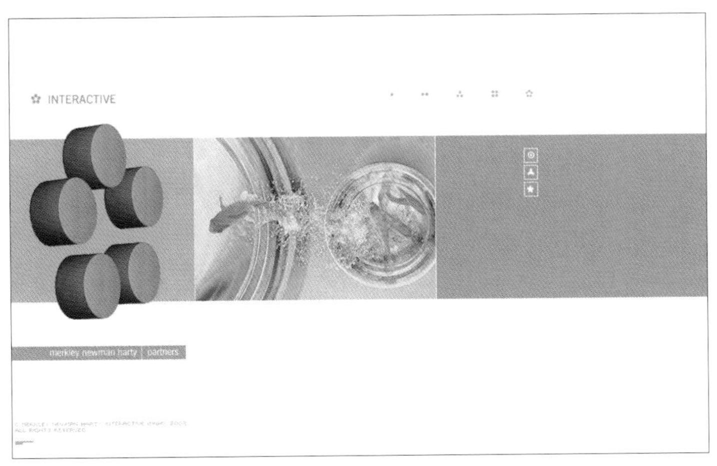

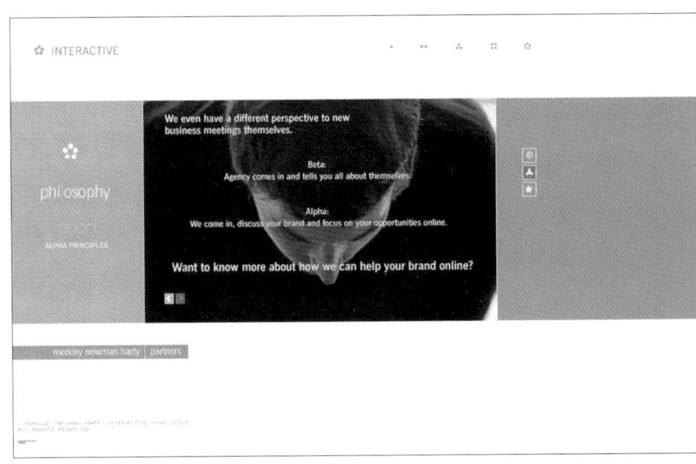

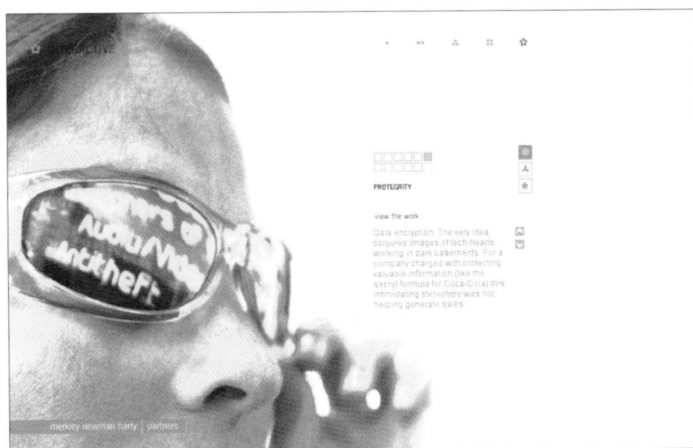

Agency | Merkley Newman Harty & Partners
New York
Client | MNHi
Art Director | Tom Moran
Creative Director | John Mamus
Producer | Michael Asaro
ID | 02170N
URL | www.mnhinteractive.com

Award | Merit
Category | **Self-Promotion — Web Sites**
Page | 230

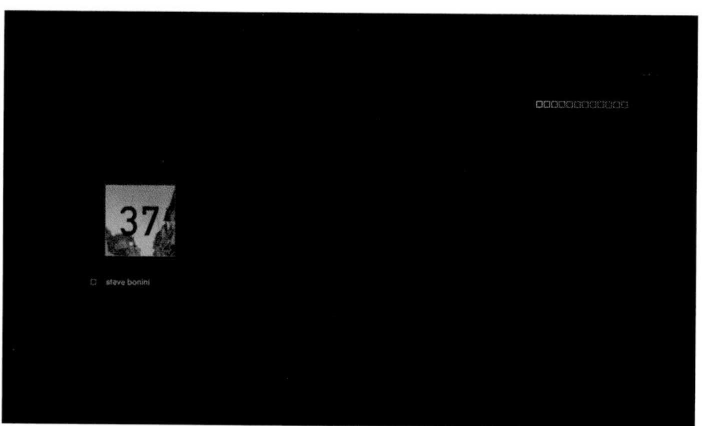

Agency	Paris France - Portland
Client	Steve Bonini Photography
Art Director	Jeff Faulkner
Creative Director	Doug Lowell
Executive Producer	Chuck Nobles
Designer	Erik Falat
Technical Director	Scott Trotter
ID	02171N
URL	www.parisfrancestage/bonini

Award Merit

Category **Self-Promotion — Web Sites**

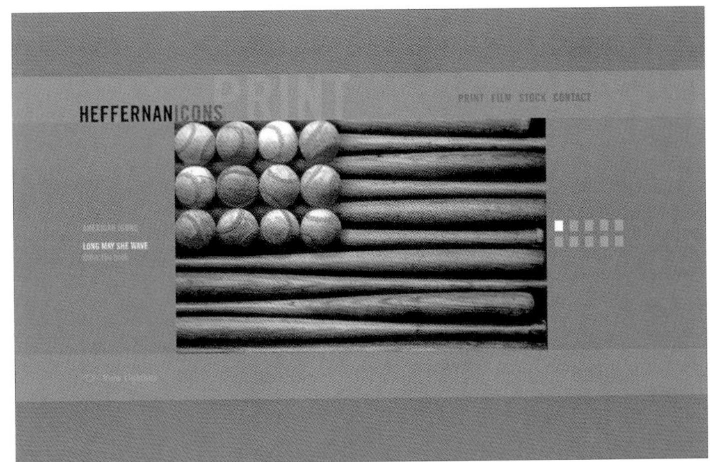

Agency	Pentagram Design - San Francisco
Client	Terry Heffernan
Art Director	Brian Jacobs
Creative Director	Kit Hinrichs
Designers	Brian Cox, Douglas McDonald
Photographer	Terry Heffernan
ID	02172N
URL	www.heffernanicons.com

Award	Merit
Category	**Self-Promotion — Web Sites**
Page	232

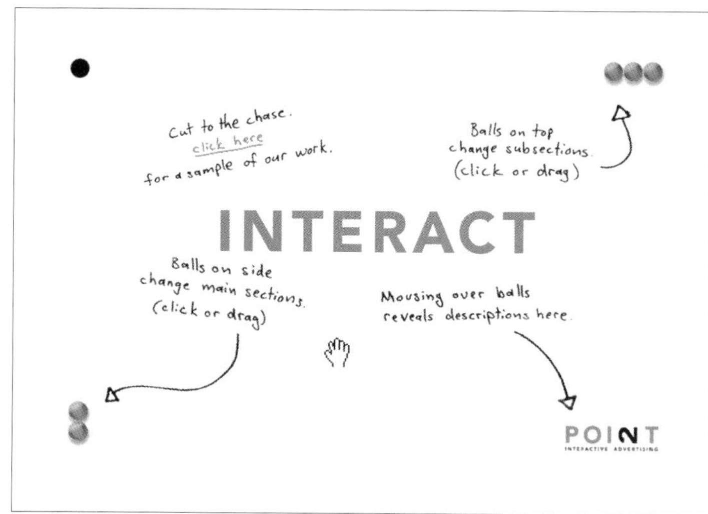

Agency	point2interactive - Detroit
Client	point2interactive advertising
Art Director	Peter Arndt
Writer	John Gregory
Creative Directors	Peter Arndt, John Gregory
Producer	Peter Arndt
Programmer	Brophy
Music/Sound	Peter Mayhem
ID	02173N
URL	www.point2interactive.com

Award	Merit
Category	**Self-Promotion — Web Sites**

1

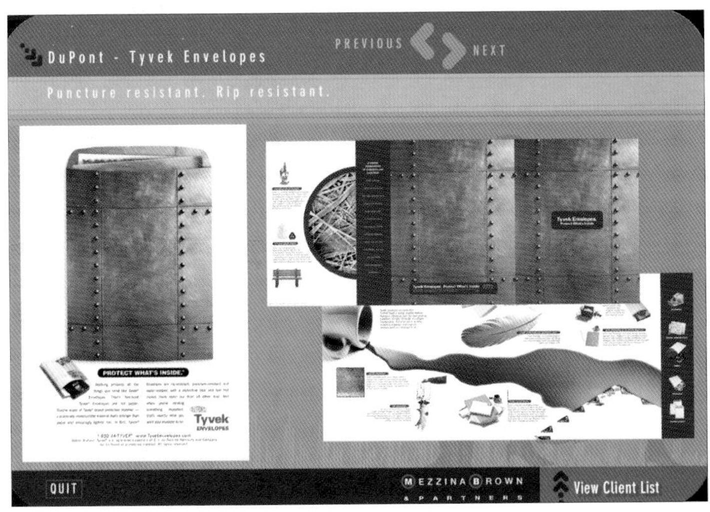

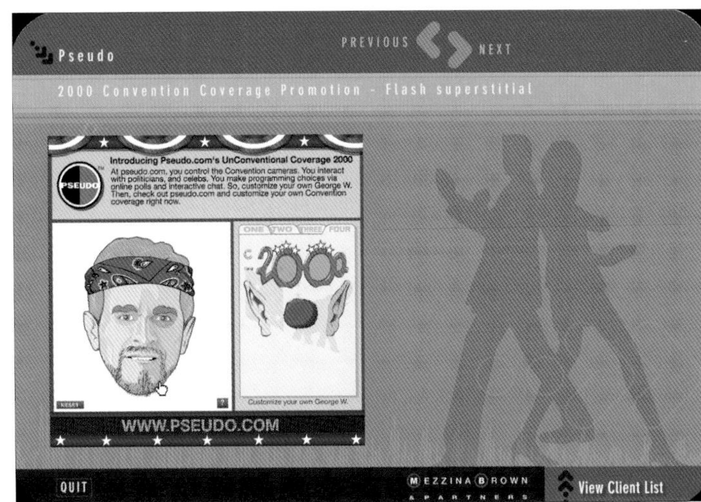

Agency	Mezzina Brown & Partners - New York
Client	Mezzina Brown & Partners
Art Directors	Chris Lenox, David Smith
Writers	Dave Pachence, Richard Wise, Clark Moss
Creative Director	Clark Moss
Designers	David Smith, Chris Lenox
Photographer	Don Sipley
Programmer	Francois Balmelle
Digital Artist/Multimedia	David Smith
Music/Sound	Richard Lainhart
ID	02174N

Award	Merit
Category	**Self-Promotion — CD-ROM**
Page	234

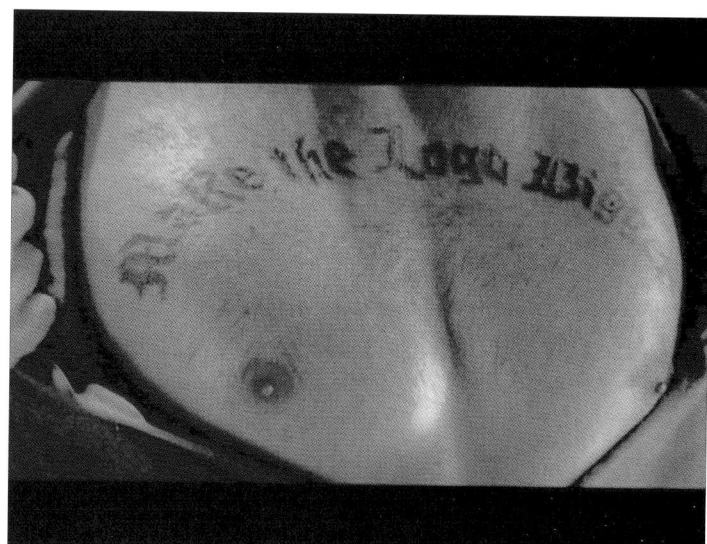

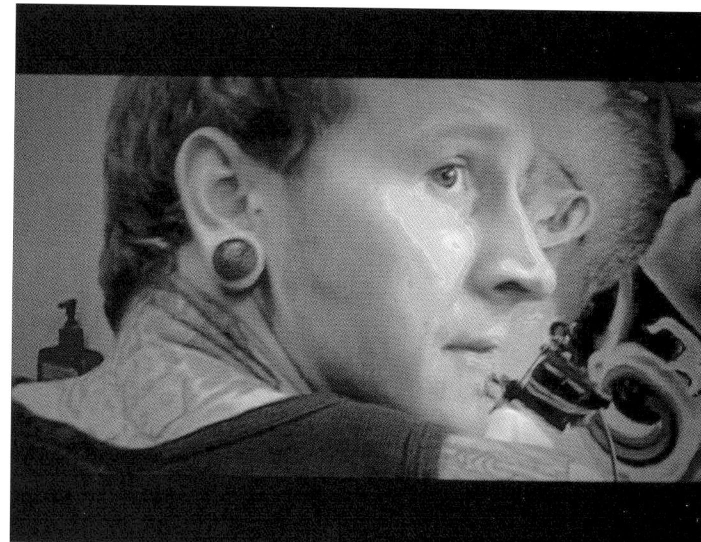

Agency	ComGroup - Atlanta
Client	ComGroup
Art Director	Don Grant
Writer	Haley Turner
Creative Director	Jim Newbury
Designer	Don Grant
Producers	Haley Turner, Claudia Goodwin-Cummings
Information Architect	Tony Martin
Programmers	Andres Echenique, Matt Howey
Digital Artist/Multimedia	Dave Ballard
Music/Sound	Chris Basta
ID	02175N
URL	http://comgroup.holiday.mragroup.com

Award Merit

Category **Self-Promotion — Other Digital Advertising**

Agency	Bent Media - New Orleans
Client	Healthy Lifestyle Choices
Art Director	Jared Coffin
Writers	Vanessa Trice, Brad Brewster Julie Koppman
Creative Director	Brad Brewster
Designer	Jared Coffin
Photographer	Mark Andresen
Programmer	Dasher Egger
Digital Artists/Multimedia	Court Batson, Dan Haugh, David Sullivan
Music/Sound	Court Batson, Dan Haugh
ID	02177N

Award	Merit
Category	**College Competition — Other Digital Advertising**
Page	236

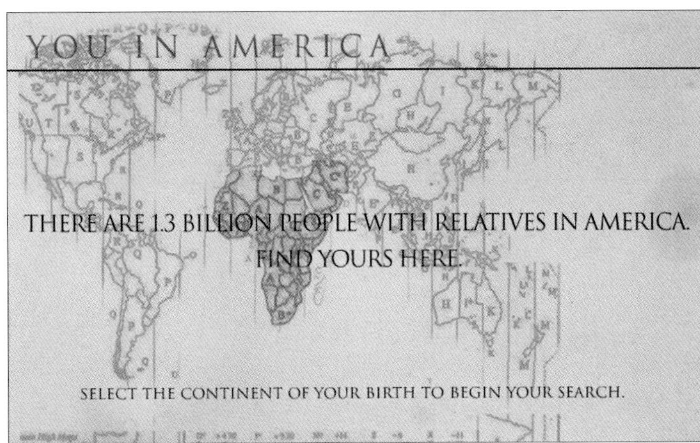

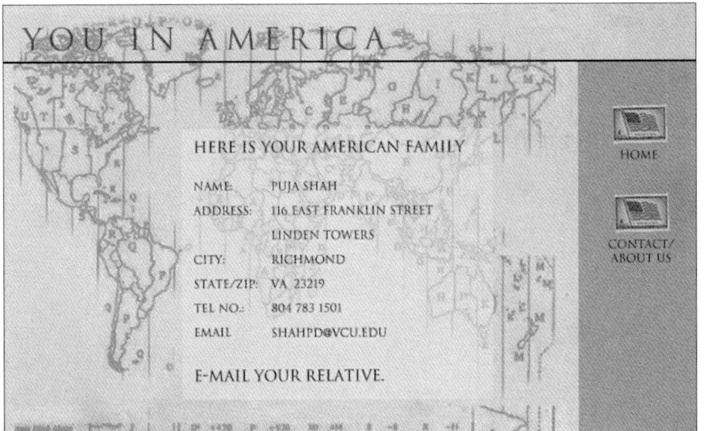

School	School Virginia Commonweath University Ad Center - Richmond
Client	USA
Art Director	Puja Shah
Writer	Jordan Sher
ID	020176
Award	Merit
Category	**College Competition — Other Digital Advertising**

Index

Agency

Agency

Art Director

Art Director

Art Director

Creative Directors

Creative Directors

Creative Directors

Designer

Designer

Designer

Designer

Programmer

Programmer

Writer

Writer